The Challenge of
Creative Leadership

The Challenge of Creative Leadership

With contributions from the
International Zermatt Symposia on Creativity in Economics, Arts and Science
by

MAYA ANGELOU   JANE GOODALL
JOSEPH BRODSKY   HELMUT MAUCHER
GERALD M. ELDELMAN   KAZUHIKO NISHI
GABRIEL GARCÍA MÁRQUEZ   EDNA O'BRIEN
WOLE SOYINKA

Introduced and edited by
GOTTLIEB GUNTERN

SHEPHERD-WALWYN
in association with
INTERNATIONAL FOUNDATION FOR CREATIVITY AND LEADERSHIP

First published in 1997 by
Shepheard-Walwyn (Publishers) Ltd.
26 Charing Cross Road, Suite 34
London WC2H 0DH

British Library Cataloguing-in-Publication Data

A Catalogue record of this book
is available from the British Library

ISBN 0 85683 168 9

Acknowledgements

The Foundation gratefully acknowledges the authors' permission to reproduce their talks
given at the Zermatt Symposia, and the contribution of the following:

Translators:	Kevin Whiteley (Helmut Maucher)
	Myrna Farage (Gabriel García Márquez)
Editing:	Myrna Farage
Photos:	Barbara Davatz (Edna O'Brien)
	Renato Jordan (Joseph Brodsky, Gerald M. Eldelman,
	Jane Goodall, Gabriel García Márquez, Helmut
	Maucher, Kazuhiko Nishi, Wole Soyinka)
	Pia Zanetti (Maya Angelou)
	Beat Wenger (Gottlieb Guntern)

Printed and Bound in Great Britian by
BPC Wheatons, Exeter

Contents

Contents

GOTTLIEB GUNTERN.
Swiss systems scientist and researcher; author

The author of several scientific articles and books on specialized topics - including the Swiss bestseller, *Im Zeichen des Schmetterlings* - Gottlieb Guntern was born in Biel, a small town in the canton of Valais, on April 26, 1939. He studied medicine in Basel and Paris before specializing in psychiatry in Bern, Lausanne and Philadelphia. In 1978 he founded a pilot medical center of which he was head physician for ten years.

A year later he created the International Foundation for Creativity and Leadership (located today in Martigny, Switzerland), dedicated to the study of the relationship between innovation and leadership. Dr. Guntern is the director of the Foundation as well as chairman of the International Zermatt Symposium on Creativity in Economics, Art and Science which he established in 1990 and is held every year.

Today Dr. Guntern is dedicated exclusively to the scientific study of innovation and leadership through a systemic approach. There is a great demand for his seminars, conferences and workshops in the economic sector. He works as special adviser for the top management of multinational firms, counseling in the fields of creativity, leadership development and innovation within companies. A Fellow of the Davos World Economic Forum, he is also a member of various international associations.

Introduction by Gottlieb Guntern

The muck of mediocracy

Our planet could be a jewel. It is not. Our society could be the best that ever was. It is not. We could brim over with confidence and contentment and even exult in triumph. We do not.

Why is this so?

Because our contemporary society increasingly opts for a general coping strategy I propose to call *mediocracy* (Guntern 1993 b). *Mediocracy* (Lat. *medium* = middle; Gr. *kratein* = to govern) *is defined as the predominance of the mindless overadaptation to what and how a majority of people presumably or de facto perceives, thinks, feels, demands and does and to how it functions physiologically.* So far, so good. After all, we do adhere to democratic principles which hold that the majority knows best which course of action should be taken to achieve, maintain and further develop a highly desirable society. Yet there is a snag. If the ruling majority does not pursue the right kind of goals or if it pursues them through inadequate strategies, then we are in for a nasty surprise.

Apart from watching passively from the sidelines how a well-paid elite (e.g., in sports or top entertainment) displays excellence in performance, the mediocratic majority is not really interested in the subject. Instead of striving for the best in all circumstances, mediocracy just muddles through. The mediocre is preferred to the excellent. Strategic long-term planning is replaced by microtactical tit-for-tat peddling. Where have all the leaders gone? To quite an extent they have been replaced by trailers, bandwagon jumpers, hams, insolent impersonators and preposterous pretenders. As a result, quality-oriented performance has gone down the drain in many a field of contemporary society. TV talk shows, the pacemakers of public opinion, prefer jerking rumps to "talking heads." Banality, shabbiness and trash increase. Religious

3

fundamentalism and parasitic sects are having a heyday. Criminality, drug abuse and ecological damage abound. Apathy, resignation and helplessness keep spreading. Quite obviously, traditional management, with its preference for habitual strategies, is no longer fit to cope successfully with the tasks at hand. Yet if you ask its top representatives why they keep doing what they do, they retort, with conviction, "Because this is exactly what the majority demands!" Such a pseudo-democratic reply, which in fact betrays a condescending, cynical attitude, is a handy mask for the muck of mediocrity.

Failing according to the rules?

In 1707 Lord Galway lost a decisive battle against the Spanish at Almanza. Later the poet and statesman Macaulay (Colville 1981, 219) said with tongue in cheek about the poor general: "He thought it more honourable to fail according to the rules rather than to succeed by innovation."

Lord Galway seems to have bred a huge progeny of epigones. The conspicuous lack of creative leadership in church and state, economics, politics, education, health care, mass media, architecture and other sectors bears witness to the fact that there are too many individuals in positions of high responsibility who prefer to fail according to the rules rather than to succeed by innovation. Reflection is out, action is in. We love the frenetic makers and shakers - and sometimes even the ruthless breakers. We approve the turbulent speeders and wily wheelers and dealers. If their failure is too great, it does not harm mediocratic complacency: less than mediocratic role players are simply replaced by their own kind.

Yet as the debacles of Almanza keep increasing, the call for creative leadership increases too. As James MacGregor Burns (Cronin 1993, 7) wrote almost two decades ago, "One of the most universal cravings of our time is a hunger for compelling and creative leadership." The number of articles and books on the topic of leadership and innovative leadership is ever more impressive. Interviews and discussions in mass media and public conferences abound. Institutes are founded for the purpose of investigating the nature of creativity and leadership.

In 1979 my wife and I established the *International Foundation for Creativity and Leadership*. Its original aims and purposes included:

- offering post-graduate teaching programs on systems science and systems therapy in order to develop creative leadership in the realm of individual, couple, family and group therapy;

- organizing international transdisciplinary symposia on these topics;

- doing scientific research and writing publications on these topics.

After a decade of such activity we decided to leave the realm of therapy and broaden the scope of our work. We redefined our aims as follows:

- scientific research and publications on the strategically relevant link between creativity and leadership;

- organization of an annual *International Zermatt Symposium on Creativity in Economics, Arts and Science*;

- public conferences, seminars, workshops on the strategic link between creativity and leadership;

- special advisor activities for the top management of enterprises and other organizations interested in developing creative leadership.

By now (January 1997) our Foundation has published a dozen books (Guntern 1979, 1981, 1983, 1987, 1989, 1990, 1991, 1992 a, 1992 b, 1993 a, 1994, 1995 a, 1995 b, 1996) on the above-mentioned topics. It has organized seven International Zermatt Symposia. The present book contains a series of contributions by leaders who were invited to speak at the Symposia because they attained a solid international reputation through outstanding performances in their specific field of activity.

The famous Hollywood diva, Mae West, once quipped, "Whenever a woman goes wrong, men go right after her." Whenever a leader goes wrong - as Lord Galway did at Almanza - things go down the drain and a lot of people are hurt in the process. The purpose of our Foundation, of the Zermatt Symposia and the present book is to show how leaders may go right and how society may develop the creative leadership so direly needed everywhere.

What is *creative leadership?* A new slogan - as empty as other slogans supposed to provide insight, vision and strategic direction? Obviously there is more to it behind all the word thrashing on the subject in public discussions and publications. Even in many of the books on leadership and/or creativity there are no definitions of these basic terms - and thus every discussion on a these topics tends to get stuck in a semantic quagmire. Where the basic terms are defined, the discussion on leadership tends to pile up heaps of data without any order or explanation of their causal connections and logical implications. To take but one example, between 1974 and 1981 Stogdill and Bass analyzed some 4,725 studies on leadership. Stogdill (Rost 1993, 4) concluded: "The endless accumulation of empirical data has not produced an integrated understanding of leadership." Evidently, piling up bricks does not suffice to produce a cathedral. Moreover, there is a lot of apodictically stated nonsense with respect to leadership and creativity and, more often than not, the complex phenomenon of leadership, creativity and the strategically relevant link between the two is reduced to an oversimplified discussion of the specific personality traits a creative individual, a leader or a creative leader is supposed to have. If all those personality traits really were a sine qua non for leadership and creative performance, no human being would qualify.

James MacGregor Burns, author of a classic on political leadership (Burns 1979, 3), stated in his prologue on the crisis of leadership," Leadership is one of the most observed and least understood phenomena on earth." It still is - and the same holds true for creative leadership. We already know enough about it, however, to enable us to develop it in every single field of our society. It is my hope that the present book will make a significant contribution to this purpose.

Basic building blocks

I define *leadership* as *a specific process of interpersonal relationships whose participants play basically equivalent but complementary roles in such a way that they become inspired and motivated for extraordinary performances.*

This definition has various implications including the following:

- Leadership is not a quality that somebody possesses. It is not something that somebody does to somebody else. Leadership is an interpersonal relationship of a specific kind, i.e., one which shows a specific order of continuous exchange of matter-energy and information signals between human beings.

- The participants in a leadership relation play specific roles; i.e., within the setting of the leadership relation, they operate (perceive, think, feel, function physiologically and behave) in certain ways and not in others, and do so according to the implicit and explicit rules defining role prescriptions and role expectations.

- Those roles are basically equivalent. A sine qua non for leadership is that there be one or more alpha-figure(s) and a group of so-called followers, the latter usually belonging to various hierarchical levels.

A president without a constituency is not a political leader but a deserted individual. A general whose signal to attack the enemy is not followed by his troops is not a military leader, but a tragic or even a ridiculous figure. A fervent believer whose exhortations to join his scheme for eternal redemption are not followed by some individuals is not a spiritual leader, but a solitary religious fanatic. In other words, it takes two to tango. So-called leaders and so-called followers are two sides of the same coin called leadership.

- The roles are complementary. If everybody wants to govern and nobody wants to obey, there is no leadership. If every member of an orchestra fancies herself/himself to be a conductor and insists on playing her/his own tune, the result will be a cacophony and not a symphony. If everybody wants to follow and nobody has strategic vision or a sense of direction, there is no leadership, either. The muck of mediocracy is what it is because official alpha-figures lack imagination, vision, credibility, moral integrity and a firm determination to reach significant goals. Lack of values, wavering and silly overadaptation to presumed or real majorities generate meek mediocracy and not a peak of excellence in performance. Due to such boneless tactics presumed leaders eventually end up lacking a constituency. A good case in point is what happened when President George Bush proposed a new budget plan some years ago. Democratic and Republican leaders accepted it, but their constituency in Congress rejected it. The day after this defeat the Wall Street Journal (Rosenbach 1993, 115) reported that Representative Silvio Conte of Massachusetts, the senior Republican on the appropriations panel, appeared in Congress wearing a hat with two visors pointing in opposite directions and with the following legend, "I'm their leader, which way did they go?"

- The basically equivalent but complementary roles are played in such a way that the role players become inspired and motivated for extraordinary performances. Here we have three elements which are important for the leadership process: inspiration, motivation, and extraordinary performance. They constitute the basic difference between traditional management and authentic leadership. *Traditional management orders and controls habitual performance; leadership inspires and motivates extraordinary performance.*

- *Inspiration* is a specific state of organismic operation in which an individual gets more and better ideas per unit of time than in an uninspired state.

- *Motivation* is a specific state of organismic operation in which an individual has a precisely defined goal, attributes a positive value to it and does everything she/he can to reach it.

- An *extraordinary performance* is an unusual, above average performance surpassing the quantity and quality of habitual performance. Ultimately it will be a set of specific extraordinary performances which will enable us to escape the muck of mediocracy and with it, a ubiquitous coping strategy I propose to call *Babbitt's ploy*. In 1922 Sinclair Lewis (1982) published his novel, *Babbitt*. The hero is George Babbitt, a prosperous self-satisfied house agent overadapted to the mediocracy of Zenith, a town in the Midwest. One day Babbitt decides to become autonomous, to develop his own ideas, make his own decisions and behave and act differently from his colleagues and fellow citizens. His straying provokes immediate social ostracism which brings him promptly back into the middle of the herd - and soon enough he forgets his endeavor for autonomy and self-determination.

A manager orders and controls habitual performance. To do so she/he may rely entirely on the institutional authority and power bestowed upon her/him by her/his very place in the hierarchical pyramid of the institution (e.g., enterprise, governmental administration, army, hospital, school, etc.) which employs her/him. Thus she/he may be - and sometimes actually is - devoid of any particular personal and professional abilities and skills - including vision, credibility and moral integrity. *Yet a leader must inspire and motivate and she/he can do so if and only if she/he has got vision, credibility and moral integrity.*

- *Vision* is a specific part of the imagination. It is a result of anticipating imagination which formulates a specific goal in an eidetic (pictorial) or metaphorical manner. Jack Welch's (Tichy 1993) "Number 1, Number 2 rule," which holds that General Electrics should get rid of every enterprise which is not able to attain the top or second position on the global markets, is not vision but an abstract and quantified statement about GE's mission or strategic top priorities. True vision is better expressed by Saint-Exupéry (1993) in his novel, *La Citadelle*: If you want your men to build you a seaworthy ship, don't give them a blue-print, wood, saws, nails and hammers; provoke their yearning for the wide open sea and they will build you the desired ship.

- Vision is not a rambling account of strategic purposes and goals, nor a magna carta of glorious intentions printed on expensive glossy paper and handed out to a great number of people. So-called vision is not vision if it activates only abstract thinking. Real vision must activate our imagination, intuition, emotions and instincts. Metaphorically speaking, it must not only address our mind, but our heart and our guts as well - and it must be anchored deep down in our marrow-bone. As the poet Yeats (Guntern 1993a, 183) once put it, "God guard me of those men who think in their mind alone; he that sings a lasting song, sings in his marrow-bone."

- *Credibility* exists if the receiver of a message assumes that the sender of that message really means what she/he says. Credibility cannot be usurped by the sender; it is attributed to her/him, rightly or wrongly, by the receiver. Yet the sender must have a track record for consistency and congruency, otherwise people will not attribute credibility to her/him.

- *Moral integrity* is also attributed to senders by the receivers of messages. Often credibility and moral integrity are held to be identical qualities, yet they are not. Let us take an example. One night you go into a public parking lot, walk to your car, insert the key, and all of a sudden you feel a sharp pressure between your shoulder blades. You turn around and find yourself face-to-face with a mugger whose grim expression, gun and unmistakable gestures suggest that you should immediately give him all the money and credit cards you have got, plus your wristwatch and ring to boot! You will undoubtedly attribute credibility to him, but you would never go so far as to believe that this creature has got moral integrity. An individual possesses moral integrity if she/he thinks and acts according to the moral standards and ethical principles valued by society.

Our definition of leadership does not specify for what kind of extraordinary performance human beings are inspired and motivated. Adolf Hitler, Benito Mussolini, Ceausescu, Papa Doc, Charlie Manson, Jim Jones and Sohoko Asahara of AUM (who ordered his followers to attack the Tokyo subway with sarin gas) were leaders because they and their followers mutually inspired and motivated each other for truly extraordinary performances. Yet such performances are not of the sort that will help us to escape the misery of mediocracy and develop a society that functions better. What we need is constructive, not destructive leadership; but not simply constructive leadership which complements traditional management - which, by the way, is important for the normal functioning of a society and its various structural components and institutions. What we need today is creative leadership.

What is creativity? What is a creative process? What is creative leadership? What is innovative leadership?

First of all, *creative leadership and innovative leadership are equivalent terms*. Certain individuals, especially if they have some training in the natural sciences, do not like the term "creative" and prefer the term "innovative." Others prefer "innovative" because they wrongly assume that only artists are creative - or that only a genius in art, science or technological invention is creative. The fact is that too many people on the art scene today are not particularly creative; they repeat, and often badly, the work done by other artists at the beginning of our century. Most art produced and sold nowadays seems to be of a mediocre nature; its mindless banality is overwhelming. The British sculptor, Henry Moore, (1964, 140) once said that authentic art must have "beauty of expression" to please our senses and "power of expression" to fascinate our mind. Similarly, the American playwright, Eugene O'Neill (Gelb 1989, 630) wrote that an authentic artist is able to "force significant form upon experience." Thus there must be a specific life experience without which no authentic art is possible. This experience must be given a specific form able to please our senses and impress our mind; in case of doubt, the latter is more important than the former. The term "to force" implies that it takes an iron will to shape correctly a rather unstructured mass of experience. This is something which too many contemporary artists are either unable or unwilling to do. Easy commercial success lights the bone-fires of vanities and keeps them ablaze, and those fires generate a warm glow of complacency and exaggerated self-esteem. With respect to the genius, we may make the following statement: whereas a virtuoso is a perfect technician who may or may not be creative, a genius is the highest expression of human creativity.

But on a scale from 1 to 100, creativity has many levels of performance and it would be completely wrong to attribute creativity only to those on the top of that hierarchy of human performance.

What is creativity?

In my view (Guntern 1991, 37) *human creativity may be defined as the ability to generate a new form which must meet four criteria of selection: uniqueness, functional adequacy, formal-esthetic perfection, and value for society.*

- The new form must be *unique.* It is quite clear that if one reinvents the electric light bulb, paints the Mona Lisa, re-writes *Ulysses,* and formulates the General Theory of Relativity all over again, one is not being creative, but is merely an epigone who imitates, copies and reproduces what has been done before. The British playwright and actor, Noël Coward, (Payn 1982) once wrote to a friend that he was "happily bashing away at awful water colors." This is not a unique but a reproductive activity because thousands of amateurs keep happily bashing away at awful water colors - and with similar results.

- The new form must *function adequately,* i.e., it must serve the purpose for which it has been generated. A unique marketing strategy that does not function properly is not the result of creativity, but of wild imagination unfettered by the structural constraints of observable reality and strategic intentions.

- The new form must be *beautiful,* i.e., it must meet certain formal-esthetic standards - in the sense specified by Moore. There is a hidden connection between proper functionalism and formal perfection. An old Roman proverb held, "pulchritudo sigillum veri" - beauty is the sign of truth. That is probably why creative individuals spend so much time in perfecting and polishing the formal expression of their creations. Gustave Flaubert (Sandblom 1987, 27) stated that he would "rather die like a dog than to save a second by leaving a sentence before it is perfect." The quantum physicist, Paul Dirac, (Goldberg 1983, 82) who predicted the existence of antimatter two years before the positron was discovered in a laboratory experiment, observed, "It seems that if one is working from the point of getting beauty into one's equations, and if one has a really sound insight, one is on a sure line of progress." Similarly, the quantum physicist, Richard Feynman (Gleick 1993, 338) whose mathematical equations did for the understanding of the neutrino what Dirac's equations had done for the understanding of the electron, wrote: "There was a moment when I knew how nature worked. It had elegance and beauty. The goddamn thing was gleaming."

- The new form must *represent a value for society.* Whatever some people may think, an authentic human creative process is not a solipsistic, self-serving activity. It always occurs - whether or not it was intended to do so - in the service of society. If a new form meets the first three criteria but misses the fourth, it is not the result of a creative process, but of some other process which, as the following example suggests, may even be a destructive one. The inventor of the infamous gas chamber sold his contraption to the Nazis with the argument that it was an original, well-functioning invention and, as he specified "a formally elegant method of killing."

My definition calls for a few remarks. First, the new form may be a matter-energy form (e.g., an object of art, an instrument, a machine, a house, a bridge) or an information form (e.g., a concept, theory, or strategy). Sometimes it may be a compound form (e.g., a production technology combining a sophisticated scientific theory, computer technology and software). Second, all four criteria are of a qualitative kind. Usually our intuition tells us that a specific new form meets the four criteria of cultural selection and to what degree. Later, as social consensus increases and ongoing observations and experiments prove the value of the new form, we may find rational arguments allowing us to define it more precisely as the result of an authentic creative process and how and why it came about. Third, the better a new form meets the four criteria of selection, the more creative is the process which generated it. Fourth, the more unique a new form, the greater will be the effort of mental adjustment and adaptation on the part of the public for properly understanding it. Most individuals who must adjust to a very unique new form experience quite some stress. Since a human organism has two physiological stress axes (Guntern 1989, 93ff), stressed individuals may enter the so-called *Selye stress* or *helplessness stress*, feeling that they are not intelligent enough to understand the new form. They may enter the so-called *Cannon stress* or *fight-flight stress* whereby they attack the new form and/or its producer or escape any encounter with it and/or its producer.

The Greek philosopher Anaxagoras was stoned by enraged citizens because he dared to claim that the moon was not a goddess named Selene but an incandescent rock. Galileo Galilei provoked the ire of Pope Urban VIII because he defended Copernicus' view that the earth revolved around the sun, while the Vatican clung to the Ptolemaic theory, which stated the contrary. Pope Urban VIII seems to have been quite an irascible fellow; his Holiness ordered all the birds in the Vatican gardens to be killed, as their song disturbed his concentration! Galilei met a better fate: he was only threatened with torture. But as he maintained his iconoclastic views, he was put under house arrest for the rest of his life and forbidden to talk or write about his ideas, let alone publish them. The French impressionists, in later times, were not permitted to exhibit their work in the Salon d'Automne. When they had the temerity to exhibit in the Salon des Indépendants, they were heavily attacked by critics and the public alike. Albert Einstein's Theory of General Relativity was denounced by Paul Weyland (Clark 1972, 317f), founder of a so-called "Study Group of German Natural Philosophers," and by the German Nobel Prize winner, Philip Lenard, who rallied assorted riffraff to give public conferences accusing Einstein's theory as being a non-Aryan compilation of well known facts botched up by some fancy Jewish mathematics. When Einstein got phone calls with threats to kill him, he emigrated to Princeton.

All these examples - and there are many more to be found in the history of cultural evolution - are but a specific expression of what I have called *Diesel's-Dilemma* (Guntern 1994, 102f). A dilemma occurs in decision making if you are faced with a choice between two alternatives both of which imply some form of severe harm or punishment. I proposed the term Diesel's Dilemma because according to the German inventor, Rudolf Diesel (ibid), ninety-nine out of one hundred geniuses perish without being discovered and the last one prevails under untold difficulties. Diesel was wrong in many respects. Geniuses are geniuses *because* they are successful even in very difficult circumstances. There are more creative individuals who are not geniuses but will be discovered than the percentage indicated by Diesel. Yet there is a grain of truth in Diesel's statement and this grain I have included in my definition of *Diesel's Dilemma* which holds that:

> *"Creative individuals and society mutually depend on each other for survival and proper development. Yet although this mutual functional dependence is of vital significance for both parties, cooperation as well as non-cooperation will invariably generate significant and, in principle, unavoidable stress."*

By now we have all the elements to answer the question: what is creative (innovative) leadership? *Creative leadership is a specific type of leadership which inspires and motivates people for creative performance.*

The weaver at the enchanted loom

Creative leadership is the weaver at the enchanted loom able to weave the patterns of unique, well functioning, beautiful forms of high value for society. The enchanted loom is called creative process. In my view, a creative process, leading from the very first and often vague idea to the final new form that meets the criteria of cultural selection, shows the following basic mechanism:

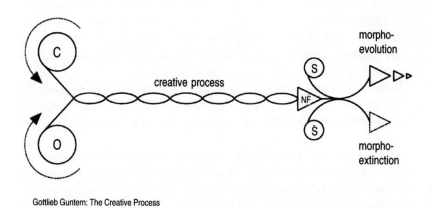

Gottlieb Guntern: The Creative Process

Figure 1 : Linear model of a creative process

There seem to be four major stages (Guntern 1991, 54ff) in the basic mechanism of the creative process:

Stage 1
Chaos (C) and order (O), chance and law, freedom and structural constraint, instinctive-emotional spontaneity and rational calculation combine in a specific way which gives rise to the germination of an idea.

Stage 2

With the germination of a new idea a multiphase process begins; it ends with the generation of a new form (NF). In my view, there must be at least seven phases in stage 2 of every single creative process:

Table 1: Phases of the creative process

Germination
Inspiration
Preparation
Incubation
Illumination
Elaboration
Evaluation

Germination consists of the unconscious generation of a potentially interesting and fertile idea.

The very moment a germinating idea enters into our consciousness and fires up our imagination, *inspiration* occurs.

Once we are inspired we begin to gather data and look for specific materials, techniques and methods; discuss with knowledgeable individuals; formulate our ideas to write, paint, compose, sculpt or do whatever we do in our specific field of activity. With that, we have entered the phase of *preparation.*

Sometimes preparation seems to run almost directly into elaboration. But a more detailed analysis of observable facts and subjective experience suggests that there is always a period of *incubation* involved. We may encounter major obstacles during preparation and further progress appears to be blocked for good. Our ideas slip back into the unconscious, where they may vanish forever. Yet if we are lucky, one day the next phase of the creative process will occur.

If all of a sudden - usually while we are in a relaxed mood and far from thinking of the unsolved problem - a solution to that problem pops into our conscious mind, *illumination* occurs. It is also called the *eureka-experience* (Gr. *heuréka* = I have found it). As soon as this happens, we enter the next phase of the creative process.

The phase of *elaboration* may last for long periods of time, sometimes years or even decades. Now we really compose our music, write our novel, make our movie, invent a machine, formulate a scientific theory, or studiously work out a new marketing strategy.

Eventually we enter the phase of *evaluation,* where we try to separate the wheat from the chaff. The more creative a person, the more inexorable the weeding out. The less creative a person, the more she/he is usually convinced that everything she/he does is great. Then it takes stage 3 of the creative process to draw out the air from the blown-up balloon of the grandiose self.

Stage 3

Once the process of evaluation by the creator has been accomplished, the new form leaves the private space-time to enter the public space-time. Now society begins to evaluate the new form and decide whether or not it meets the four criteria of *cultural selection* (S). Depending upon the verdict of cultural selection, which may well - and often does - change with time, the new form will follow one or the other of the two paths in stage 4.

Stage 4

If cultural selection decides that the new form meets the four criteria of creative performance, then *morpho-evolution* (Gr. *morphé* = structure, form, gestalt) occurs. The new form inspires and motivates its generator and/or other individuals or groups for creative performance. Sometimes a new form - for instance a new scientific theory, object of art, or invention - may heavily influence the Zeitgeist and even stimulate the foundation of new professional disciplines, art forms, industries and so on.

If cultural selection decides that the new form does not meet the four criteria for creative performance, *morpho-elimination* occurs. The new form is forgotten or physically destroyed - and sometimes (as was the case with Ford Etzel) it serves as a model of deterrence, suggesting what one should not do to achieve creative performance.

Whatever the outcome of stage 3, both morpho-evolution and morpho-elimination influence the deterministic chaos of the transactional field from which a new stage 1 of a new creative process may begin, be it in the same individual or group or elsewhere.

The basic mechanism of creative performance just outlined calls for a few remarks. First, metaphorically speaking, the model shown in figure 1 is a simple skeleton devoid of muscles, vessels and inner organs. To put it more abstractly, it suggests a simple linear process. The creative process, however, is a complex multidimensional process full of reciprocal feedback loops and redundant operations interconnecting the four stages and the seven phases in stage 2, and thus generating a host of reciprocal influences. Second, a single individual or a team may be involved in two or more creative processes simultaneously, sometimes even in different fields. For the sake of allowing the reader a rapid overview and intuitive understanding, I have preferred to remain simple and stripped my model of the above-mentioned complexity. Third, a specific creative process may get stuck in any stage or any phase of stage 2. Fourth, in every single stage and in every single phase of stage 2 there are specific opportunities for enhancing the probability of good creative performance. Fifth, every stage and every phase may last minutes or hours, months, years and even decades. Sixth, the form-generating, form-maintaining, form-evolving and form-dissolving processes of geophysical and biological evolution seem to operate according to a basic mechanism which in many respects is analogous to - but not identical with! - the creative process in cultural evolution.

Clumsy partridges and wily foxes, playing golf and playing with loaded dice

Why and for what purpose do we need more creative leadership and more creative performance? Why and for what purpose should we increase the rate and quality of innovation?

The answer is quite simple: in order better to survive and adequately develop! We will successfully reach these strategic goals if, and only if, our capacity to adapt allows a satisfying *mutual fit* between ourselves and the world we live in. But what is the concrete nature of our contemporary world?

Today's world is a *system*. It is an organized whole consisting of continuously interacting parts. What happens *here* will have consequences *there*. "No man is an island," wrote the poet John Donne a long time ago. He was right. We are not isolated from the mainland, we are an integral part of it - though we seem to have forgotten it. For too long we have indulged in a *naïve supremacy* wielding the *flail of Genesis* (Guntern 1992 a, 32ff) and subduing the earth. We have considered the earth's ecosystem, including the atmosphere, as a storeroom full of resources and robbed it. We have used it as a trash bin and cluttered it with waste and toxic materials - to the point where ecological catastrophes are beginning to remind the *greedy society* of the simple fact that our earth is a system within which everything is connected with everything else. For too long we have played the *lyre of Orpheus* (Guntern 1992 a, 47), forcing our mind - and its assistant, our will - to subdue our body. The consequences - individual illness, social misery and premature death - are highly symptomatic phenomena of the nature of our society. Both the flail of Genesis and the lyre of Orpheus are the results of the one-sided, analytical-dualistic thinking which began some three thousand years ago in Jewish and Greek thought. It put the logical, rational, detail-centered and quantitative thinking of our dominant brain hemisphere on a throne, while relegating the intuitive, imaginative, qualitative and relation-centered thinking of our non-dominant brain hemisphere (Guntern 1990, 24ff) to the position of valet. Thus a specific cultural evolution led to the functional inhibition of a major part of our complex brain. We grew smarter and smarter as we lost the ancient wisdom of man who knew that the world is, as I once put it, a seamless *swinging web* (Guntern 1983) in which each one of us is a thread and a knot all at once.

Our world is a *complex system*. Complexity depends neither on the number of structural components nor on functional processes in a system. It depends on the amount of information needed properly to describe, explain and understand a system so as to operate efficiently on the basis of that understanding. A husband and wife may be a highly complex system if their relationship is full of chaotic manipulations, dirty tricks and insidious intrigues. A team consisting of seven people, on the other hand, may be a simple system if they cooperate in a well ordered, open-minded, and efficient manner, ruled by moral integrity.

Our world is a *highly dynamic system*. A system is qualified as dynamic if it changes its structures and functions in the course of time. It is termed highly dynamic if structural and functional changes occur very rapidly and radically. Modern means of transportation and communication are fast, and the development of so-called data highways will further speed up the process of interactive connectedness. Thus, what happens here may immediately have consequences there. If the MITI in Tokyo decides today on a new strategic policy and the decision is made public, immediately the top executives of governments, corporations and other agencies all over the globe will meet to decide how to respond to the new challenge. When the former Minister of Defense, Carl Weinberger, quoted Tennyson in his hopes that the Soviet Union would perish "not with a whimper but with a bang," nobody believed it would happen - and so soon. Yet the huge and apparently petrified political structure collapsed under the impact of its own inertia and lack of creative leadership. The dust raised has yet to settle before we can see all the consequences. There are individuals who do not feel at all comfortable with unstable, highly dynamic systems. Perhaps Prigogine's (Cramer 1988, 238) observation can be of some consolation: "Matter at equilibrium is dull. The further one goes away from equilibrium, the more intelligent matter becomes." Creative leaders know how to profit from the windows of opportunity opened in the violently shaking house of ongoing structural change.

Our world shows a *sensitive dependence upon initial conditions*. In 1961 the American meteorologist Lorenz (Gleick 1987, 11ff) made computer simulations of the development of weather at M.I.T. He fed data on temperature, air pressure, wind direction and other causal factors influencing the development of meteorological conditions into his computer. Since in those days computers took some time to grind out their answers, at one point Lorenz abbreviated the six numbers after the decimal to only three. When the computer had finished calculating, there was a tremendous change in the simulated weather! Lorenz had come upon a concrete case of a phenomenon known today as the *butterfly effect* or *sensitive dependence upon initial conditions*: a tiny deviation in initial conditions may - due to deviation-amplifying positive feedback loops - ultimately generate a huge difference in outcome. It is, of course, an old human experience that tiny causes may produce huge consequences, as illustrated by the famous nursery rhyme:

> For want of a nail the shoe was lost.
> For want of a shoe the horse was lost.
> For want of a horse the man was lost.
> For want of a man the battle was lost.
> For want of a battle the kingdom was lost.

The butterfly effect is responsible, among other things, for the unpredictability of events. If you simulate a billiard game on your computer screen and set the virtual balls in motion, they will go on forever because there is no loss of kinetic energy due to friction. Yet if in the initial data fed into your computer you miss even so small a factor as the impact of the gravitational field of an electron at the outer edge of our universe, then, as Morfill and Scheingraber (1991, 54) emphasize, in about ten minutes of interaction your prediction of the ball trajectories will turn out to be wrong. Thus the butterfly effect implies that in the long run, the behavior of highly dynamic systems with sensitive dependence on initial conditions is in principle unpredictable.

Our world shows a *fractal structure with transscalar self-similarity*. This insight is due to the highly creative work of Benoît Mandelbrot (1995), mathematician and founding father of fractal geometry. Transscalar self-similarity implies that on various levels of complexity, phenomena or events may show striking structural and functional similarities.

In 1865 Whymper, who was a member of the first group of alpinists ever to climb the Matterhorn - considered at that time a challenge nobody could meet - observed that a small rock in the Matterhorn was shaped like the entire mountain. If you observe how autonomy is developed or blocked in an individual, you understand more easily how the same occurs in a team or a whole nation. Properly understanding the principle of self-similarity allows us better to cope with complexity.

As is usually the case with important cognitive principles, the concept of transscalar self-similarity was intuitively understood a long time ago. St. Augustine could see the world in a grain of sand. During the 1598 Korean campaign near Naniwa, the famous Shogun, Toyotomi Hideoshi (Suzuki 1973, 303) wrote a poem as he lay on his deathbed: "Like a dewdrop, settled, / Like a dewdrop, fading away - / Alas, this, my life! / As to the affairs of Naniwa, / A dream in a dream!" Similarly, Leibniz (Gleick 1987, 115) intuitively grasped the notion that a drop of water contained a teeming universe. And when with the help of a microscope, Anton van Leeuwenhoek discovered the sperm in 1683, he considered it to be a homunculus, a tiny replica of man.

Our world is governed by *deterministic chaos*. This is an intricate concept, and a brief historical review of the topic of causality will help us better to understand it. In the early 17th century the astronomer, Johannes Kepler (Bronowski 1973), stated that the universe was not a divine organism, as had been assumed until then, but a machine. Kepler's change of metaphors was the beginning of a far-reaching butterfly effect which eventually generated the mechanistic thinking and ideology of a technological era. Newton, Laplace and Lagrange further developed the basic idea contained in Kepler's metaphor. For Newton the universe was a kind of high-precision Swiss watch, a machine that functioned perfectly and whose events were utterly predictable. In this universe governed by rigorous determinism there was no place for chaos, chance events or freedom. All events were governed by the laws of nature, and the Lord himself made sure that the scheme of pre-established harmony was maintained and those events never went astray. Laplace (Gleick 1987, 14), taking up Newton's concept, even imagined a master mind who would know all the positions of heavenly bodies and all the forces impinging upon them at a specific point of time. He wrote, "Such an intelligence would embrace in the same formula the movements of the greatest bodies of the universe and those of the lightest atom; for it, nothing would be uncertain and the future, as the past, would be present to its eyes."

In the second half of the 19th century, Boltzmann proved in his theory of thermodynamics that, due to the intervention of chance events, the collision of gas molecules in a closed container could not be predicted with certainty, but only in terms of probability. Yet Boltzmann's discovery was thought to be no more than a footnote to Newton's paradigm, a local exception emphasizing the general rule. In 1887 Oscar II, the King of Sweden (Morfill 1991, 44), initiated a scientific competition offering 2,500 Swedish crowns for the best answer to the question, "How stable is our solar system?" Many scientists entered the unusual steeple chase that was eventually won by the famous French mathematician, Poincaré. Yet what he found was not at all to his liking, because as he confessed (Breuer and Haaf 1990, 54f), "Those things are so bizarre that I simply cannot bear to give them more thought." *Bizarre* comes from the Basque word for bearded. What was so strange and outlandish that Poincaré felt compelled to call it bizarre? He had unwittingly discovered that during the turbulent events of what is known today as the *big bang,* the supreme watchmaker had placed a little time-bomb in the Kepler-Newton-Laplacian cosmic machinery. One day the whole machinery may fly apart because the interactions between its elements will influence each other in such a way that resonant forces will produce an escalation of centrifugal forces, causing the planets to escape their elliptical orbits and be hurled into norm-deviant trajectories. Thus Poincaré had discovered what is known today as *sensitive dependence on initial conditions,* a causal principle which he clearly formulated (Breuer and Haaf 1990, 56) in 1903: "The case may occur that minor differences in initial conditions will cause major differences in later phenomena; a small error in the former may provoke an extraordinarily large error for the latter. Prediction will become impossible and we will have a 'chance phenomenon.'"

This was the second time since Boltzmann that the hissing snake of unpredictability had raised its fear-inducing head. And there was more to come. The 5th International Solvay Congress was held in Brussels in 1925. Dedicated to the topic *Electrons and Photons,* it was attended by the international crème de la crème of physics. The meeting turned out to be electrifying for all the participants, shedding some light on the nature of causality - and, I may add, on the nature of man as well. Bohr and Heisenberg (Gamow 1966, 114f; Clark 1972, 415ff; Bernstein 1974, 217ff) held that within an atom, events could be predicted only in terms of probability and not with certainty because of chance events. Einstein, supported by Schrödinger, did not agree at all with this proposition. For him chance was but a convenient label masking the fact that we did not yet know the laws of nature governing intra-atomic events. He kept repeating in the metaphorical language he loved, "God does not play dice with the world," to the point where an exasperated Bohr exclaimed, "Stop telling the Lord what he is supposed to do!" Einstein and Schrödinger lost the battle of Brussels. From then on unpredictability reigned in the interactions of gas molecules, in the outer cosmos of interplanetary interactions and in the interactions of intra-atomic particles. Incidentally, the computer simulations made by the French astrophysicist, Jacques Laskar, have meanwhile supported Poincaré's discovery that in the long range the solar system is unstable and unpredictable. He (Breuer and Haaf 1990, 57) stated, "The solar system is chaotic, not quasi-periodical. Especially with respect to the inner planets such as the earth, the predictability gets lost after x million years."

Today contemporary *chaos theory* (Guntern 1995 a) goes beyond the concrete realms of atoms, molecules, atmospheres and solar systems. It holds that all complex and dynamic systems in the universe (e.g., wave patterns at the beach, neuronal events in human brains, interpersonal relationships within an enterprise, developments in the stock exchange, relations between nations, the development of an ecosystem, etc.) are governed by so-called *deterministic chaos.* This term implies that chaos and order, chance events and natural laws, freedom and structural constraints (as well as instinctive-emotional spontaneity and rational calculation in human beings) continuously influence each other to co-determine all the events in complex dynamic systems, making their behavior completely unpredictable in the long run. More than two decades ago Mitchell Feigenbaum (1995), a brilliant young theoretical physicist, discovered how highly ordered dynamic systems may enter a transition phase of rhythmical oscillations ending in chaos. The *Feigenbaumroute* into chaos describes a cascade of period-doublings characterized by the number 4.6692016090.... This type of cascade may be found, for instance, in a pot of water which goes from rest to boiling point; in the laminar stream of water hitting a stone in a river bed and turning into a set of consecutive bifurcations ending in chaotic whirls and eddies; (this event, incidentally, inspired Leonardo da Vinci to make beautiful drawings of the turbulence phenomenon, which intrigued him as it has intrigued many great minds in the history of man); in the crisscrossing wave patterns along the beach; in the behavior of atmospheric conditions, and in many more dynamic systems. Thus, for the time being, the historical Battle of Brussels has produced an outcome which the physicist Ford (Gleick 1987, 314) has formulated as follows: "God plays dice with the universe. But they're loaded dice." They are loaded because chance events (the casual throwing) and lawfulness (the manipulated dice) interact.

Such is the overall picture drawn by contemporary science: our world is a highly dynamic system characterized by complexity and sensitive dependence upon initial conditions and governed by deterministic chaos which, in the long run, makes events utterly unpredictable. As Drucker (1989) puts it, the *age of uncertainty* has come, and it is here to stay. Thus the next question arises: What are we supposed to do to survive and develop properly in a saloon where every single game is played with loaded dice? There are many possible answers. Let us take the world of economics as an example to illustrate what they might be. Industrial leaders and managers offer basically three answers to this strategically relevant question - and not all have the same value for survival and adequate development.

The first answer is: *Get bigger!* Mergers, acquisitions and strategic alliances increase the size of an enterprise and provide it with a better leverage in the fierce global competition for increased market shares and higher profits. Top executives who believe in the unconditional benediction of big size never tire of praising the huge benefits to be expected from an economy of size and the incredible chances of a large corporation for mobilizing resources and discovering synergies. *Synergy* is treated like a fetish, a cult object to which true believers attribute magical powers. While the tribal dance whirls in frenetic enthusiasm around the cult object, nobody seems to be aware of the huge losses of time, energy and money due to the friction which invariably arises if you try to weld different enterprises with different individuals, different habitual ways of thinking and acting, and different mentalities and corporate cultures into one single unit. The huge costs of restructuring, downsizing, reengineering and the like are not always properly taken into account. Huge enterprises cut jobs, while small enterprises generate new ones. What about the people who are fired in the process of so-called *downsizing* and fill the streets with crowds of frustrated, embittered, angered, depressed or helpless individuals eagerly awaiting a charismatic leader who promises immediate redemption from all misery? What about those self-styled redeemers, often of a destructive kind, who invariably pop up whenever the established leadership fails? Have we already forgotten Adolf Hitler, who induced by the size of his inflated, grandiose self, promised the establishment of "Das Tausendjährige Reich" to a nation suffering from the pain and shame of a lost world war, huge reparation costs and a worldwide economic depression?

There is no doubt that proper size and an economy of scale offer important competitive advantages; but optimal size is not maximal size. The war cry for the *get-bigger-strategy* overlooks the fact that big systems - e.g., a huge molecule, big rocks, the dinosaurs, big political parties, the Roman Empire, the British Empire, the former Soviet Union - have an inherent tendency towards decay. Big systems, moreover, develop a lot of inertia, and they are difficult to steer - especially at a time when the world has become a complex and highly dynamic system where agility is one of the prerequisites of proper adaptation. A good case in point is IBM. It was, and still is, a big global player. It was number one in computer hardware. In the mid 1980's (Tichy 1993, 74) it was making huge profits from mainframes. But suddenly the competitive field conditions changed, and it turned out that IBM lacked the agility and innovation necessary for proper adaptation. It had fallen into the snare of *hybris,* a trap often set by long-lasting success. Continuous success easily breeds complacency, presumption and contempt for competitors. As Jack Welch (Tichy 1993, 104), CEO of General Electrics, once put it, "The worst sins are committed in boom times, when everybody feels satisfied. That's when managers get fat and arrogant." Big Blue also missed the *kairos,* the God of the propitious moment for the strategic shift from big mainframes to work stations and personal computers. Even worse, it did not perceive the window of opportunity opened by the development of an ever more sophisticated software - a strategic opportunity Bill Gates, founder and president of Microsoft, was eager to grasp. In the mid 1990's IBM's market value had sunk to almost half its 1987 level. It fell prey not only to the stranglehold of inertia but also to what I call the *spill-over effect* (Guntern1994, 69), a mechanism of sterile in-fighting and self-destruction triggered by a rapid decline of success on the markets and transforming extrasystemically deployed aggression into intrasystemic destruction. In 1993 Lou Gerstner (44f), yet another CEO involved in the turn-around management at IBM, stated, "I've never seen a company…so much caught up in its own underwear." This is not necessarily an auspicious strategic position to be in if you intend to woo your customers and scare your competitors away.

The second answer is: *Get faster!* Maximal acceleration is another fetish in our *dromomaniac society* (Gr. *drómos* = course of events, speed; *manía* = delusion, craziness, obsession). The followers of this *cult of dromomania* (Guntern 1994, 66) overlook the fact that many a frenetically accelerating fish ends up all too easily in the wide open jaws of a predator lurking in the wings. Maximal acceleration of decisions and actions generates a lot of failures, costs and other problems. Great strategists seek optimal, not maximal, speed. In 1643, a few weeks before he died of natural death, the famous samurai master, Myamoto Musashi, (1974) retired into a mountain cave to write *Go Rin No Sho,* a famous treatise on the art of strategy. In the course of his life Musashi had participated in six wars and innumerable man-to-man contests and had never been defeated. Now fencing is certainly a competitive game that demands speed - optimal, not maximal speed. Musashi (ib. 91) wrote: "Speed is not part of the true Way of strategy. Speed implies that things seem fast or slow, according to whether or not they are in rhythm. Whatever the Way, the master of strategy does not appear fast." Optimal strategy demands that the strategist tune into the rhythm of events and synchronize with the overall pattern of action. In my view, a landscape - be it geographic or transactional - is like a song: it has got melody, rhythm and harmony. If you want to dance in that landscape without stumbling and deliver a graceful and efficient performance crowned by success, then you have to tune into that landscape. *But this synchronized tuning-in is governed by the receptive mode of our intuitive thinking - not by the action mode of our dominant brain hemisphere!* (Guntern 1990, 19ff; 1992, 187ff). That is why Musashi (1974, 44) stated, "The Way of strategy is the Way of nature." Natural events rarely occur very fast - with the exception of lightning, volcano eruptions, tornadoes and certain types of avalanches. This truth, however, is not easily grasped by the firm believers in maximal speed, who keep to the German proverb, "Wer rastet, rostet!" - he who rests rusts. This may indeed be the case. Yet there is another aspect of the same phenomenon: on the heated grill of frenetic acceleration, human beings get roasted to the point of *burn-out,* a syndrome of chronic exhaustion. Exhausted troops will win no battles. A dromomaniac manager who follows the famous *panic instruction for industrial engineers* (Dickson 1978, 141), "When you don't know what to do, walk fast and look worried!" will not fare any better.

Winston Churchill, a great political leader who tended to shun any unnecessary physical exertion, once scoffed at golf players, "The aim of the game is to hit a very small ball into an even smaller hole - with weapons singularly ill-suited for that purpose." His witticism holds true for life in general. Too many ill-advised strategists try to hit the ball of their ambitions into the hole of success with methods - maximal size or maximal speed - singularly ill-suited for that purpose. Why ill-suited? Because in the competitive game played in the industrial world, almost every single competitor applies them too. When everyone in a competition does the same thing, the outcome is utterly predictable. A few will win; most will lose the fight for survival and proper development. The winners will sleep well while their opponents sleep badly; but during his restless night, a competitor may well hit on tactics that will make him win tomorrow, and the loser will be you. Thus the merry-go-round of consecutive success and failure keeps turning. A predictable strategy is not a very clever device for winning in a saloon where all the games are played with loaded dice. This is a fact which all great military strategists from Sun Tzu (1984) to Myamoto Musashi (1974), from von Clausewitz (1980) to Napoleon (Matthews 1989, 18ff) have emphasized time and again. In peace and war, and whatever the specific circumstances may be, the best strategy chosen and implemented always contains an element of surprise.

The third answer is: *Get more innovative!* This is the best answer and, of course, it may be combined with answers one and two. To be innovative implies, as we have seen, coming up with a unique problem solution. In contradistinction to the habitual solution of getting bigger and faster, the uniqueness of a creative performance implies its unpredictability and the vital element of surprise. "Not to innovate is the single largest reason for the decline of existing organizations," writes the renowned social scientist and management specialist Peter Drucker (1989, 277). He insists on the fact that in the future, social innovation may even become more important than technological innovation. Only if the rate and quality of innovation is good enough, are survival and proper development possible for an enterprise - or any other human system involved in competition. Your competitors are able to copy your strategies of increased growth, increased process acceleration and the application of all the habitual management tools (e.g., restructuring, downsizing, outsourcing, insourcing, bench-marking, total quality management, just-in-time management, customer focus, reengineering, etc.) available today. But they cannot copy the creativity of your enterprise, because this creative performance is the result of a unique blend of individuals and teams generating a unique blend of ideas, strategies, products and services. There seems to be no doubt: *the proper combination of a sufficient rate and quality of innovation is the number 1 critical success factor in today's global economic competition.* And because too many enterprises lack the necessary rate and quality of innovation, the industrial landscape is littered with the pale bones of extinct enterprises.

After this more analytical approach to the question of coping strategies for optimal survival and development, let us put the same basic message into metaphorical form. To illustrate the difference between predictable and unpredictable strategies, we shall take an example from biological evolution where predators and prey have always played and still play a competitive game whose outcome determines life or death. Biological evolution began some 3.5 billion years ago when the first cyanobacteria or blue-green algae began to populate the oceans of the earth. *In the course of biological evolution microbial, plant, animal and human organisms have developed linear (predictable) and non-linear (unpredictable) coping strategies. Although both have their intrinsic merits, organisms able to develop non-linear strategies have, by and large, fared better in the principle of natural selection that weeds out those unfit to cope with actual living conditions.* Let us have a look at the basic coping strategies of a partridge and a fox faced with a human predator.

Alarmed by an approaching hunter, a *clumsy partridge* immediately rises from its lair, blindly flying off and accelerating as fast as it possibly can. But since its flight trajectory is linear, characterized by the typical straight line of Euclidian geometry and therefore utterly predictable, the partridge stands little chance of escaping an intelligent hunter armed with a sharp eye, a steady hand and a good rifle. It will pay for its frenetic action mode by ending right where it began its coping maneuver: on the ground. It will be bagged, thrown in the frying pan, cut apart by a knife, torn to shreds by the successful hunter's teeth, and ultimately digested into molecular nirvana.

But a *wily fox,* the principle incarnate of non-linear gambling, will respond quite differently to the existential challenge it is suddenly confronted with. It will slowly rise. It will look, sniff and listen. It will sneak off, unhurriedly slipping into the undergrowth, trotting to the left and weaving to the right. It will push through dense shrubbery, take off for a little sprint, remain motionless in the shadow of a tree, jump over a trunk lying on the ground, climb a rock, have a good look at its entire surroundings, and again, sniff and listen. Thus, continuously combining action mode and receptive mode of operation, the fox cleverly exploits the conditions and strategic possibilities of the territory. In escaping its hunter, it may even catch a careless partridge feeding on berries in a clearing. Eventually it will hide away in a hole in the ground. For a long time it will not reappear. When it does, it will be where the hunter least expects. Since the fox pursues a non-linear flight trajectory, characterized by a combination of geodesic and fractal geometry, its behavior is not predictable, and its chance of escaping the hunter is much greater than that of the poor partridge. The fox responds to the existential threat and challenge with a non-linear game, using loaded dice in the strategic game played by predators and prey, and thus inducing perplexity, uncertainty and failure in its hunter.

Natural resources, fat hens and a fair race

We live in an era of rapidly dwindling natural resources. Yet *human creativity is a natural resource that is virtually inexhaustible because successful creative performances always inspire and motivate further creative performances.*

Yet many a human system - including enterprises and social institutions - do not seem to know what to do with this precious natural resource. *A manager who is not able to mobilize properly the creative human resources she/he is responsible for is like a brooding-hen, frozen to death on a cold winter's night and sitting like a block of ice on her eggs, unable to give them the thermic input to energize and break through the shell that hinders their further development.*

In every single human system there are three major resources of creativity: the human brain, the human personality, and the culture of the system. The human brain is a complex penta-megastructure composed of a dominant brain hemisphere, a non-dominant brain hemisphere, an emotion brain, a cerebellum and an instinct brain. Each one of these five brains plays a specific role in creative performance - and there are specific methods for mobilizing their resources. A creative performer must mobilize specific personality traits (e.g., motivation, endurance, stress tolerance, resilience, playfulness, etc.). Finally there is the system's culture (e.g., corporate culture in a multinational enterprise), an invisible transactional field, an inconspicuous tapestry woven by what and how all the individuals living and working in it perceive, think and feel; how they function physiologically and how they behave - including their verbal, para-verbal and non-verbal communication. This invisible transactional field is patterned and the main transactional patterns are: prevailing ideas, autonomies, hierarchies, decision-making, cooperation, conflict management, and coping strategies. These seven transactional patterns can be transformed in such a way that the rate and quality of innovation increases.

In one of his songs the rock poet Bob Dylan sings:

> "...for I am runnin' in a fair race
> with no race-track but the night
> an' no competition but the dawn."

Most people are running in a race where many of their opponents do not behave like gentlemen - or ladies. They are standing in a boxing ring where many an opponent does not honor the rules of fairness standardized in 1865 by the 8th Marquis of Queensberry to guarantee a hint of decency between aggressive fighters. Most race tracks are crowded and open day and night. Therefore it must have dawned on you that your competitors spend sleepless nights trying to find out how to beat you in the morning. Yet if you energetically mobilize your creative resources and those of your collaborators, you will prevail. You will belong to the winners and not the losers. You will hedge your risks, secure your present, and adequately prepare for the future.

"There is no substitute for victory!" exclaimed General MacArthur (Ward 1992, 81) in a speech delivered to the American Congress. There is no substitute for victory, indeed. If you have no intention of sharing poor Galway's fate, but prefer the track record of the Commander of the Allied Pacific forces during World War II who, after having been chased from the Philippines, eventually accepted the Japanese capitulation, then you must energetically mobilize the creative resources lying dormant in every single human brain, in every single personality and in every single system culture - and direct their forces toward your most important strategic goals. It can be done. There are, as mentioned above, specific methods for doing so. But the context of this introduction does not lend itself to a deeper discussion of this highly relevant topic.

The Golden Thread

To many a bewildered citizen, our contemporary world is like a labyrinth. In the context of fierce global competition, the fight for survival and proper development often resembles the hero's fight with the Minotaur. Theseus used Ariadne's thread to find his way out of King Minos' labyrinth. There is also a thread that helps us to find our way out of the labyrinth of today's existential challenges and threats. This thread is called creative performance.

In the present book, creative minds with a track record of outstanding achievement unwind the spool of genuine leadership. These leaders come from different spheres of activity. They express themselves differently and emphasize different aspects of creative leadership. Yet all of them have something in common: they are keenly aware of the strategic importance of creative performance in today's world. We have something to learn from each of them.

Hopefully, this introduction will provide the reader with a general conceptual framework enabling her/him better to understand the implications of the specific aspects of the creative process and the creative leadership presented and emphasized by the contributors to this volume.

Gottlieb Guntern, M.D.
Martigny 1996

Readers who are genuinely interested in knowing more about the International Foundation for Creativity and Leadership as well as the International Zermatt Symposia on Creativity in Economics, Arts and Science may get in touch with:
Gottlieb Guntern, M.D.
Director
International Foundation for Creativity and Leadership
P.O. Box 464
CH-1920 Martigny

Tel: +41 / 27 / 723 17 77
Fax: + 41 / 27 / 723 17 78

References

Bernstein J. (1974): *Einstein.* New York: Viking Press

Breuer R., HAAF G. (1990): Kosmos - Ein ordentliches Chaos. In: *GEO Wissen. Chaos + Kreativität.* 7. Mai, pp. 32-60

Bronowski J. (1973): *The Ascent of Man.* Boston, Toronto: Little, Brown & Co.

Burns J.M. (1979): *Leadership.* New York : Harper & Row Publishers.

Clark R.W. (1972): *Einstein, the Life and Times.* New York: Avon Books.

Clausewitz, von C. (1980): *Vom Kriege.* Ungekürzter Text nach der Erstauflage (1832-34). Frankfurt, Berlin, Wien: Ullstein.

Colville J. (1981): *Churchill and His Inner Circle.* New York: Wyndham Books.

Cramer F. (1988): *Chaos und Ordnung. Die komplexe Struktur des Lebendigen.* Stuttgart: Deutsche Verlags-Anstalt

Cronin T.E. (1993): Reflections on Leadership. In: W.E. Rosenbach and R.L. Taylor (eds): *Contemporary Issues in Leadership.* Boulder - San Francisco - Oxford: Westview Press, pp. 7 - 26

Dickson P. (1978): *The Official Rules.* New York: Delacorte Press

Drucker P.F. (1989): *The New Realities.* New York: Harper & Row

Feigenbaum M.J. (1995): In: G. Guntern (ed.): *Chaos und Kreativität. Rigorous Chaos. Das rigorose Chaos.* Zürich: Scalo Publishers, pp.

Gamow G. (1966): *Thirty Years that Shook Physics.* New York: Anchor Books, Doubleday & Co., Inc.

Gelb A. and B. (1987): *O'Neill.* New York: Harper & Row, Publishers, Perennial Library

Gerstner L: (1993): Rethinking IBM, Cover story, *Business Week,* October 4, pp. 44-55

Gleick J. (1987): *Chaos. Making a New Science.* New York: Viking Penguin, Inc.

Gleick J. (1993): *Richard Feynman and Modern Physics.* London : Abacus Press,

Goldberg P. (1983): *The Intuitive Edge. Understanding Intuition and Applying it in Everyday Life.* Los Angeles: Jeremy P. Tarcher, Inc.

Guntern G. (1979): *Social Change, Stress, and Mental Health in the Pearl of the Alps.* Berlin-Heidelberg-New York: Springer

- (1981) (Hrsg.): *Structural Family Therapy - Systemtherapie.* Martigny: International Foundation for Creativity and Leadership

- (Hrsg.) (1983): *Die Welt, ein schwingendes Gewebe.* Martigny: International Foundation for Creativity and Leadership
- (1987) (ed): *Der blinde Tanz zur lautlosen Musik.* Martigny: International Foundation for Creativity and Leadership
- (1989): *Therápodos - la via del terapeuta.* Milano, Hoepli.
- (1990) (ed): *Der Gesang des Schamanen.* Hirnforschung- Veränderte Bewusstseinszustände - Schamanismus (mit Beiträgen von Joseph E. und Glenda M. Bogen, Arthur J. Deikman, Peter F. Furst and Raymond H. Prince), Martigny: International Foundation for Creativity and Leadership
- (1991) (ed): *Der kreative Weg.* Kreativität in Wirtschaft, Kunst und Wissenschaft (mit Beiträgen von Maya Angelou, Luc Bondy, Mario Botta, Heinz Dürr, Franco Sbarro, Robert Wilson), Zürich: Verlag Moderne Industrie
- (1992 a): *Im Zeichen des Schmetterlings.* Vom Powerplay zum sanften Spiel der Kräfte. Bern-München-Wien: Scherz Verlag
- (1992 b): *Kreativität. Ressource und Lebenselexier.* Referat anlässlich des Fabrikgespräches von W & L/Dialog/Grey, Walther + Leuenberger AG, Rüschlikon/Zürich
- (1993 a) (ed): *Irritation und Kreativität.* Hemmende und fördernde Faktoren im kreativen Prozess (mit Beiträgen von François Couchepin, Zaha Hadid, Gabriel García Márquez, Helmut Maucher, Anatol Rapoport, Harald Szeemann, Eleanor Traylor). Zürich: Scalo
- (1993 b) : La crise est une chance! Finissons-en avec la médiocratie pour réinventer la Suisse. In: *Le Nouveau Quotdien*, 23.11.1993, p. 4
- (1994): *Sieben Goldene Regeln der Kreativitätsförderung.* Zürich: Scalo
- (Hg.)(1995 a): *Chaos und Kreativität. Rigorous Chaos.* (Mit Beiträgen von Gerd Binnig, Mitchell J. Feigenbaum, Abdullah Ibrahim, Benoit B. Mandelbrot, Ivo Pitanguy, Lothar Späth). Zürich: Scalo
- (Hg.)(1995 b): *Imagination und Kreativität. Playful Imagination.* (Mit Beiträgen von Gerald M. Edelman, Jane Goodall, Jon Lord, Peter Schneider, Liv Ullmann). Zürich: Scalo
- (Hg) (1996) *Intuition und Kreativität,* Zürich: Scalo (in Vorbereitung)
Lewis S. (1982): *Babbitt.* New York : Granada
Mandelbrot B. B. (1995): In: Gottlieb Guntern (Hg): *Chaos und Kreativität. Rigorous Chaos.* (Mit Beiträgen von Gerd Binnig, Mitchell

J. Feigenbaum, Abdullah Ibrahim, Benoit B. Mandelbrot, Ivo Pitanguy, Lothar Späth). Zürich: Scalo

Matthews, Lloyd J. (ed) (1989) : *The Challenge of Military Leadership.* Washington etc. : Pergamon-Brassey's International Defence Publishers, Inc.

Moore H. (1964): On Sculpture & Primitive Art. In: R.L. Herbert (ed): *Modern Artists on Art. Ten Unabridged Essays.* Englewood Cliffs, N.J.: Prentice-Hall, Inc., pp. 138-149

Morfill G.; Scheingraber H. (1991): *Chaos Ist Überall... Und Es Funktioniert* Eine neue Weltsicht Frankfurt/Main; Berlin: Ullstein,

Musashi M. (1974): *A Book of Five Rings.* Woodstock, New York: The Overlode Press

O'Neill E. (1989): *Eines Langen Tages Reise in die Nacht.* Schauspiel In Vier Akten. Deutsch Von Christian Enzensberger. Grosse Bühne, Theater Basel

Payn G., Morley S. (eds) 1982. *The Noël Coward Diaries.* Boston, Toronto: Little, Brown and Company.

Rosenbach, W.E., Taylor R.L. (eds.)(1993): *Contemporary Issues in Leadership.* Boulder-San Francisco-Oxford: Westview Press

Rost J.C. (1993): *Leadership for the Twenty-First Century.* Westport, CT London : Praeger Publishers

Tichy N.M., Sherman S. (1993):*Control your destiny or someone else will : How Jack Welch is making General Electric the World's most competitive corporation.* New York : Currency / Doubleday

Saint-Exupéry A. (1993): *Citadelle.* Paris: Edition Gallimard

Sandblom P. (1987): *Creativity and Disease. How illness affects literature, art and music.* Philadelphia: George F. Stickley Company

Suzuki D.T. (1973): *Zen and Japanese Culture.* Princeton, New Jersey: Princeton Univ. Press.

Tzu Sun (1984): *The Art of War, ed.by James Clavell,* Hodder and Stoughton, London-Sydney-Auckland-Toronto

Ward G.C. (1992): Douglas MacArthur: An American soldier, *National Geographic* Vol 181 No 3, S. 54-83

MAYA ANGELOU
American writer and poet

Born Marguerite Johnson in St. Louis, Missouri, on April 4,1928, Maya Angelou was raised in Arkansas, a rural and segregated state. She later related her upbringing in the best seller, *I Know Why the Caged Bird Sings*, a poignant account which won critical acclaim in 1970. Angelou went on to become a prominent and respected literary voice of the African-American community. Her preferred theme of love and the universality of all human lives is dominant in over a dozen books she wrote of prose and poetry, earning her a Pulitzer Prize and National Book Award nominations. Her screenplay, *Georgia,* won her an Emmy Award nomination as did her acting in the TV series, *Roots.* Maya Angelou was appointed professor of American Studies at Wake Forest University in 1981 and is an eminent lecturer.

Introduction by Gottlieb Guntern

At the age of three, when her parents divorced, Marguerite Johnson was sent to Arkansas, together with her brother Bailey. Both children had cardboard tags on their wrists, indicating their name and their destination. Raised by her grandmother in a shanty town, Stamps, she was taken to St. Louis at the age of seven, then returned to Arkansas before eventually joining her mother in California.

At the age of eight she lived through a devastating psychological experience whereby she lost her voice for four years. This was in St. Louis, and in St. Louis there is a beautiful structure, a huge arch called the Gateway to the West. Dr. Maya Angelou, as she is known today, found another gateway; it did not lead to the West, it led into silence. She later said that in order to achieve perfect personal silence, "I was to attach myself, leech-like, to sound. I began to listen to everything." It was in this silence that she discovered the beauty of poetry, the poetry of the Black poet Lawrence Dunbar and the beauty of the sonnets of Shakespeare.

After four years she started to speak again and did so by speaking poetry. She writes: "So when I was about 12, I went under the house and started to speak poetry. Until I felt it over my tongue, through my teeth and across my lips, I would never love it. That has influenced the way I hear poetry when I'm writing it; I write for the voice, not the eye."

At the age of 16, after a brief encounter with an adolescent boy, she was pregnant. She decided not to marry but to bring up her son completely on her own. Now she had to raise and feed her son and herself and she entered what she later called "a roller-coaster life," tumbling like a butterfly through the meadows of the vicissitudes of life, reaching brief peaks of happiness and satisfaction only to fall again into the ditches of prejudice, disappointment and rejection.

She worked as a waitress, as a conductress of a San Francisco cable-car, as a Madam for two aging Lesbians. She learned the bitter wisdom of

Hemingway's dictum that man can always be destroyed but never defeated. And while coping with a hard and often cruel life experience she could draw from the strength, the resilience and the indomitable spirit of her Black race that she later beautifully expressed in her poem *And Still I Rise.*

> You may write me down in history
> With your bitter, twisted lies,
> You may trod me in the very dirt
> But still like dust I rise.

Maya Angelou, never giving up hope and always looking forward to the opportunity of deploying the incredible potential that she felt she had, got her break. She became a dancer and a calypso singer. She became an actress in Genet's *The Negroes* and traveled to Europe - Paris, Venice, Rome, and Moscow - as a dancer with *Porgy and Bess.*

One day the Black writer, James Baldwin, took her to a party at the home of the American cartoonist, Julius Feiffer. That very evening she was challenged to become a writer. After some hesitation she took up the challenge, met it, and at the age of forty began to write her first autobiographical novel, *I Know Why the Caged Bird Sings.*

The title is revealing. The Finnish poet Zacharis Topelius once said: "A song is born of sorrow." She had had her fill of sorrow, and she knew how to sing. She vindicated Sören Kierkegard's observation that "a poet is an unhappy being whose heart is torn by secret suffering, but whose lips are so strangely formed that when he sighs and the cries escape them, they sound like beautiful music."

Her first novel, published in 1970, was a huge success and all of a sudden Maya Angelou was in the limelight. In rapid succession she wrote four more novels: *Gather Together in my Name, Singin' and Swingin' and Gettin' Merry Like Christmas, All God's Children Need Traveling Shoes,* and *The Heart of a Woman.* She may well become the American female Proust, a goal that is dear to her heart.

She was the first Black woman ever to be nominated for the Pulitzer Prize for poetry for her collection of poems, *Just Give Me a Cool Drink of Water 'fore I Diiie.* She performed as an actress in films and plays. She won a Tony nomination for her supporting role in Haley's *Roots,* where she played the role of the Grandmother, Nyo Boto, as well as for her role opposite Geraldine Page in a Broadway play, *Look Away.*

She has been called a Proteus because she successfully changed her roles and activities in many fields of performance. She has been married to the Greek Evaristos Angelos, to the English writer Paul du Feu, and to the African freedom fighter Make Vizumi. She has been a fund raiser for Dr. Martin Luther King, one of the great leadership figures of our century, and she was to become the collaborator of the Black leader Malcolm X, but the day before she arrived to work with him, he was shot and killed.

The Greek philosopher Diogenes once said "Kosmpolites eimi," I am a citizen of the world. Maya Angelou *is* a citizen of the world. She has been living and working all over the USA, including on a house-boat in Sausalito outside of San Francisco. She has taught dancing in Rome and Tel-Aviv. She has been an associate editor of the Arab Observer in Cairo and taught music and drama at the University of Ghana where she also worked as an editor of the *African Review.*

She has received honorary doctoral degrees from Smith College, Mills College, Lawrence University. She is a Chubb Fellow of Yale University. She was appointed by President Ford to the Bicentennial Council and by President Carter to the International Women's Year Commission. In 1975 Maya Angelou received the *Ladies' Home Journal* "Woman of the Year Award" for communication, because meanwhile she had become a lecturer much in demand throughout the United States of America and throughout the world, too.

She speaks seven languages, has cut two records, written and produced a ten-part television series, written plays and scores of musicals and directed a film. Moreover, she was the first Black woman to write a screenplay and the musical score of a Hollywood film.

Today she has a lifelong tenure as a Reynolds professor of American studies at the Wake Forest University in Winston-Salem, North Carolina.

Maya Angelou has been called "a giant among people," "a Renaissance woman" with "a spine of iron." But in spite of all this praise she has remained an authentic woman without any pretension. She says: "I'd just like to be thought of as someone who tried to be a blessing rather than a curse to the human race." I think she is a blessing.

Maya Angelou

My thanks to you for the invitation to come to this beautiful place are with some apprehension. I am not sure it is wise to look into the mystery of creativity. I always want to know that there is the creativity somewhere, near me, and that if I close my eyes and sit very still, I can poke around and find some way to get into that source and find the plum and pull it out. I do not want to look and see where I have been. I also have a feeling - or perhaps it is a superstition - that I have a friend, an entity, a thing, a spirit. I do not know if once I investigate the mystery, the spirit will think I have betrayed it and will flee from me. If it leaves me, I am dead and done for. And yet, I would try with other artists to look into this glass, this mirror, darkly. There is a poem written by Paul Dunbar, called "Sympathy." I took the title of my first book from this poem. It is:

I know what the caged bird feels
Ah me,
When the sun is bright on the upland slopes
When the wind blows soft through the springing grass
And the river float like the sheet of glass
When the first bird sings, and the first bud opes
And the faint perfume from its jallies steels
I know what the caged bird feels.

I know why the caged bird beats its wings
Till its wings are red on the cruel bars
For he must fly back to his perch and clean
When he fain would be on the bough aswing
And the blood still throbs in the old old scars
And they pulse again with a keener sting
I know why he beats his wing
And I know why the caged bird sings.
Ah me.

I do not know what came first, the chicken or the egg. I do not know if the artist is born with that particular imbalance or perfect balance, and so, sings. I do not know if the artist starts to sing, because I think that is exactly what a composer does - and the architect, and the designer, and the dancer, and the choreographer. I think all of us sing. I do not know whether the artist begins to sing and then becomes saddened or miserable or unsure or fearful or lost, or whether the person is lost first and sings in self-defense.

As for me, I have written poetry since I was about nine. I thought at one time I could make my entire body into an ear, and it could absorb all sound. I think the music of the Black Church temporized and tenderized and shifted my hearing so that I find myself able to learn languages rather quickly because I listen. I simply listen, I take it all in. All of it. I think that the artist risks everything all the time, is on the edge - tightrope-walking I think you called it - is edge-walking all the time. The artist, I believe, operates in the familiar, has baths, combs her hair, brushes his teeth, puts clothes on, says: "Good morning, guten Morgen, how are you? Fine, thank you." Don't believe it. That is the protection, I think, so that the artist operates in the familiar, does the right things or some of the things that society insists the artist do. Behind that facade, however, for me, there is constant confusion, chaos, fear, insecurity... I say the nice things and I smile nicely and I speak my language very well and try to mumble around in some others. But the truth is, I am always working. I am working at trying to create balance. So maybe the poem or the piece of music I finally get out comes as a result of my working to create balance. As a Black American I have wonderful precedents. There is a song, a slave song which I love and use all the time. The song says (sings):

> I open my mouth to the Lord
> and I won't turn back, no.
> I will go, I shall go
> to see what the end is going to be.

Now, the people who wrote that song had chains around their ankles, around their hands, around their necks, they had no license to walk one foot beyond where their owner said they could walk. And yet those people said: (sings)

> If the Lord wants somebody
> Here am I. Send me.

In what way could these artists hope to be free? To say, I will go. Of course, I will go. The song continues this way (sings):

> I'm gonna run on
> See what the end is gonna be
> I'm gonna run on...

The people could not walk, but they said they would run. For two hundred years that song has remained one of the closest of songs to the Black American, much closer than "Go Down Moses" or "We Shall Overcome." The song which really brings a group of Black people to sit and be centered, is this particular song (sings):

> I open my mouth to the Lord
> and I won't turn back, no.
> I will go...

That is amazing. So for me as an artist, I take inspiration from that magic which allowed Blacks brought to the United States in 1619, one year before the Mayflower docked, who underwent experiences too bizarre to be included in almost any normal history book, to survive. I suggest it is that ability to liberate one's own self beyond the confines of the chains and the whip and the lash. I believe this is so. So that many non-Blacks, when they see Blacks laughing, misread. They think immediately: "Oh, they're like children." Well, I don't know. I do know that the Bible - Judeo-Christian Bible - suggests that unless we become like little children, we will in no way enter the kingdom of heaven. I do not think the laughter, though, speaks of a childishness. I do not think either it is a response to nervousness. I think the laughter is a realization - maybe not intellectual - but the realization that one can survive, and therefore becomes the sweetest of testimonies. For in a dungeon, when one is being brutalized, and one can freely laugh, what does the guard think? I wonder what he does think when I see the racists watching Black Americans. Do they really think that we are so superficial? Do they really think we do not long for the Easter bunny and Christmas trees and are not afraid of the dark? I do not know what they think, but I do believe that the strength to survive for the Black American has come almost directly from that ability to go inside and free oneself from the inside out. So that our movements, our laughter, the loose body, all those external gestures are aspects, are a result of internal liberation. I believe that to be so.

I am concerned that you should know my heart, what I think is influenced by it. I do not mean to say I am only a feeling being - which is what they say in New York, "I'm feeling," - but rather that my intellect is influenced directly by what I feel. I work at that; it is not accidental. I have no accidental innocence. It is all contrived. I work for it. I work to keep my heart clean, so that in case an idea, a poem is flying around and wants to have a home, I can welcome it. I want to be ready to welcome it. The Catholics call that, I think, staying in a state of grace. In order to remain in a state of grace as I understand it, I am obliged to be as simple as possible, as direct as possible, as uncluttered as possible. I try to keep my voice quiet and I use silence a lot. I know it well, silence. It is addictive and it can be dangerous, but in moderation silence is... maybe heaven.

I want to talk to you a little bit about my Grandma. The description of the town in which I grew up can be fleshed out a bit. My grandmother owned the only Black-owned store in the town. She owned most of the land the poor Whites lived on, and most of the land the Blacks lived on. In 1903, in this small town in the South, she divorced my grandfather. Now, White women did not get divorced in 1903. But my grandmother somehow decided she would be divorced from my grandfather. She had two children, my father and my uncle. My uncle was crippled; his whole right side was paralyzed. So when my brother and I arrived in Stamps, my uncle started to teach us to read and to do our numbers. He would catch me with his good hand just behind my neck with all my clothes, stand me in front of a big pot-bellied stove, and say: "Now sister, I want you to do your sixes," - the multiplication tables. "Do your sevens." Well, I learned my sixes and sevens and nines. Even now, after a night of full libation, you can wake me up at three in the morning and say: "Maya, do your twelves." I have my twelves. I was so sure my uncle would open the door of the stove and throw me in, that I learned. Well, of course, I found he was so tender-hearted, he would not allow us to kill a moth or spider in the store.

My uncle died about eight years ago. I went down to the store in Arkansas, to see about things. A woman met me in Little Rock and said to me: "I want to introduce you to a man who says he must meet you. Please, may I bring him to your hotel?" That was in Little Rock, way up north in Arkansas. When I grew up in Stamps, I thought of Little Rock as Buda and Pest. It was exotic. This man came to the hotel, a very wonderful looking Black man with a big

Texas hat, and he said, "I know you're down here because your Uncle Willie has died." I thought, you know my Uncle Willie? My crippled Uncle Willie?" He had left the state of Arkansas twice in his life: once to go to California in the thirties, and once to go to Hope, Arkansas, which is thirty miles away, also in the thirties. He was so ashamed of being crippled, he would not leave the town. This good-looking, wonderfully turned-out man said to me: "Your uncle Willie has died, in that little town, in that village." So I asked him: "You know my Uncle Willie? He said: "The State of Arkansas has lost a great man." I said: "Uncle Willie?" He said: "The United States has lost a great man. The world..." So I said: "Let me sit down first." He said in the twenties he had been the only child of a blind mother, and my Uncle Willie had given him a job in our store, made him love to learn and to learn his times-tables. I asked him, "How did he get you to do it?" He said: "He used to grab me like this and just hold me in front of the stove. Because of your Uncle Willie, I am who I am today." He was the first Black mayor of Little Rock, Arkansas. He said, "Because of the power vested in me by the citizens, I have a police escort for you downstairs."

I went downstairs and started to weep. When I had been a small girl in that town, the Ku Klux Klan would ride over into the Black neighborhood and they... they wouldn't wear sheets, oh no, they didn't have to do that. They wore no disguises. They simply came over and we would take the potatoes and onions out of the bins, and my uncle would use his stick to get down into the bins, and then we would cover him with the potatoes and onions. He would lie there all night long, moaning, and my grandmother would sing all night (sings):

I shall not, I shall not be moved.

Now, my brother and I would look out the window at these people. There they were, with huge bellies like that, and huge guns. They looked like theatrical props. They looked so big to us. When I went downstairs with the Mayor of Little Rock, there were eight White men. Forty years later, I started to weep. I shook each one's hand. I went to each one. I said: "Thank you, in the name of my Uncle Willie. Thank you in the name of my Uncle Willie." They had no idea what I was talking about.

The mayor told me: "Now when you get to Stamps, I want you to look up this lawyer. He is a good old boy. He will look after your property. So, I expected an old, well-established Black lawyer. I went into the office, and a young White man with the Arkansas accent jumped up "Good morning, Mrs. Angelou. I'm just delighted to meet you." He said: "The Mayor called me this morning from Little Rock and told me you would come in. You know, the Mayor is the most powerful Black man in the State of Arkansas. More important than that, the Mayor is a noble man. Because of the Mayor, I am who I am today." He said: "The mayor caught me, when I was about twelve years old. I was a hellion. He made me go to school and love to learn. Today I am in the State legislature." I looked back at Uncle Willie, Black, poor and crippled. I looked at his influence. So I wrote a song for Roberta Flack. And the song is (sings):

> Willie was a man without frame
> Hardly anybody knew his name.
> Crippled and limping, always walking lame,
> He said, "I keep on movin'
> Movin' just the same."

> Solitude was the climate in his head
> Emptiness was the partner in his bed,
> Pain echoed in the steps of his tread,
> He said, "I keep on followin'
> Where the leaders led."
> I may cry and I will die,
> But my spirit is in search of every spring,
> Watch for me and you will see
> That I'm present in the songs that children sing.

Recites:
> People called him "Uncle," "Boy" and "Hey,"
> Said, "You can't live through this another day."
> Then, they awaited to hear what he would say.

Sings:
> He said, "I'm living
> In the games that children play.

Recites:

"You may enter my sleep, people my dreams,
Threaten my early morning's ease,
But I keep comin' followin' laughin' cryin',
Sure as a summer breeze.

"Wait for me, watch for me.
My spirit is the surge of open seas.
Look for me, ask for me,
I'm the rustle in the autumn leaves.

"When the sun rises
I am the time.
When the children sing
I am the Rhyme."

I think that people live in direct relation to the heroes and the "she-roes" they have. I think that the ability to make art and the ability to cherish art, two separate things, are heroes and she-roes. I think that the business person who has been told that because he is a businessman or because she is a businesswoman, that he or she cannot love ballet, is crippled and will not live long. He might exist, but he will not live long. I think we make a dangerous mistake if we suggest that the brick-mason, or the garbage collector would not love to go into an art gallery. We separate ourselves, as if making ourselves unique and valuable makes others less unique and less valuable. We remove so many possibilities from ourselves, our nations, our communities, our families and simply our own, singular selves, seeing the reactions to prejudices, especially racial or sexual prejudices. To see one side set apart and told, "Oh, you can't do that, you can't mingle with us," to become exclusive as opposed to inclusive, is anti-life. There is a difference between being a man and being an old male, or being a woman and being an old female. We do not stop often enough to examine that difference. Born with certain genitalia and living long enough, a person can be an old whatever genitalia dictates. But to become a man, ein Mensch, to be a woman, woman, is so… it may be as close as we will ever come while we live, to being angels. It is as man, as woman, that we take responsibility for the time we take up and the space we occupy. It is as man and woman that we create poetry and song and dance and sculpture and architecture and children, healthy children - I think.

I could recite poetry to you for the next seven hours, but there is one thing about the process that I see. I start off to write one thing, and the thing itself seems to have its own life. It is flying through the air, and I give it a home and think now I might be able to control it, understand it. Then it takes off and goes another way altogether. Out of respect for it and the creative processes, I try to follow it. There is a story that Martin Luther King used to tell. During the civil rights movement a man was running in the country. He would run to a farm and see a farmer and ask: "Did you see a group of young people going past here?" The farmer would say: "No." So he would run to another farm and ask: "Did you see maybe a hundred and fifty young people going past here?" Again, the answer was no. The fourth time the farmer asked him: "Why do you ask? Why are you looking for these people?" And the person who was running responded: "Oh, because I'm leading them." I believe that is so with poetry. I think I am going one way with it and then it goes another way entirely. There is a poem I am going to read called "Shaker, Why Don't You Sing?." There is a folk song called "John Henry," which I hope you know, in which we are told Henry laid rails for the railroad. He had a ten-pound hammer, and the man who held the spike for him to hit was called the shaker. In the song, the statement is (sings):

> John Henry said to his shaker,
> Shaker, why don't you sing?
> I'm throwing ten pounds from the hips all down
> and listen to the cool steel, ring.
> Listen to the cool steel ring.

So the point was that if John Henry missed this spike, it was goodbye to the shaker! *I* wanted to write a poem addressed to all people who are depressed, disheartened, lonely: "Sing! Sing!" But it turned into a love poem, right under my hands.

Reads:
> Evicted from sleep's mute palace,
> I wait in silence
> for the bridal croon;
> your legs rubbing insistent
> rhythm against my thighs,

your breast moaning
a canticle in my hair.
But the solemn moments,
unuttering, pass in
unaccompanied procession.
You, whose chanteys hummed
my life alive, have withdrawn
your music and lean inaudibly
on the quiet slope of memory.

O shaker, why don't you sing?

It goes on. But I think the artist who begins to think she or he is in control, makes another mistake. The work is always greater than the person whose hospitality it has used. It is as if the work has come, and while being housed, it has grown healthy, strong, it has used some of the paraphernalia, some of the machinery inside its host who has helped to shape it. The work goes on becoming greater. I collect art. I am a serious collector. I love Tomayo, the Mexican painter. I have a painting of a slice of watermelon: the peel is bright green; the flesh, red, blood-red; the seeds, black. When I see the piece, I think of the caricature that was drawn of Black people in the early part of this century, with the mouth like a slice of watermelon, and my heart shudders. Another person sees the same slice of watermelon and remembers summer and how nice it was to be young. Another person sees that same slice of watermelon and remembers honeymooning in the tropics. The painter has put it there for us and we bring all our equipment to it. So each one sees it differently and enlarges the possibility of the piece, I think. So for me, my responsibility as an artist, I think, is to prepare myself as well as possible for the craft of writing poetry. To learn my language so well, to respect the melody so that I can almost say what I think I think. When another person sees it, he or she is going to take it some place else anyway. I have no control over that. I wanted to read that poem in order to show you how a poem can get away from the poet, from me.

One last poem: I write songs with Quincy Jones sometimes for different singers, classical blues singers. Once I wanted to write about love, romantic love, through color. So I wrote:

Recites:

> Our summer's gone
> the golden days are through
> the rosy dawns I used to wake with you
> have turned gray.
> My life has turned blue.
> Red robin's gone, down to the South he flew.
> Left all alone. My life has turned blue.
>
> If summer comes next year
> will we be here to share its brown caress?
> Or will the color's white leave us, bareness.
> I've heard it said that when the dew will pass,
> that springs... that summers do it last.
> But till I see you, lying in green grass.
> My life has turned blue.

I heard the music in my mind, so I did not have to ask Quincy to write. I can compose, but I cannot write musical notes; I have to sing them. I have no training as a composer. So I went to a transcriber and sang him the melody, and he worked on the chords while I sat in another room. Then he called me in and said, "This is what you have written."

Sings:

> Our summer's gone
> the golden days are through
> the rosy dawns...

I had written "Without a Song"

Sings:

> Without a song
> the day will never...
> Without a song...

It had been written fifty years earlier. I do not know if I had the radio on and had heard it in my sleep, or had heard it in an elevator, but I stole every note. So when the man finished playing the piano, I said, "Thank you very much," and left.

I know that in the next few days, listening to and talking to and asking questions of all the people who are here for your enjoyment and information will make us all a little wiser and maybe a little braver. I think courage is the most important of all the virtues, because without courage, one cannot practice any other virtue consistently. So it is in gatherings where people risk everything that we stand the chance of developing a little more courage, just the courage to look into each other's eyes for a little while.

Guntern: You know, the poet Maya Angelou knows how to sing, how to use her wings. She even gave us the impression that we could fly for a short moment of time. She reminded me, in her performance, of a Siberian shaman who is able to take you on the spirit journey, throw you into the underworld and put you into altered states of consciousness. James Joyce once defined a male poet as a "hawk-like man, flying sunwards high above the sea." I do understand now that Maya Angelou belongs to the strange, mysterious species of she-roe nightingales.

Discussion

Guntern: I am taking up the word "grace." Eugene O'Neil once said, "Man is born broken. He lives by mending. The grace of God is glue." And Faulkner once wrote: "We are all bitched from the start." This does not seem to be your philosophy of life. It does not seem to be your walk on the tightrope. Could you comment on that?

Angelou: I said earlier I did not know what came first, the chicken or the egg. I do not know if we are bitched or witched from beyond the stars. I do know that Shakespeare makes us see how juvenile we are when we blame our fortunes on the stars. I believe human beings have the capability to make a choice. I do not know whether we come broken, I do not know whether the endorphins that our bodies create are simply to make us well because we were broken. I do not know that. But I do know that within every person, there is a plateau. Many times we pretend that we have forgotten how to stand on that plateau. It is easier to pretend, we think, so we commit crimes against other human beings and against ourselves, under the pretext that we have forgotten our moral plateau. It is a lie. Each and every person, the Eskimo, the Chinese, the Black, the White, the Jew, the Dalai Lama - everybody knows - what is right. But somehow we probably think that if we pretend we have forgotten, we can die more quickly and be away from the responsibility. That is my belief.

Guntern: Okay, let us continue from there, from this plateau. Graham Greene once said that writing is a form of therapy. What does writing give to you in terms of inner contentment, from day to day? Does it throw you into more anguish? Does it relieve your anguish? What does it do to you?

Angelou: I have heard it said that an autobiographer achieves therapeutic catharsis, so some critics will say: "Well, at last Maya Angelou is going to feel better, now that she has written all this hard life down." I want to believe them, but I do not feel any different. The only thing I know is that the yellow page, the tablet, remains to be filled. I feel better when I have written only because I feel I have discharged my responsibility. If I do not write, I feel like you would feel in a car with no gas. You knew the car needed gas, but you did not put it in. Then when you turned on the ignition and the car wouldn't go, you felt foolish because you had time to put in the gas. If I do not write, I feel foolish. I feel I have not done what I am supposed to do. But if I write a happy poem or a light essay, or if I try to really go down and see what pain is, physically, and write it... I do not feel any less pain. The next day I think, ah, it is right here again.

Guntern: A fox, before going to sleep, turns around on its own axis, two, three, four times until the territory feels right. Then it lays down and lifts its snout, looks around, puts its head down, brings its tail over its head, and when the ritual is accomplished, it can enter an altered state of consciousness leading to sleep. Now, before you start writing, what kind of rituals do you use?

Angelou: First, I cannot believe you have done the research you have done. Nobody knows all the names of my husbands. Nobody.

I keep a room in a hotel in my town. I get up at about five in the morning, do my ablutions and make coffee, and then drive to the hotel. When I rent the room, I make sure that they can take all the paintings off the walls. I ask the owner never to have anybody clean the room because I never sleep there. I stay there from six in the morning until about one o'clock and then I go home. After about a month, the owner slips a piece of paper under the door to ask me if they may please change the sheets, because, "We know they are moldering." I have a Bible, Roget's Thesaurus, a dictionary, a deck of cards, a bottle of Sherry, and then I do something...

Guntern: ...with your hands...?

Angelou: No. I just do something inside myself. I center. I wait. I wait until there is a moment when you can surrender. You cannot surrender right away. I can't. But there is a moment that comes when it is all right and you can hear. I don't know. I don't know.

Guntern: In his autobiography, *Little Wilson and Big God,* Anthony Burgess wrote: "Ale, Lad, Ale is the stuff for fellows who need hurts to think." What function does the bottle of Sherry have in your ritual?

Angelou: I am turning around on my axis, so I lay out the cards. I might not do it in exactly the same way every time, but if I do not hear anything, or cannot sense it, if it is really not here, it is not smell, it is something else. If I am there trying to be in a state of grace and nothing happens, I wait. Then maybe around nine o'clock, I'll have a glass of Sherry ... one bottle lasts me for two or three months in my room, while in my home I might drink one in two days, if I want to. It is just that things have to be in a place.

Roitman: Why the Bible?

Angelou: The music of the Bible, the Old Testament in particular, is the music I grew up on. It is the music of the Black Southern preacher. The Black Southern preacher was important during the years when I was a mute, which was really about five-and-a-half years. I would listen carefully to the melody of the Black preacher at funerals:

> Weep not, she is not dead
> She's resting in the bosom of Jesus
> Heart-broken husband weep no more
> Grief-stricken son, weep no more
> She's only just gone home.

So that beauty of the imagery informed my vocabulary. My grandmother used to sing, "I'm standing out on the Word of God." I would picture her standing out in space, with moons flying around her head, and stars and comets at her feet. So that is why I use the Bible. I love to open it and hear that beautiful melody in Deuteronomy.

Petrozzi: First, I would like to thank you for the gift that you have given us today. The lady here notices that the smile and the laugh, the sadness and the cry on your face almost melt. She would like to know what the secret of your intensity is and how you succeed in so deeply integrating all these emotions; how you succeed in being so in consent with everything that happens within you.

Angelou: Thank you. All right. Let me try to do that; it will take about a half hour. Black Americans for centuries were forced to laugh when they were not amused and to scratch when they were not itching. We have this line in so many songs (sings)

> You see me laughin'
> I'm laughin' just to keep from cryin'

And we have poems in which these two emotions merge. So one is always on the edge. I have a poem I wrote for a woman who is a maid in New York City. She rides the bus; if the bus stops quickly, she laughs, if it stops slowly, she laughs; if it misses somebody, she laughs; if it picks up somebody... So I wrote a poem for her which has these two emotions. The poem is:

> When I think about myself
> I almost laugh myself to death.
> My life has been one great big joke
> A dance that's walked
> A song that's spoke
> I laugh so hard
> I nearly choke
> When I think about myself.
>
> Seventy years in these folk's world
> The child I works for calls me "girl."
> I say, "Yes Ma'am." For working's sake
> I'm too proud to bend and too poor to break
> So I laugh until my stomach ache
> When I think about myself.
>
> My folks can make me split my side.
> I laughed so hard I almost died.
> They grow the fruit but eat the rind.
> Ha. Ha. I laugh until I start to crying.
> When I think about myself.

So those two emotions are not even the other side of the same coin, they are the same side of the same coin. I think that the method of integrating all the emotions is to admit they exist, that they roam throughout my body, throughout my mind and they have a place here. They are not strangers, they belong to me. You see? I do not deny them, I try to keep them in their place, sometimes, so that I do not wake up in the morning and see a stranger and say, "Good morning" and start to cry. I try to keep them under control, you know. But they belong to me. They have not invaded me; they have come with me.

Guntern: Heraclitus had a concept; he called it "enanciodromia" which means that opposites melt together so that out of the old comes the young and out of the young comes the old. Out of life comes death and out of death comes life.

Angelou: Yes. So says Thomas Wolfe. It is made as a very good point, for even in the body, in the corpse, beautiful flowers grow out of the eye sockets. I think, too, that sometimes we are so afraid of death, we become the prisoners of existence and will serve existence as slaves, rather than admit that the only promise we can be sure will not be refused is death. So if we keep it with us, just as tears are in the laughter and laughter in the tears, then I think we stand the chance of balance. I always say, " I think," but that really is because as much as I talk, I am not in love with any position. I hope to be brave enough to be in pursuit of truth. I hope. If by nightfall I am convinced that what I think today is wrong, I want to say, " Hey, everybody, you remember what I said yesterday? I don't believe it anymore." I want to be like that.

Petrozzi: I usually try to help people meditate, and I just want to say to you that today you have helped me to enlarge my meditation. I believe that is connected with your capacity to be in that state of grace that you were talking about. Thank you.

Angelou: Dankeschön.

Q. Several times this morning you have described balance as one of the things you are striving for. Could you tell us more about it?

Angelou: I use the word really trying to see the rhythm, I suppose. Everything on the planet or anywhere else we have been able to see it seems, has rhythm. Everything. There is summer and fall, and winter and spring and summer and fall, and winter and spring and summer and fall... suns go out, moons settle, tides come in, rivers move. It is interesting for me to look at Martin Buber and see that statement which suggests that the two poles, the male and female, without judgment, the positive and negative, these two poles in their pressing together create life. I don't know. But I do know that if one pushes the other over, if there is too much aggression, then we explode. If there is too much passivity, then men do not woo women, we do not build bridges, we do not live. So I think I am looking for the rhythm of balance, the balance of rhythm in everything. Always. It seems to me my output is more true because my inside is just balanced. I am sorry I cannot put it better; I have never been asked to articulate that. Maybe I do not even believe it.

Guntern: You once wrote: "If growing up is a painful experience for a Black Southern girl, the awareness of her displacement is the rust on the edge of the razor that threatens her throat. It's an unnecessary insult." But then you go and choose the autobiography as your method and by writing you become aware again and again of painful and joyful experiences. Don't you go on to insult yourself?

Angelou: No. One of the greatest American writers was a man little known in even American company and probably little known in this company. His name was Frederick Douglas, and in the 1840's he wrote a book called *The Slave Narrative*. It is great English. It is beautiful writing. But more important for me was the fact that Frederick Douglas used the "I," first person singular - Ich - meaning "we," first person plural. When I really looked at his ability to tell everybody's story by saying "I," I was intrigued. So what I try to do is write using the Black American experience, the female black American experience. I am always talking about the human being. How we weep, how we stand up, how we fall, how we betray ourselves, how we can somehow embrace each other. As a result, although it is the first person singular and I am talking about a Black girl or Black woman, one or the other of my books is required reading in nearly every university or college in the United States. Last summer I went to a White male college in Indiana. These very big men, athletes, had taken a poem of mine, "And Still I Rise," as the theme for their senior year. So there were a thousand young White men using my work. It is useable, utile, because I have tried in the work to tell the truth about the human being so that a White woman in Iowa can read my work and say, "That's true"; a Chinese man in San Francisco can read it and say "Aha, that's right. That's life. That is it." So the autobiographical form is one I am trying to work with. The book *All God's Children Need Traveling Shoes* is not the same book as *I Know Why the Caged Bird Sings*. You know, in each case I have tried to do something new, take again, look for a balance, find the rhythm of a sixteen-year-old; find the rhythm of a twenty-year-old; find the rhythm of a forty-year-old woman who is lonely. Tell the truth about it. I am a poet-autographer. I could have wished for something else, but that is what I do. I used to dance.

Guntern: You have gone a long stretch in your work, and you have done it in a very conscious manner. You have now reached a certain age. In *The Death of a Salesman,* Willy Loman says to his brother Ben: "I still feel kind of temporary about myself." How do you feel about yourself at this point along your way?

Angelou: Well, I feel very young. It's true! It's true! The week before last, *The USA Today* newspaper had a huge photograph of me on its front page and it looked like my grandmother. I do not mean I resembled her, I mean it *looked* like her. I could not believe it. I am so surprised that I am this old. Inside myself, I feel as fresh as dew. Yes, and wondering if I will be able to continue to get my work done. The temporary thing ... I think everybody feels temporary especially after a night of drinking. I think so. I want to read a poem to you if I may. It is in the new book. I have told you about my grandmother. In the church of my little town my grandmother was "Mother of the Church." You have to see her. When she died she was over six foot and she spoke very softly. I remember people leaning toward her when she was talking at the table and ask: "Sister Henderson, what did you say?" But in church, when she would sing, she had a great voice, huge voice. Every Sunday for ten years she would sit down in the Mother of the Church chair. The preacher was up there. My grandmother never looked at him, but when the preacher would say: "And now, we will be privileged with the song from Sister Henderson," every Sunday my grandmother would say, "Me?" I would be so embarrassed, but finally she would sing and when she did sing, the church would go mad. The women would get so happy, they would take their purses and throw them at the preacher. The men would jump up and dance. At home, when I would ask her: "Mamma, please sing," she would say to me, 'Go on sister, you know Mamma can't sing.'" But if you left her alone, she would sing: (sings)

> I shall not, I shall not be moved,
> I shall not, I shall not be moved.
> Just like a tree that's planted by the water,
> I shall not be moved.

So I wrote a poem for my grandmother. It is for all grandmothers. It is the Black grandmother in the South.

Our Grandmothers

She lay, skin down on the moist dirt,
the canebrake rustling
with the whispers of leaves, and
loud longing of hounds and
the ransack of hunters crackling the near branches.

She muttered, lifting her head a nod toward freedom,
I shall not, I shall not be moved.

She gathered her babies,
their tears slick as oil on black faces,
their young eyes canvassing mornings of madness.
Momma, is Master going to sell you
from us tomorrow?

Yes.
Unless you keep walking more
and talking less.
Yes.
Unless the keeper of our lives
releases me from all commandments.
Yes.
And your lives, never mine to live,
will be executed upon the killing floor of innocents.
Unless you match my heart and words,
saying with me,

I shall not be moved.

In Virginia tobacco fields,
leaning into the curve
of Steinway pianos,
along Arkansas roads,
in the red hills of Georgia,
into the palms of her chained hands,
she cried against calamity.
You have tried to destroy me
and though I perish daily,

I shall not be moved.

Her universe, often
summarized into one black body
falling finally from the tree to her feet,
made her cry each time in a new voice.
All my past hastens to defeat,
and strangers claim the glory of my love,
Iniquity has me bound to his bed,
yet, I shall not be moved.

She heard the names,
swirling ribbons in the winds of history:
nigger, nigger bitch, heifer,
mammy, property, creature, ape, baboon,
whore, hot tail, thing, it.
She said, But my description cannot
fit your tongue, for
I have a certain way of being in this world,

and I shall not, I shall not be moved.

No angel stretched protecting wings
above the heads of her children,
fluttering and urging the winds of reason
into the confusion of their lives.
They sprouted like young weeds,
but she could not shield their growth
from the grinding blades of ignorance, nor
shape them into symbolic topiaries.
She sent them away,
underground, overland, in coaches and
shoeless.
When you learn, teach.
When you get, give.
As for me,

I shall not be moved.

She stood in midocean, seeking dry land.
She searched God's face.
Assured,
she placed her fire of service
on the altar, and though
clothed in the finery of faith,
when she appeared at the temple door,
no sign welcomed
Black Grandmother. Enter here.

Into the crashing sound,
into wickedness, she cried,
No one, no, nor no one million
ones dare deny me God. I go forth
alone, and stand as ten thousand.

The Divine upon my right
impels me to pull forever
at the latch on Freedom's gate.

The Holy Spirit upon my left leads my
feet without ceasing into the camp of the
righteous and into the tents of the free.

These momma faces, lemon-yellows, plum-purple,
honey-brown, have grimaced and twisted
down a pyramid of years.
She is Sheba and Sojourner,
Harriet and Zora,
Mary Bethune and Angela,
Annie top Zenobia.

She stands
before the abortion clinic,
confounded by the lack of choices.
In the Welfare line,
reduced to the pity of handouts.
Ordained in the pulpit, shielded
by the mysteries.
In the operating room,

husbanding life.
In the choir loft,
holding God in her throat.
On lonely street corners,
hawking her body.
In the classroom, loving the
children to understanding.

Centered on the world's stage,
she sings to her loves and beloveds,
to her foes and detractors:
However I am perceived and deceived,
however my ignorance and conceits,
lay aside your fears that I will be undone,

for I shall not be moved.

Guntern: Let us move one step further. We have to be moved. It seems that the creative process, whether it occurs in art, in science or elsewhere, always goes through a number of stages and phases. You have the moment of inspiration, then you start preparatory work, then you get blocked by something, things go underground; that is the phase of incubation. Then, all a sudden, you have illumination. It jumps out at your face. You start to elaborate and, eventually, you verify. There are rarely happy movements, where all these five, six, seven stages are compressed into a single sheet. Just here, and now and then. Alexander Pushkin once wrote - and I have to read it, it's too beautiful and I wouldn't want to make a mistake: "that blessed state of the spirit... when verses lie down before your pen and ringing rhymes run to meet up with a nicely turned thought." What about the stages that you are running through? How do you go about it? How do you cope with difficulty?

Angelou: There is a time for every book when I might have two weeks of euphoria in a year. Then everything I write is right, smooth; the verses lay down in front of my pen. Now it is not one solid block of two weeks. It might be three days here, two days there, and it is so delicious. Then there is the down. That is the end of that, maybe for a month, and I never know when it is coming. I go to the hotel room, I am ready, I get everything right, then... I'm gone, I'm gone. Two days later I weigh ten hundred pounds. I can't get up, but I go to work. Words are my tools, so I use them. If there is no inspiration, I work.

>A rat sat
>on the mat.
>That is that,
>not a cat.

And I continue plugging, plugging until somehow the muse says, "Well, okay, you're sincere, I'll give you a little bit." But in those moments, in those few times, maybe that is why a person does what she or he does, just to get to that magic again, because then you are neither meat nor fowl nor good red herring, you are nothing, nothing. You do not exist. That happens two weeks a year, maybe a little more. I cannot count on it, though. I cannot do anything to induce it, to make it come to me.

Guntern: ...but perseverance. You know, this sounds like what many, many a creative person has lived through, and Hemingway once said: "Greatness is the longest steeplechase ever run. Many enter, few survive." But he said how those who did survive, survive. He said: "Il faut d'abord durer. To endure is everything." In his Nobel speech Faulkner said: "To endure is not enough, you have to prevail." Prevail by working hard.

Angelou: Yes, that is true. Well, I think the minute you endure, you have prevailed. I think Faulkner has split a hair there, because if you endure, you have said to life, "I will stay with you." The inducement, the temptation to leave life is so great, that the minute you say, "Okay, I will stay with you one more day. I can always commit suicide tomorrow," then you have done well, you have prevailed against all these forces - I think.

Q. I really love hearing and seeing you speak about creativity, sing, laugh and I believe you are a very creative person because you bring me into an atmosphere where my soul is lighter and flies away for a delicious moment. I thank you for this beautiful moment. My question is, how do you manage your success? In other words, is creativity without success possible or not?

Angelou: I do not think one is dependent upon the other. The story is repeated so many times in the world of art: the young man who wrote the book and committed suicide; the painter who becomes known only after he is dead; the composer who becomes famous after she has died or gone mad, or something. So the person has been creative without success. You can be successful without creativity. All you have to do is look at Hollywood and see that. As far as I am concerned, I think I am very fortunate to be successful. It means, for me, that certain generosities are available. I can do certain things, and I am free not to have to do certain things. What I have to do is write. Now money does not help me there, nor do success, fame or notoriety. Nothing helps me with that yellow pad and that pen. But in the other areas of my life, yes, I can do things for myself and for others if I choose. It should not impinge though, I think. One of the points made earlier by Dr. Guntern was that if a person becomes successful too soon, he or she crystallizes. I have seen that happen. I talked about that just a week ago with a friend. We knew a person who became very famous and has repeated the work which made him famous over and over for twenty years and has not grown any further. However, you do not get any response, you can become so insecure, that you do not trust the muse any more. I think that every person is worthy of his or her hire. Everybody is worthy to be paid. I do not think that we should have a society where one person makes a million dollars a week for singing in Las Vegas and another person has to starve in a garret, in a basement some place while he is trying to write music. That is out of balance, there is something wrong with that.

Steininger: If you had had a happy life from the beginning, if you had lived in a beautiful family without sorrow, without grief, without all that you had to suffer, do you think that you could be able to do the work you did and that you could be the person full of life and full of whim and vigor that you are now?

Angelou: Well, again, I do not know what came first, the chicken or the egg. I cannot even imagine. I know some people who have been born with silver spoons in their mouths and who have been able to take those spoons out and write or paint. Not often though. So, I am led to think that one had to have a rather hard life in order to be a poet, to sing, to build. If I say that, I am afraid I have fallen into the trap which is what a number of people who have money would like to say, "Well, you don't have money, you don't have any clothes to wear. I have clothes, I have money, but never mind, you can sing." Well, I mean, there is something wrong with that too. You see, in a way it lets them off the hooks, and I don't want to do that. I don't want to give them that excuse to say, "You don't have to feel for me because after all I can sing." No.

Guntern: May I just add something to your question? It seems that there is a paradox. If somebody is growing up in very difficult circumstances, if the person is very strong - to begin with the egg or the hen - he will become even stronger. If he is not that strong, he will be deformed. If he is weak, he will be destroyed. Now, if somebody is growing up in very happy circumstances, there you have the opposite. The very weak are made stronger, the middle ones are deformed and the very strong ones are sometimes - sometimes - destroyed. It is a paradox, but that is how it seems to be.

Angelou: That is true. My brother Bailey, who is the closest my family has ever come to making a genius, who is simply an original thinker, was introducing me to Thomas Wolfe, to Phillip Wiley, to Faulkner by the age of fourteen. I do not know how he knew about them. I had read every book in the Black school library, but they were old books that White schools had given away to Black schools. He got these brand-new contemporary authors. By seventeen he was using drugs. He has won a number of battles against drugs, but he has never won the war. He is still alive, still brilliant; even after all the drugs have done whatever they have done physiologically, he is still brilliant. Imagine what would have happened had he been stronger psychologically. He had the better - or the faster - creative brain than I did.

Guntern: ...and must have had extreme sensitivity.

Angelou: Extreme. My brother and I were sent three thousand miles - when we were three and four - with tags on our arms, and the Black men who worked on the trains looked after us, and read wherever we were going and helped us to change trains. My Grandmother says when we arrived at her store, and she had fried chicken under a tea-towel, my brother wept, "I want my mother, I want my mother." He was four. I said, "I want some chicken." I was three. They do tell the story. So he was and has been needy, and somehow I was not so needy. I had...

Guntern: ...autonomy?

Angelou: Autonomy.

Compernolle: You talked about freeing yourself and how the Black people free themselves from the inside out. But each time you talked about it, you made a reference to the Gospel, to Gospel singing, to the Church. So from there, my question, and I ask it as an atheist, could you have freed yourself from the inside out without religion? And how can the young ones in the same situation free themselves from the inside out without religion?

Angelou: I think that the Judeo religion - particularly the Old Testament - was almost as if it had been made for us, as if the Jews had lived their lives thousands of years earlier, so that Blacks would have something to identify with. The story of the enslavement in Egypt and the forty years in the desert and the looking for the home - all those things fit directly into the Black slaves' imagination. Had there been a philosopher on the scene at the time, that might have worked. But as it was, the slaves had to believe in something other than this tactile life, this reality that they were living. So they had to suspend themselves. And there was God, and they had come from Africa, where the religions talked about the spider, Ananse, going to Heaven on its web, to talk to Nyame, to talk to God. So when the African slaves heard that there was a man named Jacob, who went to Heaven on a chariot wheel, they said, "Yes, I can believe that." In the West African religions Nyame is hermaphroditic; it can make itself female, male, or neuter. So when the African slaves heard that Jesus was the result of an immaculate conception, they said, "Yes, I can see that." So the Bible stories worked. I cannot even speculate what would have happened. I do know that the religion without the music would not have been sufficient. But the music the slaves inherited had to be changed from its original form. For instance, there is a song the Europeans sing (sings) "Amazing grace how sweet thou sound, that save ... " I can hardly sing it that way. The Blacks took that melody, made it their own: (sings)

Amazing grace, how sweet thou sound...

Q: I want to see the secrets of your silence. Are there three secrets, two secrets, one secret about your silence? Do you understand what I mean?

Angelou: Well, yes. I was seven and-a-half when I was raped, and very badly abused. All rape is bad. The man said if I told anyone, he would kill my brother, and I adored my brother. So I went to hospital and my brother told me I had to tell who did it. I said, "But if I tell, he will kill you." He said, "He can't, I won't let him." He was eight years old, and I believed him. So I told my brother the man's name and the man was put in jail. After he came out - he had been out for about two days - I was in my mother's mother's house, when a policeman came in and told my grandmother that the man had been found dead and that it looked as if he had been kicked to death. My logic told me that my voice had killed him, and that it was better not to speak, that a person might die if I spoke. So I stopped speaking. Black people all over the world believe a person is supposed to speak. There is a book by Janheinz-Jahn on African culture in which he declares that you must give the word, you must speak. And in the South among Black people, if an older person told another older person that a young person did not speak, the younger person could get into all sorts of trouble. Somehow my grandmother allowed me the space not to speak, and she used to say to me when she would braid my hair - (old Black people would sit a child down on the ground between the legs and pull the brush through the hair): "Sister, Momma don't care what these people say about you, that you are an idiot, that you are a moron. Sister, Momma know when you and the Lord get ready, Sister, you will be a preacher." And I used to think, poor ignorant Momma; she does not know I'll never speak. Let alone become a preacher. I forgot why I stopped speaking after about two years. I only knew I loved it. If you do not speak, you are free. It is very addictive, very.

Guntern: You know, there is a line by William Butler Yeats: "Like a long-legged fly moves upon a stream, the poet moves upon silence." This was your start in poetry.

I should like to thank Dr. Maya Angelou for all she gave us this morning. She reminds me of another Maya, the mythological Maya of the Hindu, who by her dancing creates illusions which hinder man to see the truth. By using her hands, her voice, her words and her songs, she has woven this morning a magic carpet and tricked us into the illusion that every one of us - even I - can be a poet. With this happy knowledge we shall now go up and tell it on the mountains!

Angelou: Bravo, that was beautifully said!

Works by Maya Angelou

l Know Why the Caged Bird Sings. New York: Random House, 1970.
Just Give Me a Cool Drink of Water 'fore I Diiie; the Poetry of Maya Angelou. New York: Random House, 1971.
Gather Together in My Name. New York: Random House, 1974.
Oh Pray My Wings are Gonna Fit Me Well. New York: Random House, 1975.
Singin' and Swingin' and Gettin' Merry Like Christmas. New York: Random House, 1976.
And Still I Rise New York. New York: Random House, 1978.
The Heart of a Woman. New York: Random House, 1981.
Shaker, Why Don't You Sing? New York: Random House, 1983.
All God's Children Need Traveling Shoes. New York: Random House, 1986.
Now Sheba Sings the Song. New York: Dutton/Dial, 1987.
I Shall Not Be Moved. New York: Random House, 1990.
Wouldn't Take Nothing for my Journey Now. New York: Random House, 1993.

JOSEPH BRODSKY
Russian-American poet and writer, 1940 - 1996
Nobel Prize laureate

Born in Leningrad in 1940, Joseph Brodsky was forced to emigrate from the Soviet Union in 1972 and settled in bustling Manhatten. One of the most outstanding contemporary essayists, he was awarded the Nobel Prize in Literature in 1987. Not only a gifted and prominent writer, Brodsky was also masterful in translating and interpreting some of his fellow authors including Anna Achmatova, Marina Zvetajeva, Ossip Mandelstam, W.H. Auden, Konstantine Kavafis and Eugenio Montale. In 1978 he was appointed honorary doctor of literature at Yale University, received the John D. and Catherine T. MacArthur Foundation Award in 1981, and later held the Andrew Mellon Professor of Literature chair in Mount Holyoke. He died of heart failure in New York in January 1996.

Introduction by Gottlieb Guntern

I am happy to present the Russian poet Joseph Brodsky, who expresses himself, of course, in language, but at the same time creates pictures that you will not very easily forget. Joseph Brodsky has been hailed by Anna Akhmatova in the East, by Wystan H. Auden here in the West, as being the foremost voice of contemporary Russian poetry. So much praise may sometimes lie on his shoulders as quite a heavy burden. But then life has trained his shoulders to carry heavy burdens.

He was born in Leningrad where he spent his childhood. Two parents and a child shared one room and-a-half within a communal apartment. At the age of 15 he left school, disgusted by the dreariness of uninspired teaching and rote learning, which, as he put it, "bred in us such an overpowering sense of ambivalence that in ten years we ended up with a will-power in no way superior to a seaweed's." He worked then as a milling operator, had the idea of becoming a neuro-surgeon and worked in a morgue. Then he understood that his destiny was to become a poet. The state, Communist Russia back then, thought otherwise; so he was sent to a forced labor camp up north in Arkhangels, near the White Sea. In 1964 a transcript was smuggled into the West, and when we read it, we get a glimpse of the kind of trial in which he was a defendant, but also of the character, the personality of the defendant. I will read a few lines:

Judge :   What is your profession?
Brodsky: Translator and poet.
Judge: Who has recognized you as a poet? Who has enrolled you in the ranks of poets?
Brodsky: No one. Who enrolled me in the ranks of human beings?
Judge: Did you study for it?

Brodsky: What?

Judge: To be a poet. Didn't you try to take courses in school where one prepares for life, where one learns?

Brodsky: I didn't believe it was a matter of education.

Judge: How is that?

Brodsky: I thought that it came from God.

In this dramatic moment Brodsky, who was called by Nadezhda Mandelstam a spoiled darling of fate, certainly not correctly, displayed clear judgment, cunning and a lot of courage. Eventually international and national protest forced the Soviet government to reconsider the sentence and Brodsky returned to Leningrad. He was threatened to be killed unless he applied for a visa to emigrate to the West, a terrible punishment for a poet who lives in his language as does a fish in the sea. Yet even at the heart-rending moment when he left the country, he wrote a letter to Leonid Breshnev, stating, "Although I am losing my Soviet citizenship, I do not cease to be a Russian poet. I believe that I will return. Poets always return in flesh or on paper." Since then he has returned, yet only on paper. He lives in Manhattan, a peninsula surrounded by water, and he seems to like this city. Perhaps not exactly in the same way he likes Leningrad, where he was born, and Venice, where he often spends some time at the end of the year, but still he likes it. He keeps away from the celebrity cult which has already killed many a minor talent in Manhattan. He is like a highly motivated tightrope walker who knows that he has to keep aloof in order not to be smashed to pieces.

Joseph Brodsky was invited to be a speaker at our Symposium last year. At the last minute, for health reasons, he could not attend. I am very happy that he is with us today, and I am sure that he has as much to say about the topic of intuition and creativity as he could have said about the topic of playful imagination and creativity.

Joseph Brodsky

I should begin by clarifying two or three inaccuracies that have been voiced here. In 1972, when I was told by the Ministry of Internal Affairs that I had to leave Russia, I was not threatened with execution or murder, but simply with all sorts of rather vague unpredictabilities, the bottom line of which was that I would end up again behind bars. By that time I had served in various prisons, twice in mental institutions, and I didn't see any merit in trying it again.

Now, back to our subject, intuition and creativity. A paper or an essay comes in different forms - monologue, dialogue, synagogue, that sort of thing. Actually I have written on the subject of creativity, and it has little to do with the subject of intuition. However, here is what I have got to say about it. Basically, as we know, the aptitude, the parameters of our species throughout recorded history could be termed as having two trends, two tendencies, two abilities to operate, to manage our cognitive process. One is the Western way, that puts a great premium on the rational with the attendant emphasis on the individual significance. It could best be exemplified by Descartes who said, as you probably know, *cogito ergo sum*. It is a rational, analytical approach towards reality. Yet there is another option available to the species which is loosely associated with the Orient, whose cornerstone is intuition, self-negation, self-abnegation; and it could best be exemplified, I would say, by Buddha. Now, the whole point about writing or literary process - at least this is the way I have learned what the literary process is like - is rather an interesting thing because it is indeed a fusion of the analytical and intuitive processes. That is, you may set out to write a poem with a number of very coherent attitudes. But no sooner have you started, than you begin to realize that something else, something unpredictable, creeps in. These are the words, the command, the allusions, the associations and connections, which you had not thought of heretofore. So basically you may compose a poem whose chief genius would be the analytical or rational genius. And yet, you sit down and begin to edit it, to correct it, to throw things away; this is no longer the analytical process, but rather the intuitive. There is something in you, in your ear, in your mind, in your esthetic sense that tells you this word will not do, this notion will not do; let's replace it. And very often you end up with a poem you didn't intend to write. What I am trying to tell you basically is that the creative process as such is the unwitting fusion of intuitive and analytical approach. I would stretch it even a bit further and say that those who practice poetry professionally, those who employ meter, rhymes, etc., who play the game by the rules, could be billed as the most accomplished of human animals, that is, those who do not choose one method of cognition, but for whom cognition is the almost unwitting fusion of the intuitive and analytical processes. In other words, poets, up to a certain point, are the healthiest animals. This is no small matter, and I am not saying that to sell you my line of work as perhaps the most valuable line of work available. To me poetry is not an art as such, though it is an art, it's not an entertainment though it may result in entertainment. Above all it's a tremendous tool of cognition, a tremendous form of mental acceleration. And that's what hooks one into doing it. Once you have made the connections which you didn't expect to make, you can't really let it go. You would like to try it time and again, and each time, if you are successful, or at least if you are so in your own eyes, it's terribly rewarding. It provides you with the insights which aren't available (a) to you, or (b) to the public, and wouldn't be available, couldn't be attained by any other route. I indeed prize poetry more highly than any other form of cognitive process; more than philosophical inquiry, more than scientific inquiry. It may not be exactly as conclusive or binding as the scientific discovery, but then it's better when the discovery is not binding. These are my feelings on the subject of intuition and the role it plays. To isolate one or the other, and to proclaim it as the most effective *modus operandi* would be a tremendous mistake, which would find its audience as mistakes always do. I have never seen a graphomaniac who wouldn't have had a substantial following. But basically, I think, the most sound advice that one could give to anybody who is embarking on this sort of career of producing verses is just to combine intuition and one's analytical proclivity.

I am going to read you something which is 12 pages long. It's an essay - a lecture in fact - I wrote exactly a year ago for this occasion, but as Dr. Guntern mentioned, all sorts of peculiar vicissitudes prevented me from delivering it to you. So if you don't respond in any positive way to what you are about to hear, you will at least have the comfort of thinking that this is still 1994.

The title of this piece is *A Cat's Meow*. I will try to read it to you fairly slowly, as English is not my mother tongue and I do have a tendency, practically unbeknown to myself and for which I apologize, to accelerate. Actually acceleration, as every driver knows, is a form of self-effacement. So here it goes. It has three parts, part II is the footnote. And it is perhaps the lengthiest footnote that you are to experience in your conscious life.

A CAT'S MEOW.

I

I dearly wish I could begin this monologue from afar, or at least preface it with a bunch of disclaimers. However, this dog's ability to learn new tricks is inferior to its tendency to forget old ones. So let me try to cut straight to the bone.

Many things have changed on this dog's watch; but I believe that a study of phenomena is still valid and of interest only as long as it is being conducted from without. The view from within is inevitably distorted and of parochial consequence, its claims to documentary status notwithstanding. A good example is madness: the view of the physician is of greater import than that of his patient.

Theoretically, the same should apply to "creativity," except that the nature of this phenomenon rules out the possibility of a vantage point for studying it. Here, the very process of observation renders the observer, to put it mildly, inferior to the phenomenon he observes, whether he is positioned without or within the phenomenon. In a manner of speaking, the report of the physician here is as invalid as the patient's own ravings.

The lesser commenting upon the greater has of course a certain humbling appeal; and at our end of the galaxy we are quite accustomed to this sort of procedure. I hope therefore that my reluctance to objectify creativity bespeaks not a lack of humility on my part but precisely the absence of a vantage point enabling me to pronounce anything of value on the subject.

I don't qualify as a physician; as a patient I am too much of a basket case to be taken seriously. Besides, I detest the very term — creativity — and some of this detestation rubs off on the phenomenon this term appears to denote. Even if I were able to shut down the voice of my senses revolting against it, my utterance on the subject would amount at best to a cat's attempt to catch its own tail. An absorbing endeavor, to be sure; but then perhaps I should be meowing.

Given the solipsistic nature of any human inquiry, that would be as honest a response to the notion of creativity as you can get. Seen from the outside, creativity is the subject of fascination or envy; seen from within, it is an unending exercise in uncertainty and a tremendous school for insecurity. In either case, a meow or some other incoherent sound is the most adequate response whenever the notion of creativity is invoked.

Let me therefore get rid of the panting and bated breath that accompanies this term, which is to say let me get rid of the term altogether. Webster's Collegiate Dictionary defines creativity as the ability to create; so let me stick to this definition. This way perhaps at least one of us will know what he is talking about, although not entirely.

The trouble begins with "create," which is, I believe, an exalted version of the verb "to make," and the same good old Webster's offers us "to bring into existence." The exaltation here has to do presumably with our ability to distinguish between familiar and unprecedented results of one's making. The familiar, thus, is made; the unfamiliar, or unprecedented, is **created**.

Now, no honest craftsman or maker knows in the process of working whether he is making or creating. He may be overtaken with this or that incoherent emotion at a certain stage of the process, he may even have an inkling that he manufactures something qualitatively new or unique, but the first, the second, and the last reality for him is the work itself, the very process of working. The process takes precedence over its result if only because the latter is impossible without the former.

The emergence of something qualitatively new is a matter of chance. Hence there is no visual distinction between a maker and a beholder, between an artist and his public. At a reception the latter may stand out in the crowd at best by virtue of his longer hair or sartorial extravagance, but nowadays the reverse may be true as well. In any case, at the completion of the work, a maker may mingle with beholders and even assume their perspective on his work and employ their vocabulary. It is unlikely, however, that upon returning to his study, studio, or, for that matter, lab, he would attempt to re-christen his tools.

One says "I make" rather than "I create." This choice of verb reflects not only humility but the distinction between the guild and the market, for the distinction between making and creating can only be made retroactively, by the beholder. Beholders are essentially consumers, and that's why a sculptor seldom buys another sculptor's works. Any discourse on creativity, no matter how analytical it may turn out to be, is therefore a market discourse. One artist's recognition of another's genius is essentially a recognition of the power of chance and perhaps of the other's industry in producing occasions for chance to invade.

This, I hope, takes care of the "make" part of Webster's definition. Let's address the "ability" part. The notion of ability comes from experience. Theoretically, the greater one's experience, the more secure one may feel in one's ability. In reality (in art and, I would think, science) experience and the accompanying expertise are the maker's worst enemies.

The more successful you've been, the more uncertain you are, when embarking on a new project, of the result. Say, the greater the masterpiece you just produced, the smaller the likelihood of your repeating the feat tomorrow. In other words, the more questionable your ability becomes. The very notion of ability acquires in your mind a permanent question mark and gradually one begins to regard one's work as a non-stop effort to erase that mark. This is especially true among those engaged in literature, particularly in poetry, which, unlike other arts, is bound to make detectable sense.

But even adorned with an exclamation mark ability is not guaranteed to spawn masterpieces each time it is applied. We all know plenty of uniquely endowed artists and scientists producing little of consequence. Dry spells, writers' blocks, and fallow stretches are the companions of practically every known genius, all lamenting about them bitterly, as do much lesser lights. Often a gallery signs up an artist or an institution a scientist only to learn how slim the pickings may get.

In other words, ability is not reducible either to skill or an individual's energy, much less to the congeniality of one's surroundings, one's financial predicament, or one's milieu. Had it been so, we would have had by now a far greater volume of masterpieces on our hands than is the case. In short, the ratio of those engaged throughout just this century in art and science to the appreciable results is such that one gets tempted to equate ability with chance. Well, it looks like chance inhabits both parts of Webster's definition of creativity rather cozily. It is so much so that it occurs to me that perhaps the term "creativity" denotes not so much an aspect of human agency as the property of the material to which this agency now and then is applied; that perhaps the ugliness of the term is after all justified, since it bespeaks the pliable and malleable aspects of inanimate matter. Perhaps the One Who dealt with that matter first is not called "Creator" for nothing. Hence, creativity.

Considering the Webster's definition, a qualifier is perhaps in order. Denoting a certain unidentified resistance, "the ability to make" perhaps should be accompanied by a sobering "war on chance." A good question is of course what comes first: the material or its maker? For all our profound humility, at our end of the galaxy the answer is obvious and resounds with hubris. The other—and a much better question—is whose chance are we talking about here, the maker's or the material's?

Neither hubris nor humility will be of much help here. Perhaps in trying to answer this question, we have to jettison the notion of virtue altogether. But then we have always been tempted to do just that. So let's seize this opportunity: not for the sake of scientific inquiry so much as for Webster's reputation.

But I am afraid we need a footnote.

II

Because human beings are finite, their system of causality is linear, which is to say, self-referential. The same goes for their notion of chance, since chance is not cause-free; it is but a moment of interference by another system of causality, however aberrant its pattern, in our own. The very existence of the term, not to mention a variety of epithets accompanying it (for instance, "blind"), shows that our concepts of order and chance are both essentially anthropomorphic.

Had the area of human inquiry been limited to the animal kingdom, that would be fine. However, it's manifestly not so; it's much larger and, on top of that, a human being insists on knowing the truth. The notion of truth, in its own right, is also anthropomorphic and presupposes, on the part of the inquiry's subject—i.e., the world—a withholding of the story, if not outright deception.

Hence a variety of scientific disciplines probing the universe in the most minute manner, the intensity of which—especially the language—could be likened to torture. In any case, if the truth about things has not been attained thus far, we should put this down to the world's extraordinary resilience, rather than to a lack of effort. The other explanation, of course, is truth's absence; an absence we don't accept because of its dramatic consequences for our ethics.

Ethics—or, to put it less grandly but perhaps more pointedly, pure and simple eschatology—as the vehicle of science? Perhaps; at any rate, what human inquiry indeed boils down to is the animate interrogating the inanimate. Small wonder that the results are inconclusive; smaller wonder still that the methods and the language we employ in the process more and more resemble the matter at hand itself.

Ideally, perhaps, the animate and the inanimate should swap places. That, of course, would be to the liking of the dispassionate scientist, who places such a premium on objectivity. Alas, this is not likely to happen, as the inanimate doesn't seem to show any interest in the animate: the world is not interested in its humans. Unless, of course, we ascribe to the world divine provenance, which, for several millennia now, we've failed to demonstrate.

If the truth about things indeed exists, then, given our status as the world's latecomers, that truth is bound to be inhuman. It is bound to cancel our notions of causality, aberrant or not, as well as those of chance. The same applies to our surmises as to the world's provenance, be that divine, molecular, or both: the viability of a concept depends on the viability of its carriers.

Which is to say that our inquiry is essentially a highly solipsistic endeavor. For the only opportunity available for the animate to swap places with the inanimate is the former's physical end: the man joins, as it were, matter.

Still, one can stretch matters somewhat by imagining that it is not the inanimate which is under the animate's investigation, but the other way around. This rings a certain metaphysical bell, and not so faintly. Of course, it's difficult to build either science or a religion on such a foundation. Still, the possibility shouldn't be ruled out, if only because this option allows our notion of causality to survive intact. Not to mention that of chance.

What sort of interest could the infinite take in the finite? To see how the latter might modify its ethics? But ethics as such contains its opposite. To tax human eschatology further? But the results will be quite predictable. Why would the infinite keep an eye on the finite?

Perhaps out of the infinite's nostalgia for its own finite past, if it ever had one? In order to see how the poor old finite is still faring against overwhelming odds? How close the finite may come to comprehending, with its microscopes, telescopes, and all, with its observatories' and churches' domes, those odds' enormity?

And what would the infinite's response be, should the finite prove itself capable of revealing the infinite's secrets? What course of action might the infinite take, given that its repertoire is limited to the choice between being punitive or benevolent? And since benevolence is something we are less familiar with, what form might it assume?

If it is, let's say, some version of life eternal, or Paradise, or Utopia where nothing ever ends, what should be done, for instance, about those who never make it there? And if it were possible for us to resurrect them, what would happen to our notion of causality, not to mention chance? Or maybe the opportunity to resurrect them, an opportunity for the living to meet the dead, is what chance is all about? And isn't the finite's chance to become infinite synonymous with the animate becoming inanimate? Is that a promotion?

Or perhaps the inanimate only appears to be so to the eye of the finite? And if there is indeed no difference, save a few secrets thus far not revealed, where, once they get revealed, are we all to dwell? Would we be able to shift from the infinite to the finite and back, would we have a choice? What would the means of transportation between the two be? An injection, perhaps? And once we lose the distinction between the finite and the infinite, would we care where we are? Wouldn't that be, to say the least, the end of science, not to mention religion?

Have you been influenced by Wittgenstein, asks the reader?

Acknowledging the solipsistic nature of human inquiry shouldn't, of course, result in prohibitive legislation limiting that inquiry's scope. It won't work: No law based on the recognition of human shortcomings does. Furthermore, every legislator, especially an unacknowledged one, should be, in turn, aware all the time of the equally solipsistic nature of the very law he is trying to push.

Still, it would be both prudent and fruitful to admit that all our conclusions about the world outside, including those about its provenance, are but reflections, or better yet articulations of our physical selves.

For what constitutes a discovery or, more broadly, truth, is our recognition of it. Presented with an observation or a conclusion backed by evidence, we exclaim, "Yes, that's true!" In other words, we recognize something that has been offered to our scrutiny as our own. Recognition, after all, is an identification of the reality within with the reality without; an admission of the latter into the former. However, in order to be admitted into the inner sanctum (say, the mind), the guest should possess at least some structural characteristics similar to those of the host.

This, of course, is what explains the considerable success of all manner of microcosmic research, with all those cells and particles echoing nicely our own self-esteem. Yet, humility aside, when a grateful guest eventually reciprocates by inviting his gracious host over to his place, the latter often finds himself quite comfortable in those theoretically strange quarters and occasionally even benefits from a sojourn to the village of Applied Sciences, emerging from it now and then from a jar of penicillin, now with a tankful of gravity-spurning fuel.

In other words, in order to recognize anything, you've got to have something to recognize it with, something that will do the recognizing. The faculty that we believe does the recognizing job on our behalf is our brain. Yet the brain is not an autonomous entity; it functions only in concert with the rest of our physiological system. What's more, we are quite cognizant of our brain's ability not only to absorb concepts as regards the outside world but to generate them as well; we are also cognizant of that ability's relative dependence on, say, our motoric or metabolic functions.

This is enough to suspect a certain parity between the inquirer and the inquired; and suspicion is often the mother of truth. That, at any rate, is enough to suggest a perceptible resemblance between what's getting discovered and the discoverer's own cellular makeup. Now that, of course, stands to reason, if only because we are very much of this world—at least according to the admission of our own evolutionary theory.

Small wonder, then, that we are capable of discovering or discerning certain truths about it. This wonder is so small that it occurs to one that "discovery" is quite possibly a misnomer, and so are "recognition," "admission," "identification," etc.

It occurs to one that what we habitually bill as our discoveries are but the projections of what we contain within upon the outside. That the physical reality of the world/nature/you-name-it is but a screen—or, if you like, a wall—with our own structural imperatives and irregularities writ large or small upon it. That the outside is a blackboard or a sounding board for our ideas and inklings about our own largely incomprehensible tissue.

That, in the final analysis, a human being doesn't so much obtain knowledge from the outside as secrete it from within. That human inquiry is a closed-circuit system, where no Supreme Being or alternative system of intelligence can break in. Were they to, they wouldn't be welcome, if only because He, or it, would become one of us, and we have had enough of our kind.

They had better stay in the realm of probability, in the province of chance. Besides, as One of them said, "My kingdom is not of this world." No matter how scandalous probability's reputation is, it won't thrust either one of them into our midst, because probability is not suicidal. Inhabiting our minds for want of a better seat, it surely won't try to destroy its only habitat. And if infinity indeed has us for its audience, probability will certainly try its best to present infinity as a moral perspective, especially with a view to our eventually entering it.

To that end, it may even send in a Messiah, since left to our own devices we have a pretty rough time with the ethics of even our manifestly limited existence. As chance might have it, this Messiah may assume any guise, and not necessarily the guise of human likeness. He may for instance appear in the form of some scientific idea, in the shape of some microbiological breakthrough predicating individual salvation on a universal chain reaction that would require safety for all in order to achieve eternity for one, and vice versa.

Stranger things have happened. In any case, whatever it is that makes life safer or gives it hope of extension should be regarded as being of supernatural origin, because nature is neither friendly nor hope-inspiring. On the other hand, between science and creeds, one is perhaps better off with science, because creeds have proven too divisive.

All I am trying to suggest is that, chances are, a new Messiah, should he really emerge, is likely to know a bit more about nuclear physics or microbiology—and about virology in particular—than we do today. That knowledge of course is bound to be of greater use for us here than in the life everlasting, but, for the moment, we may still settle for less.

Actually, this could be a good test for probability, for chance in particular, since the linear system of causality takes us straight into extinction. Let's see whether chance is indeed an independent notion. Let's see whether it is something more than just bumping into a movie star in a suburban bar or winning the lottery. Of course, this depends on how much one wins: a big win may come close to personal salvation.

Not Wittgenstein. Only Frankenstein.

End of footnote.

III

So if we are a part of the natural world (as our cellular make-up suggests), if the animate is an aspect of the inanimate, then chance pertaining to a maker pertains to matter. Perhaps Webster's "ability to make" is nothing more (or less) than matter's attempts to articulate itself. Since a maker (and with him the whole of the human species) is an infinitesimal speck of matter, the latter's attempts at articulation must be few and far between. Their infrequency is proportionate to the availability of adequate mouthpieces, whose adequacy, i.e., the readiness to perceive an inhuman truth, is known in our parlance as genius. This infrequency is thus the mother of chance.

Now, matter, I believe, comes to articulate itself through human science or human art presumably only under some kind of duress. This may sound like an anthropomorphic fantasy, but our cellular make-up entitles us to this sort of indulgence. Matter's fatigue, its thinning out, or its oversaturation with time are, among a host of other less and more fathomable processes, what further enunciates chance and what is registered by the lab's instruments or by the no less sensitive pen of the lyric poet. In either case, what you get is the ripple effect.

In this sense, the ability to make is a passive ability: a grain of sand's response to the horizon. For it is the sense of an opened horizon that impresses us in a work of art or a scientific breakthrough, isn't it? Anything less than that qualifies not for the unique but for the familiar. The ability to make, in other words, depends on the horizon and not on one's own resolve, ambition, or training. To analyze this ability only from our end of the story is therefore erroneous and not terribly rewarding.

"Creativity" is what a vast beach remarks when a grain of sand is swept away by the ocean. If this sounds too tragic or too grand for you, it means only that you are too far back in the dunes. An artist's or a scientist's notion of luck or chance reflects essentially his proximity to the water, or, if you will, to matter.

One can increase one's proximity to it in principle by will in reality, though it happens nearly always inadvertently. No amount of research or of caffeine, calories, alcohol, or tobacco consumed can position that grain of sand sufficiently close to the breakers. It all depends on the breakers themselves, i.e., on matter's own timing, which is solely responsible for the erosion of its so-called beach. Hence all this loose talk about divine intervention, breakthroughs, and so forth. Whose breakthroughs?

If poetry fares somewhat better in this context, it is because language is, in a manner of speaking, the inanimate's first line of information about itself released to the animate. To put it perhaps less polemically, language is a diluted aspect of matter. By manipulating it into a harmony or, for that matter, disharmony, a poet—by and large unwittingly—negotiates himself into the domain of pure matter—or, if you will, of pure time—faster than can be done in any other line of work. A poem—and above all a poem with a recurrent stanzaic design—almost inevitably develops a centrifugal force whose ever-widening radius lands the poet far beyond his initial destination.

It is precisely the unpredictability of the place of one's arrival as well as perhaps his eventual gratitude, that makes a poet regard his ability "to make" as a passive ability. The vastness of what lies ahead rules out the possibility of any other attitude towards one's regular or irregular procedure; it certainly rules out the notion of creativity. There is no creativity vis-à-vis that which instills terror.

Joseph Brodsky December, 1992/1993
Rome/New York

Discussion

Guntern: Thank you very much for your brilliant introduction in your own form of self-effacement. Now, since you don't like the term "creativity," let's stick to what you call your tremendous exercise in uncertainty.

Brodsky: Now I'm going to be held responsible for what I have said - which is a ridiculous exercise, because it was written a year ago. Indeed it does reflect some thinking on my part on the subject, but I don't really remember details.

Guntern: Shall I begin with this or go a little bit further back in time?

Brodsky: Whichever you like.

Guntern: You said here, language is a diluted form of matter and you have often commented in your work about what happens if the poet floats with the language and doesn't try to control it in a rational way. I remember with respect to Dostoevski in another context you said that language will land you far beyond the point where you originally intended to go. Could you say a little bit more about this?

Brodsky: I do not really remember what I said on the score, but essentially you can't really abandon control when you operate in a language. This is true for poetry or literature in general, but poetry specifically because it is sort of condensed and right in front of your eyes; it is an incurably semantic art, it's bound to make sense. So therefore you can't really abandon yourself to the flow of the language, alliteration, sounds, etc. Now, you still at all times do control that process, that is, the rational is still there. And yet what you do perhaps, (this is going to be a bit impressionistic for your liking), but what you do is that as you proceed for the poem, the words - simply by the means of rhymes - begin to suggest the connections which you were not intending to make. Say you write a poem about the moon. Well - moon, moon, moon, what does it rhyme with? And you go through a variety of options the English language has to offer. Sooner or later you hit something - you don't want to rhyme it with anything obvious, with "soon," "noon" and so on. So you try to rhyme it with something perhaps less obvious. You look at the less obvious things and you bump into, let's say, "spoon." You think, no, no, that cannot do because what does spoon have to do with the moon? You sit down, you think, and you decide that perhaps, after all, they do have something in common. They both are inanimate - silvery, shiny - that sort of thing. So perhaps you can utilize the spoon, though initially when you set out to write a poem you didn't think about that. What occurs in the process of composition is that you begin to uncover, unearth the dependencies, the linguistic dependencies heretofore unknown to you or to your predecessors if you know them well. What you do by rhyming certain things is to establish or uncover a possibility, a semblance of certain linguistic laws. Poems, good ones especially, apart from what they tell you about the sentiments, the weather, the layout of your room, whatever, apart from their content, are above all linguistic inevitabilities.

Guntern: And what about the surprise aspect?

Brodsky: Well, that is exactly what I have been talking about. It surprises you. The rhyme does. Well, you may will a surprise, you may conjure an idea and you can sort of carry the poem by the idea, subordinate it to the idea, subordinate it to the desire, to shock the reader. Lots of people have done exactly that and there is an entire industry of that. But I think there is a peculiar, divine or diabolical economy here that gets into play. A perception may be of tremendously powerful, shocking value, of tremendous impact, and yet, if it doesn't work, if it doesn't entail, if it doesn't involve or retain the aspect of linguistic harmony, it won't survive, that is, it won't arrest one's mind. A great deal of people do write rather shocking and revealing things, especially about themselves. For the latter half of the twentieth century there has been a lot of that. And yet you read a poem, you are impressed by the statement. But when you turn it white side up, you can't repeat a line. Two days later there is no such a poem, at least for you. So there is a peculiar correspondence, or the inevitability of connection between what you are saying and how you are saying it, and the language.

Guntern: You also wrote once - to use your same picture - if you cover a poem with something that would erase all the adjectives...

Brodsky: Ah, that's about the methodology of writing a poem. I can teach you how to write a good poem. Do you want me to?

Guntern: Yes.

Brodsky: It's easy. Basically, a good poem should have a higher percentage of nouns. That is, the ratio of the nouns to the other parts of speech, like adjectives, verbs, adverbs, etc. should be far superior. So that if you have written a poem, and then you imagine covering it with a sort of magic blanket that removes the adjectives, verbs and adverbs, when you remove the blanket, the poem should be sufficiently black on the page, there should be a table, there should be some furniture, other furniture, a flower, a parquet, a bulb, those things. It shouldn't be white.

Guntern: Another aspect about physiology and poetry. You wrote somewhere: differences in meters are differences in breath and heartbeat, differences in rhyming pattern are differences in brain functions. I was struck by this phrasing. Could you tell us more about it?

Brodsky: The meters poetry employs are not simply meters. They are basically - how should I put it? - a distribution of time or restructuring of time. Every song is a restructuring of time - even a bird's song. Let me give you an example. Let's have an iambic pentameter: Ta-**ta**-ta-**ta**-ta-**ta**-ta-**ta**-ta-**ta**; ten syllables, five stresses. And then you say, for instance:

> When you are old and gray and full of sleep,
> And nodding by the fire, take down this book.

William Butler Yeats, When You Are Old [1893]

That's one version of iambic pentameter, that's one type of time. Or,

> Especially when the October wind
> with frosty fingers punishes my hair
> caught by the crabbing sun I walk on fire
> and cast a shadow crab upon the land...

Dylan Thomas

You see the different jobs, the different velocities being offered to you in the same iambic pentameter. That's what meters are, they are vessels of velocities, or the opportunities to convey various velocities. Now, as for the rhymes - they convey perhaps more than anything else the intelligence of the poet. Let's take the almost most difficult thing in English, let's try to rhyme "love" with something. English has a rather limited amount of rhymes for that: glove, above, dove and that's more or less it. So the poets are sort of locked into reshuffling those words and then along comes someone who manages to introduce a new rhyme to love. I'm thinking in particular about W.H. Auden, who managed to rhyme "love" with "Diaghilev." So it's tremendous nonsense when you hear in English - or in any other language of Christendom for that matter - that rhyme is scarce, that all the rhymes have been used up, that there is no way of doing anything qualitatively new. Garbage! At any given time, at any given epoch or year, it's a matter of individual intelligence. Of course it's difficult to rhyme, for instance, "I am" in English. But you can rhyme it, if you have enough wits, with "1 a.m." and it will do. There are all sorts of things.

You simply have to be inventive. There is something quite interesting here, since we are talking about rhyme. I used to think that the terrific ability to handle rhyme bespoke intelligence. That is not entirely true; it is, however, a mark of intelligence. On the one hand I can think of somebody like, let's say the same W.H. Auden or the great poet, Wilfred Owen, who introduced the assonant rhyme to the English language, though it hasn't been picked up for half a century. They were terribly intelligent individuals. On the other hand I have in mind poets with tremendous facility, yet what they say is not terribly interesting. So it's very tricky. It basically has to do with your taste.

The whole history of art, the whole notion of history in general, boils down to the fact that there is no history other than the history of taste. And our presence on earth, our presence in every given generation is precisely that: the purpose of our presence is to refine taste.

Guntern: Let's stay with taste and esthetic perception. You once wrote that a baby's esthetical judgment comes before his/her ethical judgment, describing a scene where a stranger comes over the cradle of a child, and then you derived the notion that the difference between good and bad is older than between good and evil. Could you say something about this interconnection of ethics and esthetics?

Brodsky: I know what you are referring to. Indeed I once made an audacious statement (by which I stick) that esthetics is the mother of ethics. I would say, even today, that our most crucial choices are based on esthetics, not on ethics. That is, you pick up your mistress or beloved not on an ethical basis, because by doing so you could end up with a dog. Esthetical judgment I think - I'm not a Darwinist, I am a Lamarckian - is indeed an inherited thing. You may try to cultivate it, you may try to refine it, and you may try to adjust it to ethics. And yet ultimately your esthetic self will gain an upper hand in the most unlikely and very often most unpleasant manner. The crucial thing for a society, for an accumulation of individuals, is to develop taste individually. Because if you develop taste you cannot be fooled very easily, you cannot co-operate with a demagogue. You cannot cooperate with anybody who frequently resorts to clichés. An esthete constantly demands an esthetical elaboration, a next esthetical step. What makes art different from life is that good old silly art always tries to take the next step. Art tries to avoid cliché, whereas life's reality or ethical reality's main medium is precisely cliché. The main medium of life is tedium.

I could go on and on and on. It is one of the most crucial things. Believe it or not, we should regard and build ourselves above all, *not* as ethical beings. It is easy to be ethical. It's easy to share values. And there is nothing easier than to court those who share values and to turn them into monsters or something monstrous. It's very difficult to make an esthete participate in some persecution or some atrocious activity. I know the return, I know the response. I know that lots of Germans were all listening to Beethoven and yet they were manning the ovens. Well, the whole point about Beethoven is that art wants you to be its maker, not just a consumer; to make you imitate it in your life. There is a famous poem by Rilke, *Torso of Apollo*, which says

> With its every muscle
> at every angle
> this torso tells you,
> change your life.

What you have to be is not merely a listener of Beethoven, you have to become a Beethoven. Then society may be safer. As long as you just buy CDs, light the fire and digest dinner listening to Sonata No. 17, you can easily become a murderer.

Guntern: Concerning the interrelationship of esthetics and ethics, you wrote about the scum of Gropius, Corbusier and the like who did more to destroy the landscape of Europe than the German Luftwaffe did during the Second World War.

Brodsky: Well, I thought that before Prince Charles. I said that twenty years ago. Architecture is rather a peculiar thing. Architecture - the muse of architecture - depends so much on money, like no other muse.

Guntern: They are paid per cubic meter, not per quality. In Switzerland architects are paid per cubic meter they are constructing, per quantity.

Brodsky: Switzerland is not such a tragic case. You have a redeeming or rather alleviating aspect here. You can do any garbage architecturally, but it's sort of alleviated by the backdrop of the mountains. So in a sense if you don't want to keep your eyes at the level of your reality you can lift them up and, well, you are still intact.

Guntern: So the grains of sand do not have to respond to the horizon.

Brodsky: Well, I do not think Gropius, the entire Bauhaus School, would have been able to dwell or to evolve in such a manner, in such full flower in the mountainous area. For that you need a flat country.

Guntern: To turn to quite another issue, people who do not do what you do and often do not know how to do what you do, somehow always know how you should do better. So because we are inviting people here, creative individuals like you, one of the reproaches that came on and off was that this meeting here is an elitist meeting. I could never understand that reproach and I was, of course, pleased when I read in *Less than One*, "for culture is 'elitist' by definition, and the application of democratic principles in the sphere of knowledge leads to equating wisdom with idiocy."

Brodsky: Not only on cultural terms... Democracy is a tremendously good concept, but the democratic principles, when applied either to culture or to science or to sports for that matter, give contra-productive results. In art it results in equating a masterpiece to a hack job; in science it would result in equating discovery to total ignorance; and in sports you simply won't sell the tickets for the game, if you're going to be democratic there. I suppose I am better off on the subject of culture, I'm not so sure. The whole point is that there is no such a thing as elitism; or the notion of "elite" is valuable only within the social-political context. In terms of art, there is no such a notion, there is no such a business as "elite." Because "elite" in art means the best of art, the highest achievement of the human being, of our species. And the higher one's achievement is, the better it shows the people their potential. It simply shows the goal, the target, for which the species has to strive. In a sense the highest achievement of art is the invitation to the people to be like that art, to achieve the same, to go in that direction. Take poetry. Poetry is the supreme form of linguistic operation of our species, it's our genetic or anthropological target. You cannot be an elitist in poetry. What you simply do, you show people their maximum, and the job of the people is to follow or to try to approach that maximum. The notion of elitism in art, in culture is pure garbage. Of course, one could be more subtle about this, but I don't really want to waste (a) your time, (b) my breath arguing about it.

Guntern: John Donne wrote a few centuries ago: "No man is an island," and you wrote somewhere, "Every writer is a universe unto himself." And then you emphasize that there is more in him that separates him from others than in others that separates others from him.

Brodsky: So, what's the question?

Guntern: The question is, I would like to know a little bit more about the uniqueness of the human being. In spite of his genetic programming and in spite of a sometimes similar educational background, human beings are quite different one from another. The more someone develops autonomy, the more he/she is different. I would like you to talk a little bit more about the value of autonomy, identity, being different.

Brodsky: Well, I don't really know how to rejoin it, but here I am sitting pontificating in front of you. All right, let me say this: I think the job of the human being upon this earth, (since this is the only chance one is given, it's the only run you have) is to be unique, to be yourself and not be like others; it's to define, to establish and to proceed along the lines of what you think is you. There is no point in aspiring to be like others; there is no point in imitating them. This is your only chance. You are not going to have any other. You know how it is going to end. So, what you have to winnow from all that chaff is what it means to be yourself. We all have been told by the sociologists, by the social thinkers, by the reformers of society that the human being is the social animal. Well, we are social animals, but we are not animals only. We are unique entities, and what we have to strive for is to define our own uniqueness. Of course, we can achieve it through all sorts of perversities. We also can define it through something that we are attracted to. If you are attracted to a particular kind of music, a particular kind of painting, or a particular kind of literature, what you have to try to do is to become like that art, like that painting, like that music, like that poem. What you have to seek is not the common denominator, but your unique numerator. That is what I think, otherwise it would be a waste of time.

Guntern: Let me just ask the people, wouldn't you like to have a break?

Brodsky: I do not need any breaks. In front of you sits the man who just arrived this morning from the North American shores. I am not trying to say that I am not responsible for what I am saying. I am responsible for that. But I am afraid I may be less succinct now and then than I would like to be. Go ahead, ask any questions. I possibly, presumably, theoretically, may even come up with nonsense. Thus far it has been easy.

Guntern: There are several settings in which our intuition seems to flow spontaneously where we get inspired, where we even get illuminations. You wrote once with respect to Kavafis' work that ninety percent of the best poetry has been written *post coitum*. There must be other settings that are inspiring, what about that?

Brodsky: Well, the human being is a retrospective animal. And I think we perform better when we think back, when we look back, than when we look ahead, than when we try to be futuristic or utopian. Essentially, it has to do with - good Lord, we're opening a huge can with a great deal of worms in it! - essentially I think we are retrospective animals, we make better historians than theologians. Both activities do have to do with our eschatological dread, with the dread of not existing. However the past, as it offers some record, is a safer bet than the future, which is all but imponderables. The opposite number of the historian is the theologian, of course. And it's easier, perhaps more comfortable, to design a coherent past than a coherent future. I don't believe I answered your question, but somehow I went in that direction.

Guntern: What are settings that you find inspiring, do you have certain settings? I know that you often spend time in Venice. You said somewhere that watching the river Neva has taught you more about infinity and stoicism than mathematics and the writings of Zeno combined.

Brodsky: Water does have that effect, no question about it. Water has a peculiar property. If you look at the ocean or at the sea, you realize that for all its wrinkles, it has no memory, and you begin to wonder about those wrinkles. Many moons ago - I'm going to sell you the old perception - I remember I was looking at the water; it was in the previous incarnation indeed, in Russia, and I thought about the opening of the Bible, about God flying over creation for an undisclosed amount of time, and there was the sea. And I thought if He was flying above the sea, He was bound to be reflected in it. I have sort of a heretical notion of what the Supreme Being is. I think the notion of the Supreme Being, as it has come down to us through the centuries, is essentially the notion of time, of infinity. I thought that what we see in the surface of the water, preferably the ocean, is the reflection of time, that all those wrinkles are time's face. So essentially I believe that looking at the water gives you immediately a sense of your utter insignificance, which is a good humbling effect.

Guntern: And what about farming in Manhattan? Walt Whitman once wrote that Manhattan is a good place for harvest, but a bad place for farming.

Brodsky: Well, this is on Walt Whitman's conscience. Manhattan, actually, is not a promontory, it's an island, I have to correct you. It's an island and if you live long on that island you begin to develop (especially if you were not born there) a sense of being a Robinson Crusoe yourself. And you begin to regard everybody else as Good Man Friday or his relatives. Well, you walk out in the morning, especially when it's snowing and you see a footprint in the snow, and you wonder if this is Good Man Friday's footprint or your own. So you gradually begin to merge with the savages, you begin to regard yourself as a savage. What more can I say? It's rather interesting that Manhattan was initially called New Amsterdam. And I'll give you one more picture of it, if you will. When you walk through downtown Manhattan, through all the skyscrapers, etc. you begin to think that perhaps it is New Amsterdam or New Venice indeed, except that the canals that you have in Amsterdam or in Venice which run horizontally, are vertical here because the buildings, the skyscrapers, mostly glass and concrete, are vertical. So when you see those canals going upwards, you wouldn't want to be a bird there because you wouldn't know whether you were flying horizontally or vertically.

Guntern: Now, you also wrote that good writing is always a dialogue between the gutter and the spheres. It would seem then, from listening to you, that the gutters are especially deep in Manhattan and the spheres, especially high.

Brodsky: Gutters are gutters. They do not possess any particular depth in Manhattan, I believe. It's a normal town, very thickly settled and very densely populated. It's a place which makes you terribly humble. Every tall building immediately reduces you or tells you about your own size. It tells you that you are practically nothing, it cures you instantly of any hubris, which is a good thing. Mostly people like Manhattan, Europeans especially, but Americans as well. The usual sentence about Manhattan, or about people living in New York, is "Oh, there is so much going on." And for years and years I tried to fathom what it is exactly that they have in mind when they say, "There is so much going on." Finally I realized that it is the traffic.

Roessler: My question concerns what you said about the history of artists, the history of taste. I understand it as the fact that works of art can only be appreciated within a certain cultural context and not without, and that they do not have any perennity outside that cultural context. I would like to understand how, if this relates to something you said in your essay about the fact that creativity couldn't be defined, either from within or from without; in the sense that there is no creativity because the only result of a creative process could be such a cultural artifact, and that is something that can only be understood in this limited context of a certain cultural world. I do not know if I am clear.

Brodsky: The parameters of the question are rather vague. What I mean by history of taste, (let me think before I open my spittoon)... Essentially, what I was trying to say, perhaps I didn't say it clearly enough and I don't believe it can be said clearly enough, is that humanity has two records: one is a so-called historical record and the other is the record of art, which can also be called historical if we like. As for the historical record, it's basically pure nonsense because it doesn't really determine or define anything. I'll give you an American example. Not that long ago, in the very learned paper, *The New York Review of Books*, I read a big article about the history of American slavery. The author of the article was trying to establish the role played by Portuguese and other European Jews in being slave merchants, in transporting the African slaves to America. It's a very burning issue in many ways, and the entire essay originated as part of an argument by radical Black extremists in the United States. The general gist of that argument is that the European Jews were instrumental in part in creating this phenomenon of Black slavery, buying and shipping the Blacks from the African shores to the United States. I thought about that and about the great paradox that lies in that argument. First of all, regardless of who and what were instrumental in conveying the ancestors of present-day Black Americans from Africa to the United States, it's totally irrelevant for a man who now lives in Harlem or the Bronx or any other Black ghetto in the United States; it's absolutely of no consequence what transpired in history. What matters to the Black man or to any man who finds himself in circumstances unpalatable for him is what to do now. And what to do now has nothing to do with what happened then. It doesn't really matter for us whether Caligula was a good or bad emperor. We have our problems right now: my salary is not high enough; what should I do to support my family? Caligula, whether he was good or bad, is of no help. In fact, the entire issue of Black slavery and its history can be regarded as White man's ploy to prevent the American Blacks from solving their problems right now; it can be regarded as an attempt to diffuse the Black man's real focus. W.H. Auden once said: "Had I been an American Negro, in order to improve my plight, I would have joined the communist party and made a social revolution." That might sound a bit extreme, but it makes sense. Because a human being, at every given point, is faced with a particular problem that has its own dimensions and presumably its own solutions. When instead of solving your problem now, you plunge into your nostalgia for an existent or non-existent past, you don't help yourself or your own kind in any way whatsoever. The problem a man faces is always here and now and has or doesn't have its adequate solutions. So in a sense, to muse about whatever happened in the 16th or 17th century, who was the guilty party, and to what degree he was guilty, is absolutely irrelevant. My feeling is that we are putting too high a price on history as such. My feeling is that when we repeat those famous words by Santagora that those who forget history are liable to repeat its mistakes, is nonsense. We are going to make mistakes, no matter what, history or no history. It's simply because we are not angels. We are human beings, we are radically bad. We are not fallen angels, we are simply radically bad human beings. Well, the whole difference between somebody like myself and a predominant majority of the liberal crowd is that I do believe in original sin and they don't. The notion of original sin is a very simple one. It means that man is not good. The liberal thinks man is good. That is how I feel.

Now, when I talk about the history of taste, I don't mean exactly taking a work of art out of its historical context. Art, for its evolution, for its occurrence, doesn't need history. It needs neither political history nor social history. Art is essentially a history of its own material, of its own devices. If we talk about painting, art is a history of the cost at this particular moment of the lapis lazuli, of the color blue, which was the most expensive paint throughout the Renaissance. The most expensive painting by an Italian artist of the 14th, 15th, or 16th century is not the one that employs a great deal of gold, but the one that employs a great deal of blue, because the color lapis lazuli was imported from India or from the Orient. So art has its own logic, its own velocity, its own dynamics, its own past and its own future. That it overlaps with the actual history of society is of little consequence. You don't need the Guelfs and Ghibellines in order to have Dante. Dante would have occurred no matter what. The same goes for Shakespeare; you don't need a particular situation in the English court to produce Shakespeare. You do not need a particular situation in the English court to become John Donne. You do not need a particular situation in the Russian court to become Pushkin or anybody else. What really contributes, what really propels or creates the dynamics of an art is the number of your predecessors in that art. Somebody wrote this poem, that poem, this set of sonnets, etc., and you are a rival. You realize: "Aha! This has been said. I have to say something qualitatively different in order for my work to be read." So the dynamics and evolution of the arts and those of society are not parallel: They are wholly independent. Art always consists in taking the next step. Art defies the general principle of society that the supply creates the demand; for art, regardless of the demand, creates the supply. You see, nobody wanted Dante Alighieri to write the *Divine Comedy*, there was no demand for it. He simply sat down one day and wrote it, and he offered it; and then the demand emerged. What I am trying to say is the dynamics of art and of society are not coincident. Very often a poet or an artist is praised for being ahead of his time. He is not understood in his own time which is therefore regarded as a sort of dumb time. Art evolves according to its own logic. There is Homer, now comes Virgil. There is Virgil, now comes Dante. The ascension of art is vertical; the line of succession is a vertical line. The new artist picks up where the greatest artist of the preceding generation left off. He has to take the next step. In the life of a society, you can repeat things ad infinitum. You can have democracy and the democracy may slide into tyranny and there will be centuries and centuries of tyranny, and then somebody will say that it's time to revert to democracy again. Life, social organization, social history operates indeed within very few available clichés. Art never does. For that reason the man who studies the history of art, the man who develops taste, advances faster than the one who studies the social history.

Guntern: Let me pull out one single thread of the fabric of your argument. You said that Homer and Dante, for instance, are quite independent from the historical, social-economic or social-political context. It seems to me that that is true for the highest creative talents, but not for the lesser talents. And the genius, I agree, always makes her/his way. But I do not think that is true for somebody who is not a genius.

Brodsky: But the purpose, the ambition of the species is to achieve the maximum, not the minimum.

Guntern: I would say the optimum.

Brodsky: Well, whichever you like. It is to go for a kill.

Guntern: (to **Roessler**) Did you wish to ask more with respect to this question?

Roessler: I just wanted to know if I understood you correctly. Before, you said you considered art as the only way to improve mankind and also to improve history. Now you say that art is always ahead and moving in a vertical direction unlike history that can go backwards and forwards. Why does art, if art is the medium that improves human beings and mankind, not help to improve the rest of history and to make the rest of history go in a more vertical direction?

Brodsky: Because we put money on the wrong things. Because society taxes its subjects first of all to sustain itself, the government, the state, the administration. What society should do is to use the lion share of taxes for the development of art.

Roessler: But who is the society, if you have all those individuals who are looking at art works all day long and going into museums to see that advanced form of art they never saw before? Why do they do other things than what they have learned from going to museums or reading poems?

Brodsky: I do not know why that happens. I suppose simply because art does not have the same status in society, because it is not associated with money. Had art been associated with money, you would pay far lesser attention to your statesmen and far greater attention to the artists. You see, the whole point is that we have our priorities screwed up. It has to do with something very basic, which is the lack on the part of the species of the desire to evolve. You all like it the way you are. You think it is okay. That is all there is to it. Now and then you have to pay an awful price, of course.

Guntern: For complacency.

Brodsky: Am I clear?

Roessler: Not at all.

Brodsky: Not at all? Let me try again: because you are bourgeois and a bourgeois values nothing more than the comfort of his convictions.

Roessler: But that is not the question. I know society does not develop because we are bourgeois and because we put our money on the wrong things and because we like to be how we are and so on. The main question, I think, is that you see two different developments, art on one side and society on the other. How can art step out of the rest of society? Why, artists are bourgeois, too, and they like to be how they are too, so how can you...

Brodsky: Art has no business stepping out. When an artist produces a work of art, either by writing a poem or doing a painting, he takes a step towards society. It's society's responsibility to meet him halfway. But society doesn't take that responsibility. So whatever happens to the society as a consequence is the society's own fault. If you want to be where you are, stay there. If you are satisfied with your condition, and you obviously are, then stay there.

Roessler: Why do artists want to move and why does the rest of society not want to move? Where does this difference come from?

Brodsky: The difference comes from a very simple thing. The artist, by doing what he does, moves. It is up to society or the audience to join him, to catch the same train. And apparently society doesn't want to do that. So society has no way to reproach the artist. When you see something beautiful, when you see a beautiful lady or a beautifully built man, you have two options: either to approach him or her, or not to approach him or her. You elect not to approach him. Because you are already tied up otherwise, elsewhere. This is your problem.

Gschwend: I am a journalist. Two days ago I interviewed a very great, but very humble architect, whose name is Luigi Snozzi, and I asked him, "What is architecture to you? What is the difference between just building and architecture?" And he said, "Architecture to me is a way of understanding who I am."

Brodsky: Oh, oh.

Gschwend: You said... I think that we also are a product of history, of our personal history and of the history of society. Don't you think that if we used history in the way you use literature, it could be a way of helping us understand who we are? I'm not talking of using history to become better or to progress. I don't believe in that. But I think it is as good a way of understanding our human condition as literature is.

Brodsky: Look, I am speaking only for myself. I represent absolutely nobody. And these are my idiosyncratic ideas about this. Now, as for the statement by the architect that architecture is the way for him to understand himself - it's a bloody costly way to understand himself!. Well, architecture is the most social art, the purpose of architecture is to serve people. An architect in a way can't be regarded as an authority on individual choices. An architect should be regarded at best, if he is a good architect, as the servant of society. That would be the best thing to say about an architect. Now, that's one thing. I do not remember the other thing you talked about, it's already gone.

Gschwend: History as a tool to understand who we are.

Brodsky: History may be a tool, but it's also regrettably, too often, an excuse. We think, "Oh, we failed in history, so why not fail now?" Why not, indeed? But when we come to that conclusion, we usually do so at the expense of lots of other people.

Kadanoff: As I understand it, a portion of your argument is based on the idea that the arts progress. Do they really progress?

Brodsky: I would not use the verb "progress," but I would certainly use the verb "evolve." They do. Faster than anything else.

von Wartburg: Can I quickly come back to poetry? When you write poetry, you give us a gift. This gift apparently is the result of your fusing rationality and intuition. This gift is wrapped in words, and these words which are the gift-wrapping of your poems, are now English words. Previously they were Russian words. How do you make the transition from a language which is extremely complex, like Russian, to a rather impoverished language like English? I am sorry ... I am just making comparisons, I did not want to...

Guntern: It's your idiosyncratic expression, it's fine.

von Wartburg: Okay. I would like to add a second question to that. What do you think of the present climate of political correctness which to my feeling, my idiosyncrasy, is further impoverishing the language?

Brodsky: Well, you asked about the transition from one thing to another. As for the political correctness, as you justly said, it is a climate; it is not even a climate exactly, it is the weather. And weather changes. It is temporary and it may do some damage, but such are the aspects of weather. And so it is not exactly a terribly interesting thing to deal with. But again, those notions, those concepts matter only to those who do embrace them and who put themselves into dependence upon them - which is a very small percentage of the people, even in the United States. The notion of political correctness is essentially the property of a certain milieu. It is basically of an academic milieu, it is basically an intramural reality. The moment you cross the road and go to a gas station, the principles of political correctness do not apply. Now, that is one thing.

Blum: Is that good or bad?

Brodsky: Well, that is certainly good. In my book it is. Now, as for the transition from Russian to English, the answer may surprise you: it has never really been a transition in the final analysis. I grew up in Russia, I was reading a great deal of Russian poetry. I was also reading the gamut of Russian poetry. Then I began to read all sorts of other people, including the English. The body of Russian poetry is a fairly limited one. Russian poetry is at best 250 years old. Granted, Russia is a very populous country and a great deal of people were involved in producing that poetry, and partly because there were so many people involved, in no time, that is in two and a half centuries, we managed to catch up with our European sisters, with the poetries in French, English, German and so forth. Still, after a certain point, I began to look elsewhere. Because when you evolve, when you grow, when you develop as a poet, there is a certain sportsmanship that takes places. You want to beat others at the game. And initially you try to beat your own people; you try to beat this poet, that poet, your contemporaries, sometimes your predecessors, which is a little harder, but still, you can do that. You may write a pastiche, you may write a lyric in the style of this and that author, but you try to beat him. Well, pretty soon it ends, then you begin to look elsewhere. And then you see before you the civilization or the culture of Christendom, with its corresponding literature. So you look into Spanish poetry, French poetry, German poetry, English poetry. By the age of 25 or 26 or 27, I began to read a great deal of poetry in English, and so much so, I read it both in translation and in the original whenever I couldn't find the text or the appropriate books. Well, of course it was very much home-made reading. I would use the dictionary, I would just try to go, I would plow through the text of this or that poem and try to surmise what was there. And half the time I would be guessing, I wouldn't know what I was reading. I would apply my intuition, based on the Russian culture, and simply hope that there was something more vast than what we in Russia had produced. So by the end of the sixties, by the beginning of the seventies, I think I was as much a Russian poet, a reader of Russian poetry as I was a reader of English and American poetry. In fact, there is something more to it. I began to regard -

well, not only I, I'm not speaking solely for myself but for the entire generation, a group of people anyway, a coterie if you will, of my friends - we regarded ourselves by that time, as individualists. And naturally enough, for the embodiment of that individualism, for the spirit of man being on his own, we obviously turned to American poetry and American literature. In a sense we became Americans. In fact, we became Americans to a far greater degree than Americans themselves are or ever have been. When some of us came to the United States, we at best recognized only certain aspects of it, because by the time we arrived in America, or what we thought was America, American culture and American literature had changed. What had previously been the literature keen on hardihood, endurance and reticence, had now become very vociferous, very emphatic, very hysterical. We can still recognize certain things in American literature, but I think we have been, we are and we will remain perhaps more American - I for one - than Americans themselves. That is the answer to your question.

Compernolle: As regards translation, could you translate your own poems from Russian into English? Does it make sense for me to read your poetry in English?

Brodsky: If you cannot read it in Russian, the best thing you can do is to read it in English rather than in German, French, or Italian. I do that. I have been doing that for a number of years, increasingly so. It is an entirely schizophrenic enterprise, but well, that is what I do.

Sikorskaia: I don't have any questions. I have a request: Could you please read some poetry, unfortunately in English. Unfortunately for me, I mean.

Brodsky: Of course I can read some poetry in English. It's a little poem by Robert Frost.

Participant: Your poem.

Brodsky: I don't care for mine. It's called "Come In".

> COME IN
> As I came to the edge of the woods,
> Thrush music - hark!
> Now if it was dusk outside,
> Inside it was dark.
> Too dark in the woods for a bird
> By sleight of wing

To better its perch for the night,
Though it still could sing.

The last of the light of the sun
That had died in the west
Still lived for one song more
In a thrush's breast.

Far in the pillared dark
Thrush music went -
Almost like a call to come in
To the dark and lament.

But no, I was out for stars:
I would not come in.
I meant not even if asked,
And I hadn't been.

And let me do something to please me more than you. Here is a poem by the
English poet Thomas Hardy.

THE CONVERGENCE OF THE TWAIN
(Lines on the loss of the 'Titanic')

In a solitude of the sea
Deep from human vanity,
And the Pride of Life that planned her, stilly couches she.

Steel chambers, late the pyres
Of her salamandrine fires,
Cold currents thrid, and turn to rhythmic tidal lyres.

Over the mirrors meant
To glass the opulent
The sea-worm crawls - grotesque, slimed, dumb, indifferent.
Jewels in joy designed
To ravish the sensuous mind
Lie lightless, all their sparkles bleared and black and blind.

Dim moon-eyed fishes near
Gaze at the gilded gear
And query: 'What does this vaingloriousness down here?'...

Well: while was fashioning
This creature of cleaving wing,
The Immanent Will that stirs and urges everything

Prepared a sinister mate
For her - so gaily great -
A Shape of Ice, for the time far and dissociate.

And as the smart ship grew
In stature, grace, and hue,
In shadowy silent distance grew the Iceberg too.

Alien they seemed to be:
No mortal eye could see
The intimate welding of their later history.

Or sign that they were bent
By paths coincident
On being anon twin halves of one angust event,

Till the Spinner of the Years
Said 'Now!' And each one hears,
And consummation comes, and jars two hemispheres.

Guntern: Can you add one in Russian, for the music of it, of yours or Pushkin's or Mandelstam's or whoever?

Brodsky: (Recites a little poem by Pushkin).
    That's Pushkin for you.
    What else?

Roessler: I wanted to ask a further question before about the fact that arts had internal dynamics that were independent of the dynamics of society. I wonder about the compatibility of the statement with what you said in your essay about example providing the function of art, that is, that artists provide examples for people to follow.

Brodsky: I am trying to say something very simple: society does not condition the emergence of art. You may have a totalitarian society, or you may have an absolutely free society. But art will emerge: a song is older than any form of social organization. You may have God knows what - ancient Rome, the Third Republic, totalitarian Russia, and yet you would have Ovid, or Virgil or Propertius. Better yet, you may have Proust, you may have Frost, you may have Akhmatova, Tzvetaja, Mandelstam, they didn't need society. They were born, particularly those three Russians - or make it four - before 1917. They would have evolved as great poets no matter what had transpired on the territory of Russia. They didn't need the garbage.

Blum: Is art the only thing in the world that comes directly from heaven?

Brodsky: I do not know whether it comes directly from heaven or not. The other things that come directly from heaven are obviously snow and rain. Sorry.

Guntern: You said somewhere that poetry is the articulation of perception into language.

Brodsky: Well, very often it is.

Guntern: Then you added that language is the best tool for this purpose, for the articulation of perception. Don't you think that a painting by Kandinsky or a sculpture by Giacometti or a nocturne by Chopin achieves the same thing?

Brodsky: I certainly do not.

Guntern: Why?

Brodsky: For a very simple reason. Poetry and literature in general, but poetry by law - and I am quoting Eugene Montale - is an incurably semantic art. It is bound to make sense. If it does not make sense, it does not exist. In painting, in music and whatever else it's possible not to make sense. In poetry it is not. And this is the best and perhaps the only hope in this life. The other arts are decorative. They appeal to your viscera, they irritate or entertain your pupil, your membrane, your senses or whatever. They are no different in the final analysis from gastronomy that entertains your bowels. Art, literature, poetry works with your mind, and that is the best thing you have got.

Q.: I do not understand Russian, but what you just did with Pushkin was music, it was lovely, beautiful to listen to. It was music. So you are a musician.

Brodsky: I am not a musician.

Q.: You are a poet, but you made music.

Brodsky: No, poetry, for your information, is a melic art. It started with a song. Robert Frost again used to say the aim was song. The aim of poetry is song.

Q.: Why does the principle of causality emphasize logic?

Brodsky: Well, logic is impossible without causality.

Q.: The artist is part of society.

Brodsky: No, no. The first question was more interesting than the second one.

Q.: Let's stay with the first one.

Brodsky: If you speak about logic, you have to talk about causality. You can't really avoid it. Mind you, I'm not entirely sold on this, on logic. But insofar as I am addressing the representatives of the rationalist culture, I have to employ or resort to the principles of logic. It's as simple as that. I would be far better off with irrationals, but then I should be sitting somewhere in India, not in Zermatt. Insofar as we are sitting in Zermatt, in this rarefied air, I may just as well address the aspects of causality, of cause and effect. Meow, what else?

Gebhardt: I have a very simple question. You suggest the poet if not as a legislator of society, at least as a model for society, for social behavior. Now we know that...

Brodsky: Social behavior I haven't said, but...

Q.: ...for good behavior, for history, for progress and I am not sure that you can speak of progress in art, the way you can speak of progress in the sciences. For instance, can poetry actually widen the range of human options? Two, even given society's willingness to accept poets as models, how do we know who are the ones worthy of being models? For we know, forgive the term, that there are just as many "bull-shitters" among the poets as in any other social group.

Brodsky: The easiest thing with poetry, to establish what is what, is simply to open the book, and if it does not make sense to you, throw it away. That is the easiest thing. You cannot really do that with painting or music. I'll give you one example. I have been engaged these days in a rather unlikely activity: translating Euripides's *Medea* into Russian. I have this acquaintance, a very famous Russian director who lives in Greece, and he has decided to produce *Medea* in Greece, but in Russian. There is some money in that, so he can do it. So I have retranslated the play. He comes to me and tries to entice me back to Greece just to discuss the production scheme with the director - who is obviously nowadays far more important than the author - and with the composer and the set designer. I wrote him a letter saying that I would not be coming because of my teaching. I told him, "Do whatever you like, but for Christ's sake, I beseech you, do not use music. Because no matter how good your modern composer may be, he may be a genius, (whatever that is), what he is going to produce is non-Euripidean, anachronistic music. What is the point of it?" The point of it is, the attraction of it (a) for the composer himself and (b) for the morons in the audience who will become only more morons because of that music. Okay? Now, I am getting back to a very simple point. Poetry makes sense, or else it does not. In poetry you can tell whether it makes sense or not faster than in any other form of art which theoretically employs new means, new idioms, etc., which are not available to you. Poetry employs words, words are bound to make sense by themselves or in connection with each other. So it is easier than any place else to tell the bullshit from the jewel.

Gebhardt: But now poetry is supposed to be the avant-garde of consciousness, as you said.

Brodsky: There is no way of talking about avant-garde. Avant-garde is the category which could have been valid presumably somewhere in the twenties or in the thirties. Now we are sitting here, it's 1995, the end of the century, the end of the millennium. An avant-garde in comparison to what?

Q.: You yourself said poetry was ahead of society.

Brodsky: I used that term mockingly in reference to the journalist or the critic billing this or that author as being ahead of society. He is not ahead of or behind his own society. He is simply following the logic, the dynamics of the evolution of the art. It may happen that the state of the art does not coincide with the state of the society. Very often, a modern reader goes to the book store, opens a book, and he does not make heads or tails of it; that's fine and dandy, as far as I'm concerned. Basically a modern reader, in relation to modern poetry, finds himself in the position of somebody boarding a runaway train; he gets on the train, looks through that window, does not know where it is going, it is going too fast, and his immediate desire is to get off as soon as he comes to the station. If he feels that way, he should.

Gebhardt: It's not poetry, I wanna get off!

Brodsky: Well, I want to get off or get on.

Q.: You suggest that society should follow poetry.

Brodsky: I did not say anything so grand. But go ahead.

Osann: Somehow.

Brodsky: Yes, somehow...

Osann: You were relatively negative when you said society does not approach poets, it put its money on the wrong things. Are you completely negative, or do you have any type of small success where you could say, "That is a success, that's the way it should go!" To give a concrete example, there is one person I know today who is in politics - Havel - what's your position vis-à-vis Havel? Or any other example.

Brodsky: And yet another can filled up with worms!

Society has no obligation. There is no way to legislate in a society what you should read and what you should not. However, every man, every member of society should be cognizant of the choices he makes on a daily basis, whether he reads Robert Musil, *Volksstimme* or *Die Ziet*. We are in a situation where you can read a newspaper, a magazine, a novel or a poem. By and large we elect to read magazines and newspapers. But we should tell ourselves that we are reading a newspaper, we are not reading literature. We are moving away from literature. There is literature, but we prefer a newspaper or a magazine. That is, we are making this particular choice. And whatever happens to us is our own fault and not somebody else's. That's one thing.

As regards Václav Havel, when the changes began to occur in eastern Europe, I thought that was a marvelous opportunity for eastern Europe and Russia to come closer. In those countries the vertical hierarchy, the authoritarian system was still intact and I thought that if they had brains, if they only had brains, they could do the following thing: the newspapers like *Rudeprawa* in Czechoslovakia or *Esuestia* and *Pravda* in Russia could have ceased being the main central organ of the state. If the people who were running the societies there genuinely had in mind changing reality, changing human predicament, what they should have done from one paper to another, from one issue to another, is to have serialized man without qualities in search of the, well, *à la recherche du temps perdu* in order to take the entire nations into readership, to give them an entirely new sensibility, qualitatively different from the one that they had been brought up with. That is, to give them not either-or, but rather at least in the case of Musil, the genius of uncertainty. Then they could have implemented, they could have changed those societies' prospects. As it is, they didn't do so. I wrote to Havel specifically about that project because Czechoslovakia is, after all, a fairly limited entity. I was trying to convince him to run this program. The government had the money to conduct this sort of thing. Havel obviously did not do that. Havel is a politician. He was elected as a politician to go with the desires or predilections of the majority. And this is the horrendous error a politician can make. He made it. Eastern Europe therefore, not to mention Russia, is doomed to repeat the quite tremendously compromised predicament of the capitalist West. Perhaps in a far coarser, slower, more idiotic, viscious way. It is a tremendous mistake, the loss of chance. It is as simple as that. Well, they are idiots, those people who run the societies in the East; and they are idiots who run the societies in the West.

E. Blum: What do you think then about Alexander Solshenizin 's projects for Russia now, to bring back the old Russian values and the old Russian culture to the people?

Brodsky: You cannot regalvanize the corpse. You may try to do that, but you have to remember that the old Russia he is trying to revive, to bring back, was precisely what resulted in 1917; it's the Russian Church and the Russian nobility that lost the country. They can't be forgiven. And the efforts to revive those things are idiotic.

Q.: I have two different questions: first, have you ever met a politician who had the intellectual capacity to memorize a poem? Second what comes first in creating a poem, the idea of the subject or the first pictures you want to paint? And may I kindly ask you not to reply, "First comes the first word," thank you.

Brodsky: I met such a politician, in fact two, in the United States. One is the Representative in Congress from North Dakota and the other is the Senator from New York. Such people do exist.

As for the second part of the question, according to my experience, a poem starts not as an idea, but as a certain hum, a certain noise; the noise which is not free from the meaning, the noise that somehow contains the idea. And as you proceed to write, it's like playing the keys, like trying to - by this or that word or this or that grammatical operation - to approach that noise to find an equivalent in meaning. It's like playing the keys, it's like trying to pick up the tune that already exists in your head. My beloved Auden used to say about the young poets, "I don't believe when a poet comes to me and says, 'Oh, I want to write about this and that and the other.' I believe rather a man who comes to me and says, 'I like this word or that word.'"

Guntern: Shelley once said that the mind is a fading coal and sometimes a gust of wind begins to make it glow. And that the poet runs after this glow, and that the best poetry has never been written because once the poet starts to write, many important things are already gone. What about this?

Brodsky: No, the best poetry has been written, I hate to contradict Percy Bysshe Shelley, but the best poetry has been written. It has been written.

Recites:
WHEN YOU ARE OLD [1893]

How many loved your moments of glad grace,
And loved your beauty, with love false or true,
But one man loved the pilgrim soul in you,
And loved the sorrows of your changing face.

William Butler Yeats (1865-1939)

The best poetry has been written.

Guntern: Okay. I think that we have come to a closure of Gestalt?

Brodsky: Gestalt? I love the word, never understood what it meant.

Guntern: The closure of a structure, a coherence where the end meets the beginning.

I have two things to do now. First, I would like to thank you very much for giving us a glimpse of your...

Brodsky: Do not thank me for anything. I am sitting here, not exactly myself, I am the sum total of what I have read and of what I remember. The moment I do not remember those things, the moment I am on the streets, anybody can knife me and that would not be a great loss. But the moment I remember, I am a treasure. I remember some lines, the lines that will perhaps go down with me, not only with me, they will stay with the others, but they will go, my idiosyncratic choice of the lines will. The whole point is that a human being should know certain lines. Not so much because they may brighten your day or help you along in this and that, but imagine yourself at the end of the road, lying down in pain perhaps, or not in pain, numb by drugs in some hospital. You may find yourself, to your great astonishment, mumbling the lines which bear no relation whatsoever to your predicament right then, mumbling the lines of certain poets. And these lines will help you to meet your last hour, will help you to die or will help you in your pain. Without those lines you will be simply scared. So you better know some poetry by heart.

Guntern: What kind of incantation will you choose?

Brodsky: Odd things. It may be Auden, in my case, or it may be Frost, it may be this. It can be any other poem by Frost, but I like this.

Recites:

PROVIDE, PROVIDE

The witch that came (the withered hag)
To wash the steps with pail and rag
Was once the beauty Abishag.

The picture pride of Hollywood.
Too many fall from great and good
For you to doubt the likelihood.

Die early and avoid the fate.
Or if predestined to die late,
Make up your mind to die in state.

Make the whole stock exchange your own!
If need be occupy a throne,
Where nobody can call you crone.

Some have relied on what they knew,
Others on being simply true.
What worked for them might work for you.

No memory of having starred
Atones for later disregard
Or keeps the end from being hard.

Better to go down dignified
With boughten friendship at your side
Than none at all. Provide, provide!

Remember these three lines

No memory of having starred
Atones for later disregard
Or keeps the end from being hard.

Meow.

Guntern: We have had a look at your tremendous exercise in uncertainty. You have transmitted to us your passion for this art, for the handicraft, for the whole world that goes with it. It was a beautiful moment. If I could choose an epitaph for myself, I would like to have a haiku by a modern Japanese writer who died some time ago. The lines go:

Tell them he is out - back in five million years.
So I hope you will be back here in Zermatt.

Brodsky: There is a friend of mine in Venice. His name is Geronimo Marcello. He comes from the old Marcello family that gave the doges and the composers and all sorts of things to the city of Venice. One evening, not that long ago, we were having dinner and he said, "Joseph, I composed a terrific epitaph for myself." I said, "What is it?" - "Here lies Geronimo Marcello, the enemy of ideology, the enemy of conventions." I said, "Well, all right, that's okay." He said, "What do you mean that's all right, that's okay? What would you come up with for your own?" And I replied, "Here lies Joseph Brodsky. I hope you can read."

Works by Joseph Brodsky
A Part of Speech, Farrar, Straus and Giroux, New York 1980.
Less Than One - selected essays, Penguin Books, London 1987
Selected Poems 1965-1985, Penguin Books, London 1988
Watermark, Farrar, Straus and Giroux, New York 1992.
On Grief and Reason : Essays, Farrar, Straus and Giroux, New York 1995
So Forth : Poems, Farrar, Straus and Giroux, New York 1995.

GERALD M. EDELMAN
American medical doctor and scientist
Nobel Prize laureate

Born in New York City in 1929, Gerald Edelman received his MD in medicine from the University of Pennsylvania and went on to obtain his PhD from the Rockefeller Institute (now Rockefeller University) in 1960. A man of varied interests, he made outstanding contributions in the fields of biophysics, protein chemistry, immunology, cell biology, and neurobiology. His research on the structure and variety of antibodies earned him the Nobel Prize in Medicine or Physiology in 1972. Among other things, Edelman is the author of a universal theory on the development and organization of the higher brain functions which help to explain so-called neural group selection. He is president of Neurosciences Research Foundation; chairman of the Department of Neurobiology at The Scripps Research Institute, La Jolla, California; and founding director of the Neurosciences Institute, an independent organization dedicated to brain research.

Introduction by Gottlieb Guntern

Professor Edelman knows everybody in the various scientific communities, from Norbert Wiener to Karl Popper to Noam Chomsky, with whom he is currently involved in some debate. Noam Chomsky has proposed the hypothesis that linguistic competence, and with it syntactic structures, are inborn and that linguistic performance depends only on human experience. This is not at all what Professor Edelman thinks about the topic.

As the following metaphor suggests, the quest for autonomy is not the same with everybody. There are sardines that always swim in the center of a school of fish. They think they are quite safe if they keep to the mainstream, renounce their autonomy, do what everybody else is doing and do it at the same time. Yet before they can really understand what has happened, sardines often wind up in a tin can. Then there are trout. Trout in a mountain stream are mavericks, they go their own way. They have discovered that in order to get to the source, you have to swim upstream. I think Professor Edelman is - and has been - swimming upstream for quite some time, and he is now exploring something that he calls the program of Darwin. That is why he has moved from the domain of immunology, where he got his Nobel Prize, to the field of neurobiology. The topic of his presentation is "Beyond Computers: Simulating the Human Brain." He firmly disagrees with the idea that our brain is a computer. He believes the Keplerian machine metaphor does not really grasp the essence of reality, and he will now present his own ideas and metaphors regarding the human brain.

Gerald M. Edelman*

I would like to talk about the most complicated material object in the universe. But before I do, I will say something about what has been happening on the scene. It is a kind of cliché to the people in my field, that in the last ten years more explosive progress has been made in understanding the brain - including the human brain - than in all of recorded history. Now, that is true because of the number of scientists involved. There have been more scientists working on the brain over the last ten years than in all of history. The really important question is: What is unique about the brain, that extraordinarily dense and complicated object? If your life depended on it, and someone asked you what distinguishes the brain from everything else, what would you say? To answer this question is one of my tasks in this lecture.

The dominant science of our time is physics. (I do not think there is any debate about that.) Physics is the most general of all sciences. It describes the boundary conditions of the skeleton of the world and in the most formal terms, the most abstract as well. Indeed it was physics that began western science, but I do want to point out that there is a difference between our enterprise and physics: the physicist takes the God's-eye view of the world. He does not include his own psyche in his productions. A person who studies the phenomenology of mind, or the consciousness or intentions, be it of animals or of human beings, cannot afford this luxury. If he does, his investigation simply leads to sterile ground.

Western science began by removing the mind from nature. Somewhere at the end of the 19th century, enough was discovered to put the mind back into

*Professor Edelman's presentation was illustrated by slides which cannot be reproduced here, but are indicated by an *.

nature, but in such an embarrassing way, that we have had a hard time knowing what to do ever since. Our task is to try to see how the mind fits into our description of nature and therefore, how we fit into our description of nature from a scientific point of view.

Let us begin with a lady poet, for however great science is, the exertions of art always lead to insights well prior to anything we do.

*Marianne Moore, a great American poetess, wrote:

> The Mind is an Enchanting Thing
> is an enchanted thing
> like the glaze on a katydid-wing
> subdivided by sun
> still the nettings are legion.
> Like Gieseking playing Scarlatti.

She saw that in the web of the brain was the constituent of the mind.
*(Descartes/Galileo)

It is certainly reasonable to propose that Galileo Galilei was the originator of western science back at the beginning of the 17th century. He saw, contrary to the thinkers of his time, that the Aristotelian method must fail, that you cannot invoke human feelings, intentions and purposes and final causes in the description of the world. Instead you have to remove yourself from the world, choose a language - he proposed mathematics - explicitly as the language of nature, and then do experiments based on hypotheses. As you now know, his famous experiments on the pendulum, the inclined plane and a variety of other things, as well as his confirmation of the Copernican point of view, which got him into a lot of trouble, literally served as the beginning of the paradigm of the western scientific approach.

In his book *De Assea* you will see that he says, "Of course I know that without animals there would be no warmth and no green and no touch. But that is not my business. I am to describe the world of physics and that is what I am going to do." In the meantime, of course, he complained a lot about people stealing his ideas, which is a chronic habit among scientists.

Some time later, René Descartes, who dreamed of "mathematizing" the entire world, came back from his campaigns in the Thirty Years War and began penetrating the questions of how he could be certain of anything. His *Discourse on Method* outlines his experience; in it he came up with a very famous conclusion which lays the foundation for modern philosophy. He indeed also removed the mind from nature, not through scientific procedure, but through a philosophical conclusion stemming from an interior monologue.[1]

He concluded that no demon could ever remove him from the consequence that he knew he existed because he could think - *je pense, donc je suis* - *cogito ergo sum* - and he thus promulgated a notion that the world consisted of two kinds of entities: *res cogitans*, which was out of time and space and could not be described by Galilean or Cartesian methods, and *res extensa*, the world of extended things which could be.

This marked the beginning of a philosophy of dualism. It has been plaguing us ever since, and I would like to make a point about Descartes: I think he was dead wrong. I think being dead wrong is not wrong; I think he posed a question of such significance, he casts into a sharp light the challenge we have in trying to explain how the mind arises in the brain. So here we have two gentlemen who removed the mind from nature in two different ways.

As Alfred North Whitehead, the British philosopher, pointed out, "The mind was put back into nature in the determinant part of the 19th century with the up-swing and the search in our understanding of physiology, human physiology and physiological psychology, notably Wilhelm Wundt in Leipzig and William James in Boston, who began the science of physiological

---

[1] **Note by Dr. Guntern**: In his introduction to the *Discourse on Method*, the epistemological basis of rationalism, Suthcliffe described the treatise as "curiously obscure" and called Descartes' plan "a caricature of logical composition."

Descartes took the machine metaphor, "The universe is not a divine organism but a machine," from Johannes Kepler, pulling it down from the stars, so to speak, and planting it in the organism. By claiming that the human body was "a machine made of blood and bones," he legitimated the body-mind dualism posited by the Orphics, followers of a Greek mystery cult in the seventh century BC. Descartes thus became a pioneer of mechanistic thinking and paved the way for the twentieth-century architect whose credo, "the house is a machine for living," equipped the soulless human automaton with the machine for living he deserved. (G. Guntern, *Im Zeichen des Schmetterlings. Vom Powerplay zum sanften Spiel der Kräfte.* Scherz-Verlag, Bern/Munich/Vienna 1992, pp. 47 ff.)

It has been common knowledge since time immemorial that actions originate in thoughts. Actions produce consequences. We have become very aware of the alienation human beings experience when they are treated like machines. If we wish to eliminate this unwelcome consequence of the mechanistic mind-set, we have to replace dualistic body-mind thinking with organismic thinking. Organismic thinking understands the human being as an indivisible unit and the human mind, not as a thing locked into the skull or brain, but as one of the ways the human brain or the whole organism operates, or even, as anthropologist Gregory Bateson suggested, as a way in which the unified structure of man and environment operates. (In: *Steps to an Ecology of Mind*, Ballantine Books, New York 1972.)

psychology. We were faced with the problem that no longer could we take the comfortable position that we were gods looking at nature with mathematical precision, but had literally to deal with such things as feelings, sensory perception, attention, consciousness and other such subjects."

Let me now say something about the brain. There is no better way to begin than by looking at one of the beautiful plates produced by Andreas Vesalius. He was a great artist as well as an anatomist of note of what we now call the cerebral cortex, that wrinkled, convoluted plane of nerve cells which covers our entire core brain like a mantle. Let me give you a general idea of its complexity. If I unfolded the human cerebral cortex, it would be about the size of a large table napkin and about as thick. It would contain 10 billion neurons and a million billion interneuronal connections. If I counted one connection per second, I would finish counting them in 32 million years. If I computed how many different possibilities they have of combining with each other, it would be 10 followed by millions of zeros. When we consider that the number of particles in the entire universe is 10 followed by 80 zeros, that will give you a picture of what we are dealing with. If someone says that this approach could hardly explain esthetics, feelings and what have you - be aware of the numbers.

Recently I moved from New York to California, to the Neurosciences Institute in La Jolla. This institute has been constructed for a specific reason. I should like to emphasize that if we are to get anywhere in understanding the human brain, we are not going to be able to do it in the usual athletic way prescribed by modern science. Modern science has the failure of success. My own laboratory, at the Scripps Research Institute, is completely separate from the Neurosciences Institute. Thirty people work there. Today's scientific centers tend to be large institutions with many competitive groups grinding out a lot of ideas. Yet these superstructures are not necessarily apt to penetrate deep theoretical matters. That is why our own institute is apart from the rest, a kind of scientific monastery with a 350-seat auditorium. There is a Theory Center with theoretical fellows and visiting fellows from all over the world who discuss a variety of subjects ranging from mathematics to philosophy to psychology, psychiatry and so on. There are laboratories in which mainly young people are working under somewhat less athletic conditions on some things that I believe will intrigue, if not amaze, you.

*Here you see a structure called Darwin IV, and there is a Darwin V about to be born.

They are, to my knowledge, the first non-living things that truly learn. They are not computers. I shall return to this topic later.

Let me summarize my argument up to this point. Physics is, of course, the queen of sciences. We need physics as the constraint of every other science, but the position of physics simply will not deal with the problem we are dealing with. This we must embed in the order of the matter of the brain in order to find an explanation for how the most remarkable of sensibilities, including language and consciousness, arise. We have also to understand their operation within the framework of our relationship to other animals.

Of course, I will not be able to do this without getting into some technical detail. So please take my advice, and if you come to a hard part, hum it. I want you to get the overall picture. These are not easy things and knowledge is not the same as skill. Skill requires habit and silence and practice and no one - no matter how endowed - is going to achieve skill in thirty minutes of talk. So please do not feel hesitant; I am sure you will comprehend more than you feel confident with. The reason you do not feel confident has to do more or less with skill.

I shall embed this pact I want to make with you in a story. There are two Jewish tourists who go to Israel for the first time. They have a wonderful time in Tel-Aviv and go to a night club to see what an Israeli night club is like. There is a comedian doing stand-up routines, telling one-liners in Hebrew. After five minutes one of the Jewish tourists falls on the floor, laughing hysterically. The other one looks down and says, "What are you laughing at? You don't even understand Hebrew!" His friend looks up and says, "I trust these people." So if you will do the same for me...

Let us begin with a short course in neurobiology.

*This is the cerebral cortex. It has a six-layered structure, and each layer has a specific thickness and architecture.

*What is it made of? Here is a cartoon of a nerve cell. Like every other cell, it has a nucleus that contains DNA, the genetic material to be found in every single cell of the organism.

This cell body puts out tree-like ramifications called a dendritic tree, and each one of these is called a dendrite. On the other side of the cell it sends out a very long and interesting process called an axon. At the end of the axon is a very specialized structure which allows it to connect to yet another neuron, let us say of the same type. This connection is known as a synapse. One of the great discoveries of modern neurobiology is that the synapse is not electrical in higher organisms, but chemical.

When a particular neuron, or cell, receives a signal from another one connected to it, an electrical impulse passes down the axon, reaches the synapse, and releases a chemical called a neurotransmitter. This diffuses into a little cleft which binds to the receptors on the other side, the post-synaptic neuron, making that neuron fire. You might be tempted to think that this is the biological counterpart of a computer or an electronic circuit. It is not so, and I hope to show you why.

Evolution has produced this cortex with its cells and their ramifications and connections. This maze of connections is often arranged in so-called maps.

*Here is an example of a map. A map is a structure where an element or arrangement, which are distinct one from the other, share a neighborhood relation. There is a structure in the frog's brain called the tectum. Now I can put an electrode into the neuron of the tectum to measure its electrical activity. Then I can shine a light into a specific sector of the frog's eye. What I will discover is that this light stimulation of a specific sector A of the frog's eye will produce an electrical activity in a specific area A of the frog's tectum. If I do the same thing in sector B of the frog's eye, I will get an electrical activity in the corresponding sector B of the frog's tectum. The biological fact is that the map in the tectum is rotated, but the correspondence between the map in the tectum and the sectors in the eye still remains the same. My conclusion, so far, is that the brains of higher organisms show maps.

In short, brains are made up of neurons, and neurons connect with each other in very definite ways. They connect in such a way that an electrical signal in the neuron releases a chemical substance which then causes another electrical signal to fire away down the line. All these routes and connections resemble the arrangements of chips in an IBM computer.

The number of routes is staggering: it is a structure of intricate complexity. Yet in spite of the superficial resemblance to a computer or a television transmitter, this jungle of nerve cells is different from the nature and complexity of a computer chip. To see that difference you must dive deep into the microcosm of this jungle. Let us imagine you are sitting in a little helicopter which you can shrink, and you dive deep down into the jungle of the cortex. You dive down through layers I,II,III,IV,V and VI. Then you see that layer II, right in front of your eyes, resembles exactly layer II over there. You dive even deeper down into the jungle of layer II. You fly a helicopter length over to the right, and all of a sudden you are lost. You do not know where you are anymore, because the spot looks completely different, because the structure is so individual, so stochastically arranged, there is no man-made device that has that kind of ordering. We still do not understand that ordering completely.

So much for the structure of the brain. Let us now confront the issue of the structure and the functioning of computers.

*This is ENIAC, the first practical computer. It is essentially a room full of vacuum tubes. This machine would handle about 8,000 instructions per second. That is how computer people measure things. (I shall explain what an instruction is in a minute.) People said ENIAC could not possibly work because it was full of vacuum tubes that would pop. They did. A rather brilliant mathematician by the name of John von Neumann, however, pointed out in a brilliant paper that it does not matter if they blow up, because there is always another one to take up the task. Indeed ENIAC did work.

*Here is the modern version - we have a couple of these at the Neurosciences Institute - an expensive hairdryer, really. It is called an N-Cube, and is a massively parallel modern computer. It has 1,024 individual processors acting in parallel. Each processor is more powerful than a modern PC or an old workstation and they all act at once.

This carries out billions of instructions per second, and this parallel processing can be used, as we shall see in a moment, to simulate the brain.

*I am going to tell you how computers work because I want to get to the remarkable idea of a British mathematician named Alan Turing. Computers work by concatenating effective procedures, and I shall describe what an effective procedure or an algorithm is. Here is one for boiling an egg. It is exactly what I would write if I programmed in an N-Cube how to boil an egg. I would say, start! - Put water in the pot! - Turn on the heat! - If the water does not boil, go to step 3! (Step 3 is a wait loop, you just wait.) - Then put the egg in the water! - Set the timer to three minutes! - If timer has not gone off, go to step 6! (It means wait.) - Turn off the heat and cool! - When you are finished, retrieve, peel and crack the egg! Notice that every single step is described effectively with precision, without ambiguity. Everything must be done precisely, otherwise the computer will not work. That is an algorithm.

So we have this hair dryer with all these electronic circuits in it. They simply switch zero to one and one to zero. That is a kind of electronic abacus, only instead of beads, think of electrons. Now electrons move at the speed of light, and that is why computers are the most interesting invention of the 20th century.

Alan Turing, the great British mathematician, was an extraordinary fellow, a most remarkable mind. You may read about him, and I think it is well worth doing so, because he embodies a personal tragedy, a scientific tragedy and a social tragedy, combined with a most remarkable gift - but that is not my point here. Turing invented **the** mathematical theorem about computers known as Turing's theorem. In his mind he invented a machine called the finite-state-automaton. Finite means it does not go on forever, but stops. State means the sum of all the yea's and no's inside. An automaton is a self-acting machine.

It had a tape that would go on indefinitely. It wrote ones and zeros and could do very limited things. It could either read or write a one or a zero on this block here as the tape moved through this head. When it did, it would decide to go to the right or the left, it would change its state, namely all the numbers of yea's and no's, zeros and ones. It would consult the program, which is a collection of actions and conditions for the actions and it would make the next move. So here it would go on merrily reading the tape, two steps to the right, erase the zero, replace it by one, 15 steps to the left, etc. This kind of thinking is amazing, and what Turing showed was even more amazing: a Turing machine of this kind can replicate any effective procedure, from boiling an egg to solving a quadratic equation, to doing a simulation of a star bursting, etc. Indeed he invented something called the Universal Turing Machine which would emulate every other Turing Machine in the universe! These mathematicians have incredible ambition.

Why then, would I insist that the brain is not a computer? I belonged to the $1/2 MV^2$ school, that is to say, just as you could describe a falling object or planet or whatever with Galileo and Newton and finally Einstein, I thought if you had enough time and proposed enough scientific questions, everything would come out that way. You could have an equation for Jane Goodall, one for Dr. Guntern, one for me. But then erosion and wisdom set in, and my position has changed.

I shall now tell you a fable dealing with Newtonian physics, science, and human intention. It will demonstrate the pitfalls of reductionistic explanation.

It is about a young man in New York who thought his girl was carrying on with somebody else. One hot summer day, he came home early to the cold-water flat they were living in in the Village to discover his rival. He looked in the closet, he looked under the bed, he started shouting, and his girl denied everything. She said, "You're crazy, there is no other guy! Forget it, you're just nuts! You're paranoid!" He soon found himself at the back window of the apartment, trembling with rage, when out of the corner of his eye, he saw a guy on the fire escape below, loosening his collar and wiping his brow. At that point he flew into an even greater rage, grabbed hold of a huge refrigerator, smashed it through the window, aimed it and dropped it on this man's head. The man dropped dead. Now, the scene switches to heaven and Saint Peter is admitting three men, saying, "You fulfilled all the criteria to enter heaven, but you have to tell me how you died for the records." The first fellow said, "Well, I thought there was some hanky-panky going on, so I came home early to catch my rival. My girl said he wasn't around, but I finally saw him on the fire escape below. I must have had an adrenaline fit, I got an enormous superhuman surge of strength, grabbed this massive refrigerator and dropped it on his head, and then I must have had a heart attack." The second man said, "I don't know, it was hot. I don't have enough money for an air conditioner in my office. I came home early to have a drink. I had the drink and stepped out on the fire escape. I loosened my collar, wiped my brow and then this damn refrigerator falls on my head." The third man said, "I don't know, I was just sitting in this refrigerator, minding my own business."

So you see the challenge to reductionism. It is not easy to fit in an equation, especially if you include the emotions.

*I do insist that physics is the skeleton of the world, but not necessarily all of the flesh. In fact, if the physicists say, as they are tempted to do these days, that they want to construct a theory of everything that would be self-consistent, that is wonderful. But where is the physicist? I know where the refrigerator is, but where is the physicist?

Here is where the problem begins. The first is one of the homunculus. If I have a thought and I am interpreting vision, or a touch, what is it that is going on to decide that it is a scene, and not just a splotch of color and moving things? Is there a "neural executive" on top, or is there a little man inside my brain, as is the case with a computer? Then the question arises: who is inside this homunculus, who reads and interprets his "brain processes"? Another homunculus? When does this thing stop? That is called the endless regression of homunculi. There is no homunculus. That is the key problem. How do you put it all together inside your head? You see, in a computer you have a homunculus. **We** are the homunculus, we have a linguistic structure achieved in speech communities, we have history, we have logic, we have a description, we put the description in as a syntax. It has no meaning inside; when it comes out, we give it meaning again. If you assume the brain is a computer, you have got to answer this semantic question: who is saying what is going on? Well, the naive answer is - me. Right? Except when you go to look at what "me" is. So that is the first problem.[2]

*Here is the second problem; it is a structural one: how your brain is put together. I have told you before how neurons are and how they connect up to make this intricate neuroanatomy. This is how it begins, in a plate of cells. If we take the chick, a fertilized egg rapidly divides the cells and makes a plate, called the blastula, composed of 100,000 cells. Then the plate receives a special signal and wraps it up in a tube called a neural tube, shown here. This neural tube fills with fluid, bends, grows, as every other part, and at a certain time, these neurons that started the whole thing divide and make daughter cells. They also move up and down in the layers of the cortex, landing in layer III or in layer IV or in some other layer. They also move from one part of the tube to another, and the final result of all of that intricate and myriad set of processes is this cortex with this kind of structure that tempts you to think it is like an electronic circuit.

There are, however, problems with this kind of thinking. The first problem is that the single cells do not move in fixed ways. If I took twins and I colored or numbered their cells and then followed the developmental paths of the corresponding brain cells, I would see that they move along different paths. Their respective movements are not governed by a strictly deterministic process. In other words, chance events influence their movements. Furthermore, in the formation of the nervous system, up to 70 % of the cells die, and not always the same ones. Then there is the spinal cord, which is part of your central nervous system and is connected to the cortex. Up to 70% of the cells of the spinal cord die in the course of its making, and you cannot tell which cell will die when you are in a local neighborhood. Try to do that in a computer factory. You will be fired promptly. That is the second problem. The first problem is metaphysical; it is a deep question of what you would do to reach some

---

[2] **Note by Dr. Guntern:** The mathematical theory of communication published by Shannon and Weaver in 1948 formed the basis for information transfer by machine (e.g., in and between computers). Shannon was an engineer interested solely in how information could be transferred reliably (i.e., without loss of information) from machine A to machine B. As machines are totally unconcerned with the meaning (semantics) of signals (C.E. Shannon, W. Weaver, *The Mathematical Theory of Communication*, University of Illinois Press, Urbana/Chicago /London 1972), his theory excluded the problem of semantics. Present-day communication specialists do the same when they maintain that the brain is a computer. The meaning of a signal (of a message) is of fundamental importance in both human reflection and interpersonal communication, for the semantics of a signal determines the thoughts and actions it will elicit.

interpretation if you were going to conclude that the world is a piece of tape and the brain, a computer.

*The second problem is one of neuroembryology. Whatever happens to a specific cell during its development does not simply depend upon the genetic program. The genes do not determine where and when a cell will move. The movement of a specific cell, the timing of that movement and the definitive position of that cell in the space of the brain also depends on so-called epigenetic factors. Whatever influences an individual at a specific time (e.g., influence of some environmental factors) will also influence the developmental movement of that cell. Genes define certain constraints for the development, not its fate. Since the positions of cells count, you cannot say that the connections of your brain are already preprogrammed in your genes. A human being has some 100,000 major genes in his/her chromosomes. I just told you how many billions of interneuronal connections you have - you do not have enough genes for those connections. That is a salvation. That will solve the problem of individuality, ultimately, when we understand the brain.[3]

*Here is a real picture of a neuron that comes from a structure called the thalamus in the center of the brain, which projects from the thalamus into the layers of cortex that I showed you. I am looking at the three lower layers: you can see the branching of the axon. The reason is this: although the fibers that come in could lie one next to another like electronic lines - when it diverges out into a tree, it branches absolutely individually into a tufted structure like this one-millimeter axon, which is big for this neuron. The neuron itself is 50 micrometers inside and it sends out this tree. Another neuron would overlap it at least 70%, like this. Now imagine you sat on any synapse of any two of these trees and you asked where this synapse came from in the jungle of things that are overlapping like that. You could not tell. So unlike the electronic engineer, you cannot sit there and say, "The red wire goes to the yellow post, the green wire goes to the orange post," or "This voltage that I am measuring came from the green post or the orange post." No way. So there lies the

---

[3] **Note by Dr. Guntern:** Our chromosomes are as little responsible for our fate as is the constellation of the planets at the moment of our birth or the emotional-sexual experiences we had as children. Our fate is decided by so-called deterministic chaos, in other words, by the unceasing interaction of coincidence and law, chaos and order, freedom and structural constraint, spontaneity and calculation, both in ourselves and in our relations with the physical and biosocial (micro-organisms, plants, animals, human beings) environment. Human beings are to some degree autonomous, i.e., self-determined, and to some degree heteronomous, i.e., determined by factors over which they have little or no influence.

whole problem, and it is a very deep problem, indeed. The gist of my argument is that every single individual in this room has a unique nervous system, never repeated before, and very unlikely to be repeated again, unless time goes on infinitely.

*Now let us turn from these structural matters to perception, which I believe has to be the problem you must solve before you go to anything more ambitious. I have just come from a conference where some influent politicians discussed about fifty gigantic problems in one hour. We take one problem in a lifetime and employ 10,000 people with grants to try to get two inches ahead. It is always astonishing to us what virtuosos those politicians must be to deal with the problems of conservation, ghettos, money, etc. all at once. You get that distinct - I hope not haughty - feeling that either they have some kind of magical intelligence, or that perhaps they are not really facing the issue. Scientific knowledge, physicists, are corrigible. Our conclusions are going to change as we learn more and more, and must constantly be revised. I do not want you to think that I am taking a rigid position whereby these men are wrong and I am right. What we can do at best in science is poke our noses in a certain direction. Scientific exploration in the domain of human creativity or elsewhere consists of people who intuitively decide where to poke their nose. They do not give the ultimate description; there is no ultimate description. I believe that the most fundamental problem we must solve to link psychology to all that neurobiology is the problem of perception.

What is perception? Perception is the discrimination of one object or event from another for adaptive purposes. There is something very weird about perception, which is going to kill the computer boys again. It is not a fully solved problem, but I want to explore it now with you. Here we can have a bit of fun.

You are going to do an experiment with me. So remember what I said about perception: it is for adaptive purposes, for your survival. You want to discriminate what you call an object or an event from the background in order to flee in case a predator comes along. Perception depends on context; it depends on where you are and how you perceive.

Second, perception is not necessarily veridical. Veridical means that if I am a physicist and someone says something is out there and I am measuring an energy difference with my instruments and someone else is measuring it, too, and they agree, it must really be out there. These physicists are naive realists. They believe it is really out there; they are not metaphysicians.

Perception does not necessarily follow that rule, as I am going to show you. Sometimes it does, sometimes it does not.

The third thing that is absolutely astonishing about perception is that on very few encounters, even non-linguistic animals can generalize on their experience to a degree that no computer and none of our models can completely emulate yet. I emphasize that. There is no getting around; it is not some fancy emulation or computer algorithm. There is something there we have got to understand. It is not like anything we have ever invented. The final thing about it is, there is no judge in nature. There is no one telling us, "Go and get red." That is the problem.

*Here is a face drawn by a really distinguished artist - I will not say who. Look at it a while. Here is the same face, along with a poem by Wallace Stevens entitled, *Frogs Eat Butterflies, Snakes Eat Frogs, Hogs Eat Snakes, Men Eat Hogs.*

Wallace Stevens is, in my opinion, the greatest American poet. He was an insurance man, an esthete and a millionaire, and he once had a fight with Hemingway - which is a distinction, I suppose. He had a penchant for these strange titles. In his poems he describes our metaphysical situation better than anybody, including Mr. Eliot.

*Here is a frog eating a butterfly, a snake eating a frog, a hog eating a snake, and a man eating a hog, and once I say that to you, you are not going to look at this picture the same way. Now I have cheated; I have employed higher-order linguistic use. I am not going to do that to show you the context dependence that I am talking about.

*Here you are looking at the Wundt-Hering illusion. Wundt, along with William James, was the first to invent physiological psychology: he invented this illusion. You look here and these lines are parallel. You look here, and they appear to bow in; you look here and they bow out. Now we are going to do some physics together. I say, how do you know that they are not parallel? You measure here and here, you do some statistics, and you find out within a certain limit of your measurement instrument that the measurement is the same. The lines are parallel; but they do not appear to be. It is an illusion. Now, that is a terrible word because an illusion is a reality. You are constructing reality for very good reasons: You would not be here today and you would not have survived if you played it by the physicist rules. Imagine a tiger entered this room and, like a good physicist, you went to measure the stripes in order to find out if it really was a tiger. You would not survive that maneuver. Thus if you want to survive in order to adapt to changing circumstances, it is very important that your perception proceeds in another way. If you go and measure the stripes, you will be dead before you have verified your original perception.

Perception is not necessarily veridical, it is constructive. I want to say one more thing - it can be generalized to a degree we do not fully understand. That is really the theme of this lecture when I show you these automata, because it is our task to try to understand that generalization. You see, science cannot leap. We cannot go and say, oh, forget about perception, we shall get concepts first. Oh, forget about concepts, let us go to language and declare that it is syntactic generative grammar. You become famous, but your work is wrong. You have got to go step by step. If you do not understand this one, you are just not going to get ahead.

*This one is a killer. Dr. I. Cerilla at Harvard took oak leaves - *cortis alba* - and projected a picture like this in front of a pigeon. The pigeon was operantly conditioned so that when it saw an oak leaf, it would peck a key and was rewarded with some food. After some trials, more than 80% of the time the pigeon would distinguish all oak leaves from all other kinds of leaves. In fact, it over-generalized, because as you can see, some oak leaves are not very distinctive as compared to *cortis alba* here. You may think that after all pigeons evolved in forests, and these shapes are familiar to them because the neurons have adapted to them.

*Dr. R. Herrnstein at Harvard then took a thousand pictures of trees, picked out 80 at random, put them in a carousel projector, presented the pigeon with this picture, and it got the food. After about eight or nine trials, the pigeon recognized that this was a tree and rejected pseudo-trees. Now, let us be clear: the pigeon was not pronouncing the word "tree"; it was simply doing something, indicating that it recognized what you, the independent judge, called a "tree." So what? Pigeons evolved in these trees, so they have a limited number of these pictures. Herrnstein hired a scuba diver to take pictures of fish and rock and seaweed at all possible kinds of places. He got a thousand of those, picked out eighty and showed them to the pigeon.

*That took a little longer and the performance was not as good. It was in the 80% range, but the pigeon recognized fish. Now, ladies and gentlemen, pigeons do not live with fish, they do not eat fish - except maybe in New York, desperately - they do not evolve with fish and yet, this pigeon is taking all kinds of fish against all kinds of backgrounds and giving a positive response. That is extraordinary. At first I could not believe it - until I found out that four of our laboratories replicated this, which brings me to another thing I want to say about science. Someone asked me recently why scientists are so skeptical, so hesitant in talking about their ideas. Partly it is because they are proprietary and selfish like everybody else, and the only credit they are given is for discovering something. Yet skepticism is necessary because the cost of making a mistake is high to the community. You have to be careful about what you are saying. This skepticism has been applied here and, believe me, it looks pretty sound although we cannot be absolute about it.

*Motion is another problem. In order to perceive, you have to move. You cannot put the little baby in Lucite, even a chimp, and expect things to happen and have it integrate everything. It has got to move, to get around in its environment. This is the startle response of the armadillo. There is not just physics of motion, there is the biology of movement which is itself an entire story of extraordinary complexity and beauty, which I am not going to discuss; but take my word for it, you need it to understand perception.

Now let me summarize what I have tried to say so far:

First of all, the world is not a piece of tape. If the world were a piece of tape, then there would be only one species - the guy who figured out the code. The world is not a labeled place, although it follows the rules of physics. Physics does not tell me that a chair is a chair and not a table. It does not deal with the problem of categories. The world is an unlabeled place, that is the problem.

Brain order shows enormous variance and you cannot write it off as noise. In a television set, if you see a little flicker, you write it off as noise. That has to do with the theory of electronics and random movements of electrons. It will not do here, there are too many variances, and that is the lesson in biology: diversity. There are too many variances to sweep away. You get a very impoverished non-animal if you try to trick with the variances. So really reductionism does not work.

Perception is adaptive, context-sensitive as you heard, capable of enormous generalization.

Motion is essential. Perceptual categorization, the way a particular animal of a particular species carves up its environment and world into objects and events for adaptive purposes, involves generalization and that is a fundamental thing. With that, we have reached a sort of turning point.

So if the brain is not a computer, what is it? That will be, I believe, the main challenge in neuroscience in the next decade or so. I have just come from inaugurating the decade of the brain in Switzerland - at the Association for the Decade of the Brain. There is a general feeling that brain science is going to have the most enormous influence. If you interpret it very broadly, it is not just neurons and chemistry, but in the larger sense deals with animal behavior as well as human psychological function. It is going to have the largest single impact of any branch of science, and you might even throw in cosmology for that matter. We are on our way. But if what I have said is correct, it is not good enough to say what something is not. You have to say what something is.

Here I must turn to a proposal of a theory, and that theory is based on the contribution made by the most important theoretician in all of biology, Charles Darwin. What did Darwin invent? He invented a new kind of thinking called population thinking. In thinking about the problem of species, he asked a very sensible scientific question: how did they originate? Before him only his grandfather Erasmus had thought about that. Other people believed in Aristotle who had assumed that species - such as tigers, dogs and human beings - had been there forever. But Darwin was a singular example, a most remarkable, powerful example of the scientific mind, carefully putting together evidence, spending an entire lifetime trying to understand. What was the important question? The important question was the origin of species. His answer, independently also reached by Alfred Russell Wallace, was as follows: Species are not defined top to bottom by some logical-mathematical scheme. They are not the result of purposeful, goal-oriented evolution, either. There is no preexisting master plan for their evolution. Although Darwin did not have a useful genetic theory, he understood the basic principle of evolution, after having read Malthus' essay on the struggle for survival. Darwin's principle of the evolution of species operated as follows:[4] by means of chance events differential production leads to a specific variation. Then a principle of

---

[4] **Note by Dr. Guntern:** Eleven years before Darwin's birth, the British economist Thomas Malthus published his *Essay on the Principle of Population*, which contained the term "struggle for survival." Malthus put forward the following hypothesis: the increase in a nation's food production is linear, i.e., in an arithmetic progression (1, 2, 3, 4, 5, 6, etc.); the growth of a nation's population, on the other hand, is exponential, i.e., in a geometric progression (2, 4, 8, 16, 32, 64, etc.). As time passes, the gap between the two lines of development widens, with the result that the nation can no longer feed its population. This leads to famine, distress, disease and war; they, in turn, act as positive checks and reduce the population once again. If two nations fight over scarce foodstuffs, the struggle for survival will be won by the stronger nation.

Although Darwin took over the idea of the principle of selection from Malthus, he never spoke of the *survival of the strongest*, only of the *survival of the fittest*. In other words, in the struggle for survival among animal species, it is not necessarily the *strongest* that will survive but the ones best adapted to their surroundings (i.e., the *fittest*).

selection intervenes, separating the wheat from the chaff. This principle of selection acts according to the criterion "How does this specific variation fit to environmental circumstances?" If the variation is compatible with circumstances, if it provides even a very slight advantage for survival, then it is selected. If not, the new variation of species vanishes into oblivion. He understood that about 99% of all species that ever existed vanished again. He also understood that even the slightest advantage in reproduction would - over x generations - lead to a great increase in population.

With this idea he not only created a principle of explanation but also an empirical theory of classification, not simply composed of philosophy, logic or mathematics. This is the most fundamental theory in all of biology. If a biologist does not embrace this theory, then he is a quirky biologist, maybe even a crackpot.

I should like to emphasize that according to Darwin's theory the whole process was not goal-oriented. There was no master plan, no Turing machine. There was only the principle of selection which generated the differential reproduction of those individuals which were fitter to given circumstances.

*Here you see two different populations of fruit flies (*drosophila melanogaster*), barred ones and clear ones. There are more barred ones because the principle of natural selection has favored them against the clear ones, which were less fit. The genetic material of these fruit flies is continuously influenced by external factors (e.g., cosmic rays continuously streaming through their bodies) generating new variations.

*Here you have a picture of an antibody molecule of the immune system. It too is influenced by natural selection, and I have spent fifteen years of my life studying (with the help of several marvelous colleagues) the immune system. That is what an antibody molecule looks like if you blow it up trillions of times. It is the centerpiece of immunity recognizing the difference between self and non-self. This enables it to fight foreign invaders (antigens). It has a symmetric structure with two ends or binding sites for antigens. On the lower part you see the region attached to the surface of a body cell. There would be about 100,000 antibody molecules attached to a cell as big as this house. Now if a foreign body, an antigen, such as for instance a virus, a microbe or a chemical substance X, enters an organism, and if it happens to fit this nudge at the two ends, then something will happen.

Let me make a short commentary here on the fate of scientific theories. When I first entered the field of immunology, there was a theory proposed by

Linus Pauling.[5] It turned out that his theory was wrong. Great scientists can be wrong, too. But they are great because they take the risk of proposing new concepts. Pauling's theory was a theory of instruction. Its basic assumption was that, in the immune system, a foreign molecule transferred information about its shape and structure to a particular site of the antibody molecule. It then removed itself (the way a cookie cutter would be removed from dough) leaving a crevice of complementary shape that could then bind to all foreign molecules with regions having the shape with which the impression was originally made. It is obvious why this is an instructive process: Information about a three-dimensional structure is posited to be *necessary* to instruct the immune system how to form an antibody protein whose polypeptide chain folds around that structure to give the appropriate complementary shape.

Then came MacFarlane Burnet and proposed the so-called *clonal selection theory*. Burnet maintained that prior to confrontation with any foreign molecule, an individual's body has the ability to make a huge repertoire of antibody molecules, each with a different shape at its binding site. When a foreign molecule (e.g., a virus or bacterium) is introduced into the body, it encounters a population of cells, each with a different antibody on its surface. It binds to those cells in the repertoire having antibodies whose combining

[5] **Note by Dr. Guntern:** Creative individuals tend to be extremely performance-oriented people whose burning ambition is the source of energy that drives their creative motor. Occasionally that ambition can be so great as to impair critical thinking, human decency and moral principles. Linus Pauling provides a perfect case in point.

Pauling received a Nobel Prize for his brilliant work on the nature of chemical bonds. But that was not enough for him: he urgently wanted to win a second Nobel Prize (evidently inspired by Madame Curie, who had won two). To this end he began investigating the chemical nature of genetic substance. But in the race to decipher the genetic code, he was beaten to the finish line by Watson and Crick. One of the reasons for the two men's success was that they had engaged in a kind of industrial espionage: Pauling's son worked in their lab and used to read them his father's letters, which always described the scientific progress he had made!

Pauling was later awarded the Nobel Peace Prize for his efforts in the cause of nuclear disarmament, but now he wanted a third Nobel Prize. So he resolved to find a scientific explanation for one of the great evolutionary enigmas - schizophrenia. Urine samples of hospitalized patients showed that these patients were suffering from a significant Vitamin C deficiency. But in the excitement of his discovery, Pauling failed to heed the words of the Chinese philosopher Mencius, who said: "All people perpetually seek Tao far away. And yet Tao is always nearby." In other words, he overlooked the obvious explanation that this vitamin deficiency was caused by the one-sided diet at American state hospitals. Consequently, he put forward the hypothesis that high daily doses of Vitamin C could cure schizophrenia. The result was that he became the father of so-called "orthomolecular psychiatry," the butt of his colleagues' jokes, and the prophet of a popular movement that generated an abundance of nonsense, stress, confusion and unnecessary suffering - which it sporadically continues to do.

sites happen to be more or less complementary to it - as a master key would fit into those locks more or less complementary to it. When a portion of an antigen binds to an antibody with a sufficiently close fit, it stimulates the cell (called a lymphocyte) bearing that antibody to divide repeatedly. This results in many more "progeny" cells having antibodies of the same shape and binding specificity. A group of daughter cells is called a clone (an asexual progeny of a single cell) and the whole process is one of differential reproduction by clonal selection. The composition of the lymphocyte population is changed by selection - individual experience plays a role in it.

*So here are cells with all the antibodies, a total number of 10^{11}, one hundred billion, each different. One cell, one antibody. One blue, one red, one green, one violet, etc. The virus comes along and happens to find it fits red. It says, make more - and this cell divides like crazy and makes more, just like a population produces more offspring in evolution. That is how antibodies work, that is how you defend your body. No two of you have the same population, even though you are defending yourselves against the same invaders. That is important, no two of you have the same population, even though you are defending yourselves against the same typhoid shot, the same allergen, the same hay fever or whatever it is. That is how selection works.

Now here comes the nub of how we are going to solve this problem of the nature of the nervous system.

*This is the part for which I have to apologize. Einstein said a theory should be as simple as possible, but no simpler. This is the simplest I can make this. If someone else can make it simpler I should be very grateful to him. This theory has three parts:

Remember what I said. Talking about neuroembryology a while ago, I said that these neurons are moving around like gypsies in order to build up the layers of the brain. A lot of them die in that process. Now if they punch into each other and fit, they connect to build a circuit. In a specific part of the brain these circuits will look alike - without being identical, like different faces may resemble each other - and in other parts of the brain they will again look alike. Thus the process of development generates a lot of diversity in anatomy. These repertoires already exist at a baby's birth, even in an embryo before the organism has had an experience of perception. This is the first assumption of my theory: that there is developmental selection of repertoires of circuits.

The second assumption is that individual experience will selectionally strengthen or weaken specific synapses. If a specific synapse is strengthened, then incoming signals will travel across that interneuronal bridge. Where synapses are weakened, no signals will travel anymore. If that process of selection goes on in vast populations of neurons, then new structural patterns will arise in the brain.

The third assumption is that maps - remember the frog! - are connected to each other by so-called re-entry, i.e., by millions of parallel interneuronal connections. That is, there is a selection of parallel connections which help to correlate neural signals in both space and time.

Now, the unit of selection in the brain is not the individual neuron, but a neuronal group, a cooperative local set of neurons which are more tightly coupled by synaptic bridges than distant neurons.

*Here is some adventurous neurophysiology. What you do is, you take a glass electrode and impale a single cell, hook it to an amplifier and measure its electrical activity. On this slide you see background electricity; every time that cell fires, there is a spike, a voltage like that. Note that there is a whole train of them in time. Now what Wolf Singer and his colleagues in Frankfurt did was to measure the electrical activity of a single neuron at the same time they measured the electrical activity of neurons all around the one that they had impaled. Thus they obtained what is called a *local field potential.* They fed the data thus collected into a computer and asked the following question: would the field potential correlate in time with the individual neuron when given a signal?

In a newborn cat, many neurons are already tuned to respond to specific stimuli. For example, the signal coming in from a light bar will stimulate those neurons tuned to the orientation of that bar. Singer and his colleagues measured the electrical activity of those neurons in the vicinity of their electrodes and they correlated the activity of individual neurons with that of the surrounding population. They found the population activity (field potential) correlated with the individual spikes at 40 hertz, 40 oscillations per second, when the light bar is on. This is evidence for the existence of neuronal groups, because locally connected neurons behave in a highly correlated fashion.

Neurons do not just correlate locally to form groups, but they establish correlations over long distances between maps; this is evidence for reentry.

*Mike Merzenich at the University of California, San Francisco, did a very interesting experiment with monkeys. He chose owl monkeys because they have a very smooth cortex, so that you do not have to enter the convolutions of the brain if you want to record, point after point, the electrical activity of the so-called somato-sensory cortex. This is the part of the cortex containing neuronal groups firing whenever somebody touches your hand or your foot. The map shown here is from Brodmann's area 3b. If you touch digit 1 of a monkey, then a specific group of neurons in the corresponding map will fire. If you touch digit 2, then another group in the map will fire. It turned out that every monkey had an individual map. Individual maps resembled each other, but they were not identical.

Then he trained the monkey to tap. After 100,000 such taps the map of that finger encroached on the maps of the remaining fingers and all the borders rearranged. Then he cut the medium nerve of that animal. The medium nerve supplies this thumb, this finger, this finger here with its smooth surface. He then immediately went back before the nerves could try to regenerate and he mapped again, and this is what he saw: the whole map was immediately rearranged. Dark areas took over where there were no signals coming from that nerve of those fingers - a complete rearrangement of the borders. If he left it that way a whole new map was now shared by the remaining nerves. Every monkey did this individually. The map that was formed was just as good at sensitivity of 2 point discrimination as the original map.

I have told you about the nervous system. I have told you about computers. I have tried to give you the evidence of why as a biological system, a nervous system could not be a computer. I have then tried to explain what it could be, and I have invoked Darwin's kind of thinking. I have used a population thinking model to tell you your brain is not an instructional device, but one which makes selections. It consists of populations just the way chimps do and humans do and cats do, except the populations do not breed and differentially replicate, they differentially amplify. The trouble is that our brains do not make new neurons when they are injured. That is the tragedy of neurology. The central nervous system does not repair itself in the way the rest of your body does, and that is why strokes are a tragedy. Instead, the thing is very plastic and it will readapt to your individual experience, and my claim has been that that is going to account for these properties of perception.

Now I should like to talk in some detail about the concept of re-entry.

*Here is a map, and you must imagine it is full of neurons; here is another map, part of the brain, imagine full of another kind of neuron. Now, one map, by genetics and evolutionary selection is to do, say a visual task, like the one I showed you: the units there will describe reactions to things moving this way, this way, this way, etc. You are born with that. The other map will be responding to how your hand crawls around an object with movement and touch. Now imagine that these maps are linked to each other by a massive number of fibers. Now I am able to say what makes a brain more distinct than anything else in the whole known universe. The brain you see is more like a jungle than it is like a computer. Jungles are more complicated than brains, but not as nifty in certain ways. They have correlations because the animals signal and use a remarkable set of symbols, and these signals will induce an animal population to do remarkable things. Pure physics is not able to deal with a signal that means "Get out of here!"

In spite of all its complexity, a jungle does not have re-entrant connectivity. The trees in the rain forest of the Amazon are not connected by millions of long vines carrying signals back and forth. The brain, however, is the most re-entrantly connected physical object known in the universe - the Internet and the entire telephone system of the globe included.

You have probably heard of the *corpus callosum*, an interneuronal structure connecting the left and the right hemispheres of the brain. There are some 200 million nerve fibers firing off every twenty milliseconds or so in all the possible combinations from one map of your brain across the corpus callosum to another map in the other hemisphere. The neuronal fibers in the corpus callosum contribute massive parallel connections and 90% of them are re-entrant.

I have tried to tell you that the brain is not a computer and I have tried to explain why. A computer does not think. A computer has no semantics; it does not know the meaning of anything. It only has a set of rules that determines little scratch marks - zeros and ones, plusses and minuses - in an order which we have mapped onto what we have established in our society with our thought, our logic, and our mathematics, so that it does it very fast, much faster than our brain. Our brains are wet and slow, for they work by table salt - ions of sodium, chloride, potassium and calcium. A computer works by electrons, which work at the speed of light. We know how to manipulate them and we have a logical scheme with effective procedures. Our brain is not wired that way, it does not have a tape. The world is not the tape, the world is variously interpretable, and I want you to take solace in that. It is the richness of our lives. If the world were like a tape, it would be terribly boring.

So the next thing I said was that the brain had singular ways of putting itself together, and if you had to describe what it was, you would say it is the most re-entrantly connected device there is. It is the idea that you map maps to each other by an extraordinary kind of wiring, so that different parts of the maps can select, out of the billions upon billions, *that* circuit which responds best after the event. So if I have to describe how our brain works, it is the following way, the way the lady in the English novel by E.M. Foster said,

"How do I know what I think until I see what I say?" That is how our brain works. Take solace in that, too.

Now I am going to describe what you are going to see. In the film you will see in a moment, Darwin III is an automaton or artifact; it is not a machine because it is not the Turing machine. The reason it is not a Turing machine is it has no effective procedure in its ultimate action, because we put in dice-tossing. Every gambler will tell you that if you toss a dice, you do not know what number is going to come up; you only know the probability. The minute you put in dice-tossing, every mathematician will tell you it is no longer a Turing machine because there is no effective procedure. I am going to show you a simple organism called Darwin III, which consists of a head, an eye, a four-jointed arm and a sessile. By that I mean it is stuck in one place. We want to make this thing simple.

This is the third attempt we have made: today, we are up to our fifth. Darwin III sits there, and objects come past it; let us call them food. They are about the same scale as its body. In other words, I do not see bacteria, I see a doughnut or a croissant. Consider that the equivalent of doughnuts and croissants are floating past Darwin III. Consider that we are not going to make them float according to any program; we have a random number generator. So there is no way you can describe when the next event is going to occur or what the event is. That is a random number. We have tricks that are almost like that for computers and we use them to float a selection of objects by. We do not cheat and Darwin III does not cheat. What would it cheat for? Well, it would cheat if I told it, this is good to eat, when you see an orange object going at such-and-such a speed, grab it. That is what you do with computers. We do not do that. We act as if we are evolution and development - we build a brain of a certain type. We follow the principles, we allow it to be very diverse so that no two are alike, no two creatures are alike; individuality matters. We build in molecules, and we build in synapses and we build in nerves - all these words, you have heard. We build in an arm with muscles that can move it and an eye with four muscles that can move it.

We build in one other thing which is terribly important for our discussion and that is: value. What we have discovered in designing these artifacts is, if you do not build in value, then they will not go anywhere because they have no program. A program, you see, embeds both categories and values. When I tell a computer to do something, I know what I want, that is the value. I am hungry for an answer - that is a value. When I ask, "Well, how do you get the answer?" that is a category. I have got to write the right equation. But Darwin III by definition is a selectional device, like your brain is a selectional brain, so it does not have any category once it is in the world. It is very important you understand two things: the first is, yes, we designed it and we used the computer. It sounds like I am contradicting myself. No, we just use a computer because it is much cheaper. We use the capacity of a computer to simulate, just as you can simulate a wind tunnel with the plane flying in it - you can simulate a neuron. We can actually do that and we have a vast program that does it. It took thirteen years to build and it can make neurons, hook them up, and the computer does not duplicate a nervous system, but it simulates it - with all these principles. No cheating though, no electronics, no logic, nothing of that kind.

So we have acted in a certain proud way, like evolution and development. But we have not told it what it is going to encounter, where it is going to encounter it and what to do. Now, at that point you might say, oh yes, you really did that when you embodied values. But have you noticed that a new-born baby has a rooting reflex if you touch it here, it goes like that for the breast. If it does not, it is selected out: a dead baby! If it does not have the sucking reflex when a breast goes in its mouth, it is an unfed baby: a dead baby! So there are values that evolutionary selection give as envelopes shaping basic fundamental actions of your life.

Here is what we do: we build in these random number generators and we put them in in such a way that the initial activity of the nervous system is also random - so there is no cheating. There are random objects moving by. Then we watch. But since it is simulated, we can look inside its brain while it is doing something. Every single set of experiments that it has is individual. We can do each experiment ten times or more and compare. Then we can store every single event, in its brain and in its behavior, up and down the levels of organization. That is why this subject is difficult.

Esther Thelen, from the University of Indiana, is studying the movements of babies. When she saw Darwin III, she got very excited because her studies of babies reaching out correspond exactly to what we have concluded. Babies reach, each in its own way, just the way your signatures read in your own way.

Bernstein, a great Soviet scientist, pointed out that it is impossible to reach in the way engineers describe movement. He used the example of putting a dot in space and asking someone to reach for it three times and touch it, and he would score the person. How could a computer make one do that? After all, it is done with missiles that track airplanes. You have got a computer. You have a feedback loop. You correct it like crazy. It looks very much like it is intelligent, but it is not. Yet that is not the way to do it. Bernstein pointed out that if you did it that way, your brain would have to compute the center of mass across every joint of your body, compute 1,600 simultaneous equations once every ten milliseconds. The number of degrees of freedom of your arm alone is too great to accomplish that. You have tens to hundreds of degrees of freedom: there is no way you can compute movements the ordinary way.

Second, he pointed out that individuals reach like this, but the minute they do so, by Newton's third law, the body goes backwards. The brain has to compute that, but the individual is going for his next movement before his body comes back to equilibrium. So what is the solution to Bernstein's problem? Olaf Sporns has provided it. Out of a repertoire of quite clumsy movements, the fine movements of a virtuoso violinist eventually emerge by selection. They are selected upon value by strengthening specific synapses. So that is the first lesson.

Now I am going to show you Darwin IV. Darwin III is the world and the brain simulated in a computer. But now you would like to know what happens outside the computer, in the real world of directly observable phenomena, so we made Darwin IV.

*Now Darwin IV is truly interesting in several ways. It has its own playpen, and underneath it, is a real robot. What do I mean by real robot? That thing underneath is moving a light. I have a PC programmed to move that around following instructions, that is to say, turn in a vector of 35 degrees, go so many time-steps, turn this way, turn that way. If I lose a byte, the thing stops, just like any computer crashing. It is a real robot. But this thing is not a robot, this thing has a brain down the hall in another room. The brain is much more complicated, as you might imagine, than in Darwin III. It is in an N-Cube supercomputer. It is really stupid. I mean, it is an insect learning to be a dog. In its most sophisticated form it has only about 100,000 neurons and a few million connections. I want to give you a feeling of how puny our efforts are. If I took a match head of your cortex, it would have one billion connections. Feel proud!

So we want to work with a Darwin IV (as opposed to a Darwin III) because now Darwin IV has an eye - you will see that eye in a minute on the video - but now it is in the real world. The brain is simulated down the hall and we have a little transmitter here that takes the television signals, converts them through a computer into muscle movements going to the wheels. We are not smart enough to make muscles yet, so, we just use wheels. But that is not cheating; it is just turning the brain's signals into actual wheel movements. It does not actually control the movement itself.

(Video)

Here is Darwin IV. It has an eye, which is a CCD camera. A television receiver/transmitter unit communicates with its brain, a simulation in a computer outside the device. It has a German computer that translates its muscle commands into wheel motions. It has a snout, and on this snout is a big magnet which picks up blocks and tastes them, except the taste is a conducting circuit. After being born it moves around in its playpen. It can turn, it can translate forward, and it has been given (by evolution and development) the value stating that light is better than no light. But it has no instructions as to where to move, how to move and what to see and what to do.

On top of Darwin IV's head is an arrow. The light it is supposed to be tracking is being moved by the robot in a random movement. Here is what is happening: every time that arrow moves away, its brain changes and selection occurs, and synapses are weakened and strengthened, and every time it hits the object, they are strengthened, etc. Every experience it has - positive and negative - is important. Mistakes are just as important as the others. It does this 3,000 times and now watch what happens. Its brain changes so that some connections are weakened by selection, others are strengthened and we can watch its brain doing that, while it is doing its behavior. There is no perfection. In evolution perfection implies death. Thus, Darwin IV makes mistakes, learns from its own experience and changes its own nervous system. Now comes the next step in our experiment. We put in an opaque floor and a bunch of light steel-cubes which are colored red and blue. Some of those cubes, the blue ones, have faces covered with conducting plastic. Imagine that this conductance corresponds to a kind of taste, a bitter taste. Now you see, Darwin IV approaches a blue object only once and when its snout grabs it, it gets a "bitter" taste. From now on it will avoid the blue blocks. It will get near them, it will get what the Catholics call "a near occasion of sin," but it will not grab it. Do not forget, it has never been instructed about what to do and when to move. When Darwin IV stops for a while, you might be tempted to indulge in anthropomorphism and to assume that it is sitting there thinking. It does not think at all. Let me repeat once more. Darwin IV has no description of an object. Yet it is a recognition automaton working by selection.

What I have tried to show you is the next step of a scientific theory. The theory I put forth and have written about is not adequate. It is not adequate because I think it is wrong. It is inadequate because you have to get to the details. God is in the detail. You have to show that the theory will really yield something that does what you say it does. You have to test it. Notice that I cannot use mathematics any more. There are no mathematics that can describe what I have just shown you, yet. There may be some day, but right now there are not. We have used the computer as a tool, but not as a model, mainly for financial reasons. That does not mean that we could not build these kinds of things outside; it just means it would be very costly.

What does this mean for computation? I have some friends at the Massachusetts Institute of Technology that work on artificial intelligence. They are great innovators, they come, they look at this, they say, "Gerald, we can write a 300-line program that will do more than that." My answer is, "Sure, you wrote it, you told it what to do. Nothing new happened; it just keeps doing the same old thing and you're proud of yourself. You're wasting your time." We have big arguments and then I say, "Okay, you want to go hunting. You want to go to swarm for birds, and I'm going to give you the Air Force computer in a tea cup, and it's going to be friendly, it speaks English. Would you take that or would you take a dog?" Most of them say they would take the dog. You ask why, and they are hard-pressed to say why: no number of smart guys at Harvard or MIT can program a bird hunt. Dogs have been evolved to recognize novelty. The way they recognize novelty is the way I have just described. They make mistakes. They select those things which happen to match, like the pigeons do with the objects, and then they train the dog by rewarding its values. But it does not know what a rifle is. It just has to be trained, so it does not jump and run away when the rifle bangs in its barbarous activity and you do not know what is going on in the dog's brain either.

Well, now imagine a perception-Turing machine. Take 10 Darwin IX's, hook them up to a vast data base in a regular computer and you will have a world revolution. All you have to do is train those Darwin IX's according to whatever is in your electromagnetic spectrum, just like the dog, and they will report back. In other words, these Darwins will be able to do what computers cannot do. It is stupendous. Yet remember, what scientists are interested in is our original question, how do you think? Now, have you noticed that I have not mentioned thinking at all? I have talked about perception and these things that I have shown you are not even conscious, and those automata do not have concepts. They do not know the difference between the concepts up, down, inside, out.

Let me talk, however, about something that relates to the beginning road, to concepts, because Dr. Guntern and I conspired to talk about it as it relates to creativity. What about memory?

I have never met anybody, lay or scientific, who is not interested in memory. I want to draw the distinction between computer memory and your memory. If what I say is correct and it stands to be tested, let me leave you with this: I believe it is correct, we have proven its self-consistency. That does not mean it is correct science. We must do experiments to show re-entry, and we are beginning to do so now.

Here is how computer memories work. They do not work by selection, they work by instruction. You give them the instructions. You write a detailed algorithmic program. It is syntactic. What does that mean? Syntax refers to a set of rules about how you make scratches on paper or yea's and no's on a computer. It does not have anything to do with meaning, although it is an aid to meaning. Reliability is accuracy. If you drop a byte in a computer, it usually crashes. In order to prevent it from crashing, you write something called an error code. But you just cannot keep doing that. It will eventually crash, and that is what a bug is. Reliability is accuracy, it is not creative. (Guntern, I put this down before I heard of you.) It is not creative, it cannot be creative because it cannot make mistakes. Your memory is not a code of syntactical elements which is read out from the memory address, interpreted semantically by an operator as a computer code is. Your system works by selection; just like Darwin IV, it is semantic. That means it must put significance above anything else. Because it has not got a program with someone else hiding the meaning. Its reliability is not efficiency. It is achieving the goal. What is the goal? Well, that depends upon the value.

In the end, of course, it is creative.

Now let me talk about real memory and creation. There are different kinds of genius. I want to talk about two. This is a true story. Fritz Kreisler was the only genius of a violinist that Jasha Heifetz admired. Believe me, I am not sure whether Jasha Heifetz admired God, but if you are admired by Jasha Heifetz, you are in. He was playing Grieg's C-minor sonata - actually, not Grieg's greatest work - with Rachmaninov in Berlin in 1930, and they were planning to record it. They are two different kinds of geniuses, just as there are different kinds of scientists, different kinds of dogs, different kinds of everything. My message is, individuality is essential in a selectional system, that is why you must not abandon it or be apologetic for your prejudices or your individuality or whatever. That is the message. So the two musicians were very different. Rachmaninov is a great genius, but he practiced all the time. Kreisler went out to night clubs, and in fact he never practiced. He practiced in his head, just imagining the movements. So the night before the recording he went out night-clubbing, came in all bleary-eyed and said, "Sergej, let's record." Rachmaninov retorted, "You're not ready. I've got to practice with you, so the hell with you." Kreisler insisted, "Let's just get on with it." They had a big argument and he won. Rachmaninov very unhappily did the recording. You can buy it, it is on Victriola, mono, 1930. It is unbelievable. It takes a rather banal piece of music and transports it.

About six months later they were playing in Carnegie Hall. They started the second part of the program by playing that same Grieg Sonata. It had been triumphant up until then. In the second movement, Kreisler suddenly forgot, but as he was Fritz Kreisler, he made up the cadences. He was no longer playing Grieg, but something Grieg-like. So there he was, making it up as he went along, and everything was fine. All of a sudden he got a little anxious, and he leaned over and said, "Sergej, where are we?" Rachmaninov looked at him and said, "Carnegie Hall."

So, memory works creatively and in many different modes, but never with the kind of rigid, fixed, coded accuracy, and that should console you, too.

*Here is the picture of a darling genius, William James, one of the co-inventors of psychology, who I think would be very pleased with this. He would have welcomed the idea that you can find a biological basis for these psychological events, because if you consider the alternative, you are split from your body in a very curious way, and you know something is wrong with that. William James, who wrote *The Principles of Psychology,* really came closer than anyone else to defining the psychology of the inner life at the conscious level, unlike Freud, who dealt with the unconscious. I would like, therefore, to summarize some general conclusions.

Obviously I have gone through a lot of different things, but I think I can synthesize what I have to say. The evidence, I believe, points overwhelmingly to the fact that what is going on inside you at this moment is a little bit like an evolutionary process. Instead of a jungle filled with different species and breeding which leads to the evolution of the species, selections are occurring individually inside your head across a repertoire of neurons each of which is unique, coupling with your body and coupling with your experience so you are embedded in the world and there is no way you can pull free. You are part of the world and the world then becomes part of you, not as a mirror, but in the way you saw in Darwin III and IV.

137

The second conclusion is that error is absolutely necessary in such a system, since there is no judge and no one giving you marks, except the eventual performance.

The third conclusion is, value is important. You must have already had selection going on in evolution to pick a set of values which will constrain you, but not terribly. I mean you can write an infinite number of fourteen line sonnets and some of them could be great if you were Shakespeare. So it is not a question of declaring ultimate freedom. But there is nobody sitting around writing you a little program. You have to do it through your own experience.

The final message is that we are not computers, we are not machines, even in the Turing machine sense. We can be represented by Turing machines after they see what we say, but until we see what we say, there is nobody to say what is going to be the case. And if that is the case, as James himself stated, freedom does exist. It is very limited, you cannot have everything, but there is a freedom in your ability - and this, we have not discussed - consciously to imagine a future and make a choice. Combine that freedom with the freedom to make errors, and creativity begins to emerge. It emerges not as a result of any even very gifted individual, it emerges from the interaction and within a tradition given by the necessary coupling of all of us human beings together.

So I shall conclude as I started, with a lady poet, Emily Dickinson, who said,

> "The Brain - is wider than the Sky -
> For - put them side by side -
> The one the other will contain
> With ease - and You - beside -
>
> The Brain is deeper than the sea -
> For - hold them - Blue to Blue -
> The one the other will absorb -
> As sponges - buckets - do -
>
> The brain is just the weight of God -
> For - Heft them - Pound for Pound -
> And they will differ - if they do -
> As Syllable from Sound. -

Emily Dickinson

Science is imagination in the pursuit of the verifiable truth. Not all of the truth, but it is the one form of truth which we can skeptically continue to test, the results of which are eminently practical, the largest single, mutual cultural engine of all civilizations, necessarily creative, starting like art, ending as a little line in a text, packed into it the work of very many imaginative and creative intellects, and I think one of the splendors of our species. Thank you very much.

Discussion

Lambelin: My question is in two parts. You stated that the local potential of the electromagnetic field is in correlation with a form of cooperation by groups of neurons. Does this mean that if we could consciously make a greater number of neurons participate in this process of cooperation, the resulting energy potential would be proportional to the number of neurons which participate? That is the first part.

Edelman: If I understand your question, what you want is an explanation of how you correlate taste with visual activity in terms of groups of neurons. The idea is something like this. After it learns about light, since different colors reflect different amounts of light, it will discriminate one color from another. It does not have true color vision: for example, it cannot distinguish shades of pink. We are currently working on a new model that can discriminate true color. The present model can, however, distinguish the reflectance, which is a very big part of color of different objects. Now, what happens is, certain neurons are selected in its visual brain. It also has a smell-taste brain there, the activity of which goes up, and those two are connected. If it gets a taste that already says it is a bad value, then anything that happens to be active at that moment tends to be weakened, but you cannot say exactly which neuronal groups they will be. It depends on what happened at that moment. It is correlated as you have implied, and that correlation sets up a probability that the next time that combination comes along, you will not strengthen that connection. Therefore, over time, it will stay away. Now, this does not work perfectly all the time. It will sometimes go twice to a blue object, but usually not. Each time we train Darwin IV, its behavior will converge, but never the same way twice. One other thing related to your question: the key principle about how reentry works when there is no message - only neural signals - is that the brain is an engine for converting space into time and time into space. So if in a certain time things are firing together, they have a higher possibility of connecting up across space. In turn, neurons that are connected in space tend to fire together in time. So if there is a spatial organization that is converted in time, then the next time around there is a higher probability Darwin IV's behavior will be correlated the right way. Which way it behaves is another story. The numbers are scary. They are combinatorial, and they go on to infinity; they are really unbelievably large numbers.

Lambelin: Thank you. The second part of my question is is it possible to show a cause-effect relation between the way of thinking and the energy displayed in the process?

Edelman: The question is whether there is a possibility of connecting up the organization with the energy of the processes. Not directly, and that is a very interesting thing. You see, your brain uses up more oxygen and glucose than your liver. Your liver is the engine of your body, the biochemical engine of your body and a great generator of heat. But your brain is even more so. Your brain just buzzes along, and that is why not having oxygen or being deprived of glucose can cause permanent brain damage very fast. Within one minute you start losing nerve cells terribly fast. By the way, it may cheer you up to think that every time you have a drink, you lose thousands of them. Good luck! But then, what are a few thousand neurons for people so rich in trillions of connections? There is no direct connection between the energy expenditure of a particular neuron and a particular valuable act, if you will. What there is, however, are certain energy relationships in your muscles, which will weigh on other systems that feed your brain, that say you are not going to reach for the table that way, you are going to try to minimize energy as you reach there, in the larger group. But if you made an energy map in the brain, it would not correspond. It takes probably just about the same energy to commit a mortal sin as to grasp Einstein's theory.

Reiser: Has your research led you to find out about conditions or stimuli which enhance creativity or the brain? In other words, can you say what differentiates the replicative activity of the brain from the non-replicative activity? What stimulates the non-replicative activity?

Edelman: That is a good question. Of course, you realize we are working well below the level of your question, and that may be a good entry into concepts and creativity, because, you see, it will not do. If I have told you the basis of perceptual categorization and it turns out to be this way, I have not even touched upon conceptual matters, and that even hardly begins to talk about the matter of the relationship of concept to a new kind of memory called language, in which we intend when we point to an object and say "video" (points to video projector). Under the auspices of that symbol we intend the same thing, even though different neurons are firing in your brain and mine when we look at the video. We have not even touched upon that. If you like, I can comment on it. There is no direct relationship, it would be absurd for me to extrapolate from these results to messages having to do with human creativity. But one can see a potential path of research, one can see what it is you would have to learn.

If you ask a philosopher what a concept is, he will tell you it is a propositional term or a sentential term - sentences subject to falsification, true or false, having to do with generalization across a set. Now, I believe that is all right, but it is not what your brain does. It begs the question. If you had to do that, you would have to claim that because cats did not have language, they would not have concepts. Now you know very well your cat has a concept of milk, and what a moving object is. You do not know exactly what it feels like to be a cat with a concept, because your concepts are already contaminated by language which makes you into a philosopher, which makes you say it is a sentential proposition. So the question, scientifically, is: could you get a concept out of perceptual categorizing, of the kind we just showed you with the automaton? No, no matter how many times a Darwin IV would go around and categorize objects according to its values, it would never generalize to the point where it would say "up," "down," "inside," "out," regardless of the nature of the objects. Supposing I made a tunnel out of salami and another tunnel out of flasks, with no inside or outside. A conceptualizing animal would ignore the question of whether they were flasks or salamis, and there would be no inside or outside. That is the universal represented by a conceptual event. My proposal has been that the way the brain develops, the concepts are not sentential, they are functions of the brain which precede language and which have to do with the frontal cortex, the pyramidal cortex and the temporal cortex - these higher order brain maps which do not map to the outside world by touch, sound, kinesthesia, smell, taste, but which map the maps of the brain. Now imagine that you can map and categorize those maps that relate to movement, those maps that relate to taste, and you have a way of mixing the results and categorizing, which you can, I believe, get to a universal.

Now we are going further into Dr. Guntern's favorite precincts. You have to come to terms with language and consciousness. You do not think with language. Language is the secretary of your concepts, so that language is a speech-community interaction which has evolved, obviously, for very great advantage, in which under the auspices of a symbol - ba, wa, da, Hebrew words - or any other - you can categorize your concepts into a lexicon. Does the thinking occur in the language? No. The thinking occurs in the conceptual portion of the brain, but once a baby has a lexicon of 50 words, with enough verbs and nouns in a semantic meaning related to its values conceptually, an explosion occurs of the kind that happened with Helen Keller. On a crucial day this blind, dumb, deaf person of high intelligence felt water and realized that water was "w-a-t-e-r." She went nuts and wanted to invent everything in the world. At that moment she suffered the epiphany of language. She saw that water meant any kind of water, not just the thing trickling here. Then she wanted to know about tables, chairs, and wanted to name everything. The reason is that at that point, the number of possible ways of imagining through memory and creating a future concept of a world explodes, whereas if you do not have that, because there is not any syntax, you get just so far. It will be like these apes that have been taught and can do a certain number of things, but do not have the syntactical skill to build up endless chains of sentences. So, according to this theory, yes, language then adds to concepts immeasurably, just the way video adds to my capacity to change gestures or whatever. Or just as computers change my capability of solving equations. But it is not the real underlying thing.

Guntern: Let us talk about metaphors and understanding the world in which we live. In the 17th century Johannes Kepler introduced the machine metaphor. He said the universe is not a divine organism, but a machine. Fifty years later, in the 6th meditation, Descartes said the body was a machine made of flesh and bones. One hundred years later LaMettrie said, "L'organisme est une machine," which also includes the mind. Today computer specialists tell us the organism is a computer machine. Now you come and introduce not the divine organism, but the ecosystem as a metaphor for the brain. Could you tell us a little bit more about the interplay of imagination, metaphors and creative process, because you have been creative in many fields, and you still are.

Edelman: Who knows? I want to say something about machines first, because you have to be careful here. You can use that metaphor to an excess. I have argued against the machine model of the mind. If there is a machine model of the mind, you are slaves, because economics will couple to scientific discovery in such a way as to use you as part of a mega-machine. There is no doubt about it. Ask any businessman in the crowd. That is what his human resources division is about, to indulge in that curious softening of arbitration and force. It is important to be very clear about what you mean by machine. A machine is a Turing machine. A machine is a device with an input and an output, with a defined set of effective procedures to carry out a task and replicate that task. A Tinguely sculpture is not a machine, especially if it explodes differently each time. The universe is not a machine. The lady novelist in England, when she was asked what she thinks of the universe, said, "Thank God there is only one of them." It is not a machine because there are not two of them and you would not know whether it would replicate its behavior; you would know under the law of physics that it might converge to certain things. The universe is not a machine. If it is not a machine, there is no way of writing an equation down, except to say what constrains the universe. That is not the same. That is the history of the universe. So a machine is a Turing machine. It would have to follow that the most general kind of machine is a Turing machine, that is why these people say it is a computer. They feel they can generate everything with their computers. Well, I have challenged them, I have said, "Do you think evolution is a Turing machine? If so, please tell me what we are going to look like 350,000 years from now or even better, 2,000,000 which is a very small amount. Do you think we will look the same or not? Tell me. Predict it. You can't."

Now, the machine model is very attractive. Human beings like to control the world in which they live. There is nothing so remarkable as being able to control your machine. But, you know, being in control is not good for art, that is for sure. Bad art cannot substitute imagination. If you force it like a machine, you know what you will get. So, I understand why scientists do that. It is a natural temptation for people to do that because of course at one level, your heart can be treated as a machine, your brain can be treated as a machine, and your kidney can be treated as a machine. Your heart has a certain work function, it has the same thermodynamics as a gasoline engine. There are no miracles, you have to put in so much energy to get the muscles to do this and they pump so much blood in, it increases entropy the same way as anything else. But that is not our message. Our message is, that is not what we mean by us and by our brain and by these categories. Our brain is a machine in that sense. If I cut off the blood supply, the machine in that sense of input-output of energy will collapse, and I am dead. By the way, do you know how de LaMettrie died? De LaMettrie wrote *L'homme machine*. Even the French who were rather liberal, given the way things were then, kicked him out. He went to Holland. So he wrote this book *Man as a Machine*. Then in Holland he wrote, *L'homme plante - Man as a Plant*. They kicked him out of Holland. He landed up in the court of Frederic the Great and he decided that science was for the birds - eating was what counted. So he ate especially in the company of very powerful people, following Sam Johnson's credo, "Dine with the rich, laugh with the wise." One day he fell down to the ground in the middle of a meal with terrible abdominal pains, and three days later he died of peritonitis. He had what is known as volvulus. Volvulus is when your intestine twists around its own artery, loses its blood supply and gangrene sets in. It is very bad news even today. When Frederic the Great heard of his death, he said, "Did he renounce his atheism?" And they said, "No sire." And he said, "Good, I will write a eulogy." Now, de LaMettrie was the most extreme example of a mechanist of the body. Descartes was more subtle. First, he did not want to get into trouble with the Church, but secondly, he was genuinely convinced, *je pense, donc je suis* . Furthermore, Descartes was very much ignorant, as great as he was, of a little sentential proposition. He did not realize that in talking to yourself, you are always talking to a hidden interlocutor who is somebody else. That is how you do language, so when he concluded from his own linguistic thinking that he could declare himself free of all mechanical things in a sort of ideal space, he did not realize that what he was doing was conditioned by what we know today: that when you talk to yourself, you are talking to your great school teacher, your mother, all of the people who in fact infused you with language. If you want to describe the human tragedy instead of creativity, it is very simple. It is tragic that evolution has built us to be totally selfish, as it has every other organism, and necessarily so. It is also sublime that in order to speak language we must interact with each other and in a very, very rich and cooperative way - or we are out. That is counterproductive. So, of course, human resources are constantly tested by this paradox. If brain science shows that in every individual brain a unique historical path has occurred, both in development and in exposure to this rich world, such that creativity results because of that complex history and not because of a single thing and that nobody can write down a formula for it, then it is perfectly clear you are not a machine. It cannot be proven today, but I believe it will be in future. There are now devices which are able to look into a living brain and see what happens when you pronounce this word versus that word. We will be going down to millimeter resolutions, but don't let us confuse those firings with what we mean by a word. There will be a theory which will relate language to this activity, and I believe what it will confirm is that the historical process is very important. Now, for a machine a historical process just means wearing out. It is called down-time. Every machine has a historical process. After a certain point, you retire it and replace it with another machine. Try it with any of you, would you resent it?

Of course, that is not a scientific statement; that is an article of faith on my part, but it does follow from this kind of theory that, like evolution and like immunity, you are unique and significantly so, and it must follow that you could not be creative otherwise because there must be a formula by which we could replace you by what you do. Schoenberg was the greatest theorist of music in his day, because listening to his piano pieces is enough to make you commit suicide, unless Maurizio Pollini plays them, then it is different. Schoenberg was playing tennis with Gershwin. You know, Gershwin was not trained as a musician. He was a Tin Pan Alley pianist, and they were both living in Hollywood. They played a set of tennis and they came to the net. Gershwin said, "Arnold, I think I'd like to study composition with you, you know, harmony and all that, I don't know much about that." He said, "George, how much do you make a year?" He said, "Well about 200,000." He said, "I'll study with you." Technique is politeness. You can study all the rules of counterpoint and harmony until you are blue in the face, and that is not going to guarantee a single thing.

Guntern: If you compare the brain to a rain forest, then your metaphor sums up a very important result of your brain research. A metaphor is a pictorial mapping of a specific aspect of the world and because it is an element of language, it is also a linguistic mapping. At the same time it is the jumping board for new inspiration, because metaphors are inspiring. Do you see other functions in the creative process that pictures, imaginations, metaphors can play?

Edelman: My personal belief is that those linguists known as cognitive linguists are closer to the issue than Chomsky is. Do not misinterpret what I am saying. Chomsky is a remarkable figure even though he has attacked me vigorously in the last couple of weeks. He is charismatic and has transformed the entire field. Yet I believe he is dead wrong. There are a group of people called cognitive linguists who begin in exactly the opposite way. Instead of saying a baby is born with genetic rules for syntax, like a computer, the fundamental operation of the brain according to these people, is metaphor. A man named George Lakoff in Berkeley loves my book because my book says our problem is to find out how we embody the mind. Of course, Lakoff also believes that the way a baby creates language is by first being given a speech center and then being able to vocalize and recognize co-articulated sound. By the way, that is an incredibly fascinating thing. If I take the sound "b," the phoneme "b," and I break it up on a tape to the initial plosive part of it and the "ou" sound, and I put the latter part of the tape in this ear and the initial part in this ear - in this ear I hear "oui" and in the other one I hear "oh." If I put them together, I hear "b." Your brain synthesizes that. You have evolved a system for recognizing co-articulated sounds and the baby has that. Lakoff has a hypothesis whereby you embed your body functions in metaphor. The way your body works and is built and its values and its phenotypes construct a set of primitive metaphors. Here is an example. I want some water. He calls that source - path - goal. So I have a way of categorizing the way I showed you. I have a value: I am thirsty. As a result I move my body with this brain conceptualizing: have a source - path - goal. Lakoff says meaning arrives from that vague sound of a metaphor. Arnold Modell, who is a Professor of Psychiatry at Harvard, who thinks from his analytic experience - and you (to Dr. Guntern) might comment on that - much of what is going on in an analytic session is metaphorically derived. The patient does not really love you the way he loves a woman, even though he is having a transference. He knows you are not that woman, but he is metaphorically transforming you in that act into something to re-categorize his experience. That fits exactly with the notion of memory, which is not a replicative, absolute machine-like thing. So it is a truly attractive notion that the real way in which our brain begins to work is by metaphor. It is not unrelated to, say, poetry, which, by the way, brings up quite a problem to anybody who does ordinary computer analysis. He reads a poem and tries to figure out all the ways in which words acquire new meanings by being next to other words. He will never make it. So I think this idea of metaphor is very rich.

Einstein, of course, was asked about his creative processes, and in this respect, I have two really amusing stories. I have friends who knew him rather well, although I never met him myself. Asked if he thought in words, he replied, "Absolutely not."

He definitely thought in images.[6] His idea of the theory of relativity all began when as a child he dreamed about riding on a light beam. He wondered

[6] **Note by Dr. Guntern:** French mathematician Jacques Hadamard once asked several of the scientists of his time how their creative ideas began. Einstein replied: "with images or muscular movements." This answer, which can, incidentally, be heard again and again from creative individuals, indicates that creative ideas evidently begin, not in the linguistic portion of the brain, which engages in logical, rational thinking, but in the conceptual portion of the brain, which thinks intuitively, and in the cerebellum, which is characterized by sensorimotor "thinking."

In other words, creative ideas begin in the older (evolution-wise) portions of the brain and can easily be nipped in the bud if logic-linguistic thinking tries to get a rational grip on them all too quickly. Logical, rational thinking is sterile rather than creative: it can deduce from premises only what is already implicit in them. And yet it plays an important part in the creative process by furnishing the critical means of separating the wheat from the chaff. The greater the creative mind, the more unrelentingly he or she will scrutinize his or her results. Less creative minds consider everything their imagination brings forth good. (G. Guntern, *Sieben goldene Regeln der Kreativitätsförderung.* Scalo, Zurich 1994; also *Irritation und Kreativität.* Scalo, Zurich 1993 and *Der kreative Weg. Kreativität in Wirtschaft, Kunst und Wissenschaft.* Verlag Moderne Industrie, Zurich 1991.)

what would happen if he sat on a light beam, what things would look like. But there were no words in his head. Other people might imagine in words. But I believe there are old primitives in the brain, and concerning memory, there is a rather interesting anecdote: Valéry, the great poet who wrote a great deal about imagination and creativity, went to see Einstein at Princeton. I have checked this story out, for I did not believe it when I heard it. He said, "I'm writing a book about creativity, and I'd like to hear what you do every day." Einstein said, "Well, I get up, I shave with regular soap, I don't put on any socks - I don't believe in a complicated life - I take a walk; I think. By then its lunch time. I have some lunch. I try to think, but then I'm pretty tired, so I take a nap or I may sail a little boat. Then I take another nap, I try to think, but forget about it. The next day the same thing happens." Valéry suggested, "I suppose you keep a notebook." Einstein reeled around and looked at him, "What on earth for?" Valéry, "You know, to write down your good ideas." Einstein looked at him and said, "Listen, I don't get very many, and don't worry, when I do get one, I don't forget it." That is a true story; I heard it from a student of Einstein's.

Pitanguy: Is memory more comprehensive than intellect, as Proust suggested? Would you please comment on that topic?

Edelman: First of all, I would have to say that Marcel Proust was one of the most intelligent and complicated creatures that ever lived. He made a marvelous statement: "What is the greatest military virtue? Flight!" Memory is absolutely the largest instrument of a higher brain. It is the basis of consciousness which we have not discussed. It is the mechanism by which you can reorder in the absence of events, because if you had always to be saturated by events, you would be so busy that you would not be able to reconstitute and reform them. You live de facto in a remembered present, as I have said in one of my books. Your consciousness of present-day physical time is real. Our discussion is really happening now - physicists could measure it. But your concept of the past and the future is not the same as your experience of the present. You fuse them as if they were all one, but do not kid yourself. Have you noticed, as you grow older, that things seem to be going so fast? This is because it is a concept, not an experience. You are reconstituting your memory, you are constantly re-categorizing your experience. If it were otherwise, imagine what a new experience would be like against the fixed set of memories. So memory is absolutely essential for all of the higher functions beyond perception. You could argue metaphorically about Darwin IV, that it has a kind of memory. It does, it is in the synaptic mechanisms that stabilize some synapses so things move faster there than in other synapses, but it is a very low-level memory. Perhaps the statement should be this: Proust, who as a genius was thinking introspectively with language, was not considering the fact that in fact you have thousands of kinds of memory in your brain. Memory is a system property. If I showed you Darwin III and IV again and I asked you where the memory was, you could not answer me. It has been one of the category errors of modern neuroscience to say memory is stored in synapses. But every time I show you a performance, it uses another combination. So it cannot be that. It is not coded. What is it? It is the dynamic interaction of the entire system of selection, favoring a probability of repeating a performance.

Guntern: Thank you very much, Professor Edelman, for your brilliant, inspiring and quite complex presentation. We have learned a lot about the human brain today, and it is quite obvious that we have to reconsider quite a number of our traditional assumptions and concepts if we are to reach a better understanding of man and human creativity.

Works by Professor Edelman

Neural Darwinism: The Theory of Neural Group Selection.
   Basic Books, New York 1987
Topobiology: An Introduction to Molecular Embryology.
   Basic Books, New York, 1989
The Remembered Present: A Biological Theory of Consciousness.
   Basic Books, New York 1989
Bright Air, Brilliant Fire: On the Matter of the Mind.
   Basic Books, New York 1992

GABRIEL GARCÍA MÁRQUEZ
Colombian author, Nobel Prize laureate

Born on March 6, 1928 in Aracataca, northern Colombia, "Gabito" (his childhood nickname) grew up with his maternal grandparents in a house inhabited mainly by women (his superstitious aunts) and ghost stories. Such were the foundations for his future literary works. He gave up his law studies at the Universities of Bogotá and Cartagena to turn to journalism in 1949. Earning his daily bread was not always easy, and his many and varied jobs included editing magazines, advertising, writing sub-titles for films, and script writing. Considered one of the pioneers of "Magical Realism" and thought by many to be one of the world's greatest living authors, Gabriel García Márquez' amazing literary talent was rewarded in 1982 with the Nobel Prize in Literature. Today his home is in Mexico City, where he lives with his wife, Mercedes, in the perpetual state of "writing a novel."

Introduction by Gottlieb Guntern

It is no easy task to introduce a person who not only is renowned for his great creativity, but who encompasses so many personalities that he has become a myth himself. A myth tells the story of the origin, the preservation, the development and the dissolution of a human system, from the individual to its overall, transcultural constitution. All myths have heroes, and all are structured similarly, regardless of the culture to which they belong. First of all, there is the hero's birth, which can be more or less striking and may be connected with some sign, such as a sudden snowfall. Then come the crises - leaving the family nest, losing loved ones - which are followed by an even more painful loss: the dismemberment of a personality which inevitably accompanies a crisis. By withstanding such hardships, the hero indeed dies a symbolic death, but is re-born to a new dignity.

Most journalists who publish "interviews" have never actually met Mr. García Márquez. Part of what will be said today may also appear a bit contradictory; we should keep in mind that it is a poet's right to describe a single reality in different ways, depending on his ever-changing point of observation. Mr. Gabriel García Márquez does not wish to give a lecture, but rather to discuss the nature of the creative process and what positively or negatively influences it.

In the latter half of our century, no author - with the exception of Hemingway - has stirred the fantasy or the imagination of people the world over as has Gabriel García Márquez. He is a legendary figure. Because of this, especially after his Nobel Prize for literature in 1982, he has also become a public figure, hindered by the burden of glory which not only threatens his private life and his existence as a writer, but renders them quite impossible. He knows only too well the weakness of power and the solitude of the marathon runner, and even worse, becomes a target for every kind of projectile. Day and night he is pressed by people who want something from him. He takes his responsibility seriously and works like a forced laborer, striving not to let himself fritter away. He writes at a steady pace, so as to produce a new book regularly, such as *Love in the Time of Cholera* a couple of years ago. He is a man of many trades; how he can pack everything he does into a 24-hour day, one cannot imagine. He studied law, but fell in love first with poetry and then with literature during his studies. And as he became acquainted with Virginia Woolf, Faulkner, Pablo Neruda and others, he found his law studies increasingly commonplace and eventually gave them up. He began working as a journalist, paid by the line, which meant he had to write miles and miles to be able to get by. At one point he even considered buying an encyclopedia in La Guajira, a sparsely populated peninsula in the Caribbean, where people would not expect anyone with an encyclopedia to pass through.

García Márquez was born in 1928 in Aracataca, a small village in Colombia. His grandparents on his mother's side came from the flatlands of La Guajira in the Caribbean area, where the tropical vegetation thrives, as exuberantly as the imagination, narrowing the gap between those who observe their surroundings through scholarly eyes and those who observe it intuitively. The area is rich in beliefs and superstitions, and over a century ago intuition gave birth to a unique image of the world. The mixture of Indian, Black and White chromosomes created a very special breed of people, driven by the Mediterranean effusion of an immense *joie de vivre* on the one hand, and yet reserved and even inclined to sadness on the other. Such indeed are the "tristes tropiques" (sad tropics) of Levi-Strauss.

Gabriel's grandfather took part in the civil war which tore through the land at the turn of the century, as a colonel on the side of the liberals, who were seeking to overthrow the conservatives in power. Gabriel García Márquez was born on a continent which for hundreds of years was looted by White colonists and where the natives in power staged one coup d'état after the other, proving true to the motto: "Plus ça change, plus ça reste la même chose" (the more it changes, the more it stays the same). Power, weakness, death, solitude and the military were not the private obsessions of Gabriel García Márquez, but rather the themes of an entire continent echoed by Pablo Neruda, Jorge Amado, Mario Vargas Llosa, Isabel Allende, Carlos Fuentes, Octavio Paz and so many others. The great voice which rang true from this land to give all the others a stronger identity, however, was his.

His song is a "canto hondo," surging from deep within as the poet Yeats so perfectly expressed: "God guard me of those men who think in their mind alone; he that sings a lasting song, sings in his marrow-bone." His song indeed springs from the marrow, and I am happy that we can now venture into this world together.

Gabriel García Márquez

Y ou cannot imagine how difficult it is to be a myth and to be sitting here. Of all that Gottlieb has said about myths, there is one important condition which he forgot - or was too discreet - to mention: being invisible. The quality of being invisible helps a myth to grow, strengthening and sustaining it at the same time. It is a snare into which I have fallen. I am practically invisible, not because I am a myth, but basically because I am shy.

This is the first time in my life I find myself before an audience. I have never given a conference, I have never taken part in a writers' congress. I have great respect for writers and for their congresses, but I have always thought, albeit I may be wrong, that we writers are made only to write. Life is the substance, the raw material and the product of the profession of writer. A writer who does not live is dead from the beginning.

When I am not writing, I am usually in the company of a small group of old friends. I discover that through some inexplicable mystery, I am in several places all at the same time. I remember being in my home in Mexico, reading the newspaper at eight in the morning, and there were all the details of a conference, absolutely untrue. However, I have honestly had to admit that if I had really given that conference, I would have said exactly what was stated in the newspaper, for it corresponded exactly to my way of thinking, and even to my own words.

I am very hesitant to give press interviews or television interviews. First of all, it takes a great effort on my part to overcome my initial reluctance, and secondly I have the impression that it is always the same interview. I am always asked the same questions and I always have the same answers ready. Despite my reticence, there are many interviews of me, some good, some bad. The best one was in a Montevideo newspaper. It was an absolute fake, but it is the best interview that has ever been published, a synthesis of my way of thinking that I had never succeeded in conveying in an interview. I found it so interesting, I wrote the newspaper to find out who the author was, and that created a terrible state of confusion. You see, the person who had signed the interview did not exist; it had been mailed in spontaneously, and as it was so good, it was published. The greatest confusion is that the newspaper people, who were so delighted with the interview, were very disappointed in my curiosity about the author, because they thought it was a self-interview which I had signed with a pseudonym so as to be able to express my true thoughts at long last!

It is very funny to see how I inaugurate writers' congresses, give speeches, make statements, visit presidents and personalities all over the world, when in fact I am quietly at home, waking up at five in the morning to work until eight on the mass of papers left over from the night before. I suppose I could get up at five, but it is such a lonely hour! I have the impression that the whole world is asleep and only I am awake, and that fills me with a terrible sensation of loneliness. So I prefer to work in bed until eight; I write from eight in the morning till two in the afternoon. In the afternoon I always have a lot of appointments for a host of things - although not as many as Gottlieb said. There are some, and the others are taken care of by all the García Márquezes out there, whom I don't even know. There is the one who studied law, the one who goes around with presidents, the one who proselytizes, and even the one who sings. I know of a tape that people say I recorded singing at a party. I do sing at parties, but at this one, I neither sang nor was present. Besides, I wouldn't like the tape to be mine, because I sing better than that anyway.

Now, why am I here? I am here first and foremost because after forty-five years of writing every day, of having sustained my own myth, I asked myself: Why do you write? Why does one dedicate one's entire life to inventing stories? What does that creative vocation, to which one sacrifices everything, consist of? Why does one practically immolate oneself for it, doing something which, in my opinion, is very honestly no good for anything? In other words, there came a time when I began thinking seriously about the mystery of artistic creation, and in my case, of literary creation. Why does it happen, and above all, what is the process through which one can make it happen? Even more difficult, what is the process through which one can make it happen well, to such an extent that one succeeds in deceiving mankind, making everyone believe that it is a very important thing? As I asked myself these questions, I decided to open a workshop for scriptwriters, trying to set a trap for the mystery, to see if I could capture it. Every year for three weeks I get together with a group of ten young men and women from Latin America. (There are more women than men, so it must interest them more than the men.) The ten of us sit around a table with a tape recorder, the door closed, for four hours every day, inventing stories. The principle is always the same: who has an idea? One of the ten expresses an idea, and from there, all together, we explore the possibilities of the story and see it through to the end. We have never failed. Every idea winds up being a story. Of course you need a moderator, someone with experience - which is where I come in. At one point I take command of the idea and see it through. The wonderful thing is that we prove to ourselves that you can make a story out of anything. We know that what we are inventing has been happening to a lot of people for a long time. We're merely putting it together differently to come up with a new ending. The last time we held our workshop, we decided to think of half-hour subjects for television. In the three weeks it lasted, we came up with forty-three valid subjects, and the last one, we did in three minutes. I looked at my watch and said, "We've got five minutes until the end of this year's workshop, let's do a story." We did it in three. One person got up and said: "A young social worker goes to visit a young prisoner and they fall madly in love. What happens?" Someone else said: "She helps him escape so they can be happy." Fine. How does it end? Someone else said: "They're terribly unhappy, so he decides to turn himself back in so she can continue visiting him in prison and they can be happy forever." Three minutes! Of course, then we developed the story, who he was, who she was, how he managed to escape, but that was the easy part.

Guntern: You have told us how you come up with film scripts through a creative group process. But for a long time, most of the time, you wrote by yourself; you built pictures in your mind, you created characters and invented relationships, all alone, without the help of any team. *Poiesis* means the act, the deed, the design. A creative person must first have a sense of perception. When I read *Big Mama's Funeral,* for example, I was struck by the following sentence about an old priest: "He did not realize that he had become so subtle in his way of thinking, that for the past three years during his moments of meditation, he had not been thinking at all." You once said in another context: "I only write about things that I have observed." How do you reach this paradox?

García Márquez: I have often repeated that there is not a single line in my work that does not stem from something that actually happened. I am always very impressed when people talk about my extraordinary imagination, my capacity to fabulate, when I know that I am terribly subjugated to reality; I cannot write anything which does not begin with a true happening. The sentence concerning the priest that had become so subtle in his way of thinking is no more than a literary toy, a manner of speaking, a play on words. As a person, the priest exists in real life, I knew him. My work is full of priests because I was reared in little towns in Colombia where the most important person was always the priest. So every priest in my books is a sort of collage of bits and pieces of various priests: the eyes of one, the mouth of another, the legs and way of thinking of yet another. I reached a point where for many years I really thought there were priests like those I had made up from bits and pieces of others. For a long time I wrote without being really aware of where the things I wrote came from. I woke up after a time, above all by reading what the critics said. I am not at all afraid of bad critics; they don't say anything worthwhile. It's the good ones that frighten me, because usually they take apart the elements that I wrote unconsciously and make me aware of them and lay them before me on the table. Ernest Volkening, a great German critic who lived in Colombia, would analyze my early stories and discuss the way I treated the women in my books. It seemed evident to him that for me, the women took care of things within the home while the men went out making all sorts of blunders. I went back over my books with that observation in mind, and I discovered that it did indeed seem so; it showed through my work, although I was not conscious of it. What hurt me was that at the time I was right in the middle of *One Hundred Years of Solitude*, developing the character of Ursula Iguarán, who had that very function. From that moment on, I had to make a tremendous effort, for I no longer knew if I was developing the character that I wanted to develop, or if I was already consciously developing the character that the critic had said I wanted to create. In short, I didn't know if it was I or the critic who was writing. I had the fabulous luck of surviving what the critic had said and go on developing my character, but those who have read *One Hundred Years of Solitude* are certainly aware of the problem. In the outline I had made of the book, Ursula Iguarán was to die when the wars were over. When the time came for her to die, it dawned on me that if she died then, the book would collapse entirely. I did not keep to a chronology, for I did not want to limit the time in *One Hundred Years of Solitude,* but just let it flow in such a way that one wouldn't know the characters' ages. I reckoned that if the novel had been limited in time, Ursula, who was already one hundred years old then, could have reached the age of one hundred and fifty or one hundred and sixty, had she lived through the wars. So I decided then and there that it didn't matter, that I had to go on, and I did - until the moment Ursula died, which was after the banana plantation disaster. She was going to be too old anyway, but I realized that if she died at that moment, her character had such an impulse, it would carry the book to the end through inertia. So on I went, forgetting one detail which I only remembered about five years ago, as I was going through papers. I found a note according to which Ursula was not supposed to die as she dies in the book: she was supposed to start shrinking, until at one point she was buried alive in a shoe box. I had forgotten about that part, and it hurt me so much to have forgotten, that I wanted to rewrite the book twenty years after it had been published. What happens is that as a rule, I never re-read a book once I've corrected the printer's proofs; I'm too afraid of discovering incorrigible mistakes. And of course, I would never go back and correct them. But this is just an example to show that all my characters and all the events in my books are inspired by real things. I don't believe I have such a great imagination and such great fantasy as people say, but rather a certain power to transmit reality poetically.

Guntern: Your original idea of Ursula growing smaller and smaller reminds me of an experience that the sculptor Alberto Giacometti also had. His sculptures kept getting smaller and smaller, and in the end he would carry them around in a matchbox in his pocket. One day, when he was in Paris, he ran into a very good friend of his who asked him how he was, and he replied, "Lousy." His friend asked, "But why?" So he took the matchbox out of his pocket and said, "Look at this." His friend took a look inside, perplexed, and Alberto said, with deathly sad eyes, "They keep getting smaller and smaller." But he did exactly as you did, he decided they shouldn't get any smaller, and they ended up, as everybody knows, growing rather big again. Another example from *Funeral* is a hero named Damaso. He breaks into a billiards room, steals three balls, takes them home, and then many strange things happen in the village. Finally one night he breaks into the billiards room again with the intention of putting the balls back because he has noticed that since the theft, there has been a lot of hatred and confusion in the village. The second time he breaks in, he gets caught and the chapter ends with a crazy sentence: "You will be punished, thrown into prison or shot, not because you have stolen these balls, not because you have committed a crime, but because you have become so stupid." How does this story fit in with reality?

García Márquez: This is the only story which is absolutely true, written exactly as it happened, except the end. In real life Damaso, the main character, remained the suspect for the theft of the billiard balls, but never confessed to it. Instead they punished a Black man who wasn't from the village, exactly as related in the story. This happened in the same village where the crime in *Chronicle of a Death Foretold* took place. The story is absolutely true. I wasn't a direct witness to *Chronicle of a Death Foretold* because for some reason I wasn't there at the time, but I knew all those involved, I knew all the details of the story, I had all the information at hand. At that time I was a journalist; I hadn't published any books yet, I was just a journalist trying to write the story. But my mother asked me not to. It would have been my first book. I mean, it was the first impact I had had of a real-life event that inspired me to write something. My mother was a very good friend of the family's of the boy murdered in *Chronicle*. Those who have read the book remember that when he goes to seek refuge in his home because they want to kill him, his mother closes the door and he is killed against the door. My mother told me her friend would never be able to bear seeing in writing the moment when she shut the door, thus causing her son's death. So I kept the story a secret for almost thirty years until the mother died. I was in Barcelona. I received news of her death and I called my mother and said, "Can I write the story now?" She replied, "Yes, but be very careful." I wrote it exactly as it happened, only with my own interpretation, from my own point of view. It's a drama of youth, everything happens between young people, and the adults are like shadows that don't understand what's happening. The book was published, the journalists discovered it was a true story and went to look up the protagonists who were - and are - still living today. They talked with them and it was really very unpleasant. My mother was scared when she saw that the book was selling like my books do sell in Colombia, that is to say, at the city streetlights, like smuggled cigarettes. When she saw that the entire country was finding out that her friend had closed the door, my mother phoned to ask me to call back that edition. I told her: "Mother, there are seven hundred thousand copies in the streets. It's impossible to call them all back." She replied, "It doesn't matter. You can do anything." And it dawned on me right then and there that my own mother had swallowed the story about my being a myth. Now I'm a bit more resigned.

I should like to talk about that invisible boundary that exists for me between an article and a novel. I think they are two different things stemming from a common source and with a common end. *The General in His Labyrinth*, for instance, I consider more than a novel. It is an article about the last days of Simón Bolívar. To write *En este pueblo no hay ladrones* (In This Town There Are No Thieves*),* which you mentioned, I did the research of a journalist; the style and all the action, the development of the story is more journalistic than literary. That is why I am so interested in *Chronicle of a Death Foretold*; it is a total reality which has been transposed poetically.

Guntern: When I read *Chronicle*, I had the impression I was reading Sophocles. As a young boy I was in a boarding school founded by the Jesuits,

Gabriel García Márquez

and Greek was one of our main subjects. I have quite forgotten exactly what Sophocles and Euripides wrote, but I have remembered two concepts: one is the concept of *Moira,* which is the inexorable, ineluctable course of a process; the other is the concept of *Nemesis,* which consists in taking revenge for some reason; and often it is not the doer who takes his revenge, but most often something happens to avenge him without his even being conscious of it. The inhabitants of the village stand by like a Greek chorus, watching how this revengeful murder slowly comes about and cannot be prevented. They do talk about it, but more like the chorus in most of Sophocles' tragedies, standing on the side, watching and giving some stereotyped comment. How much have you been influenced by, for example, the ancient Greeks in your writings? To what extent have they helped you find certain layouts of reality?

García Márquez: Curiously enough I think there is a very strong and very constant influence and I hope it lasts all my life. But also curiously enough, this influence begins with the structure, the form. When I read Sophocles, and particularly *King Oedipus*, what impressed me most was how perfectly it was structured. It is absolutely invulnerable; it is a building which cannot be dynamited. It is no less a perfection of structure, than the scheme of a detective who winds up discovering that he himself is the murderer. That is one thing I feel has never been superseded. I read Sophocles at a time in my life when I was trying to discover precisely how to build a solid structure in literature. I think that novelists are very good readers, but the best readers are poets. Poets in general are people who acquire a great culture. We novelists only read to find out how other books are written. We read a book, and if it really interests us, we turn it around, we take out the nuts and bolts, we lay out all the pieces on the table, and when we find out how it has been written, we throw everything away and keep just the experience which is of interest to us. The first book I tore apart was Sophocles' *Oedipus,* without knowing that this is what all novelists do and that was what I was going to be doing all my life. Why is it this way and not that way? Why does it say this and not that? Of course Sophocles had the great advantage that the oracle already knew everything and had already written the book before he actually came to it. The fact that you could have a structure with no outlet of any kind is what impressed me about Sophocles and what I best retained; and if there is a story among my books which allowed such a structure, it is *Chronicle of a Death Foretold.* Now the strange thing is that the fate in the story, the part which cannot be helped, its Greek side, is no invention of mine; I related it exactly as it happened, and if by chance I made some literary addition, it simply concerned the problem of the collective responsibility that could have led me to a typical sort of analysis, which I have always tried to avoid. I think I even tried to lay out the plot without admitting the judgment. That is why the Greek flavor, the Sophocles part of *Chronicle of a Death Foretold,* is the mechanism of its structure. And the *fatum* part, the inevitable outcome, is the story as it actually happened. We might think that life keeps on repeating itself. The years go by, the centuries go by, but the human cycles are always the same, and life goes on repeating itself indefinitely. So said the critics about *One Hundred Years of Solitude,* although I never intended to write a cyclical book. I simply wanted to write a book where everything happened. Perhaps not everything did happen, but just about everything.

Guntern: You have described how a novelist reads: he takes one part at a time, unscrews what is still interlocked and spreads everything out on the floor. In other words, you do the same thing a child does with a toy to find out how it's put together. You give the toy death. Death is a theme which is present in all your books as a major part of the plot. My question is: what do you feel when you have created a character - with a spinal cord, skeleton, ribcage, muscles and blood vessels through which the blood flows; with a nervous system and a memory, endowed with the power to think; with a complete physiological system, prone to infection; a character of changing behavior - and then, one day, you have taken your creation so far, that he has to die? You have lived with him, you have grown fond of him, and then you strike him with death, kill him. What do you feel then?

García Márquez: You said, to begin with, that when a book is taken apart, it is treated as a toy. Of course the literary result is also a toy, but be careful with toys! Many years ago I was walking down a street in Bogotá where a lot of people were selling all sorts of things. One woman was selling little turtles which moved their heads around, and very much surprised, I asked, "Are those turtles plastic or are they alive?" She replied, "They're plastic, but they're alive." I never forgot that because that's a bit what we do. They're words, they're paper, they're toys made of words, they're toys made of paper, but they're alive.

Probably the most difficult thing for a writer or novelist to explain is the conception, the development and the death of his characters. Oddly enough the best experience I've had in creating characters, and probably my most important literary experience altogether, was with *Love in the Time of Cholera.* I shall take the liberty of giving the facts. I was creating Fermina Daza's family when she was very young. This is how I had imagined it: the father, the mother, the little girl and an unmarried aunt, the father's sister. I would put them in the house, I would sit the women down in a room to embroider, I would sit them all down to dinner. I knew what the father was doing, I knew what the aunt was doing, I knew what the little girl was doing but I did not see the mother. I would describe her, make her sit down at the table again, and she was just fake. She did not fit in at the table. This set me behind in my book for a long time, because she was an important person and was supposed to be an important character. Then I realized that the mother did not fit anywhere in the house because she had died a long time ago. That explains why there was an unmarried aunt; the father had had to find a substitute for the mother so he wouldn't have to bring up his daughter alone. The moment I realized this, I decided the mother had died in childbirth. And right then and there that character which did not exist, began to exist with such force for having died, that I continued writing, knowing that her presence could be felt in the house at all times, contrarily to when I had sat her down at the table to eat, or had made her embroider. She had a substitute, which was the aunt, who was a very important character for the little girl, but never really could replace the mother. There you have an example of a character who had to die before being born as a literary character. Yet the major problem related to a character is when he dies - not when one kills him, that is impossible to do. If a character is phony, you can kill him at any time. If he is real, if he really does exist in the book and consequently in life and consequently in the world, you cannot kill him. The great problem is to decide when he really dies, and if you hit it right, the character is valid; if not, he just floats around and there is nothing you can do about it. I have already given you the example of Ursula Iguarán whom I could not kill when I wanted to for purely technical purposes. I wanted her to die after the wars, because from a technical point of view, I didn't need her, I could go on without her. Well, she withstood, she refused to die before she had to. There was nothing I could do about it.

For me the most important case is that of Colonel Aureliano Buendía. Now I don't like him at all. He is exactly what I would *not* have wanted to be in life. He is a man who went through thirty-two wars and lost them all. It is obvious he had to lose them. He was carrying them on out of selfishness, out of resent, and for various reasons that are not worth going into at this point. When your characters come from the inside, they always carry a tremendous autobiographical weight. You do not know any experiences better than your own. So you inevitably give your character a lot of your own elements. I would say that Colonel Buendía was full of characteristics of mine that I wanted to exorcise, and yet, to my surprise, it hurt me a great deal when the time came for him to die. I suppose I am so attached to life, it hurt me even when the bad part of me died. I tried to let him live and invent something else for him. I thought about having him leave the country and converting him into one of those exiles you find in various parts of the Caribbean. During the war I had him fight in Central America thinking he might go back there afterwards. I even wanted to send him to Martinique, but it was not possible. I did not know how to end the chapter because I am basically a stylist and the problem with stylists is not only the word as such, but the great drama is the ending. A stylist always has to wind up with a great ending, if not, he is not satisfied. So I had Colonel Buendía urinate under a tree. I could not continue having him do trivial things and just wander around the house; I could not come up with anything else. And suddenly, as he was urinating, it occurred to me that the only thing that could happen to him was that he die. So very simply, I had him die. I work until two in the afternoon and it must have been one or one thirty or so when I wrote that, and I was terrorized that he was dead. But I realized there was no other way out, because that was the best ending to the chapter that I could find. So I went upstairs and cried for a whole hour.

If we start to analyze the deaths of my characters, we could probably write an anthology. First of all, because I feel that the only really important thing that happens to a human being is death. Everything else is a series of experiences that lead directly to death and nowhere else. You can say what you like, inevitably it leads to your death. This, for a narrator, for a witness and for a reporter like me is the most poignant drama there is. I am not afraid of death; I am afraid of the circumstances and the moment of death. But it doesn't hurt me to have to die; what hurts me is not going to be able to write about it and relate it as a capital experience. You see, I am going to end up relating all my experiences, and the one which is really worthwhile is going to be told by somebody else; yet nobody will be able to tell it better than me because nobody will know it better than me. So every time I face the problem of having a character die, I try to save him in every way, I try to beat around the bush, to let him live a little longer, and there comes a time when I just cannot any more. Therefore the best illustrated, the best worked-over, the best thought-out episode in each of my characters' lives is his death, simply because I always try not to let him die while death conquers him. And it conquers me. So your question is very pertinent. Death is so real, that even fictitious characters die; but it is death - and not the author - that kills them.

Guntern: I do not believe a person can mature and become a decent human being when he refuses to face up to his negative or despicable elements or tries to cover them up; when he denies his own development because death is inevitably in sight; when he or she tries all the tricks of the trade to do so. In *For Whom the Bell Tolls,* Hemingway leaves his character lying under a tree or under a stone by the Jordan River, his thighs broken, saying, "Dying isn't so hard when it doesn't last too long and doesn't hurt so damn much that one loses his dignity." Dignity - not pompous dignity, but the dignity that comes from within. You certainly have enough of such dignity and you also have several personalities, so I am sure that one of the many Gabriels within you will manage to write about the death of Gabriel.

Through your conception of the poetic reproduction of reality, we have dwelt on the theme of Death, which was very strongly imprinted on you by your family. As far as I know, you spent the first seven years of your life in your grandparents' house, and for years you wanted to write a novel entitled *La Casa (*The House*)* and that developed into, I believe, *One Hundred Years of Solitude.* You had aunts who were so familiar with death, they hardly knew the boundaries between life and death. Your grandmother, Tranquilina I believe was her name, would tell you, "If you're not a good boy, Gabriel, the ghosts will come for you!" And you also had an aunt called Francisca Simodosea, who sat down one day and began to weave a shroud. When asked what she was doing, she would reply, "I'm getting ready for my death." And when her shroud was finished, she lay down on it and died.

The culture of the peninsula of La Guajira, which combines Gallic, African and Caribbean influences, seems to be a very rich one, one which spontaneously integrates death into daily life, without put-on fears. As Heraclitus said, all life is governed by *Enantiodromia:* life leads to death, youth to old age, old age leads back to youth, bad leads to good, and great to lowly. Can you say a bit more about these childhood experiences which gave you a very natural and very early relationship with death?

García Márquez: The way you talk about my childhood makes me recall another interesting factor. Of course my grandparents' house in Aracataca and my childhood have greatly influenced my books. But when I hear you and others talk about my childhood, I realize that now my books are also influencing it. You talk about that house and that family not as they were, but as you see them through my books. The comparison is interesting because in the case of Francisca Simodosea, it happened exactly so. They saw her weaving her shroud, but she didn't die as soon as she had finished it, she died some time later. When I was writing *One Hundred Years of Solitude* the time came for Amaranta to die and I used the episode of Francisca Simodosea weaving her own shroud. What does the poetic transposing consist in? I had the image of my aunt weaving the shroud. I decided to quicken the entire process in Amaranta. She weaves her shroud and announces that she is going to die, gives a date and asks the people who want to send letters to their dead to write them quickly so she can take them with her because she's going to die in the afternoon. After writing that, I remembered that Aunt Francisca used to say something similar. Not necessarily when she was weaving, but she did say that she would like to take messages from the whole village to the dead. Thus I discover the origin of Amaranta's letters.

Yes, my major literary experiences do come from that house, and do so because it is located in the Caribbean. The Caribbean is endowed with an extraordinary magic. I think this is due to the fact that it is a sort of crossroads of three cultures - African, Indian, Andalusian or Gallego - which share a common, important if not basic element, and that is magic. I was not really aware of this until I went to Africa. Suddenly in Angola I started coming across domestic articles that I hadn't seen since my childhood. I had never been conscious of those objects that I had seen in my house and in all the houses in Aracataca and that I had forgotten. The discovery hit me like a concussion. Then I remembered an extraordinary experience that I would like to share with you.

When I arrived there (in Angola) my children were in New York. I tried to phone them, but for two days it was impossible because of bad connections. I became terribly desperate. On about the fourth day, I dreamt I was a child in Angola and I wanted to talk to my children but couldn't because I had to wait for many years until they were born. This is an extraordinary experience which shows to what extent those Caribbean cultural elements are anchored deep in my soul, in my personality.

That cultural region which is the Caribbean should also include Brazil. The Caribbean is referred to as a geographic area, but it is above all a cultural area with many specific elements. In a way, those three elements were accumulated in my house in Aracataca because my grandmother and aunts lived there; it was a house of women. The only man around was my grandfather, and he was always going about his business and was very different from everybody; he was a bit "out of it." Men cannot imagine just how much they are outside the circuit of everyday life in the house. They do not realize that what I discovered as a child - that my grandfather was a stranger in his own home because he was surrounded by women, and I was a corporate part of that totally matriarchal society - is, to my way of thinking, at the origin of the "macho" behavior. "Machismo" in the Caribbean springs from that matriarchal force within the home which took care of all the decision-making so that when grandfather came home in the evening, everything that had to do with the household had already been taken care of. He would come home, giving orders because he had been a colonel during the war, and all his orders were executed. What he didn't realize is that his orders were exactly the same ones his wife and the other women had already given and had already been carried out. He would come home and say, "I want to eat chicken." But of course the chicken had already been prepared, and I was in on the women's secret. So I learned to look at the world from that point of view, from within the home, to the extent that my first desire to write something was a whole story that happened within the house and never stepped out of its boundaries. That's why my first novel was going to be entitled *La Casa* (The House). But it evolved into *One Hundred Years of Solitude* because everything that went on could not be contained within the house. I let it overflow into the town, but life went on inside the house. There were my aunts, who were of mixed blood, and my grandmother who was almost pure Gallega; there were the Indian maids and the Blacks who did all the heavy jobs. Within the house, of course, you could find all the social conventionalisms proper to a small rural bourgeoisie, but as human beings, we were all equal. And I began to think that everyone was like the people in our house, that the whole world was like our house, that life was like the life in our house. I found out later on that there were differences, and those differences alone served to give me a perspective of the house. I believe I was happy there, living amongst women, dependent upon them. And so my life goes on. All my relations, my wife, my literary agent, my colleagues, my best pupils, my best friends are women, and I do not regret it. I am doing splendidly.

Guntern: Let us discuss the significance of images in literature and poetry.

Throughout your entire work the images are very strong, very important. The reader has the impression that they are at the core of a crystallization process which slowly develops. I shall never forget the first scene in *One Hundred Years of Solitude*: clear water surrounded by polished white stones which look like prehistoric eggs. The image grasps you and does not let go throughout the book; it is a timeless one.

García Márquez: I have already said that everything I write comes from a visible reality. Consequently there is a visible image at the starting point. Gottlieb has just talked about the sentence in *One Hundred Years of Solitude* which describes "…a river of clear water which ran over stones, white and enormous as prehistoric eggs." That is a childhood memory I have of when we would go and bathe in the river. I saw these stones when I was very young and had not seen them again when I wrote *One Hundred Years of Solitude*. When I went back to the site after the book, I realized that I had written what was in my memory. The stones which had seemed so enormous to me before were not all that big. But during that trip I navigated again through the huge marshes which lie near Aracataca, the Great Marshlands where the rivers which run down from the Sierra Nevada throw themselves into the ocean in a sudden drop. That is why they accumulate stones and why the stones are so polished: because the currents are so strong.

Not so long ago we took a canoe trip up one of those rivers. I was with some friends who had read *One Hundred Years of Solitude* and they were very surprised to see the stones, but more so to see that the canoe advanced through clouds of yellow butterflies that I remembered so well from my childhood. They noticed it and the owner of the canoe said, "Look, I was born here and I can swear that neither the stones nor the butterflies existed before *One Hundred Years of Solitude*." He was convinced that they had appeared afterwards. I think he was right. He had seen them but not taken any notice of them until the tourists started coming and looking for the yellow butterflies. The bookworms found the yellow butterflies and the stones, and this is becoming a phenomenon in Aracataca. Students, teachers, simple readers, a lot of people come from all over, and there are some children in the village who live off this. They wait for the visitors at the station and take them to the tree where Colonel Aureliano Buendía died; they take them to the garden where Remedios, the beautiful girl, went to Heaven, body and soul. They have found places all over town which correspond to the places in my books. Then there are the people who see yellow butterflies which have always existed but say didn't exist before. The butterflies are images of my childhood and they are the starting point of many episodes in my books.

One *Hundred Years of Solitude* was for years merely the image of an old man who would take his son to become familiar with ice. That image is my own, but curiously enough, I was not taken to be familiarized with ice. What I remember is the day I was taken to see a camel in a circus which had just arrived in town. I do not know how far my grandfather had got in his schooling, but I do know that he would always look things up in the dictionary. I remember he took me to the circus, showed me the camel, and when we got home he consulted the dictionary to find out the difference between a camel and a dromedary. Oddly enough, with time the camel turned into ice. But there I was recalling an image which actually belonged to another period, which is when a fish arrived in town completely frozen. There were no refrigerators, but my grandfather had told me he would take me to see how they brought in the fish. They opened a box of fish in the market, and I saw smoke come out and imagined it was boiling. When I put my hand on the frozen fish, I felt I was burning myself with something very hot. From that tableau, *One Hundred Years of Solitude* took off.

Now, where I can define perfectly how an image was the starting point for a story is in *The Autumn of the Patriarch*. I knew that I wanted to write the story of a very old dictator who lived alone in a house, but I didn't see the house, I didn't know how it was, I didn't have the slightest idea. I had tried my hand at the book several times, but I just wasn't able to grasp it. One summer day in Rome, in a book shop in the Piazza di Spagna, there was a color photograph book open in the display window. It showed the picture of an Indian palace in ruins with cows browsing through its mosaic and marble rooms, eating the vines which hung from the ceiling. At that moment my book was complete. I knew exactly what I had to say, where I had to start, I had it all, the length, the style, the method, the technique, everything. Because I had already solved all the problems except that one image which conditioned it all; the instant I saw it, before I even finished looking at it, all those dispersed elements had fallen together like the pieces of a puzzle. Then it was simply a matter of putting words to them, which was a long and difficult process. It was probably my hardest book to write and the hardest to read, but it is the one I consider most interesting from a literary point of view. I firmly believe that had it not been for that picture, my book would not exist. I bought the photograph book and of course I have kept it with deep gratitude not only because it provided me with the solution, but because it awakened me to the fact that all of my books stem from an image.

I knew then that *Leaf Storm (Hojarasca),* my first book, was born from an image of myself in that house in Aracataca, sitting frozen and terrorized on a chair. When I lent the original to Cecilia Porras, the Colombian artist who designed the first jacket, she came back the next day with a drawing of the little boy sitting down. It is an image which was not described specifically, but which undoubtedly is evoked throughout the book, and it is that very image that captured her. The little boy was I. To keep me quiet at night, the women would fill the rooms with ghosts, fill the house with fright. They would tell me that I could not go into such and such a room because Aunt Petra had died there; that I could not go into another room because there was a woman with no head. So reduced to a state of terror, I was confined to the chair and would not dare move until someone took me to my bedroom. That memory of myself was the starting point of my first novel. I do not know if it was very long, but let me tell you how it came about because it is the first episode of my memoirs. Yes, I am trying to write memoirs - not chronological ones, but around a theme. I am trying to explain - to the reader and to myself - the origin of each episode of my books. The aim is to sum up all the episodes in my books to wind up with a summary of my life. Perhaps the end result will be another fiction behind the fiction; but it doesn't matter as long as there is another book.

The first chapter is the detailed account of my first return to Aracataca, which I had left at the age of eight. The house had fallen to ruins, the family had been dispersed, the elder members had died, and one day my mother asked me to take her to sell the house. I agreed without giving it a second thought. I was almost twenty at the time, had already published at least three stories, and had begun the novel I told you about, *La Casa,* which had to do precisely with that house. The return was a terrible impact because the huge, happy, bustling town I had known was completely dead, dusty, and hot at two in the afternoon. I can recall walking through the town very quietly with my mother in mourning. There wasn't a soul to be seen. I knew what she was thinking. We came to a small pharmacy across the house, went in, and there was a woman behind the counter, at her sewing machine. My mother called her. She looked up, sprang to her feet, and they hugged each other and burst into tears without saying a word.

Now let me tell you something very seriously. At this point I had already written three stories, I was halfway through a novel, I had an entire column in a newspaper, and I was convinced that I would be a writer, and that nothing and nobody could keep me off the path I had already traced out. Looking back, however, I realize now it was *at that moment* that I really began to be a writer. In an instant, my life changed completely. As a child, one is not conscious of the past, simply of the future. One always thinks about what one is going to do, about coming exams, about school, about the next birthday, or when the circus will be in town. But the moment I saw the two women crying, I woke up to the immense past, not only my past, but that of humanity as a whole. I realized that there were ten thousand years of literature behind me that I had to become familiar with if I was to know when in the world I was writing, and how very tiny my voice could be within the enormous context of universal literature. I knew exactly, though, which that voice should be. In an instant I knew what place I already had in the world as a writer and what place I could have. I knew exactly what I had to do. I knew that everything I had written until then was of no consequence. I had a raw vocation, an intuition that told me I had to relate something, but I hadn't known what it was. Then suddenly, I knew! So the trip was a disaster because we had gone to sell the house and all I could think about was returning to Barranquilla, where I was living at the time, and start writing.

When I got home, I tore up all my rough drafts and started all over again with *Leaf Storm*. On the way home by train, we passed by a banana plantation called Macondo, and when I began to write *Leaf Storm* I decided that although Aracataca was a pleasant name, it was not a very poetic one. Macondo seemed much more appropriate for the world I had to rebuild, so very simply, that is how Macondo came into being, despite all the impossible interpretations the critics may come up with. Another thing is that Aracataca was too easily accessible by train, whereas you could never get to Macondo. I consider Macondo not as a place, but a state of being: mine on that hot afternoon that I had come home with my mother. So if you want to find Macondo, there is no point looking for it in Aracataca. You have to find the same state of being I have tried to render in my books. Every book, every line I write aims at instilling in the reader the same feelings that were mine at the moment I wrote them. If I do not succeed in conjuring up these feelings when I am writing, I have the impression that what I am writing is completely false. In a certain way it is still the same book with variations around a same theme, namely trying to find out why the things that happened to me happened; why one is born a writer, why one writes, how one writes. As Gottlieb stated, everything comes from an image or many images, never from an idea or a concept. I am a radical anti-intellectual. I feel that intellectuals try to accommodate reality to their schemes instead of taking their schemes from reality, which is what I try to do. As an anti-intellectual, I believe that had it not been for those memories that I succeed in recalling as though I were re-living them, I never would have been able to write anything. So if I begin to give examples of the images which have inspired my books, they are indeed numerous. In *No One Writes to the Colonel* I can remember perfectly well a very old man dressed in white at the market of Barranquilla, watching the river flow by. He reminded me of my grandfather who had lived to be very old, awaiting his civil war veteran's pension. My grandmother had always said that they were in a bad way, but that it did not matter because the pension problem was about to be solved, that the money was surely going to come through, because there had been a change in government. My grandfather died saying not to worry because he knew the pension would come through, even after his death. It never did. And that is what brought about *No One Writes to the Colonel* and *One Hundred Years of Solitude*.

Guntern: Metaphorically speaking they say that an initial creative idea is born in the bones, in the stomach, in the heart or in the mind. But strictly speaking, we know that the oldest part of our brain is the one that houses our instinct and is already found in reptiles. Federico García Lorca once said, "Instinct is the poet's only *raison d'être*." Arthur Miller, in his autobiography *Time Bands* says, "The chaos of our instinctive life is the fuel which turns our motor on." Metaphorically speaking, this would be at the level of the stomach, our instinct from within.

Behind the instinct part of the brain lies the smaller brain, which is probably as old as the instinct brain and which is responsible for our balance and co-ordination of movement. This comprises only ten per cent of our brain mass, but fifty per cent of the nerve cells, and evidently has a very important role to play. Einstein, when asked where his ideas originated, replied that they did so in motion - neurobiologically speaking, that is in the smaller brain - but he also said that they originated in images. Above the instinct part of the brain, we have our emotions. When you saw, for instance, your mother hugging her friend, and the house where you had experienced so many things, at that moment something happened. Although you had already published some articles, it is then that you became a writer in the true sense of the word. The emotional part of the brain is, metaphorically speaking, the heart.

Lastly, in the development of the brain, came the reasoning part, the mind, which comprises two hemispheres: the right, which is older and more closely linked with the emotions and houses intuition and images. You said, "My images set the whole process into motion." An abstract sentence or a mathematical, abstract, arbitrary symbol do not appear to spark off a creative process. Our left hemisphere, that of rational thinking, does not instigate anything new. New ideas spring from other sources - from the bones, the stomach, the heart - which help us to construct something.

García Márquez: If I had known everything you have just explained, I would never have been able to write a single letter. Let me explain: not because I underestimate what has just been said, but because it would be a scientific conditioning with which my method of writing could not cope. In reality, first I write how I think things are, and then I check my work to see if I am being illogical or contradictory, and I do so very seriously for quite a while. I correct my books until I am satisfied. But after forty-some years, experience has taught me that there are other ways - I could not say which - to reach either the same point or some other absolutely inexplicable and mysterious one. I shall give you just one example out of many: *The General in His Labyrinth,* whose historical facts were rigorously checked. Even the character's subjectivity, which is essential to the book, is strictly documented in Simón Bolívar's letters. When I came to an element that nobody could prove with documents, I was in seventh heaven because I could do what I wanted and nobody could contradict me. I am always very wary of the fact that the slightest detail which may provoke the slightest doubt can be picked out by the reader who knows that such or such a detail is true or false. It is surprising how much people know. There will always be a reader who finds a mistake that one would never have imagined was made.

It was in the first or second chapter of *The General in His Labyrinth* that I had to describe Bolívar's first night of exile. I knew the place, I knew what it was like, so the geographical description was no problem. But as regards Bolívar's likely state of mind that night, I figured there must have been a full moon. I had to describe that full moon and the ghostly light it shed on the town, the eerie atmosphere it created, because it was a moon that could very well have been in pace with Bolívar's state of mind. I finished the book and at the second or third revision it suddenly dawned on me, "But this is the night of May 8-9, 1830, and it is questionable whether or not there was a full moon." Somebody was bound to know and if they found out it was not true, they were going to think that all the other facts were false. So I consulted the Academy of Sciences and asked them to give me the phase of the moon on that night at that place. Was I in for a surprise! What I thought was an easy question, turned out to be terribly complicated. I learned that in order to find out when the full moons had occurred, you had to start with the eclipses, for there has to be a full moon in order to have an eclipse. They managed to establish many of the full moons of the first thirty years of the nineteenth century, and on the night of May 8-9 - any one of you can verify - there was indeed a full moon. This sort of thing happens to me quite often. Of course I have a perpetual calendar so I know what day of the week such and such a date fell on, but I always guess first, and when I go back and check, I am seldom wrong - at least as concerns the facts that can be verified.

When it comes to flowers, I have a big problem. I like having flowers and birds in my books, but I choose them for the lyricism in their names. So I put geraniums on the beaches of the Caribbean, and when Mercedes reads that, she makes such a fuss, because she is an expert on flowers and knows that there cannot be geraniums in the Caribbean. But I leave them there because they have a nice ring; I need them to sound nice and above all to smell sweet. The curious thing is how to know when the reader is going to accept something arbitrary and when he is not; that is a mystery. It might take place on I don't know which of the floors in that cerebral building you spoke about, but I don't care to know. Hemingway, in his very famous interview in the Paris Revue where he spoke about his method of work, gave two or three lessons which were vital in my life. One of them is the famous iceberg theory, whereby the immense iceberg could not keep above water if it were not for the seven eighths of its volume below the surface. That made me realize that for each sentence, each episode, each risk one takes in writing, there have to be seven eighths below to support it. The first thing I do is describe the visible part, then I investigate the seven eighths below in case there might be a flagrant contradiction. But basically I feel that when one plunges into arbitrariness and fantasy, another distinct logic is created which is equally respectable. Arbitrariness also has its rules and one has to know them to respect them; otherwise it will lack poetical and literary meaning. Hemingway's advice taught me that you can invent what you like as long as you can make it credible. The reader is always on his guard. A writer does have the right to deceive him insofar as he is willing to be deceived, to accept the impression that he is being hypnotized, but not insofar as he is not willing to be deceived, for the entire book would end up losing its value if the reader found an error.

That is why I said at the beginning that I am afraid of critics: they make me conscious of what I am doing. When a writer cannot leave free reins to intuition and to that entire unconscious battery which can be found in every creative process, if he becomes aware of all that unconscious battery, then he is not able to move; even worse, he is not able to live. So I think you are right, but I am also right in defending myself from your arguments, and I have to take care that they do not tear apart what I have written. The problem is that writing is much more difficult than people think. The hardest thing to do is to make what one has written appear easy. I have gone back over an edition for an entire month because of an adjective I did not like or with which I was not satisfied. As long as I have not found the exact word, I have the impression that the reader is going to know and is going to punish me for not having worked hard enough to convince him one hundred per cent. It is very difficult. I write every day of my life, from nine in the morning to two in the afternoon, according to my program, but at least four hours and hopefully six. Sometimes I feel happy if I've gone forward just one line. Normally I write a page a day, and usually

I take it to bed with me and tear it apart. If I manage to write a page a day, I consider myself lucky, and there is no greater joy than succeeding in writing what you wanted to write. But it requires a tremendous effort. It means attacking all fronts, re-inventing life, but with the immense presumption that it is better than life.

Guntern: You have shown very clearly and used many examples to illustrate how you build the crystals of the iceberg underwater with unbelievable care. If the creative process is never to run out in art, science, or any other field, chaos and order must dance a tango together and each lead in turn. They have to go from slides and glissades to sudden stops, abrupt breaks and many crazy things. There are creative people who work better if they follow a strict order of things - da Vinci, for example, used to say, "Lavorando ostinato rigore." Hemingway, whom you mentioned, once said that a writer had to polish each sentence until it became as sharp as the *estoque,* the sword used by the matador to kill the bull. Flaubert went even further when he stated, "I would rather die like a dog, even if only to gain one second, than to leave a sentence before it was perfect." These are two men of literature. Picasso, a master of pictures, was more inclined to chaos and felt that, "Quand c'est fini, c'est foutu." (When it's finished, it's done for.) Sometimes he would have wanted his work to remain imperfect. Now you are a man of letters and a man of pictures. How do you get round this tango of chaos and order?

García Márquez: Quite simply. I work in a chaos, but a strictly rigorous one, otherwise I could not manage. I wish I could remember the brilliant arguments of St.-John Perse, who dedicated his Nobel Prize speech to the theme "The Relation of Methods in Poetry and Science." Unfortunately I don't, but it would be interesting for you to keep his speech in mind for the next crazy writer you may get here.

I could never be an academic because I believe in the chaos of life. If I did not, I do not think my books would be read. I intend for them to resemble life. That is why I do not want *One Hundred Years of Solitude* to appear on the screen. Note that I do work in the film industry and have a great respect for it, although the only thing I have studied academically is the cinema. I attended the Center for the Experimentation in Cinematography in Rome because at that time I thought that the cinema was probably the best way to express myself much more deeply. Later I found out it was another story when you took into account all the technical and economic conditions that go with the cinema and which you do not find in novels. The work of a novelist is the loneliest in the world. In other fields, one can ask scientists and technicians for help and find

173

out about everything, but the moment you have to make a decision at your typewriter, you are absolutely alone; and the moment what you are doing starts looking good is absolute bliss. I could not see it any other way. I cannot imagine a greater sensation of happiness than when you feel that what you are writing is being dictated by someone within you, and you are simply taking it down. But I think I have gone off the subject, and I cannot remember what I was going to say.

Guntern: Time in the left hemisphere is linear; we have twelve, then one and then come three and four. Time in the right hemisphere, in the imagination, is circular. Time is always at hand; it is at hand now. Before we begin with the second part of our dialogue, I should like to read a sentence from the English translation of *No One Writes to the Colonel*. It is a dialogue between a young doctor and the old colonel waiting for the letter: "To the Europeans, South America is a man with a mustache, a guitar and a gun," said the doctor, laughing over his newspaper. "They don't understand the problem." I hope that we can continue to build together the imaginary realm, the true realm, the realm of the poetic reproduction of reality.

Discussion

Q.: Mr. García Márquez began his talk by saying twice that he was profoundly convinced that literature is useless. This rather surprises me. I should think he is not patient enough with his work. I feel that a person who writes books generally does so with the overall aim of helping people to progress. Is his literature indeed useless, do his books not allow us to progress?

García Márquez: This is a question I find very flattering, because it means some of you find that books are useful. I am speaking of novels.

To tell the truth, a little humility does not do us writers - especially famous writers - any harm. It does us good to believe that our work is not as good as we think it is at the bottom of our hearts. There is a bit of coquetry in that, to see if someone tells us we are really good. And then, of course, if one is convinced that the things he does are really useful, he probably will not continue to make the same, continuous and honest effort. So I should say that writing is useless, but you think it does serve a purpose, and let us hope that we all find it very useful.

Szeemann: It strikes me that when Gabriel García Márquez talks of images - maybe this has to do with his reporter's side - they are always pictures at eye level. When you lower your eyes, the images become crystal clear, be they the stones in the water, the child on the chair, and so on. This expansion of a precise view into the time dimension, combined with a strict regulation of distance in time and space, is something admirable. I also find it wonderful that tourists today are suddenly discovering the stones and yellow butterflies. Here we can draw a parallel with Felix Vallotton and the famous collector, Heidi Hahnloser, when she seemed to discover a cherry tree for the first time shortly after Vallotton had suggested she buy the little cherry tree painted by Hodler. He said this lovely phrase, which also applies to you: "La nature nous suit toujours." (Nature follows us always).

Now, about what is normal and what is exotic... Yesterday I quoted a sentence by James Joyce, who unlike you, goes from a concept and says, "I want what is normal, not what is unusual; that I leave to the journalists." Of course what is "normal" is relative. "Normal" in Colombia is simply more colorful as shown by your cliché. But I find it wonderful that this normal can end up in a coherent text through unusual and hard work. Take for example Kafka's executing machine which is credible only because it is text; or a woman turning 180 and getting smaller and smaller. This is possible in a text and it is just as real beyond the text. This is great literature. It follows up to what I feel when I read Márquez: that this union, this marriage between the historical and the extra temporal dimensions, this web, although it results from a precise outlook, is also interwoven in a person. Remember the words of the priest or of his characterization. The development of a human being is reflected in a single sentence: from being absorbed by religious issues to quietness to idle motion - all in one sentence - the development of fulfillment in a single formula. Tremendous.

García Márquez: Thank you very much. Let me just take a phrase he mentioned regarding Kafka and normality to express something I wanted to say somewhere along the line. When I read Kafka's *Metamorphosis,* I was in a students' boarding house in Bogotá. My roommate lent me the book, I settled down with it and read the sentence: "That morning Gregory Sansa woke up turned into a gigantic insect." Until then I had only read rhyming poetry. When I read that sentence, I thought to myself, "Ah, if this is allowed, I can probably do something in literature. If saying this is possible without it being taken as an absurdity but accepted as something real, then I can probably become a writer." This was a long time before I went with my mother into town. My discovery consisted in how naturally Kafka could make extraordinary assertions. There is another one that goes: "I have a small animal, half cat, half lamb," and he affirms this in a most natural way. You can feel that he

175

believes it; and if he believes it, there is a ninety-nine per cent chance that the reader is going to believe it too. He says, "There was a vulture pecking at my feet. It had already done with my socks, and now it went on pecking at my feet." He has such a natural way of relating things that would seem terribly abnormal but which wind up being perfectly normal in the story. I did not want to omit that experience because I also think it was fundamental for what I did afterwards. So I am very grateful you brought it up.

Kohler: I have a question concerning the images which are solidly anchored in reality and which you bring into your literature with such tremendous evocative force. Do they relate to the transmission of images in a film, if there are different degrees in images? I am thinking specifically of the screen adaptations of *Eréndira* and *Chronicle of a Death Foretold*.

García Márquez: That is a good question in the sense that I have been thinking a lot these days about the relationship between literature and the cinema. As I said this morning, I always used to think one could go much further in the cinema than in literature. But from what I have seen of the economical and technical drawbacks in films, literature is freer, more independent. I took the decision of going ahead with literature, but I have not been able to abolish the temptation to go into films. So for the time being I am doing both, and I have reached the conclusion that I have to keep literature and the cinema completely separated. This is precisely what I had intended to say at the end of the morning when I lost my line of thought.

I have decided that my novels not be made into films, particularly *One Hundred Years of Solitude,* because the screen image imposes faces on the characters, which cannot be eluded. Things have to be the way the director decides through the actor and not otherwise. In a novel there is a margin of possibilities for the reader to finish it as he sees fit and in a way come up with his own novel. As far as I have seen in conversing with some of my readers, one thinks Ursula Iguarán looks like his grandmother, another thinks the Colonel in *No One Writes to the Colonel* looks a lot like his uncle, that they're cousins, and they end up identifying the characters with members of their families. This is possible thanks to the extent of participation the reader has when he reads a novel. In films, and I am saying this in favor of the film industry, the image is so imposing, it is that way only and there is no imagining it any other way. So I have decided to continue working on my literature as literature and on films as films. They are two completely different, not interchangeable things, and many years of experience have taught me that there have been many good films made from bad novels, but very few good novels have resulted in good films - or at least in better films. The example is not very good, because I find it unjust that every time someone comes out of the cinema having just seen a film based on a novel, you hear, "The book was better" or vice versa. They are rather crude comparisons, but since they do exist, we have to deal with them. I feel that a writer of novels should go on writing novels, and if he has an idea for a film, he should participate in writing the screenplay. What happens with a scriptwriter is that he requires a great deal more humility than a writer of novels, who is the sole and supreme owner of his work. In the cinema, he has a subordinate position, for it is the director with all his staff who are going to wind up being the true authors. The scriptwriter is their humble servant and I think that is the way it should be. So the writer who wants to work in the cinema has to have humility, just as the director has to have full authority. I think that is very good for the cinema and good for the novel as well.

I very much like the example of *Chronicle of a Death Foretold,* which is actually the result of a happy weakness of mine. The book was made into a film. Francesco Rosi and I are very old and very good friends. For many years we had been talking about working together, and we had been thinking precisely of doing something on the life of Porto Ricans in New York. Francisco was very interested in the subject. So we came to an agreement which would really have been worthwhile if done by both of us. But the producers in the United States told him - and this is an example of how creation can be obstructed - that because people in the United States were particularly sensitive to the problems of Porto Ricans in New York, they could produce any theme except that one. That was that. Francesco and I went on with the idea that we had to make a picture together. When I was in Paris, Francesco called me from Rome and told me that he was going to come, so we had a long lunch together. We talked about everything and the next day, Tonino Guerra, Francesco's leading scriptwriter, phoned me and said, "You guys are imbeciles. You've had lunch together, you've been talking all day, and you haven't said a word about the cinema. Francesco went to Paris to propose doing *Chronicle of a Death Foretold.* But you are so negative about novels being made into films, that he didn't dare say anything." So I felt a bit guilty and phoned him up and said, "Francesco, do you want to do *Chronicle of a Death Foretold* ?" and he said yes. So he made the film and I think he did a good job, even if it has little to do with the book. It is an excellent film, and if it has not been more successful, it is because it has not been accepted in Latin America. The reason is they feel there is a cultural barrier which Francesco didn't succeed in overcoming. It's not his fault. It's the fault of the impenetrability of national cultures which is something one has to respect very much. Then I remembered having proposed that he make the same drama, but located in Sicily, because culturally and morally speaking, it is a drama which could be Sicilian or Andalusian. For production reasons, Francesco preferred making it in Spain. I think if he had made it in Sicily, which is his country, which is where he had worked, where he had the experience of other great films like *El Giuliano*, I think he would have done better. So this experience gave me an extra argument for not letting my books be made into films, but I am fully disposed to find arguments in favor of the cinema and I am constantly working at it.

In short films and novels, there are two completely different worlds sharing a lot of common factors. Doctors do not do engineering, nor do they aspire to build bridges. That is the way it should be, although the comparison may seem a bit strange. At any rate it explains very well what I am trying to say.

Compernolle: I have appreciated every second of what you have said. I am a child psychiatrist, and due to a series of coincidences, I work in Belgium and Holland not only with extremely disturbed children, but also with intelligent and sometimes very creative ones. This is to better situate my question. Last year, in searching for sources of creativity, I was impressed by the fact that with people like Botta, Sbarro, Maya Angelou, their creativity and their choice of expression - writing, inventing, building - was influenced by a childhood dream. Maya Angelou, as a very young child, was captivated by literature. Sbarro wanted to invent a water bicycle. These very creative people strike me as making a childhood dream come true, or even better, the child within them seemed to be extremely alive, active, stimulating the creative process. You just said that your life as a writer began when you were a young man; that you stopped your law studies to become a journalist, and that you were finally convinced by the encounter of your mother and her friend. I wonder, however, if you too are not fulfilling a childhood dream, if somewhere inside you, there is also a child's experience which pushed you to become a creative writer instead of a creative sculptor, a creative painter, a creative journalist or a creative businessman.

García Márquez: By "dream" do you mean an illusion or do you mean the experience one has when one sleeps? Is it an image I had while I was sleeping or is it something to which I aspire, an ideal?

Compernolle: The latter.

García Márquez: The only dream - ideal - I have had in my life is to be a writer. I have never thought of being anything else nor have I ever wanted to. I have had to do lots of jobs during my lifetime. When I began as a journalist at the same time I began as a writer, I was told: "Be careful, journalism kills the writer." I went on with journalism, I went on with my novels, and when I had to do some publicity, I was told: "Be careful, publicity kills the writer." Later on, when I started working with television and cinema, they told me: "Be careful, television and cinema kill the writer." The experience I have today shows that the only thing that kills the writer is death. Nothing else can kill a true writer for the simple reason that a writer writes because if he does not, he dies. Rilke said something that I will never forget: "If you think that you can live without writing, then don't write." And I always thought the only thing a writer could say is: "I know the day I have to stop writing will be my death day." There is no doubt about that, and I think the only thing that has ever kept me from writing a single day is health. I have an idea that may be very Hemingwayish: if you want to be a professional writer and always produce the same quality of work, then you have to live like a boxer. That is, you have to be in excellent health every day. I like having a drink or two with my friends, but I am always careful, because a hangover is terribly dangerous for a writer. Generally you begin a job in a given frame of mind, and the next day, if you do not continue the job in the same frame of mind, there is likely to be a change in the quality of your work. I take care to read the newspapers after work, and I never listen to the news on the radio or on television until I have finished working for the day, because they impress me. I have to keep the same frame of mind as the day before, and I take very good care of my health.

There was just one time I had to write when I was in very bad health, and that was during *One Hundred Years of Solitude*. I had very painful boils in the armpits - which kept recurring; they would heal then come out again. At one point I felt really terrible, but I had to keep on writing, and it was very painful. So much so, that I quite understood why the boils are called "golondrinos" in Spanish: because you have to go around with your arms up, like a swallow. The pain was tremendous while I was developing the character of Colonel Aureliano Buendía. As he kept winning his wars, I realized I had to give him a great handicap so things would stop going so well for him in life, so I decided on the armpit boils. I know the illness better than anyone, having gone through it for three or four months. I gave Buendía golondrinos that were even worse than mine. The reason I am telling you all this is that when I finished giving him the armpit swelling, mine disappeared for good, and that was twenty-five years ago. This leads to another mystery that I leave to you. Perhaps I am contradicting myself and it is better, after all, to write in bad health to live through an experience such as this one.

Compernolle: I liked your answer, but again, you begin your life as a writer the moment you become a journalist, as though there had been nothing before that, and my question concerned what came before that. Did you really become a writer the moment you decided to become a journalist, or was there something before that, in your youth, your childhood, was there some encounter with literature, with books, with a writer, a neighbor? I find it so extraordinary to become a writer one day as a young man of about twenty-three. All of a sudden, there you are, a writer, as though there had been nothing before!

García Márquez: I think I was a writer from the day I was born. Moreover, I think that every writer is a writer from the day he is born. I think that the fact of being a creator is a biological way of being. Some detect it, others detect it and develop it, others do not heed the divine call and do not go on. I detected it from the beginning. I can remember perfectly well when I did not know how to read. But I know the first thing I read were the pages of a book which was falling apart and came out of a drawer in the house in Aracataca. So without knowing what I was reading, I began to read these loose pages and for me, it was a marvelous revelation. Only as an adult did I find out that they were *The Thousand and One Arabian Nights*. But to me flying carpets and genies and magic lamps were not surprising because this was the sort of thing I would hear about all day every day in the house. My grandmothers talked about ghosts and the dead walking around the streets and they would tell absolutely fantastic stories, so I thought this book I was reading and the stories told by my grandmothers were all the same. I lived within a legendary world from the beginning, and then, at a very early age, I discovered poetry. Actually I started off with a poetic formation. I began with the short poems of elementary school, and as soon as I was able to read "adult" poetry, which was at around the age of twelve, I started doing so. There came a time during my end of schooling exams where I could recite by heart the most important poems of the Golden Century of Spain. Those are things you learn at a certain age and never forget. So I was giving myself an education in poetry, which is undoubtedly the literary base of everything I have written. On top of that, life kept setting traps for me so that there was no way I could escape from literature. Colombia at that time was a very centralized country. I lived in a town. There was a child born in our house every year; I am the eldest of sixteen children. The time came when I realized that the house - once my grandparents had died - was a sinking ship and the first rat to get away was me. "I have to get out of here or we're all going to drown. I'm going to escape!" Now escaping from that situation in Colombia at the beginning of the Forties was no easy task. I had to take a boat up the Magdalena River to Bogotá and take an exam with other students my age from all over the country to get a scholarship. If I lost the scholarship, I would have to go back home. The trip alone cost my parents a lot of money. But I made it, and it was risky, because I had to make it eight times during the exam period. The entire book *Love in the Time of Cholera* is based on my experiences during those trips and that last book, *The General in His Labyrinth*, is the trip up that river. I would never have known that river the way I know it today if it had not been for those trips. I suppose we could say it the other way around: that I thought up the stories because I already knew the river. In the case of Bolívar, his life and his character would have interested me, but without that river, I would not have been able to write about him. The point I want to make is that I obtained a scholarship for Sipaquira, which is a town near Bogotá. It was a laic boarding school, but the building was an old 17th century convent. They would get us out of bed at 5.30 am, and since there were no showers, they would take us out on the patio to be hosed down. But at that hour, at an altitude of 2,600 meters, it was just as cold on the patio as it is outdoors here now. Every day after our bath, they would inspect us to see if our fingernails were clean, our hair was combed, our shoes were shined. It was a hard life, very disciplined; (I do not believe in writers with no discipline). Inspiration and talent have to be accompanied by one's own strict regime and nobody else's.

I have never been able to write in pajamas and slippers. I wake up at 5.30 am, correct whatever was left from the night before, and at seven or eight I always have a cold shower. I get dressed - not with a tie, mind you - but clean and presentable like to go to the office. All this is part of a discipline which has been very useful to me in life. As there was nothing to do on Saturdays and Sundays in school, I would go to the library and read. I read all the books in the library in the six years I was in the school, in the order in which they were arranged. There was a bit of everything; books left by teachers; books left by people who were just passing through. Now that I think of it, there were three enormous volumes which I know now were written by Freud. I can just see myself at the age of 13 or 14 reading Freud page by page and with as much fascination as I had had for the *Thousand and One Nights*. And now I know why: they were clinical stories. They were personal dramas which he transcribed directly as the patients related them. I was as interested in Freud as I was in Quixote and Lazarillo de Tormes, and everything I read afterwards. I left school with a poetic education which I think was quite good, thanks to all this chaotic but rigorous reading. I acquired a theory and technique of my own in literature, for nobody ever taught me how to read or write. I went about constructing my life with what I found, which was life itself. From that moment on, I never read systematically; I would just read the books as they came and as far as I enjoyed them. I am a thoroughly self-taught man who, as all self-taught men, lives his life by filling up holes. I was greatly comforted when I saw Hemingway's library in La Havana. It was exactly like the library in my school, but obviously built up by himself for his own purposes. I have a great number of dictionaries - angel dictionaries, botanical dictionaries, witchcraft dictionaries - because dictionaries have the advantage of creating exactly the knowledge you need at a given moment, and then you can forget it forever. So whenever I am writing and some theme crops up, let's say cholera, I study everything I can find on the subject, and once I have finished my book, I forget about it and never have to remember it. That is how it was in Hemingway's library. You could tell he would send for books that he needed as he needed them and then would put them aside, and it ended up being like in my school. So when I talked this morning about rigorous chaos, I can demonstrate it at any moment as I have just done so now.

Wise: I have so enjoyed your stories of how you manipulate your characters at times, for example by giving someone swelling in the armpits. Your characters also manipulate you at times, and they may refuse to die, until it is right for them to do so. However I have noticed in your books that there is rather little dialogue. Sometimes I have to write drama serials for the BBC, and the story-line will go for two or three years only through dialogue, without any narration. I am interested in the difference between creating dialogue and creating narration. Perhaps I find dialogue easy, because of my Englishness, or the Shakespearean tradition, where there is very little narration. Perhaps you find the creation of dialogue too stressful, and therefore your creation comes in a narration with you as the observer?

García Márquez: That is a good question which I have been asking myself for some years. The truth is I have always been afraid of dialogues. In Spanish there are oceans between the written dialogue and the spoken word. This poses a very serious problem in the Spanish theater, because when the dialogues are written and then spoken, you can tell they are not natural. I could never get around the situation. Since I began writing, I have always shunned dialogue because it sounds phony. I have the impression I am not telling the truth. Now when I read Hemingway, I was greatly confused because I found his dialogues admirable. Then I discovered that they had nothing to do with real life but only with the reality of his literature. Then and there I decided to relate the dialogue in the general text and use only a few quick lines now and then, more for purposes of effect than for communication.

There came a time when I became seriously interested in the cinema, and I was faced with the problem of how to make films for the cinema or television without dialogue. So far it hasn't been possible, but I can humbly say I think I am learning. You can imagine how much I admire scriptwriters, especially Italian. I have never seen a country where they speak in the cinema or on television the way the Italians do. You could hear dialogues on Roman buses that were so coherent, you did not know if they were real or out of a movie. That is not the case with Spanish. People speak one way and write another way. So I am trying to learn to write dialogue, but in Latin America we have a problem: you can write a story for all the Latin American countries, but the colloquial dialogue changes every hundred kilometers! Writing a general dialogue for Latin America and Spain is very difficult for me. I do not think I am going to succeed. I do the themes for movies and someone else does the dialogues, but I am never satisfied with them. That is why there are so few dialogues in my books: not because I haven't wanted them, but because I haven't been able to write them. There is another technical problem: the duration of the dialogue is generally contradictory to the internal time of the narration. That is, I can put two centuries into four lines of narration, but a dialogue lasts only as long as it takes to say it. That is a very complicated technical problem over which I ponder in the solitude of my office, and with which I do not want to embitter anybody's life. I keep it to myself and consider it simply as one of those greater or smaller failures which we all have silently and which we shall try to take with us when we go, until some intelligent writer comes along and asks the question in public, and you have no choice but to answer it.

Billeter: I would like to come back to the question of the ordinary and the extraordinary, the exotic and the routine, the everyday and the exceptional or eccentric. I am asking this question as a journalist and a reader, more as a connoisseur of Kafka and a reader of Márquez. As somebody said before, as a journalist I have to produce the extraordinary day after day, or at least reflect it. Most of the time I perform it as well, and I realize that there is indeed nothing more boring than the unusual. I wonder why things take such a strange turn. But then I also think that having cakes every day would be unbearable too. I produce the extraordinary only in bits and pieces, day after day; consequently it is also consumed day by day and it disappears; nothing is left. Whereas in Kafka or Márquez the extraordinary becomes structure, cosmos, continuity, which does not leave me as long as I am reading. Something else has drawn my attention: the pope of surrealists, André Breton, who often gets on my nerves because he always wants to be so eccentric, has also said some wonderful things. He distinguishes between "le miraculeux" and "le merveilleux." "Le miraculeux" is wonderful in the sense that the priests and religion give it and in the sense of what is eccentric; it is a vertical shooting down, a phenomenon as quick as lightning, as fleeting as a moment, and it encompasses the negative surrealism that aims at bewildering by the unusual, for example, the latter Dali - the latter, not the former. "Merveilleux," however, defines the wonderful that is at the same time routine. In the fine arts, for example, if we stick to surrealism, we have Margritte; in fiction, we have Kafka on the one hand and Márquez, in a totally different manner, on the other.

García Márquez: We would have to begin with defining what is wonderful, what is magic, what is extraordinary. You are no doubt using French words that have the same meaning in Spanish, but at any rate, I think we could agree on one thing: that wonderful, the problem of what is wonderful or extraordinary lies in the measure, in the control; in knowing just how far you can go. We who write see this every day, and here too lies a mysterious factor. I am going to set a little trap; I am going to hide a bit and follow a path where we shall certainly find some answers. Writing *One Hundred Years of Solitude* left me many experiences, for instance, that of the beautiful Remedios ascending into heaven. Originally this episode was much simpler. She was sitting down sewing with the other women in the corridor, and at one point they looked up and Remedios was gone; she had disappeared. But I realized this was the lazy way out and the reader would not forgive me for that. I needed something precisely more extraordinary, *extraordinario*. There are many cases of levitation in Catholic mythology as well as of privileged beings who ascend to heaven, body and soul. So why not have Remedios do so? That is prepared almost like you would prepare the location for filming in the cinema. Where would the best place be? Not in the room, because of the ceiling. It had to be outdoors, in a garden. So I started working on the idea that she was cutting roses and suddenly she went to heaven, body and soul. I wrote it I don't know how many times, but it simply didn't happen. I didn't believe it myself and if I didn't believe it, the reader wasn't going to either. This was a particularly intense phase of work. I was so caught up in it, that for a long time I didn't go out. As a matter of fact, during that part of the book, it had been at least three months since I'd even gone into our garden. This was due primarily to the intensity with which I was working and secondly to the fact that I knew Mercedes was in a hurry for me to finish because there wasn't anything left to hock in the house. I couldn't afford the luxury of putting things off for much longer. And this is a consolation, for if I had had money, *One Hundred Years of Solitude* would be three or four volumes long; I had to omit at least two generations for want of money. Being in such a hurry, I was almost ready to give up on Remedios' ascension to heaven, body and soul. Fortunately, one day I went out into the garden for a bit of fresh air and I saw a woman who came to do our laundry struggling with the wind to hang out some sheets. I had the impression that if she clung to the sheets, they would take her away. So I went back to my desk and introduced the sheets into the scene (those of you who have read the book will remember the episode) and when they started folding them, they flew up ever so naturally. Remedios, the beautiful girl, also went to heaven ever so naturally. So how can we explain the miracle that made me go into the garden and see the sheets? There is another levitation scene in *One Hundred Years of Solitude* which is even more mysterious. I had always heard in my grandparents' house that there was a very holy priest who, at the moment he elevated the Host, was elevated himself a few millimeters from the ground, and I decided that I could have a levitating priest. I thought it could be at the moment when he took the wine, but I had two problems: one, it might seem as if he were drunk and this definitely did not coincide with the tone of my narration. Two, I had already made him drink wine several times and he had never levitated. So I had him drink all sorts of things and still he would not go up - until I had him drink chocolate - the thicker, the better, and then, up he went. What rule leads me? Very simple: if I end up believing it sincerely, without any sort of traps, then the reader will believe it. If the reader ends up believing it, it is the truth. Therefore the ascension, body and soul, into heaven is true, and if you do not believe it, read *One Hundred Years of Solitude* and you will see that it is so. And now we're back to the beginning.

Steiner: I appreciate what you have already told us, and I would like to try to go back a bit to the beginning of our interview this morning. You came here attracted by the concept that at this Symposium we would discuss the phenomenon of creation - artistic in your case. Yesterday we talked about creation in another context. Today you described various cases in which I had never seen the phenomenon of creation from so close up, like a mind, like a hand touching ice and a concept, an idea appears. My question is: as you were telling us about it, did you come closer to your question of how you create or how creation comes about within your person, or is the question still open?

García Márquez: I have not grasped very well what the distance between creation and creativity is. Probably it is just a hint.

Steiner: I believe what we are trying to find out in this Symposium is whether there is a link between creativity and world problems, for instance; whether you can take people's creativity and channel it so they can do something positive. Or does a person create only by the grace of God what he has the capacity to create? I believe we are trying to find out if creativity can be defined and if something can be done with it. In your case you have told us how you have done it, how you are creative and you came here attracted by the question. Have you come closer to the question?

García Márquez: For me the time we have spent here is a great experience because I feel I have learned a lot. I did not come to teach, but to learn. Now this is often said hypocritically. In my case it is very sincere because I am interested in going deeper into the process of literary creation and more concretely my own literary creation, which is the only thing I can answer for. I am interested in this because, as I was saying this morning, for a long time I have been asking myself why I do this. The memoirs I am in the process of writing will be more interesting if I can go even further in exploring my own literary processes. I should like to leave my readers a sort of big joke and tell them, "OK, I've created a world for you, you believed in it, and now I'm going to tell you how many lies and fabulation and untruths there were in that world I invented." But as I write, I realize that that very fact is creating another world behind the one I created; and consequently my memoirs may be the most fantastic of my novels. I am seeing this here with every passing minute, because I am very much aware of your reactions. I know exactly where you were more interested and where less and that is very important for one reason, namely that I write to be read. I have even gone as far as to say, more obscenely, "I write to be loved," so that my friends would love me more. I try to do my best each time so as to be loved more each time, because the need to be loved is an absolute, infinite sentiment, there is no end to it: voracity without cure. I am very interested in how to continue along these lines and I hope I can go on for the rest of my life. You can be sure I shall continue writing until my last breath, because I shall continue needing to be loved more and more until the end. What is more, I have been discovering lately with the book I am writing that there is a lot of drunkenness in narrating; it's a drug. So I shall continue narrating and searching and exploring and perhaps in the end I shall contradict everything I have said this morning, which is quite useless. Maybe it serves to make one loved, which is a lot in itself.

Guntern: Just another remark concerning the extraordinary and the construction of the extraordinary. We spoke of "merveilleux" (wonderful, marvelous) and "miraculeux" (miraculous). The ancient Greeks had an expression, *taumazein*, which describes the capacity to wonder with respect about what exists and to see what is particular therein. But this *taumazein* is the exact opposite of spectacular. When one talks of creativity, there is often a great misunderstanding as regards originality. Originality is not the enforcement of the spectacular; that would be extremely easy and even silly. If a schoolboy, for instance, showed up in school one morning with a cow instead of his homework, he would not be original. He would just be wanting to show off in a pathetic and crude way. The wonder with Márquez is that he makes wonder happen with the most subtle mechanisms and we, as readers, find ourselves in the position of the *taumazein* more often than not without even realizing it.

Q.: You told us how you wrote *Chronicle of a Death Foretold*. I would like to know what other of your works came from journalistic writings.

García Márquez: The things I wrote as a journalist until 1960 are published in six volumes. Thirty years have yet to be published. There will not be as many as the first phase during which I worked intensely in journalism. But I have used many more letters in journalism than in literature. As I spoke of a certain incompatibility between the cinema and literature, I must say, as I have been doing so for many years, that journalism is a sort of literature. Especially as I see it. Chronicles and reports are literary tools very useful for the novelist, just as being a novelist is very useful in journalism. In other words, the job of a journalist is important for the novelist because it makes research easier. At the same time the writer brings the journalist literary beauty and the precision of language. The most important journalistic contribution for a writer is that it keeps his feet on the ground; he never loses touch with reality. My books are full of journalistic means and ways. Those who have read or still read my articles, on the other hand, find them full of fiction. It's simple: I see the same reality in journalism as in literature and I feel that the boundary between the two is constantly growing smaller. What is happening is that great reporting in journalism is becoming extinct. I was formed by great American reporters. An entire generation (mine, from the forties and fifties) brought the reporting style into Colombia and other Latin American countries. This consists in making the newspaper reader know exactly what has happened as though he had been there. I think the expansion of radio and television is what has pushed reporting a bit behind the scenes and has ended up practically eliminating it and substituting it with interviews. Interviews are considered essential on radio and television. Not only that, journalism itself has been basically reduced to interviews. I know it and I suffer from it. I have spent hours with young journalists who have not learned a thing from what I have said because they always wind up asking for an interview and then they ask me two questions which are not any more important than everything they could have learned from a conversation. We will have been talking here for six hours and there are journalist friends waiting for us to finish so they can ask two or three questions. I was hoping they would ask them here, quietly, and we could have got that out of the way. Ah, well, I have great respect for the profession and I consider myself fundamentally a journalist. I think I am a novelist and a journalist. I want to continue being so because I do not find any difference between the two. From my journalistic writings, for example, there is a work known as *The Story of a Shipwrecked Sailor.* It is an article. There was a sailor who got shipwrecked and remained on a raft for fourteen days. I got hold of the news when it was no longer news. They had written all sorts of interviews, articles, asked questions and I got to see the man when nobody cared to hear about him anymore. So I told him, "If you were stranded on a raft for fourteen days, obviously you had to do something every minute of those fourteen days, so let's see what you did." I simply helped him think. We managed to reconstitute the story completely, almost minute by minute. It was published a chapter a day over fourteen days. The newspaper began selling better and by the time the whole story had been published, distribution had doubled. Some people from the newspaper itself were convinced that it was pure fiction, but there is not one single line of fiction in the story. The book is considered like one of my novels, but in reality it is an article and they teach it in schools not as an example of reporting, but as literature. The same goes for the journalistic works. So if we have not spoken specifically of journalism, it is because I consider it one and the same with literature. The laws I lay down for literature I use for articles. The sources of information are the same, the manner of elaborating the material may be the same, and hopefully the style and the way of writing are the same, because since the dawn of the tape recorder and television, many of my journalist friends who could have been very good writers do not even bother to try.

Q.: The way you describe how you worry while you are writing whether your pictures, your metaphors will be understood is very impressive. When I read your books I ask myself if I, a European, as compared to readers in Latin America, am actually capable of understanding what you have written or if I only think I do. Is this something that preoccupies you? What does it have to do with the creative process? Reading and understanding a book is also an act of creation which should go hand in hand with what the writer wanted to express.

García Márquez: I believe, and I believe I have already said so here, that novels reserve a margin of creation for the reader. But on the part of a European the question is very interesting. I don't think one can be a writer outside a reality with which one can fully identify. This is the case for me in Latin America, but the distances and the differences between the Latin American reader and the European reader, and ultimately the Asian reader, are so great that it makes one wonder how the book managed to sell in so many different languages. This brings me to believe that deep down, all human beings are the same. They are very interested in things about other people. I think this is one of the reasons they read remote books as if they were from their own country. I have, for instance, a very old letter from a woman in Germany, who was furious because in *One Hundred Years of Solitude* I had used facts related to her and her family. She wanted to know how I had found out about them and considered that in a way I had infringed on her privacy. As for what I think of the translations of my books into other languages, I always relate the following experience. I met in Paris a Japanese writer who only read Japanese. We were discussing *One Hundred Years of Solitude* in French. I don't know if the nuances, the definition of the characters and the atmosphere in the book were well transmitted or not into Japanese, but the Japanese man and I were talking about the same book and that is what matters.

There is an interesting experience I should like to tell you about to finish with all this. When I write, I take the readers all over the world into consideration. For instance, I am finishing a book of stories about things that have happened to Latin Americans in Europe. I started writing these stories many years ago, I took notes and ended up with some seventy. One day, perhaps five years ago, when I was tearing up old papers, I tore up the notebook with the notes about those Latin Americans in Europe. So I started to reconstruct. I found that there must have been the Hand of Divine Providence somewhere, for I could remember only those that really interested me. I managed to put together fifteen which will be published next year; the book is practically finished. But I did come across a problem. In the Caribbean I can do as I please, invent what I like, do as I like, take the cathedral of one city and put it in another; but this only within my cultural context. Those stories occurred in Madrid, Barcelona, Geneva and Rome. So I did not dare publish them until I could go back to those cities I had described from memory. And I had to come back just for that, no more than twenty days ago. I went to Geneva to make sure that the Mont Blanc Bridge is where I remembered it was, that the restaurant the character went to is really there and really existed before 1955, which is the year the story happened, because that's the year I came to Europe for the first time. I made a minute check-up of all the places, of distances, and I discovered mistakes such as having the "jet d'eau" in winter. I had to come back to know that that was a terrible mistake. I thought the flowers around the monument to Brunswick were daisies because a person comes by, picks a daisy and puts it in his lapel. I came and I realized that they are not daisies, but pansies. In Rome I went to visit the trattorias where we used to go at the time and I found that indeed they exist, but they have changed completely. In the boarding house where I used to live in the Piazza Ungaria, there also lived a tenor who used to get up very early in the morning, open the window and start his voice exercises. When he would hit lower C, the lion at the Villa Borghese zoo would always roar. I wanted to meet this lion because he was like part of the family. So I went with the tenor to meet him, and I can recall he was in a pitiful state of decrepitude and sadness. We stood in front of the lion and the tenor came out with his lower C. The lion roared. So I went back to the place to make sure the lion was there and the Romans would not say I was "building Macondo" in Rome. Unfortunately I was told that the lion had died a long time ago. If I am telling you all this, it is to point out that I have to be very careful when writing about a foreign culture. I do not dare take all the liberties I do in my own country, not with cultures which are unfamiliar to me. I have been exceedingly careful with these stories and I have found Rome, Geneva, Barcelona, Paris and Madrid much more beautiful and they have truly become an integral part of my nostalgia, more so in the fifteen days I spent checking all those details than in all my other numerous carefree visits. This probably does not answer any specific question, but I think it is a way of thanking you for your patience today.

Guntern: Some 2,500 years ago, Greek philosophers, Leukippos, Demokrit, maintained that the entire universe was made up of atoms. They imagined them as tiny, indivisible parts, eternally the same, which could combine to form lamps, stones, vases, human beings. This theory was forgotten until it was dug up again in England at the end of the last century by a person who believed in the existence of atoms, whereas most people considered them fictitious. As the majority were non-believers, they declared the believers fools and even more foolish the attempt to look into these mysterious things. Some people, such as Niels Bohr, nevertheless, went on to investigate. He discovered that an electron, when jumping from one energy level to another radiates color, like a rainbow. And he had the vision that these so-called spectral colors were a window through which one could look into the mystery of the atom. This afternoon Gabriel García Márquez has opened such a window. He has displayed marvelous spectral colors and given us food for thought; but a sort of thick fog has disguised the mystery and will probably always do so. What touched me most - among many other things - is the seriousness, the tremendous discipline, the respect with which his genius has reached out to meet us.

García Márquez: Thank you very much.

Works by García Márquez

No One Writes to the Colonel, and other stories. Harper & Row, New York 1968

Leaf Storm and other stories. Harper & Row, New York, 1972

The Autumn of the Patriarch. Pan Books / Picador, London, 1978

Innocent Eréndira, and other stories. Harper & Row, New York, 1978.

In Evil Hour. A Bard Book / Avon Books, New York, 1980

One Hundred Years of Solitude. Pan Books / Picador, London, 1983

Chronicle of a Death Foretold. Pan Books / Picador, London, 1983

The Story of a Shipwrecked Sailor. Jonathan Cape, London, 1986

Love in the Time of Cholera. A.A. Knopf, New York, 1988.

Clandestine in Chile: The Adventures of Miguel Littín. Granta Books / Penguin Books, Cambridge, 1990

Strange pilgrims. Jonathan Cape, London, 1993

Of Love and other Demons. Jonathan Cape, London, 1995

JANE GOODALL
British ethologist and author

One of the world's most popular women researchers today, Jane Goodall saw the light in London on April 3, 1934. Armed with a PhD in Ethology from Cambridge University, England, she was a pioneer in ethological field research, and is one of the best known women scientists of our time. Her keen observation and study of wild animals - notably chimpanzees - over her thirty years in Africa have revolutionized scientific theories and prejudices on the subject and won her numerous honors and awards. Jane Goodall is not only a keen observer and theoretician, she is also a gifted writer, capable of transcending the jargon of the trade to express almost poetically the results of her captivating work in an endless series of papers, articles and over half a dozen books. Traveling extensively and lecturing the world over, she is the Founder and Scientific Director of the Gombe Stream Research Centre in Tanzania; Honorary Visiting Professor in Zoology at the University of Dar es Salaam; and associate to the Cleveland Natural History Museum.

Introduction by Gottlieb Guntern

Poetry is made up of a lot of varied things. It is a specific power of expression combing playful imagination, metaphorical language, vision, rhythmical flow, musical sound and much more. Poetry is a gift that not all know how to appreciate, particularly within the scientific community. During the Renaissance, when science began to contest some of the teachings of the Church, it tried at the same time to get rid of metaphorical language and certainly of poetic expression. If you read a scientific article today, it is most often written in very dry language, which in its attempt to be utterly precise, has become withered and insipid.

Now chimpanzees are much better at poetry. One female chimpanzee was taught the American sign language of the deaf-mute. She not only learned to master quite a lot of different expressions, she learned, if this is the term, how to combine them in a poetic way. When she was presented with an Alkaseltzer drink for the first time in her life, she immediately called it "sing-drink." Isn't that a beautiful poetic statement? Another one called a cucumber a green banana. Many great scientists - Darwin, Einstein, Schrodinger and others - used a language of poetry. But most scientists do not. Now I shall read a passage from a book by a famous contemporary scientist.

"All around the trees were still shrouded with the last mysteries of the night's dreaming. It was very quiet, utterly peaceful. The only sounds were the occasional chirp of a cricket, and the soft murmur when the lake caressed the shingle, way below. As I sat there I felt the expectant thrill that, for me, always precedes a day with the chimpanzees, a day roaming the forest and mountains of the Gombe, a day for new discoveries, new insights.

Then came a sudden burst of song, the duet of a pair of robin chats, hauntingly beautiful. I realized that the intensity of light had changed: dawn had crept upon me unawares. The coming brightness of the sun had all but vanquished the silvery, indefinite illumination of its own radiance reflected by the moon. The chimpanzees still slept."

This is the introduction on page 1 of the latest book by Jane Goodall, *Through a Window*. It is a little *magnum opus*. It combines precise scientific observation, cognitive conceptual model-building, metaphorical poetic language and the deep wisdom of a scientist who for more than thirty years has shown excellence in creative performance in a most unusual way - even in the world of highly creative scientists.

Jane Goodall

How exciting that the idea we discussed ten years ago is now a reality! Let me provide a biological setting for our symposium on "Playful Imagination and Creativity." First, I should like to bring you a greeting from the chimpanzees. You, Dr. Guntern, mentioned that I was poetic in my writing. Well, this greeting shows that the chimpanzees can create a sort of poetry - though perhaps "song" would be a better description. (Imitates chimpanzee panthoot): "Huuu-hu-huuu-hu-huuu-hu-huuu!" This is the closest the chimpanzee comes to singing. The call is made in the evening when all is well in their world. They call back and forth, from one nesting group to another and, as I said, it is their version of singing.

Let me begin with four stories. The first is about a young male elephant. He would at times station himself on a path that was used by buffaloes when they went to drink each day. He would hide in the undergrowth and then, as the buffaloes appeared, burst from his hiding place and charge towards them, ears out, with a great trumpeting sound. Startled, they would scatter in all directions. At the time there were no other young elephants in his herd with whom he could play.

The second story is about a little boy who occasionally hid nasty things in a friend's bed - we call that an "apple pie bed." Then the boy would hide to watch his victim 's startled reaction.

The two stories have one thing in common: the element of surprise. The buffalo did not expect, when they went down to water, that an elephant would charge them (at least, not the first few times), nor did the boy's friends expect to find unpleasant, slimy things in their beds. Clearly, the little boy demonstrated the ability to plan and used his imagination. What about the elephant? Was he, too, demonstrating a capacity for imagination and planning? Surely to suggest that this was so would be anthropomorphic, unscientific in the extreme! Certainly most of those studying animal behavior, until very recently, would have held this view. Some still do.

The next two stories concern a different kind of playful imagination - play with words, making jokes. In a joke, it's the punch line at the end that makes us laugh, because, as was the case in both stories above, it is unexpected, surprising. This first joke fits into the theme of my talk. A man bought a young dog. He took it for a walk in the park. Presently they came to a river and the man picked up a stick and threw it into the water. The little dog ran across the surface of the water, picked up the stick, ran back and dropped it at his master's feet. The man, thinking he must be dreaming, picked it up and threw it again. And the little dog ran over the water and retrieved the stick. The dog's owner, unable to keep this amazing phenomenon to himself, approached a passer by: "Hey, look at this. I've got the most amazing dog. Watch!" he said, throwing the stick. The little dog ran over the water and fetched the stick. "Huh!" said the passer by, "Your dog's no good - he can't swim!.."

That story surely demonstrates a type of playful creativity that is unique to humans - or is it? This fourth story concerns a lowland gorilla, Koko, who is well known in America for her ability to communicate using American Sign Language, ALS. Her trainer, Francine Patterson, claims that she knows over 700 signs. One day a new student, fluent in ALS, was rehearsing Koko on her knowledge of signs for the different colors. Koko had been taught all the more commonly used colors and knew them well. The young woman picked up a white napkin. "What color this?" she signed. "Red," answered Koko, without hesitation. "Come on Koko, you know better than that. What color?" replied the helper. "Red," signed empathetically. "Koko, if you not tell me correct color, I not give you apple juice," signed the exasperated student, sure that Koko was making fun of her. At that threat, Koko reached out for the cloth, picked off a *tiny* piece of red fluff, held it out towards the young woman, and, laughing, signed "Red! Red! Red!"

Where, after all, do we draw the line between human and non-human? When I began my research 34 years ago, I was studying ethology in Cambridge, England. If I had, at that time, wanted to make a study of the animal mind, I would have been told that animals did not possess minds, in the usual sense of the word. It was not always so. In the early 20's both Wolfgang Kohler and Robert Yerkes published results of their studies of chimpanzee intelligence. The apes were given a variety of problems which, it was asserted, they solved by reasoning and even imagination. Their results, however, were not generally accepted by the scientists of the time. Pavlov wrote that such studies were anthropomorphic and "disgusting." The American psychologist, Watson, proposed a strictly mechanical process to explain apparently intelligent acts in non-human beings. Animals, he maintained, were incapable of reasoning; they functioned through innate responses to stimuli. Even though it might appear that they had minds, it was not so. Nor did they have feelings - despite similarities in the brain and central nervous system. Only human animals, it was held, felt real pain if burned or beaten. Animals might *look* as though they felt pain or experienced feelings of joy or sadness, but to suggest that they actually *did* so was anthropomorphic fallacy. In 1960 it would not have been possible for me to have studied the mind of the chimpanzee within the ethological framework acceptable to British science at the time. As for any suggestion that non-human animals might be capable of imagination... witches in the Middle Ages were burned for lesser heresies.

Gradually, however, scientific thinking changed, partly as a result of the field studies of non-human primates that began during the sixties. Suddenly ethologists were confronted by careful descriptions of highly complex social behaviors, and attempts to understand these, using the old simplistic explanations, often failed. Today we know that many non-human animals are capable of sophisticated cognitive performances, and it is quite fashionable to study the workings of the non-human animal mind. Without doubt, studies of chimpanzee behavior, particularly the longitudinal observations at Gombe and elsewhere have played a major role in helping people to understand the nature of non human animals. Let me, therefore, briefly describe the lifestyle of wild chimpanzees and some of the facts that have emerged regarding the cognitive abilities of our closest living relatives.

As more and more information was collected about the behavior of chimpanzees, both in the wild and in captivity, the many similarities in the behavior of chimpanzees and humans became increasingly obvious. We differ, in the structure of the DNA, by only just over one percent, and there are striking similarities also in the composition of the blood, the immune responses and so on. The structure of the chimpanzee brain and central nervous system is extraordinarily like ours. And this appears to have led to similar emotional expressions and intellectual abilities in our two species. Our own success as a species (if we measure success by the extent to which we have spread across the world and altered the environment to suit our immediate purposes) has been due to the explosive development of the human brain. Our intellectual abilities are clearly far more sophisticated than those of even the most gifted chimpanzees. Nevertheless, there is now good evidence for sophisticated mental performance in the apes and other higher animals.

Chimpanzees can solve simple problems through processes of reasoning and insight. They can plan for the immediate future. They can learn, as mentioned, 300 or more of the signs comprising ALS, the American Sign Language of the deaf, and use them to construct sentences similar to those used by deaf human children. They can be taught other complex human communication systems - they learn the meaning of lexigrams, picking them out in correctly ordered sequences from computer keyboards or printed boards. This helps to demonstrate their powers of generalization, abstraction and concept-formation as well as their ability to understand and use abstract symbols in their communication. One chimpanzee was able to grasp the nature of problems faced by a human actor in video sequences. In one, for example, she watched a man shivering and kicking at a faulty electric fire and then, from a series of photos, picked the correct solution, the one showing a broken cable. Chimpanzees can recognize themselves in mirrors. They clearly have a concept of Self.

Some captive chimpanzees enjoy painting or drawing. They show great concentration and make pleasing patterns, each one with his or her own distinctive style. Sometimes those who know ALS will, spontaneously, sign what it is they have represented with their work. Usually it does not look like anything much to us - but if the artist is shown the same picture a month or so later, he or she will usually label it the same way. Chimpanzee representational art!

The most intelligent captive chimp I know is the female Ai (which means *Love* in Japanese). Professor Tetsuro Matsuzawa, with great understanding and sensitivity, is investigating the upper reaches of the chimpanzee intellect in "partnership" (as he describes it) with Ai. The moment she sees her partner she is eager to leave her large outside enclosure, where she lives with eight other chimpanzees, and go to her computer. She performs many tasks better and more quickly than high school students!

It is clear that not only is the structure of the chimpanzee brain similar to the structure of the human brain, but, in addition, chimpanzees often use their brains in the same way that we use ours. One of the evolutionary pressures that helped to develop chimpanzee intelligence was, I believe, their complex society: they need to use their brains to cope with the problems of daily life. (Although, of course, this is a chicken and egg situation, since only a complex brain permits a complex society!)

Chimpanzees live in groups of thirty to fifty individuals that we call communities. Within a community the individuals recognize each other and spend varying amounts of time in each other's company. Mostly they move about in small temporary groups which may be comprised of males only, or females and youngsters with or without males. The composition of these little groups keeps changing as one or more of the members split off to move about alone or to join others. There are strong affectionate bonds between some individuals that may last throughout life, fifty years or more. Communication between community members comprises, in addition to many different calls, a rich repertoire of postures and gestures, such as kissing, embracing, holding hands, patting one another on the back, swaggering, punching, hair pulling, tickling. These are not only uncannily like many of our own, but are used in similar contexts and clearly have similar meaning. Friends greet with an embrace, and fearful individuals may be calmed by a touch, whether they be chimpanzees or humans. Chimpanzees are capable of sophisticated cooperation and complex social manipulations. Like us, they have a dark side to their nature: they can be brutal, they are aggressively territorial, sometimes they even engage in a primitive type of warfare. But they also show a variety of helping and care-giving behaviors and are capable of true altruism.

Wild chimpanzees live in male dominated societies - adult males, except on very rare occasions, are able to boss females of any age. The males, most of the time, are ordered into a dominance hierarchy with one male, the alpha, emerging at the top. Chimpanzees, like other social mammals, typically solve their disputes by means of threatening gestures rather than by attack, although fights do break out. Most aggression between males, including fighting, takes place in the context of social dominance, and conflicts leading to a change in the top ranking male may be particularly severe. Mostly, though, males try to intimidate each other by means of their dramatic *charging displays* when, with lips bunched in a ferocious scowl, they charge across the ground slapping their hands and stamping their feet, dragging great branches and hurling rocks, leaping up to shake the vegetation. They make themselves look larger and more dangerous than they may actually be and often intimidate rivals without having to risk a direct, physical attack, where the attacker, as well as his opponent, might be wounded.

It is important to point out that each chimpanzee has his or her own unique personality. They are as different, one from the other, as we humans are. Even individuals growing up in the same social group at the same time have their own unique life histories. Let me relate part of the story of Mike. In 1964 he was almost lowest ranked of fourteen fully mature males. He was a small chimpanzee, just past his prime with one canine already broken; but he was characterized by a strong motivation to improve his social standing, determination, and a high degree of intelligence. One day, during a charging display, Mike seized and hit an empty four gallon kerosene can from my camp. It made a loud and unusual noise as it clanged and banged along the ground, and a couple of senior males rushed out of the way. Over the next few months Mike began, systematically, to incorporate these cans into his displays. He learned to keep as many as three ahead of him, hitting and kicking, as he charged directly towards males who were, at that time, his superiors. Alarmed by the noise, they fled. Within a period of four months Mike rose to the coveted top ranking position in the male hierarchy without, so far as we know, having to fight at all! The point that should be made is that every male had the same opportunity as Mike to use those cans. Moreover, every male was seen to use a can at least once during a display. Only Mike had the intelligence - and dare I say the imagination - to capitalize on a chance experience and turn it to his own advantage.

Before moving on to discuss creativity and imaginative play in non-human beings, we should first ask one key question: What is play? Scientists have great difficulty in providing a precise definition of play in animals, even though there is usually a high degree of agreement among observers as to what is and what is not playful behavior. Behavior that is typically described as playful occurs only in warm blooded creatures, perhaps because they store more energy. It is difficult for reptiles to play because they don't have enough energy to waste on non-goal directed behavior. One scientist maintained that his turtles were playing when they moved their flippers in a certain manner, but after studying play in lions and wolves, he agreed that what he saw in his turtles was something quite different. Although, as mentioned, we usually know when an animal is playing, it is not always clear-cut. For example, when animals investigate the world around them, touching, picking up, tasting, biting, and so on, while it looks as though they are playing, we cannot be sure. When a human toddler "plays" with bricks, is this play, or "work"? All we can do in these cases is to make our own working definitions.

Play probably begins with simple rhythmic movements which may even occur in the womb. The most common patterns described as play in almost all mammals and birds comprise variations on upward springing, turning around, and tumbling over and over. The patterns may involve pirouetting, turning and twirling, twisting around, leaping and swinging in the trees, turning somersaults and, if the animal has a tail, chasing around after it. These play movements may be repeated many times. It is possible that the repetition of newly learned phrases by young songbirds, such as blackbirds and nightingales, may represent a type of vocal play.

During play the actor may change the mode very quickly: one moment running as though fleeing, and the next chasing or pouncing as though attacking. In many species the young play with objects, particularly young primates and young carnivores: they pounce on feathers, pieces of dried skin, dried dung and so forth. During bouts of social play, youngsters tumble and wrestle together, chase and flee from and bite one another. Sometimes play partners take it in turns to be the "aggressor" or the "victim," but in some cases the larger or more assertive individual consistently assumes the dominant role.

Many actions seen during play occur, in similar form, in adult communication sequences in a variety of contexts, but it is usually very obvious when the behavior is performed playfully. Moreover, there are special signals that clearly indicate playful intentions, such as the "play face" and the "play walk." And there are many ways in which an animal can signal its desire to initiate play, as any dog owner knows. When a play session involves partners of different age, the older typically adjusts his or her behavior so as not to hurt the younger playmate. Sometimes squabbles break out during play, typically when one of the playmates hurts the other. Usually this seems unintentional and the rough individual quickly tries to reassure the other, and then play continues. When a real fight is triggered, bystanders, particularly mothers or another family member, may become involved, joining in to support one or other of the youngsters. Or a dominant male may charge over to stop the fight, thus restoring social harmony.

The more complex the animal's brain, the more varied and complex is the play. Stuart Brown related a wonderful example of playful aerobatics in ravens. This was observed in California, at a site where a great cliff rises from the ocean. When huge waves crash against the rocks of the inlet below, there is a tremendous updraft as air is forced up the cleft in the face of the cliff. Sometimes, when this wind is at its strongest, some ravens fly low over the edge of the cliff, directly into the updraft. The wind seizes them and tumbles them head over heals, over and over. So rough is the wind that sometimes feathers are torn from the birds and swept away in the air current. Finally, when they manage to get out of the updraft, they fly away only to turn back and do the whole thing over again. Clearly they are enjoying this extraordinary activity. Ravens have been observed playing in other ways. One report relates how they fly towards a telegraph wire, seize it with their feet, and then describe a complete arc, still holding on with their claws like an Olympic gymnast performing on the high wire. Often the birds run out of impetus, and are left hanging upside down. Then, with a great flapping of wings, they gradually work up momentum, swinging back and forth until eventually they attain an upright position on the wire. Ravens have also been seen landing at the top of a snowy slope and skidding down. Otters have been seen to slide on mud or snow, and even elephants may slide down muddy banks on their large posteriors.

Another example is taken from my own observations of spotted hyenas in Tanzania. One evening I was watching two youngsters at a den, a yearling male, Baggage, and his infant sister, Brindle. The small cub found a large smooth stone. She tried to pick it up, but the stone was large, her mouth small. She persevered and seemed about to succeed when Baggage, who had been watching, gave her ear a sudden pull and she lost her grip. Again she tried to pick up that special stone - and again, just as it seemed she would succeed, Baggage pounced on her so that she lost her grip. This happened three times more - then suddenly Brindle darted behind Baggage and pulled his tail. Quickly Baggage picked up the coveted stone and ran off with it, Brindle in hot pursuit. During phase two of this teasing game, Baggage repeatedly slowed down so that Brindle caught up, but as soon as she jumped up to try to grab the stone from his mouth, he ran on again. Finally she knocked it from her brother's mouth, at which point phase one began again. Eventually, ten minutes or more after the start of play, Brindle suddenly moved away, as though no longer interested. She bit at some twigs, broke one off and began tossing it in the air, then pouncing on it. Baggage, who was watching with the stone in his mouth, could not resist this new game. He dropped the stone and ambled over to try to grab the twig. For a few seconds they had a tug of war, and then, suddenly, Brindle let go of the twig, rushed back to the stone and again tried to pick it up. But this time, when Baggage bounded over, Brindle turned to face him - and sat firmly on the stone. The game had ended!

Dietmar Todt observed fascinating play behavior among semi-free ranging barbary macaques. The monkeys were living in a large sanctuary. Water was provided in a trough, filled each day from a pipe. When the water was turned on, some of the young monkeys hurried up to play. One put his hand at the end of the pipe so that the water squirted in all different directions causing the actor, and all his companions, to jump back. Then another approached and put his hand in the stream of water. And so it went on, the monkeys taking it in turns to spray and be sprayed. At other times, when the water was calm, some of the monkeys would sit motionless, apparently gazing at their reflections. Then one would take a stick and very gently poke it in his or her reflection, so that the image became distorted by ripples.

Play in animals is rich and varied, and it occurs frequently in many species including our own. It has been estimated that up to twenty percent of the energy needed for daily survival is expended during childhood play. Animals may even take serious risks, especially monkeys and apes playing high in the trees. So why do we play? It must surely serve some useful function.

There is no doubt that locomotor play, along with object play, helps young animals to learn about their environment, to develop muscles and coordination, and to prepare them for adult life. Play provides opportunity for youngsters to become familiar with an arboreal environment so that, as adults, they will be less likely to fall during sudden flight through the treetops. Playful exploration provides information about the nature of the environment that will be useful in hunting for food, escaping enemies and so forth as they grow older. Social play provides information about the strengths and weaknesses of an individual in relation to others in the group. In other words, play teaches young animals what they can and cannot do at a time when they are relatively free from the survival pressures of adult life - when they are dependent on their mothers to take care of their needs. Thus they have time to explore, to test, to learn about the world around them.

The play drive is at its strongest at a time when the brain cells are developing new synaptic contacts. These expanding electro-chemical links, especially those in the cerebral cortex, increase the developing youngster's capacity to observe, to react, and to initiate new behavior, all of which is expressed in playful behavior as he tests his relationship with the environment and with his companions. It has been suggested that play during childhood serves to integrate inborn behavior patterns in the brain and behavior, and helps to ensure maximum flexibility in the development of the individual.

Young chimpanzees are full of energy and engage in high levels of active play. Because all chimpanzee mothers spend a good deal of time away from other adults, a firstborn infant, particularly if the mother is not very playful, must learn to amuse him- or herself. All manner of innovative performances are observed during lone play. Objects such as stones, oddly shaped twigs, pieces of dry skin, hollow gourds and so forth are picked up, thrown, carried, even used as tickling tools when the youngster rubs them in ticklish neck or groin. Two infant females occasionally tickled their own genitals with sticks, while laughing. Three infant males sometimes carried small rocks, set them down, then made thrusting movements against them with their erect penes. Water play is also quite common: youngsters poke the surface with twigs, throw stones into it, slap it, stare into it.

During their playful exploratory behavior young chimpanzees often perform activities in a seemingly purposeless way - but those same patterns may subsequently appear in goal-oriented performances. For example, small infants play with bits of twig and sometimes poke them into crannies in a tree, or holes in the ground. This is done in a careless manner, but when they are older, twigs become tools and are inserted into termite passages with great skill and concentration. Psychologist Paul Schiller found that captive chimpanzees were able to use sticks and branches as tools, only if they had first become familiar with sticks, and the properties of sticks, during free play. Wolfgang Kohler made similar observations.

Chimpanzee youngsters not only show great interest in the behavior of others, but are, in addition, able to imitate, or try to imitate, what they have seen. An infant male is fascinated by the vivid aggressive patterns of a big male, and after a charging display he may pick up the very rock that was thrown and try to throw it himself. Many animals, having watched the behavior of others, are then stimulated to do the same thing. In other words, some behavior is contagious so that young animals learn when to act in certain ways. But chimpanzees, in addition, are capable of true imitation - they can even copy motor patterns that are not part of the normal chimpanzee repertoire. A home raised chimpanzee, for example, learned to purse her lips in order to apply lipstick!

It is because chimpanzees are curious and watch unusual actions with close attention, and because they are able to learn through observing the behavior of others, that a novel performance, if adaptive, may be passed on to others in the group. It is during infant or juvenile exploratory play that we most often see unusual behaviors. A juvenile, Freud, once threw a strychnos fruit - which is round, hard and tennis ball sized - into the air and, to our amazement, caught it! He spent the next ten minutes trying to repeat the performance, going after the "ball" every time it rolled off into the undergrowth. Another infant "invented" a game with sand, lying on his back and dropping handfuls down from above, trying to catch it in his mouth without getting it into his eyes. Had other youngsters been around, they might have imitated the behavior which, for a while, might have become a "fashion" in play, as described by Kohler when he observed his captive colony at Teneriffe. One Gombe youngster, Gilka, developed an idiosyncratic gesture - rapid flapping movements with one hand. She "flapped" at insects, other chimps, humans - and sometimes apparently at nothing. A novel performance like this seldom persists over time. Occasionally, though, it may be incorporated into the behavior of the growing child, and even imitated by other youngsters. Thus Gilka's "flapping" gradually became, for her, a gesture that she used to threaten conspecifics. The gesture was imitated by juvenile Fifi who also used it in an aggressive context. Eventually, though, both youngsters stopped using the new gesture.

One infant, Wilkie, sometimes played with trails of ants, poking at them with little sticks and watching as they scattered in all directions. (My son, growing up in Africa with no TV, liked to do the same!) The same youngster was watched as he poked a twig into a hole in a tree, then darted back as some large black carpenter ants swarmed out. His mother, who was watching, came over and picked the ants off the branch with her lips. The chimpanzees living a hundred miles south in the Mahale Mountains area regularly fish for these carpenter ants, using an *anting* technique similar to that seen when the Gombe chimps feed on termites. But this type of *anting* was not once recorded at Gombe in thirty-four years of study. The incident described above suggests how a chance action could result in the "invention" of a new tool-using technique. A performance that could, if adaptive, spread through the community and be passed, from one generation to the next, through observation, imitation and practice. Given the fact that chimpanzees have been seen eating a variety of insects throughout their range, and that young chimpanzees so often investigate their environment by poking at things and into holes with twigs, it is hardly surprising that the use of twig and stick tools for insect eating is one of the most common tool-using patterns across Africa.

In West and parts of Central Africa chimpanzees use rocks or heavy pieces of wood to open hard-shelled fruits - a "hammer and anvil" technique that has never been seen in any of the East African chimpanzees studied; at least, not yet. The *pattern*, however, is available at Gombe: one infant was seen to use a rock (once) and, on another occasion, a wooden club, to pound playfully at small insects on the ground. Thus, since the patterns necessary for nut cracking are present in the Gombe chimps, the use of hammer stones in feeding at some point in the future is not an impossibility.

It is clear that play not only functions to teach growing animals a great deal about their physical and social environments as well as their own strengths and weaknesses, but also serves as a medium for the appearance and nurturance of innovative performances - performances that may become integrated into the social traditions of a group. Play can also be used innovatively as a social tool, to influence the behavior of companions. Among chimpanzees, play is often used to distract. Sometimes the aim is deception, as when an adult male initiated a tickling session with a higher ranking male who was eating meat: during the game the initiator managed to steal a piece of meat without the other noticing. More often, play serves to distract an individual from his or her goal. When an older child makes repeated efforts to play with or carry a small infant, the mother, rather than punish the child, often starts a tickling game, and the baby is temporarily forgotten. Sometimes a mother uses play to distract her child during weaning depression - when the child approaches to suckle, whimpering, the mother starts to play. Usually the child, after a moment, responds and yet another conflict is, at least temporarily, shelved. An adult male chimpanzee in a zoo learned to use an exaggerated play invitation - an upright play walk and a big play face - to distract the alpha male when he was working himself up into an aggressive frenzy. Often the ploy worked. Humans use similar tactics. Police in Los Angeles were told to joke when they were making dangerous arrests: sometimes the joking broke the tension and averted violence. Shakespeare knew that laughter can relieve built up tensions, which is why, in his plays, a scene of tragedy or horror is always followed by an interlude of comedy.

Of course not only young chimps show innovative performances during lone play. We see exuberant play and the appearance of new, often idiosyncratic patterns in all the so called "higher" mammals. Iranus Eibl-Eibesfeldt made an interesting comment concerning lone play that occurred in a badger that he raised. After hours of watching playful exploration he wrote, "Not only does this badger invent quite new behaviors in play, but in addition, when he is playing, it seems that he is freed from the kind of tensions that constrain him when he is doing his day-to-day activities, non-play activities." Perhaps, Eibesfeldt speculates, it is the freeing of our own imagination from day-to-day activities that gives us our special uniquely human freedom. In humans playful imagination may serve during times of stress, as an escape mechanism. I recently read a moving book about play in the Nazi death camps. Young children play acted the horrors around them; their elders sometimes seemed to escape into a world of their own, playfully imagining themselves in happier days.

For the most part, the frequency and form of spontaneous play, in human and non-human alike, serves as a sort of barometer by which we can deduce something about the mental state of the individual. In young chimpanzees, for example, the first signs of what we have labeled "weaning depression" (when the mother increasingly prevents access to her breasts during the fourth year) is a drop in the frequency of play. Once they begin to recover, play levels start to rise again. It is the same with us: when we can no longer smile, then we are usually very stressed or very depressed and it becomes increasingly difficult to "snap out of it." Stuart Brown, a psychiatrist, found that those people who are the most innovative and the most mentally fit are also the most playful.

Let me close with a few more examples of imaginative play in non-human animals. The first concerns Washoe, the first chimpanzee to be taught ASL. During her childhood she was given a bath every day by her human "family," after which her skin was rubbed with oil. She had a small doll that she liked to carry around with her. One day, observed by Trixie Gardner, she went and filled a can with water, then did to her doll exactly what was done to her - she washed it with water, then got the bottle of oil and rubbed it over her toy. The next observation concerns an infant at Gombe. I was watching her mother feeding on vicious driver ants, pushing her long peeled stick down into a nest, waiting for a moment, then pulling it out and, with one swift movement, sweeping it through her free hand and quickly and frantically crunching up the mass of ants that had swarmed onto the stick. She had climbed onto a low branch to keep away from the insects that swarmed out of the nest and aggressively fanned out over the ground. Suddenly I noticed her three-year-old daughter, Wanda. Like all small infants, she was keeping well away from the biting insect. She had climbed onto a branch and, perfectly imitating her mother's actions, was reaching down to the ground with a tiny stick in her hand, then running it through her free hand. The only difference was that she was not eating any ants - for there were none there! She was not unlike a human toddler "cooking" like mother - carefully stirring a pot that has nothing in it.

Is it only the non-human primates who are capable of imaginative play of this sort? I think not. The following observation comes from *The Hidden Life of Dogs* by Elizabeth Marshall Thomas. She went to visit a friend who had two dogs, one an old, rather bad tempered individual, the other a youngster whose repeated attempts to play with his companion were rejected. One day she watched the youngster, who seemed to have located a rat, or some small burrowing rodent, out in a snowy field. His tail was up, his ears pricked, and he was barking, scratching at the snow where, she presumed, the rodent had gone to ground. Suddenly, as though a rat had emerged and run off, the dog gave chase. He ran in a huge circle, nose to the ground, yapping. The rat, it seemed, ran right back to the same hole and the dog, close behind and barking furiously, again scratched at the ground. After a few moments the rodent, to her amazement, seemed to emerge and again raced off in the same huge circle with the dog in hot pursuit. This was repeated three, four, five times. She became curious. She went over to see what sort of crazy rodent was behaving in such a suicidal way - but there was no rodent. Nor had there been: there were no tracks in the snow, and no hole.

Nor is that the only example of canine imaginative play. My own dog, Rusty, used to play hide and seek with me when I was a child. I would tell him to sit, and wait, in a tree covered area. Then I hid. He never looked round. He must have known where I was - I tried to be quiet but he must have heard me. I crouched down, then called him. At once he bounded from his place, running here and there, gazing eagerly around him, often passing really close to where I hid. He must have known I was there. Finally he decided the game had lasted long enough and he would suddenly rush up and "find" me, grinning, immensely pleased with himself.

One last tale. Chimpanzee Vikki was brought up, from birth, in the house of two American psychologists, Cathy and Richard Hayes. Her "parents" recorded all her behavior carefully. Vikki behaved very much like a human child. She even went through the pull toy stage, busily pulling her wheeled toys around on their strings, pulling shoes by their laces, her animal toys by their tails. One day, as Cathy Hayes was brushing her hair in the bathroom, Vikki's behavior caught her attention. The little chimp (dressed as a child) was going round and round the toilet *as though* she were pulling a toy. Her arm was extended behind her, her hand appeared to grasp a string, and occasionally she looked back, as though to make sure all was well. But there was no toy, no string. Vikki went on, round and round, and Cathy Hayes stood and watched. Suddenly Vikki stopped, made tugging, jerking movements with her hand, then sat, and as though holding a string with both hands, leaned back and pulled. Then, noticing Cathy watching her, she breathed one of the only four words she was ever able to learn: "Mama!"

Discussion

Guntern: Thank you very much, Jane, for this marvelous introduction. We have heard something about the phylogenetic precursors of human imagination. Now, there is a technique in applied creativity research called synectics. Synectics consists in finding creative solutions to problems in economics, for instance, in scientific research and other settings, by finding analogies. And the main strategy today is - as Gordon put it decades ago - to make the familiar strange and the strange familiar. So hearing about the playful imagination of chimpanzees has now set a first stage for our discussion: it has made the familiar strange and the strange familiar.

One of the first questions that comes to our mind is: what are the social settings that trigger, inspire or foster playful imaginations and what are the social settings that hinder them? Why is this question of so much importance? It is quite easy to see why. If we do not permit a specific kind of social interaction in our social institutions, in political parties, in corporations or elsewhere, then the setting is obviously wrong, and no playfulness will occur. Imagination will be blocked and no creative process can possibly start. Now in human beings there are quite a number of settings that will certainly kill playful imagination. To take but one example, imagine that you are members of a team and you are supposed to be creative by playing with certain items, ideas or whatever. Now somebody makes a tentative proposition and somebody else, for whatever reason, comes along with an ironical, sarcastic or even cynical remark. This will kill off the creative process from the start. To take another example, if you have two or three quite ambitious members in a team, each one will block the other's ideas because he thinks if these guys' or these ladies' ideas will make it, his will not and she or he will make a career. So they will try to kill off the other person's ideas. There is something like competitive inhibition in such teams. This is quite well known and every one of you has had this kind of experience in her or his professional settings.

Now let us come back to what Dr. Goodall said and try to build bridges by analogy, find out what we can learn from chimps if we want to improve the quality and the rate of innovation in our professional domain, and perhaps in our private family domain as well. Jane, I was struck by the following things: Due to playful imagination combined with keen observation Mike, the chimpanzee, who took these cans, learned that his display behavior tremendously impressed the others and this allowed him to climb the social ladder, the hierarchical ladder, quite quickly and to establish and maintain a ranking order at the top. What do you think about creativity in human beings and ranking orders? You went through the experience yourself twenty-five or thirty years ago, when you tried to say certain things. The established scientists did not allow you to use catch words like motivation, kissing, caring, adolescence, childhood, and many more. How did it, being blocked by established authorities, intervene with your own creativity?

Goodall: When I first began the work at Gome I did not want to become a scientist, I just wanted to learn about animals. Because I had watched and loved them all my life, and because I was older than most students starting on their academic careers, I had enough self-confidence in my understanding of animal nature that I "knew" intuitively, that it was okay to use words like *personality, motivation, adolescence*, and so on. And I "knew" it was appropriate to provide my subjects with names rather than numbers. As for how I developed my self-confidence in the first place, I need to spend a few moments discussing the important issue of childhood experiences, especially the mother-child relationship. During my childhood, when I was about eight years old, I decided I *had* to go to Africa. I had been fascinated by animals from a very, very early age, but it was when I started to read about Tarzan that I determined to go to the African forests. All my mother's friends said, apparently: "But Jane can't do that. Why don't you persuade her to dream about something she can actually achieve?" Because you see fifty years ago young English girls did not go tramping off into the African forests - except missionaries' wives. There was no precedent for someone studying animals in the field. Fortunately I had a wonderful mother. She said: "Jane, if you really want something, and if you work hard enough, and if you take advantage of every opportunity, and if you never give up, you'll find a way." I think it was that advice that helped form my character. So I was able to confront those paternalistic scientists (they were all males) who told me that what I was describing was not correct when I asserted, for example, that chimpanzees had characters, could reason, had emotions, and so on. I did not believe them any more than I had believed my mother's friends who had said, "Jane, you can't do it."

Part of your question was: what enhances creative imagination? You answered that yourself: I think it is having the right people around you, and having a relaxed relationship with them, as well as having faith in yourself and your ability to answer the challenge; one or the other, and preferably both. A challenge from a good friend might be optimal, I should think!

Guntern: Right. So one condition then would be a close person or several close persons, who foster your identity or ego-strength by telling you you can do it. And the opposite would be a field condition where they not only tell you that you cannot do it, but even why you cannot do it. So one field condition that often blocks creativity in the industrial world or elsewhere, is when older persons who have authority and ranking orders say, " Well, this idea that you brought here is quite nice; we tried it twenty-three years ago and it didn't work out then." There was a famous Zen master, Lin-chi, also called Rinzai in Japan a thousand years ago and he said, "If the Buddha blocks your way to the truth, kill him." How did you kill your Buddhas, i.e. the persons of authority who blocked your way?

Goodall: I have never tried to kill them. I have always tried very quietly, simply to change the way they thought.

Guntern: How did you go about it?

212

Goodall: Well my main mentor was Robert Hinde who has a very incredibly crisp, clear mind. He taught me all I know about scientific writing. But he was the one who basically said, "Jane, these things may be true, but as a scientist you cannot write about them." That undermined my faith in science, because if scientists were thinking one thing and saying another, I felt that was wrong.

Guntern: It was a form of hypocrisy?

Goodall: Yes, At any rate, I invited him out to Gombe, and after spending a week with the chimps, he changed. I have a letter from him saying that "One week did more to change the way I think about the world around me than anything else that's ever happened." If you cannot take the person with you, you can show him or her slides and films and talk about the human-like qualities of the chimps very objectively. Then the listeners will make the jump to human inferences themselves.

Kaufmann: I do not think it is so much the problem of the ranking position or the hierarchy which prevents playful imagination. It is much more the pressure for performance, the not-having-time to develop playful imagination. I have heard that in Japanese firms there are so-called window watchers, people who have nothing else to do than to walk around the firm, look out the window and observe, come up with proposals for improvement. I think the most important thing is to give people time to develop playful imagination and not place them under performance stress. They just need enough time to develop playful imagination.

Goodall: It has been shown that a chimpanzee, when under great pressure, finds it difficult or impossible to solve a problem. For example, if food is placed outside the cage of a hungry chimp, unused to using sticks as tools, he usually will not solve the problem immediately even when a stick is placed conveniently nearby. However, if he gives up and begins to play around with the stick then, quite suddenly, he may solve the problem - take the stick and use it to rake in the food. The point that you made is a very good one. If you are under a lot of pressure to do something new quickly, you are not free to think - unless you have a mechanism for cutting off the stress.

Guntern: Absolutely. I would agree with that. Vishnu can only start his playful imagination when the field is relaxed. That is a fact. High pressure tends to put people into an action mode with a target fixation and then the free associative play in their brain is blocked. Up to now we have come up with two interesting topics. The first one is the significance of a relaxed transactional field versus a tense transactional field. *Transactional field* implies the whole context pattern generated by the continuous interpersonal signal exchange and by the signal exchange between individuals and their physical environment. A relaxed field versus a tense field, field meaning the relationships, the signals exchanged between people working at some place. The second topic is the interaction between ranking order and creativity.

Domeniconi: I think that the dichotomy which you mention exists. It seems as if the higher ranks feel challenged in their authority or whatever by creativity and playful imagination coming from the lower ranks, and they might wish to squish it. They might instinctively also feel that imaginative new solutions may put in question all the old solutions by which they have lived and by which they have made their careers. If one is high enough in the ranks to allow oneself to let go and give in to those instinctive reactions, then that may suppress imaginative solutions from the lower ranks.

I should also like to make another comment on what you said earlier about peace and quiet for playful imagination to come up. I seem to observe that people who are professionally creative, like in advertising and so forth, always seem to need to build up pressure, whether it is time pressure or whatever other pressure to be creative. In German we say: "Not macht erfinderisch" - want breeds inventiveness. Thus they create the need so they can be creative. There seems to be a contradiction; or is creativity possible under both conditions?

Goodall: I was going to say the same thing. Some of the best writing I have done has been when there is a deadline and you sit up all night and are completely exhausted and something takes over. I think something from the subconscious comes out if you are under enough stress and then you relax. Up to a certain point, pressure blocks creativity; but if you have really done your homework, if all the pieces needed are stored away in your brain, then in that state of near desperation, you relax, almost give up - and suddenly the inspiration comes.

Guntern: My comment on that would be that each organism performs in a kind of homeostatic equilibrium. If you have an excessive overstimulation, this will block your playfulness, your imagination, and other phases of the creative process as well. If you are extremely understimulated, then it will block it too. So every organism looks unconsciously for the optimum stimulation and that is why there is no contradiction in it. That is why you can have beautiful new ideas in the highly relaxed field; you are creative as well in the long stretch running towards the goal, when your attention is highly focused and you have a deadline. It is just because the two complementary conditions push your organism into the right state of operation where creative performance occurs.

Pitanguy: I have got an island off the coast of Brazil, and there I observe two families of monkeys. In one family the mother was able to concentrate fully on her offspring, which developed in a normal way with a lot of playfulness. In the other family, the father was so jealous that the mother was continuously disturbed while rearing her offspring. These youngsters became very neurotic and not playful at all. In your own case, you had a mother who told you: "If you want to go to Africa you can to do it, Jane!"

Goodall: Over the years of observing the chimpanzees at Gombe, it has become increasingly obvious that the mother - her nature, her position in the hierarchy - plays a crucial role in shaping the behavior of her offspring. If she is high-ranking and assertive and affectionate, then her children will have a much, much better start, and are likely to become high-ranking and assertive themselves - and leave a lot of their genes behind them.

Guntern: I should like to pull a few threads together to form the web of our understanding. First, playful imagination and creative performance are possible only if the organism is in an optimal state of operation generated by optimal internal and/or external stimulation. You can only be creative and imaginative if you are in the right kind of stimulus, external, internal stimulus. There is an optimum. It is not the complete under- and not the complete overstimulation.

Second, you can only become creative if during the first two years of your life you receive the necessary proteins to build up the hardware of your brain, meaning a minimum amount of interneuronal connections. We have about a hundred billion neurons in our brain and they are capable of building up to one million billion interneuronal connections. These are only built up if you run the same kind of information time and again through your neuronal circuits.

The repetitive activity of playing all kinds of roles establishes a repertoire of well-oiled patterns which can, under normal or excessive stress conditions, later be mobilized and used in a purposeful way.

Third, the higher ranking order in itself does not foster or block the creative performance of those who have a lower ranking order. The question is how the individual of a specific ranking order or hierarchical position plays her/his role, i.e., how she/he assumes the rights and obligations inevitably connected with a specific position. A parental figure must, for instance, find the right combination of support and confrontation or criticism. If a child or an adult person must be confronted with an undesirable performance, then the criticism should only aim at the inadequate performance and not at the person itself. Too much criticism ad personam is destructive. It kills self-confidence and, with it, ego-strength, which are necessary prerequisites for creative performance.

Mock: I would like to come back to the importance of hierarchy and creativity. I believe that all people are basically the same. There are various states in our company comparable to physical states. We must not forget that the hierarchy within these states serves to increase the efficiency of a system. Of course hierarchy, from a creative stand, is contraproductive. Creativity has a lot to do with dreaming and playing. I might compare this with a gaseous physical state. The highest possibility of reaction lies within a gas-forming state. Stress, certain constellations and provocative situations help to affect creativity. That's the way it is. This mixture of functions makes that creativity corresponds to the gas forming state. Hierarchy, on the contrary, corresponds to a solid state. If a hierarchical system is to function, both states must be accepted; the "solid state" must bear in mind that the ideas come from reactions in the "gaseous state" and the "gaseous state" must know that its ideas have to be transposed if they are to be productive.

Guntern: What about the liquid state?

Mock: Liquidity is the state of technical development, which must be close to reality. Normally, in a company, you have hierarchy and productivity. The gaseous state is literally the highest free state, which indeed goes along with a minimum productivity in the number of designs and ideas. The state is a chaotic one, requiring pressure, energy, catalysts, if it is to be able to give rise to a product. It demands strong flexibility to reach a liquid state and a solid state, respectively. Productivity, (unfortunately) must first be attained through the hierarchy.

Guntern: Thank you very much. We have a very interesting argument here. Mr. Mock is the man who invented the Swatch, a very inexpensive watch. There was a manager who wanted to build a watch that costs ten Swiss Francs. Everybody thought it was impossible. Mock, as he told me once, did not have much experience; he was very young then, so he was not hindered by structural constraints. He went off, let his imagination play, and constructed the watch in a very imaginative, creative way.

Schneider: I think what we are all interested in is the influence and the manipulation of creativity. My question to Dr. Goodall is: during your thirty years, was your role solely to observe patterns, or did you use your presence to influence creativity and obtain results by proposing different activities to stimulate their playful activities?

Goodall: We tried very hard not to influence them, but of course we did. We were present physically, intruding into their environment. The boxes in which we enclosed bananas so that we could somewhat control them when we dispensed them, presented a new challenge to the chimpanzees. This resulted in various unplanned field experiments: they learned, for instance, to use sticks to try to pry open the lids of the boxes. Another accidental experiment occurred when the chimps arrived when my husband was using his large shaving mirror to reflect light onto the insect subjects he was trying to film. The chimps thus saw themselves for the first time in a mirror. Some went to look behind it - to see whether the strange chimp was there. They could not figure out what was going on. So although we tried not to influence their behavior deliberately, we did. There are field biologists such as Hans Kummer who *deliberately* set up experiments to enhance their knowledge.

Von Wartburg: I come from Ciba, which is a pharmaceutical company among other things. We have a few chimpanzee families right in our research labs, and we use them to find out whether their behavior changes when they are given a certain amount of a specific drug, and if so, how. It is a much more sophisticated kind of research than the research usually done with guinea pigs. All these families who have lived for decades within our research environment have very specific behavior. You have the alpha-animal, the beta-animal, the gamma-animal, etc. and they always behave in exactly the same way. In that respect it is a very hierarchical behavior. We once had visitors from the Highest Federal Court at Ciba and they said it reminded them of a situation at court, for the routine allowed them to know exactly what was going to happen next. What strikes me now is the following: on the one hand, we say playful imagination takes place if you do away with the hierarchy, while we are watching the hierarchy in chimpanzees as the kind of ultimate stable order. If they were given drugs, which all of a sudden would lead to playful order or playful imagination, we would immediately stop exploring those drugs, because they would have impeded something which we think is the natural order within a family of chimpanzees. Now, can you help me out of this problem?

Goodall: I don't think I can help you out. What I can say is that your situation is totally abnormal when compared to chimpanzees in the wild. At Gombe the hierarchy is stable for much of the time. However, there are always young males on the lookout for opportunities to better their rank. So, Number One, the alpha, must be watchful all the time. He has to use his imagination to stay on the top, particularly as he gets older. When Mike started to get old, his hair brown and his teeth worn, the only way he could continue to dominate the young ones who were trying to usurp his place, was by planning his strategy very carefully. When he heard a group of chimps coming, for example, he sometimes hid. He often positioned himself so that he had a strategic advantage - uphill from the other chimps or up a tree. Then when they got close, he had the value of surprise as he charged out. In that way he managed to stay on top longer than if he had relied on his physical strength. With regard to your chimpanzees, I have not seen their setting. I probably would not like it very much!

Von Wartburg: So the setting might be the impairment of natural order and the impairment might lead to stability in terms of social interaction.

Goodall: It might. What is your setting?

Von Wartburg: It is the setting of a zoological garden, basically.

Goodall: A zoo, an old-fashioned zoo, probably.

Von Wartburg: They don't run around. It is obviously an old-fashioned zoo.

Guntern: Let me just comment from my perspective on Dr. von Wartburg's question and statement. If I have given the impression that I do consider a ranking order as something that hinders creativity, it is completely mistaken. That is not at all what I think. The function of ranking orders in animals and human beings is obviously to hinder the unnecessary and mainly destructive chaos and to put some order into a system; to diminish the amount as well as the destructive quality of interindividual aggression. Now, it depends completely on how the role player of a specific position plays her/his role. Depending on the mode of her/his operation, a specific ranking order can be killing, or it can be fostering creative performance. There is, for instance, a study by Zuckerman on Nobel Prize winners and the conditions that helped them to strengthen their ego, to become self-confident and to develop a high creative performance. Zuckerman investigated a number of Nobel Prize winners in science and found that over fifty percent of them had formerly worked under the direction of a Nobel Prize laureate. Now, the most important thing was the social role model they actually had. One higher-ranking older scientist showing them not only the theory, but actually practically how to go about the business of creating something from day to day. The younger scientists were watching them as keenly as the younger chimpanzees were watching their elder sisters, brothers, uncles, mothers and fathers. So ranking order can be very helpful. It can be neutral with respect to creativity: it can be destructive. It can be everything depending upon its mode of operation.

Reiser: I happened to talk to Mr. Mock during the coffee break and he gave me a wonderful example of exactly how authority may work in both ways: by killing creativity or enhancing it. He tried to explain to me in a few minutes how the Swatch was born. He said there were two young engineers at the fourth or fifth level of the organization who had this idea of building this very inexpensive watch with a new concept. The concept was to make the watch with inexpensive materials. He said the entire concept was created in one week, the two of them playing around with ideas. They knew that the objective was to have an inexpensive watch. Nobody in the organization knew how to go about it. So they played around with ideas and came up with the idea of making the watch out of new materials. They made a project and sent it up through the hierarchy. The technical directors said it was rubbish, nonsense, it would never work, so they killed the project. But somehow it reached the desk of the top manager, Mr. Thomke, and he said, "Well, I don't understand this, but at least I want to hear from these two guys what it is all about." So he called Mr. Mock into his office, gave him twenty minutes to explain his project, and Mr. Mock said, "Actually, we had only been playing around, so we had only childish drawings of how this would be." That was sufficient to arouse enough interest in the top manager who said, " I don't know whether it will work or not, but I'll give you the chance to do it," and he approved the credit. So they got the money to start this project. The four layers between them and the top manager had been trying to block the project, saying it would never work, and they continued trying to block it almost till the very end. Mock and his colleagues were only able to do it because the top manager gave the money and encouraged them to go ahead. So you see, this example illustrates both modes of operation in the hierarchy of management. There was a top manager fostering creativity; then there were several layers of lower ranking managers trying to kill it.

Pitanguy: I have another question for Dr. Goodall, because actually I felt that ranking order is extremely important. I have been teaching plastic surgery for over thirty years, and I realize that one of the most difficult things is day-by-day teaching, this corps à corps. I realized that the teachers have to control their ego. They have to make clear what they know and also what they do not know; otherwise the teaching department will not be a good one. Now, when you said of the chimpanzee that he always tries to preserve his hierarchy by hiding uphill in the bushes or climbing a tree, we can learn that we should not hide our knowledge in order to maintain our hierarchical position. It is our responsibility to share it with those whom we teach.

Goodall: Well, I have another comment. There was an intelligent young male at that time, Figan. He was fascinated by Mike and, over a number of years, followed him around and learned all his techniques. Then, when Figan took over from Mike, another bright young male, Goblin, followed Figan and learned the same techniques. So Mike's "surprise tactics" were passed on, first to Figan and then to Goblin as a result of the fascination that a high-ranking male holds for a highly motivated youngster.

Bornstein: My question concerns making art... Human conceit has, of course, insisted for a long time that humans are the unique language animal; it also insists that we are the unique art-making animal. I am sure you are well acquainted with the work - quite some while ago - of Desmond Morris and Alexander Allan, with the anthropology and the biology of art. They gave paints and brushes to chimpanzees, who did wonderful paintings and drawings. According to some of the writings, some of the chimps enjoyed the painting so much, that they preferred painting to eating, which was quite an incredible revelation. I guess we are all well aware that their art resembled that of abstract expressionists. In many ways their art also looked like the work of very young, pre-kindergarten children, and there was even a gallery in New York that sold their work and it was very popular. At any rate, the making of art seemed to be introduced to the chimpanzee. My question is, in your observation of the chimpanzees, is there anything that you observe that can in any way compare to the idea of making art, and making art for its own sake?

Goodall: I have asked myself the same question with regard to wild chimpanzees, and I would say the answer is probably not. Sometimes young chimpanzees - always young ones - make marks in the sand with their fingers, but I would not describe this as art (though the motor patterns could lead to art). The thing that fascinates me about "art" in captive chimps is that every one has his or her own characteristic style. Thus Ai, the female in Japan, loves to make circular flowing lines around the page, various colors criss-crossing. Another artist, in the same lab, is Chloe, an individual who has had a more restrictive life. Her drawings reflect this, I think; they are comprised of short lines. One of the chimpanzees we have been helping in an African zoo, JouJou, seemed to express his improved condition through his drawings. On his first paper he made a tight little knot of marks. Then, as his frustration level dropped, his drawings were slightly more free-flowing. That is what fascinates me. I wish we could see, in the Gombe chimps, behavior that could be described as the precursor of art - perhaps we shall one day.

Guntern: I would like to follow up on Dr. Bornstein's question about the rhythmical pattern. You said, and I was fascinated by this, that every play begins with a rhythmical pattern. Now many creative people, whatever their field of work, use music as a field relaxation and to get into the right mood. I remember reading that the painter Paul Klee often could not hold in his pent-up energy when he made his drawings. He would jump up and dance a while, until he built up the optimum tension once again and then he would continue to draw. Could you talk a little bit more about this importance of rhythm in play? Could you perhaps connect it with the rituals of the rain dance that you have observed?

Goodall: The play walk is slightly rhythmic, almost as though the chimpanzee is going to dance. The head moves a little from side to side, and the mouth is loose, relaxed. This clearly signals a play mood.

Dr. Guntern is very fascinated, as indeed am I, by the behavior of chimpanzees who are suddenly confronted by very heavy rain, especially when there is thunder, or when they come across a waterfall - which, of course, is always there. On these occasions they may perform very spectacular and very rhythmic displays. I suspect there is something of the play element in those displays. In a usual charging display, when one individual challenges another, and is in a way showing off, he runs flat out with lips bunched in a scowl, and hurls rocks and branches. But when he is doing one of these rain or waterfall displays, he shows rhythmic movements from side to side, and he bends down and hurls rock after rock, randomly, while maintaining the rhythm of the performance. He may do this for twenty minutes. This display is often accompanied by a deep roaring pant-hoot, *huu-he-huu*. I so often wonder what emotion lies behind such a display - an *elemental* display I have called it. It seems to me that it must have been similar emotions that led to early human primitive religions - the worship of water, sun and so forth - worship of something that you cannot understand, something magic that generates wonder and a feeling of awe. If chimpanzees had developed a spoken language, if they could discuss together the feelings that stimulate the "rain-dance," might it not develop into some kind of a religion, or worship of the elements? But since they lack language, those emotions are trapped within the individual performers.

Saemann: The slides showed beautifully the importance of play for the chimpanzees to learn, to grow up, to become. If we make an analogy for human animals, the schooling process from kindergarten up to university or through university, the element of play in this process of learning and becoming, have you given some thought to applying the rules learned with chimpanzees to our human education processes?

Goodall: I have recently become involved in education - conservation education and teaching people about the true nature of animals. We are dealing with pre-school up to university. The role of play is very interesting. Particularly in the United States teachers are beginning to realize that what is fun is learned more easily than what is absolutely boring. Yet I think you can go a bit too far in efforts to make everything fun - we need a happy medium.

We had a meeting of environmental educators the other day, and there was one absolutely incredible man from Oklahoma who has been working on teaching children of different ages about the environment. He has established a number of clubs and then moved on to another school. Somebody asked him: "Tim, how is it that when you leave, your clubs last and when anybody else leaves, the club disappears?" He replied: "It is because I made the clubs fun. If the kids don't get fun, they're not going to bother to go and do things like clearing up litter and all the hard work of planting trees. But if you reward them with fun, they will do those things." So, yes, I am thinking a lot about making things fun. I think fun is a desperately important part of our lives. If we do not have fun, if we do not have a sense of humor, we just may as well give up and dig a grave and jump in.

Guntern: But you also apply what you have learned with the chimpanzees to get in touch with street gangs, deprived youngsters. Could you expand a little bit on that?

Goodall: This does not completely have to do with play. We had a little conference in Connecticut. Among the forty children there, who came from six different states, mixed ethnic groups and social-economic backgrounds, we also had seven black kids from the inner city of New Haven, who joined the group at the last minute. Somebody asked if they could come and they did not know what it was about. They did not know why they were there. They had no teacher with them, and they did not want to join in. When I finally got them on their own, what they were fascinated in, was the chimps. The moment we began talking about the chimps and relating chimp gang warfare to their gang warfare, they were interested; more so by the fact that for young male chimps violence and aggression are fun, they seek it out, even though they are frightened. I asked them if it was like that for them and they said, yes, that they were fascinated, but frightened. They would have actually liked to give it up, but did not know how. For them, all this was part of learning about the chimpanzees. I was using the chimpanzee as an entry into those kids. They looked at some of the National Geographic films and saw me as a peculiar Beauty-and-the-Beast figure. They were fascinated, you know. Who is this peculiar woman? I mean, how does she work and why does she do it? We made the whole thing fun. When I talk to these kids, I demonstrate calls and tool using and show what it is like if drive ants bite your feet. I do all kinds of silly things, and they get very tuned in, turned on, or whatever the word is.

Sigg: You created a dilemma in me today and perhaps you will be able to help me out. It has to do with your last notion. My first observation is that this is a very harmonious world, an ideal world, the chimps live in, provided that there is no interference from the human animal, no thinking. Observation number two is that our world is totally inharmonious, far from ideal, yet infinitely more creative. I mean, we are having a Symposium where we talk about chimpanzees, they are not having a Symposium talking about us. Now, these two observations only have a value if it is true that the chimps and ourselves descend from the primates. My question is, what went wrong or what started the differentiation between us - the human animal - and between the primates, at some point of time in the past? Could creativity have something to do with it? I put the question to you because yesterday you mentioned that a population of chimps in a certain place found that they could eat ants, yet another population was not able to do so. Could creativity have something to do with this differentiation if there was one at some point of time?

Goodall: If I could answer your question I would be very famous indeed, because that is a question that has been exercising the minds of many very well-known paleo-anthropologists. Anthropologists - anybody interested in human evolution - have pondered over this. What was it that set us on the road to becoming the very unique species of primates that we are? There have been many theories put forward. One theory, which is more or less disregarded now, is that it was because this was the only niche that we could occupy in a rather hostile world. Having no claws or fierce teeth, we had to exercise our minds in order to escape danger; and of course, the more you use something, the better its development. A number of people have suggested that we learned to talk because we became hunters. We had to communicate our plans as to where to go, where to meet afterwards, and so forth. Clearly, this is not a compelling reason; there are many really good hunting animals which do not talk. Nor do they need to: they pass signals to each other. Indeed, it seems to be important *not* to vocalize since this might alert the prey. And animals certainly do not need to talk in order to meet up at their home base.

But we must assume that some kind of environmental pressure acted on the group of pre-human primates that eventually evolved to become human. We now know that there were many other kinds of pre-men or ape-men, which became extinct, probably because of one group killing off the other. We know how very aggressive chimpanzees can be to individuals of other groups and how very aggressive we can be to "non-group" members. Darwin even suggested that it might have been interspecific conflict - war - that led to our increasingly sophisticated human brain; the clever groups, because they could make better plans, killed off the less clever ones. In other words, smart thinking helped to ensure survival.

Humans and chimps differ genetically in the DNA structure by only just over one percent - a remarkable fact. Indeed, there are many striking similarities. which help to pinpoint ways in which we differ. The most important of these, I believe, is that we, and only we, have developed a sophisticated spoken language. Chimps have the cognitive ability to learn human types of language - not involving speech, but using signs and computer keyboards and so on. They can understand many words of human speech; but they have not developed a way of communicating sophisticated ideas. It was Konrad Lorenz who said that once you have words, you can teach other people in your group, you can teach your children about things, about objects and about events that are not here physically at the time. And that is something that chimpanzees, as far as we know, cannot do. The young ones can learn about things that are going on around them, but the mother cannot tell her child about what to do in this situation or that situation. She cannot say, "Last year at this time something bad happened over there." My belief is that it was because we developed language that we gradually developed an ever more sophisticated intelligence.

I suspect - at least, speaking for myself! - that playful imagination and creativity have led to theories as to *how* we developed language, *why* we developed language. I have mentioned one theory - hunting. I personally do not think that is a viable suggestion. It is not really very imaginative, and not particularly creative. The theory I have come up with is at least as good as that of anyone else's. And it is also an idea that is fun, an idea that is playful!

Let us start by imagining what happened when, at some point, early humans lost their hair. First, how would this effect the mother-child relationship, the relationship that is, I believe, at the heart of social interactions? So many of the postures and gestures of the adult communication system in chimpanzees can be seen to originate in the communicative signals that pass between mother and child. What would happen if a chimpanzee mother suddenly lost her hair? For one thing, her baby could no longer cling to her, and the mother would have to support the child. At Gombe there was a chimpanzee female who got polio and lost the use of one arm. When she subsequently had an infant she had to support it very frequently as it was a sickly child, not able to cling very well. As a result, and because she only had one functional arm, the mother had to walk upright a good deal of the time. Could the loss of hair add a new factor to the discussion of why we humans developed our strange upright stance?

Let us imagine a pre-speech ape woman who has lost her hair. Perhaps it was due to a mutation - no one knows. (There is a theory that postulates that we lost our hair, like hippos and seals and whales did, because we went through a stage when we lived in the water, but that seems a bit far-fetched). Anyway, for whatever reason, her hair has gone or almost gone. She is supporting her child. She may be carrying something, like a tool, and she has moved out from the trees and into the long grass of the savanna - where early man is thought to have developed in Africa. Now let us imagine that she stops to do something, such as collect food with a digging stick. She would need to set her infant on the ground, since it cannot cling. She might even, as she worked, move just out of sight of her child. This would create a quite new and very powerful need for more sophisticated auditory communication signals between mother and child, specific messages from the mother, like "It's okay, I'm here." The infant would also benefit from the development of more specific vocal signals to convey its wants. This kind of auditory communication is almost completely unnecessary between a chimpanzee mother and infant because the mother *feels* the needs of her infant - if it starts to slip, or wants to nurse, or something. Anyway, that is my theory, and, as I said, it is as good as any other.

Guntern: Human beings have put their own playful imagination to the use of developing, cheating and lying and have become quite sophisticated at it. If I remember well, you wrote in your big book - *The Chimpanzees Of Gombe* - about an instance where a young chimp was lying about a pretended snake in the grass.

Goodall: Yes, actually that is a good point. It is hardly *play*, but chimpanzees do lie and deceive. On the particular occasion to which you are referring, Fifi joined a group that included a large aggressive male, Humphrey. He started to bristle his hair and it was obvious that he was about to charge Fifi, and stamp on her, a typical aggressive "greeting." Fifi, presumably, knew this. Instead of uttering worried pant-grunts of submission, she looked away from him and made small sounds of concern "huu! huu!," which means "I've seen something a bit frightening." Humphrey at once sleeked his hair, and he stared and stared where Fifi looked. But there was nothing there! There are other incidents which seem to demonstrate deception. I mentioned yesterday that infants become very depressed when they are being weaned from the breast at about four years of age. During this traumatic period, they are not only depressed, but also quite demanding and, when rejected, cling to the mother, or run off and throw tantrums. The mother is not only preventing them from nursing, but also encouraging them to walk on their own four limbs. Often, as a child follows the mother, one hears loud whimpering "hoo hoo hoo." It goes on and on and on. Often the mother does not relent, and the child is not allowed to climb on her back. On three quite different occasions, involving three different infants, I observed behavior which seems to represent lying. On each occasion the infant, who was following the mother and whimpering, suddenly stopped, stared into the undergrowth by the trail, and screamed. The protective response is strong in mothers (they will even go to the aid of adolescent and adult offspring). So when these infants screamed, their mothers rushed back to gather them up. The youngsters got their way, and were carried off, riding their mothers backs. When, on each occasion, I went to look at the place where the supposed danger was - there was nothing to be seen!

Another example of deception concerned Figan, a very intelligent young male. It was at a time when we had not yet got our feeding system worked out. We were extraordinarily unsuccessful in creating a method which would allow us to ration the bananas so that the big adults did not take the lot - despite our human imaginative, creative intellect! Each time we thought we had devised a fool-proof plan, the chimpanzees proved they could outsmart us. Eventually we decided to fill the boxes for the adults, and hide bananas (early in the morning) up in the trees where the young ones could search for them. The system worked quite well. On this particular occasion, the banana frenzy was over and the chimps were resting. Two of the big dominant males were sitting grooming each other. I happened to be watching Figan just as he looked up and noticed a banana hidden on a branch just above the two males. Chimpanzees very quickly notice the eye movements of their companions; when one of them looks intently in one direction this is likely to cause others to do the same. Figan, having spotted the banana, very quickly looked away. He knew, of course, that it would have been impossible to climb and collect it - the big males would have snatched it away. It seemed that he also realized that, had he stayed there, he could not have prevented himself from looking at the bananas! At any rate, he moved right out of sight. The instant the adults moved away, Figan very quickly went back, climbed up and took his reward.

Another example concerns a young captive bonobo, Kanzi. Kanzi had a remarkable playful imagination. He learned a human language based on lexigrams printed on boards at the language lab in Atlanta, Georgia in the USA. Kanzi communicates with the people around him by pointing to the correct lexigrams on his board, one after the other. The researchers take him (and his board) into the forest. There are different areas where there are a variety of different activities for the bonobos: some have food, some have

226

games and so on. Kanzi indicates, on the board, where he wants to go - and why. Sometimes he may indicate other wishes. If, for example, he is with Sue, he may sign "Sue tickle me," then run off, laughing, hoping to be chased. Or he may communicate a more complex message. If, for example, John is with them, he may sign "John tickle chase Sue" - then climb up into a tree to watch the fun! There is, of course, a complex cognitive process going on in the brain - there is a world of difference between "Sue tickle me, Kanzi" and "Sue tickle John."

Guntern: As we go up the phylogenetic ladder from the Darwin finches at the Galapagos to the Egyptian vultures - which you described in your book *Innocent Killers* - to the tool-using and tool-making of the chimpanzees at Gombe, we can see an increase in the sophistication and diversity of purposes. Could you say a few words about this?

Goodall: A Galapagos finch uses a little twig, or cactus spine, to poke insects out of crevices in the bark. Dr. Eibl-Eibesfeldt has studied these birds in captivity and found that the youngsters play with little twigs from a very early age. They do not need to see an adult poking out insects in order to perform this tool-using behavior - which, presumably, is encoded in the genes (though aspects of the performance such as modifying a twig by breaking off a side growth is probably the result of experience). However, if he deprived them of the opportunity to play with twigs during development, they could not use them in the problem-solving situation. Egyptian vultures throw small rocks at ostrich eggs to break the shell, then eat the contents. We (H. van Lawick and myself) tried to find out more about the nature of this tool-using behavior. We carried out a series of experiments to see what triggered the throwing response. We set out a very large fiber glass "egg" - about one and a half meters long - and the vultures that arrived became very excited. They threw stone after stone after stone - although obviously they could never have seen an egg that size! They did not throw at cubes or other shapes. When presented with an ostrich sized fiberglass egg, they continued to throw and throw until we stopped the experiment - we felt so sorry for them! (The lamageier, a large vulture, often drops bones on the ground to smash them open. There is one report of a lamageier dropping a stone onto an ostrich egg).

The point I want to make is that the tool-using patterns in birds - certainly in the Galapagos finch and probably in the vultures - appears to be primarily genetically determined. What about the chimpanzee's use of objects as tools? Young apes show a predisposition to play with and manipulate objects of all kinds, both in the wild and in captivity. A young chimpanzee, confronted with an object that interests him but which he cannot touch - or of which he is frightened - typically investigates with a twig or stick. For example, he inserts a stick into a crevice in a tree, or uses it to touch a dead snake, then sniffs the end. We call this an investigation probe. Sticks were used to try to solve the novel problem of opening banana boxes. In other words, there is a strong tendency not only to manipulate objects, but also to use them to learn about the world. Thus it is not difficult to guess how the various tool-using patterns observed in chimps originated. An ingenious individual finds that he can obtain food, previously out of reach (such as termites), by using a twig. He repeats the behavior. Others watch and imitate. The behavior eventually becomes part of the cultural tradition of his community. We have never recorded the start and spread of an adaptive performance; but we have observed a novel but non-functional performance "invented" by one infant and subsequently imitated by two others. One day Flint greeted a female by touching her genital area with a twig rather than his finger. He did this again and again and soon two of his companions were doing the same. The new behavior, however, gradually faded. Kohler writes about similar fashions in play in his chimpanzee colony. One such fashion began when a female found some material, draped herself, and walked around in an upright position. Soon all the group members were frantically searching for pieces of material so that they could emulate the behavior and they then walked round in a circle, all upright, and all draped. The fashion lasted a couple of weeks and then another took its place. Thus, in chimpanzee society, there really is a good deal of imaginative, creative playful activity.

Guntern: I would like to make a few remarks to wrap up what we have discussed yesterday and today with Jane Goodall: I think that whatever human beings are, what they do, whether they are aware of it or not, is governed by sets of rules. I happen to think that there is a fourfold set of rules or code. There is a conceptual code telling us how to describe the world, how to explain it, how to understand it. There is a technical code specifying how to do something in order to accomplish it efficiently. There is an ethical code with rules specifying what is morally correct and what is not. And there is an esthetic code specifying what is beautiful, formally perfect and what is not. Now, whenever an individual, a couple, a family, a group, a team, a culture, reaches a certain degree of maturity and wisdom, then there is a congruence between the four codes. There is a harmonious mutual fit. Whenever these patterns break apart, as they are doing today in Yugoslavia, then you have a lot of destruction and Shiva is dancing the world once more into a sea of flame. Now, one of the great experiences that I have had time and again over the years whenever I have been in touch with Jane Goodall, either face to face or over the phone, is that there is a mutual fit of the four codes. That is why she is such a marvelous human being. Thank you for your contribution, Jane.

Works by Jane Goodall
In the Shadow of Man. Fontana/Collins, London 1974
Innocent Killers. Collins, London 1976
The Chimpanzees of Gombe. Patterns of Behavior. Belknap Press of
    Harvard University Press, Cambride, Mass. - London 1986
Through a Window. Houghton Mifflin Company, Boston 1990

HELMUT MAUCHER
German business executive

A child of Eisenharz, Germany, Helmut Maucher was born 1927. After having graduated from High School in Wangen, he did his commercial apprenticeship at the Nestlé Factory in his home town before being transferred to Nestlé, Frankfurt. He continued his studies of Business Administration and Economy at Frankfurt University, from which he obtained his BA. Between 1964 and 1980 he held various positions within the Nestlé company in Germany and in 1975 became President and Chief Executive Officer of Nestlé Gruppe Deutschland GmbH, Frankfurt. On October 1st, 1980 he was appointed Executive Vice President of Nestlé S.A. in Vevey, Switzerland, was nominated Chief Executive Officer in November 1981 and in 1990 became Chairman of the Board. He is also currently Vice Chairman of the Board, CS Holding and Credit Suisse, Zurich; Member of the Board, ABB Asea Brown Boveri AG, Zurich, Deutsche Bahn AG, Berlin and L'Oréal Paris - Gesparal; and Member of the International Council, Morgan Bank, N.Y.

Introduction by Gottlieb Guntern

Mr. Helmut Maucher is chairman and member of the Board of Directors of Nestlé, a large Swiss company and one of the world's major corporations. He is responsible for ensuring that this colossal firm, so impressive from the outside through its sheer size, does not fall into inner inertia, but remains an agile organization that can adapt rapidly to the constantly changing conditions of the business environment.

Anybody in such a position knows that as a rule there are plenty of people in broader circles of society who know exactly how things should be done properly. This is understandable because at the end of the day none of these unsolicited advisors has to produce evidence that the formula he is advocating actually works.

The French poet Alfred de Musset once wrote: "Qui s'élève, s'isole" - (he who rises isolates himself). Similarly the German poet, Rainer Maria Rilke, who at the time was secretary to the sculptor Auguste Rodin, spoke of the "circle of loneliness" that surrounds the sculpture on its pedestal. Individuals in a hierarchical top position are sometimes compared to figures who stand high on a pedestal in solipsistic contemplation, their heads almost in the clouds, aloof from the mundane cares of everyday life. It is my view, however, that anybody who really does justice to his outstanding position in top leadership is more like the ridge of a roof: together with the walls it supports the roof that affords everybody living in the house protection against the elements. The function that goes hand in hand with this structure implies a finely-balanced integration of autonomy and uniqueness on the one hand and dependency within the framework of solidarity-based cooperation on the other.

Mr. Helmut Maucher was born in a village in the Allgäu (southwestern Germany), that gave him a specific upbringing and shaped his relationship with reality. A down-to-earth attitude and a sharp sense of observation, coupled with good intuition and sound common sense, have forged in him a personality and management style that is by no means pretentious, dramatic or pompous.

In discussing with him, one soon notices that he listens attentively and expresses himself clearly. Above all he is accurately informed about whatever he is talking about. He is up-to-date on important conceptual developments and findings in behaviorism, communication theory and cybernetics. He is interested in biological and anthropological interrelationships.

What is less well-known is that he is a born musician. In his youth he spent as many as three or four hours a day on music; he played several instruments and conducted choirs. Accordingly, he knows from long experience how an ensemble whose elements often tend to drift apart dissonantly has to be orchestrated and conducted so as to play in harmony.

Helmut Maucher also has a sense of humor. When, for example, he noticed that suddenly everyone in the business world was beginning to discover ethics and produce a lot of rhetoric and phrase-mongering in the process, he remarked dryly: "It's astonishing; today we are living in a world of verbal inflation and conceptual deflation."

He will now discuss the factors that foster or inhibit creative processes in business life.

Helmut Maucher

I should like to begin with a simple remark. As the Nestlé Group, we are naturally interested in fostering creativity in order to achieve greater success. We are not interested in creativity per se if it yields no benefit for our company. But success or, as the case may be, long-term development and earnings optimization do not depend solely on creativity. They involve many other factors, e.g., product quality, brand image, know-how, organization, cost structure, quality of management and employees, etc. Today the promptness with which a company predicts trends and takes and implements decisions is also playing an increasingly important role in its success. (It is no longer so much the big fish that swallow the small fry as the swift ones that gobble up the slowpokes.)

Nestlé probably has an average position when it comes to creativity; this is shown by the expansion of our company and by our success. But it could be much better. My philosophy is that a boss must attend to things that are not yet adequately developed in a company. What is more, creativity is important not only in research and development of new products but in all areas of a company's activities.

I shall now attempt to describe, using some key words, what *measures, techniques* and *considerations* exist in a large company like Nestlé *to foster creativity*:

First of all, our aim should be to release creativity in accordance with our general philosophy of being more person- and product-oriented than system-oriented. (Of course, we do need systems in a large, complex company but this is a matter of priority.) The rule is: bureaucracy impedes, system releases.

Regarding the quality of our management, we feel that in addition to professional knowledge and experience, the following qualities are important:

- courage, nerves and composure;
- ability to learn, sensitivity to new things, ability to imagine the future - vision, as people call it today;
- ability to communicate and motivate internally and externally;
- ability to create an innovative climate;
- thinking in contexts;
- credibility, practicing what one preaches.

Thus one of the important points is also the ability to create an innovative climate.

A further aim should be to define personnel management policy and organization policy from the angle of fostering creativity. On this subject I have found the following table in Professor Gertrud Höhler's new book, *Spielregeln für Sieger* (Rules of the Game for Winners, Econ Verlag 1991):

From *ad rem* organization	to *ad personam* organization
from functional specialization	to interdisciplinary generalization
from the search for synergy	to competition between the units
from stressing hierarchy	to horizontal communication
and status	and cooperation
from inherent centralism	to a decentralized, flat structure
from external organization	to self-organization

Furthermore I think it is important from time to time to recruit managerial staff from the outside, as it were, to invigorate the company's blood (while it remains a priority to develop one's own managerial staff).

Another point is to further a free and - particularly - horizontal flow of communication. With a flat organizational structure we promote permeability between the individual echelons and encourage creativity at every opportunity. In addition, within the framework of our personnel policy we at Nestlé have recently implemented a new policy under the heading *Management Commitment and Employee Involvement*.

We tried to set up an *Invention Committee*, but it was not very successful. On the one hand, it talked too much nonsense.(That, in any case, was our opinion in accordance with our internal corporate culture, which perhaps is not correct; I myself sometimes intervened sharply and discouraged people by doing so.) On the other hand, people were making contributions that were so clearly structured, they could have been presented in exactly the same way and the same form at any other meeting.

Moreover, we are endeavoring to base our long-term planning less on quantitative objectives and forecasts and more on qualitative considerations; that means developing a vision of the future and deriving concepts for the company from it. As the basis of our long-term planning, we have created an arrangement by which the top management (about nine or ten people) meet once a year out-of-house for two days without any fixed agenda in order to come up with ideas and reflect on future options and priorities.

As Dr. Guntern has stressed on many occasions, a creative and innovative climate appears to mean different things to different employees, e.g., the physical or staff environment, working conditions, etc. Apart from the general measures imposed, individual conditions favorable to creativity obviously have to be created for certain people or departments, and this is not easy.

The question has been raised on several occasions whether Vevey, in the canton of Vaud on Lake Geneva, is a good location for an international headquarters or whether the atmosphere might not be too provincial. All in all our experience has been positive. Firstly, the area offers a very good quality of life and secondly, the managerial staff travel a great deal and consequently are always in touch with the whole world.

On the subject of *creative employees*, it is also worth considering the question of *which types* of employees we need - or rather still accept. On the one hand, they have to fit into our corporate culture and accept a minimum of rules and forms of behavior; on the other hand, there has to be a lot of liberalism so as to promote creativity and spontaneity. How far we can go also depends partly on the place or locality where employees work, or on their job position (in certain areas like advertising, research, etc. more independence is accepted than elsewhere). In many cases a problem can be solved by taking somebody on as a consultant without recruiting him.

On this subject, here are two more quotations from Gertrud Höhler's book *Spielregeln für Sieger*:

- "Imagination has rebellious traits, and management must constantly be checking whether it is restricting the firm's visionaries too much. The company's jesters need the management's protection."

- "Make sure the corporate intelligence has the creative spark of those who come up with ideas. Allow the creative ricochet to explode in the midst of the conventional organization. The torch of vision has to be lit."

I would also like to quote Professor Dahrendorf, who for decades dedicated himself to liberating human beings from institutions, only to come round to the view in recent years that freedom in the long run can only exist *within* institutions. Perhaps he could have saved himself a lot of trouble if he had read Goethe earlier on. I would like to quote here the end of Goethe's poem on nature and art:

"So ist's mit aller Kunst wohl auch beschaffen.
Vergebens werden ungebundene Geister
Nach der Vollendung reiner Höhe streben.
Wer Grosses will, muss sich zusammenraffen.
In der Beschränkung zeigt sich erst der Meister
und das Gesetz nur kann uns Freiheit geben."

Thus is all Art indeed composed.
In vain the spirits do unrestrained unreel
Which to the fulfillment of purest heights aspire.
Who greatness seeks, must first himself compose.
In restrictions is the master first revealed,
And through the law only can we freedom acquire.*

* Translation by the International Foundation for Creativity and Leadership.

We should not hide the fact that more creativity is also achieved in a company by an appropriate *fighting spirit* and under the pressure of competition. This is sometimes forgotten amid all the ethical and social babble that is in vogue at the moment. We already know from evolution that creativity is one of the best strategies for survival (although I do not wish to deny the importance of measured and serious ethical and social responsibility).

Corresponding processing of information can also lead to the promotion of creativity. (In my opinion, intuition and creativity sometimes mean creative utilization of information!) One way to foster creativity in a large company is by an intensive exchange of experience *(cross-fertilization)*.

Recently some experts in one company also recommended more chaos, as opposed to a perfectly-organized structure. A true core is certainly still preserved here, so long as the right balance is maintained.

There is also the *brainstorming* method for stimulating creativity. We have used it particularly when looking for new brand names or advertising slogans.

Another interesting and well-known method is so-called analogy conclusions. There are many examples of this in our company too, which I would like to mention only with some key words:

- application of the instant powder concept, which had been developed for milk powder, to coffee (result: Nescafé);

- the mousse concept for products like ham, liver, etc.;

- transferring the idea of pasta from pasta products to rice, etc.

Once again I should like to come back to personnel policy: a creative atmosphere is developed by deliberately selecting employees on the basis of their creative, innovative talents (Goethe: "If you don't feel it, you won't hunt it down.").

Likewise, the coupling of different experiences and mentalities develops more creativity. The keywords are internationalism in management.

But creativity can also be fostered by a corresponding organizational structure. We once carried out a re-organization that served this purpose, among others. In a large, well-established company such changes are often an end in themselves: the employees have to be shaken up from time to time by changes. In this connection I sometimes like to use the *Management by Provocation* method. Some examples are as follows: Are you helping us in the solution or are you part of the problem? - More pepper, less paper. - I would not object to paying some top managers; what bothers me, though, is the damage they cause.

Recently *intrapreneurship* has been advocated. I am skeptical though, because one cannot be inside and outside a company at the same time.

Other methods of promoting creativity are unlocking and destroying hackneyed patterns of thinking. Some examples:

- in our company it was impossible for a long time to sell normal roast coffee in addition to Nescafé;

- as "milk people," we were in principle against vegetable fat;

- in Asia we had a purely *trading mentality* but we have now gradually developed an industrial culture;

- the continental concept of standard chocolate bars and chocolate candies prevented virtually all chocolate manufacturers on the European continent from developing such products as those with which *Mars* and *Rowntree* conquered the world (for example, chocolate bars of very different shapes and very different contents).

Regarding packaging, we were set on the concept of the tin can for a long time and only gradually introduced other forms of packaging.

There were some countries (Italy, India and Egypt, among others) of which traditionally we did not think much and it took a lot of effort to get our Organization to take an interest in them.

I would now like to mention some *concepts* that promote *creativity* and *point it in a specific direction.* Some examples of this:

- the *double strategy* concept in Nestlé's product policy: this means, first of all, selling and disseminating our conventional products in developing countries; secondly, developing new products based more on local raw materials that adjust to local taste habits and thus usually offer a less expensive solution;

- the whole concept of *targeted nutrition and health;*

- the concept of *convenience* in food (preparation, safety, handling, shelf-life, etc.);

- our *Somep* (soft medicine) project. The object here is to obtain ideas for products and product quality from the field of empirical and alternative medicine.

Next, I would like to make some comments on the path of the empirical and creativity curve.

At the outset of a person's career the empirical and creativity curves grow stronger, whereas in many cases in the final phase of a career only experience is present and creativity is declining. That is why two curves have been plotted for creativity in the final phase of a career.

As far as the connection between size of the firm and creativity is concerned, size tends to require more rules, more bureaucracy, more administration and a greater division of labor. This kills off creativity; therefore measures have to be taken to counteract this (decentralization, creation of smaller units and *business units*, personalized management style, application of the "subsidiarity" principle, acceptance of mistakes, etc.). We do not want to be a faceless *société anonyme* or a firm that consists of people "who either sign or resign" (internal dismissal). In this respect Nestlé has a relatively favorable structure - despite its size - because our business is distributed over the entire world (in more than 400 plants, *inter alia*) and nowhere do we have too great a concentration of people in one place.

Creativity in advertising does not call for "producers of gags" but rather "high-spirited preachers." One has to be convinced of one's own cause (it is not difficult for the convinced to be convincing). Commitment is important. Advertising must be done for the consumer and not for the Cannes film festival, colleagues in advertising or decision-makers in companies. People say yes, one third of advertising is done for the product and the consumer, one third for the advertisers and one third for the colleagues in the industry. Too much so-called creativity does not help a firm's sales. Above all, the advertising themes should not be changed so quickly.

It is possible to be creative by deliberately not always doing just what everybody else is doing, because they have the same training and the same techniques and do the same market research. I am talking here about a kind of *anti-marketing*. One example of this is the introduction of Nescafé in Japan. The French say "penser à côté."

"Me too" products are in general frowned upon by marketing people, but there are creative "me too" concepts within the framework of which "me too" products are further developed, for example, with new benefits for the consumer or at lower prices, etc.

Should the head of a company himself be creative or should he just foster and understand creativity or both? Normally, both. But there is a certain danger of so-called peculiar creativity, when the latter is connected with the power of implementing ideas that are crazy or wrong.

Where do we need more creativity? In marketing or research? The marketing idea is usually straightforward and does not need any special additional creativity. It is then decisive to investigate whether a particular idea can be put into practice, for example, achieving the same taste experience in food with less fat, less sugar and less salt; developing a really good anti-aging cream or a means to stimulate the growth of hair on the head, etc.

Thinking in the context can foster creativity. Recently people have been talking about *holistic*; someone who knows only chemistry cannot do this.

Does art in the company promote creativity? That is a question I ask myself! Many people believe they are being creative by behaving and dressing "originally."

I should like to come back once again to the subject of *blocking* and *unlocking*. I have taken the following excerpt from the book *"Die anonymen Kreativen"* (The Anonymous Creative People) by Ingeborg Nütten and Peter Sauermann (Frankfurter Allgemeine/Gablers 1988):

10 rules for blocking creativity

1 Consider every new idea coming from below with mistrust - because it is new and because it comes from below.

2 Insist that people who require your permission for taking action also have to get permission from several higher echelons.

3 Urge departments or individuals to criticize each other's suggestions. (This saves you the trouble of deciding; you only have to reward the survivor.)

4 Express criticism uninhibitedly and suppress praise. (That keeps people under pressure!)

5 Treat the discovery of problems as a slip, so that people do not stumble on the idea of letting you know when something is not working.

6 Check everything carefully. Make sure everything that can be counted is counted often and checked accurately.

7 Take decisions on reorganization secretly and spring them on the employees unexpectedly. (This also keeps people under pressure).

8 Insure that requests for information are always justified and be careful that information is not made available without reason (information must not get into the wrong hands!).

9 In the context of delegation, transfer to subordinate managers particularly the responsibility for executing economy drives and other threatening decisions. Get them to do it quickly.

10 Above all, never forget that you, as a member of the higher grade, already know everything important about the business.

Finally, there are two more remarks about creativity that deserve reflection:

In *Manager Magazin* 10/1991 I read an essay by the philosopher Gerd Achenbach entitled "Being different at all costs - about forced creativity," to which I would like to refer readers. Selecting what is meaningfully creative within the limits of the objectives is, as I already said in my introduction, particularly important.

There are firms that apparently have done right everything the books say about creativity. A few years ago a book was published with the title *"In Search of Excellence"* by Thomas J. Peters and Robert H. Waterman, Jr. (Harper & Row Publishers, New York, 1982). This book and the above-mentioned work, *Die anonymen Kreativen*, describe examples of how well-known large companies grew successful. These firms also strove to foster creativity; they created leeway for creativity; they experimented - and despite that, some of those big companies are in difficulty today.

So what is it that produces meaningful, profitable creativity? What is important? What is wrong? There are certainly no simple answers and I say, thank heavens. What is it that makes or breaks a company or a manager - despite all the books, all the research and all the discussions? There are few words that are terser and more apposite in the German language than in English. One of them is the translation of "management." The German word is "Führungskunst."

Although our company is successful, my greatest worry is that creativity is being stifled by factors that are in themselves positive: pride in the company, motivation or a positive attitude. These factors can also lead to a situation in which we do not ask any more new questions and think we are doing everything right. Thus we lose our *alertness*, our sensitivity to new things. But, to echo Harald Szeemann, we do not want to become a museum for obsessions, we want to be a company *with* obsessions.

I should like to close with two maxims. The first was coined by André Gide: "One cannot discover new continents without having the courage to lose sight of old stretches of coastline." The second comes from the philosopher Marquard: "The future needs an origin." It will be important for Nestlé to find a *happy medium* between these two maxims if it is to remain creative, and thus successful, in the future.

Discussion

Guntern: Mr. Maucher has given us a glimpse of a world in which most of us do not move about daily, knowledgeably, humorously and with a quality without which there can be no creativity, namely enthusiasm. The word *enthusiasm* comes from the ancient Greek, *en* meaning in, and *theos,* god. *Enthusiazein* literally means having the god of enthusiasm in oneself. The French call it *le feu sacré*. If the top leadership in the management is imbued with enthusiasm, a company cannot, in principle, do too badly where creativity is concerned.

Wehowsky: I wonder whether Mr. Szeemann and Mr. Maucher are talking about the same thing in their discussion of creativity. I have the impression that the imaginary museum is an accumulation of complexity, whereas in the economy very great reductions take place with the aim of selling products. So are we talking about the same thing? And, for example, would Mr. Szeemann say I am creative in the same sense as Mr. Maucher and vice versa?

Maucher: I think Mr. Szeemann can answer that question better than I can. But first of all I would just say that even if creativity is geared to the firm's benefit - however that may be defined - we have discovered that if creativity is overly guided it cuts short a development and therefore probably does not achieve the objective.

Szeemann: One common feature struck me in your presentation. When you spoke about your "innovation and invention committee" and said you burst in too early, I noted the superior's impatience is the beginning of non-creativity. Basically, that is how it is. I think we need patience, both you in your company and I in mine. Mr. Bauer [head of research at Nestlé - editor's note] has just pointed out to me that I am also offering a product, namely the exhibition. The difference is that I am asked whether I would like to hold an exhibition; I am in a similar position to that of an artist. But you do not ask the Japanese whether they would like to drink Nescafé; you *want* the Japanese to drink Nescafé.

Maucher: I would just like to make one more brief comment to clarify my point. You say "You *want* to introduce Nescafé." This is correct, of course, but we know perfectly well that we can only sell something people want. We have found out that people feel a need to imitate others: on the one hand, they want to retain their own culture and identity, but at the same time they would like to visit London, drink late-vintage wine from the Rheingau and now

Nescafé, which those crazy Westerners drink. That means satisfying this need without abandoning one's own identity and that, ultimately, was why it worked. I believe there are more limits than is assumed to the possibilities of manipulating people and "terrorizing" consumers - which are often talked about. We are all the more successful if we aim at something that is already in people's predisposition. That does not necessarily mean the habit already exists or is obvious, but it is present in latent form. It is the fact that when a person is offered something, he or she suddenly says "Aha, yes, that's just right." This is basically the good thing about the market economy: at the end of the day it is the consumer who decides - the options for manipulation are thus limited.

Once I showed a French Nescafé commercial at the end of a Nestlé conference we hold about every two years for the heads of all our markets. A baby was sitting on a throne and fawning courtiers were running around and asking: "Dear baby, what would you like, what can we do for you?" and so on. At the end came a voice: "Voilà, le président." Then I said "Friends, you've now spent two days listening to me; that was very nice of you, and I definitely try to be a good boss and chairman of Nestlé; but the real chairman of our company is the consumer, for example this baby. If we lose sight of this, we're doing something wrong and won't be successful in the long run." So much for the limits to *wanting*.

McPherson: You have explained very clearly what role creativity plays with regard to your company's aims. I come from a university where corporate creativity is very efficient in terms of social responsibility. At Wake Forest University we have Maya Angelou as the Reynolds professor for American studies, which means that Reynolds Tobacco pays for this chair. In Wake Forest I teach at a predominantly white university. But we have been able to increase the proportion of minorities at Wake Forest University by 120% because *Reynolds, Heinz, Sarah Lee* and many other companies put up considerable sums for grants. What is Nestlé doing in this respect? Switzerland is a very rich country and maybe there is no need there for social responsibility. But in some other countries in which you operate, for example in Africa or South America... How do you define creativity with regard to your social and moral responsibilities in those countries?

Maucher: Your question gives me an opportunity to clarify a few points. Of course, I do not have the same problem as *Reynolds Nabisco*, that is, I do not have to compensate for selling cigarettes by doing good deeds. But I would like to make a few points, and I will be very clear and honest: our first and foremost social responsibility is to do our job well, to perform well and supply a competitive market with good products that serve the consumer's interests. We have to do this in an efficient way that is creative and innovative. Competition and the free market are not there for the benefit of the entrepreneur, as many people think, but for that of the consumer. If one overlooks this fact, the whole system does not work.

We have very clear priorities. If we do not do our job properly, if we are not successful and cost-conscious in the market and do not sell at competitive prices, the company will not survive.

That brings me to the second point, and here I totally agree with you. As a large company, we also have to be creative with regard to ethical, moral and social responsibilities. In this respect we have developed many things. We shoulder our social responsibility and do so also in the long-term interests of our company. In today's world no company that refuses to accept its social responsibility will survive. Thus it goes without saying that we do a great deal in this respect.

You mentioned India. Whenever we build a plant somewhere, it takes a long time until we make a profit. Such investments are made from a long-term perspective, and it would be wrong not to stand by them. But at the same time we do a great deal for the local people. We show the farmers how they can do various things, increase per-cow production. Such a task lasts about ten years and of course everyone can take advantage of it. More people will have work. The farmers will have a higher income and higher profits, which means they develop a greater awareness of quality and such. Consequently the whole society benefits from such an idea. Apart from this, we certainly spend millions and millions in every country on supporting social events and helping here and there, with child nutrition and many other areas and programs. Today that is part and parcel of our world and our life. And of course one has to keep stating a priority over and over again.

Many years ago we set up a foundation for management training in Switzerland, into which we poured a lot of money. We still support this project because we think that we need responsible managers - professional managers - if we are to create a flourishing business and through it make a contribution to the economy. Particularly in the East we are aware now that things are not working, partly due to an education deficit there. So we see our commitment as a long-term contribution to the development of society. Yet at the same time I would like to stress that we can only do this kind of thing so long as we are making a profit and are successful. If that is not the case, we will still be "nice people," so-called good corporate citizens, for a few months and then it will all be over. For this reason I think we have to get our priorities right. We have to accept this, and it looks as though the philosophy of a private company in a competitive world with all the freedom and pressure that you or anyone else can exert on us could trigger most aspects of a society's development. It also leads to more justice. If we are living in a genuinely free world, everybody can criticize us and push us in the right direction should we do stupid things. A company that is receptive to long-term trends and takes a serious interest in them will listen to this criticism in its own interests. In the long term we are in the same boat. Now as far as the so-called developing countries are concerned, when my employees come along with their projects, I never ask if they are in our interests. I know perfectly well that these people have calculated the right profit margins and know what they are doing. My question is therefore always: Is this investment in the country's interests? If it is not in the country's interests, it will not work in the longer term.

Gschwend: You said you wanted to contribute to the development of society - and, naturally, you would also like to make a profit. I wish to come back again to the subject of *Nescafé in Japan*. I think the idea of how you sold Nescafé in Japan was a creative one, but is it creative to put Nescafé on the market in Japan in the first place? These people were, after all, relatively happy with their tea. Even if a latent need had existed, it should not necessarily have been aroused. It was not necessarily creative to arouse this need. Quite frankly, I do not think it was particularly creative either to market an old product in another country. But I would find it very creative if you as a food group were to look for solutions to the world's food problems - with new products that would then also have to be profitable, but not necessarily with a product that a country does not need.

Maucher: The two are not mutually exclusive. In a free society in which the consumer can choose whether he or she drinks tea or Nescafé it has to be permissible to consider whether there could be a market for Nescafé and to come up with a creative idea as to how it is eventually to be sold. This is not intrinsically bad.

Regarding the second question, it is actually quite important that a large part of our creativity should focus on how we are to contribute to feeding humanity in the future and avoid malnutrition. This is a very serious concern on which we are reflecting deeply. Professor Bauer, our head of research, who is also here in the room, can testify to this. He knows exactly how much he spends on research in this area. We have set up a *Nutrition Council* in which professors and scientists from many parts of the world participate in order to find answers here. I cannot discuss this at length today, but I would just like to repeat briefly: the idea is to market as an alternative products that are less expensive but have a higher nutritional value than many things that are eaten in the countries concerned. We want to offer products that are based on local raw materials, are cheap and help to save foreign exchange. Incidentally, this was to a certain extent my own idea. I am very proud of it and pleased this kind of thing is possible.

In this connection I would like to allude to two problems: humanity cannot feed itself the way the industrial world is feeding itself at the moment, consuming about 60 to 70 kilograms of meat or sausages per person. These proteins are too expensive and cost too much energy. Humankind cannot afford it. We have already seen - thank goodness - a slight reversal of the trend with a move toward vegetable foods, cereals, etc. So we have to find foods the production of which does not take the detour via animals. The detour via animals is about seven times as expensive as for products obtained directly from plants. That was one reason why I decided to go into the pasta business as well as into cereals.

At the moment only about 1% of plants is utilized to feed humans. We are putting a lot of money into soy research and similar projects in order to eliminate or improve its unpleasant characteristics - the taste, texture or the dry feeling in the mouth. We aim to develop a whole range of products and beverages that are cheaper and have an excellent nutritional value. Vegetable fat has qualities which, from a nutrition physiology viewpoint, are better than those of animal fat, contain excellent proteins and a number of other things. Every day we bring out more plant-based products which are not only cheaper, but, what is more, better-suited to those countries' eating habits.

We are also conducting a lot of research into the connection between health, nutrition, the body and well-being. According to the WHO definition, health is physical, psychological and mental well-being. In other words, a *total-quality* concept. Of course, we are not just doing this philanthropically for humanity. But I am pleased that via research, that is by means of a longer-term commitment, we are probably making a bigger contribution to the nutrition of humanity than can be achieved with handouts and development aid. At the same time we are investing in our own future, as there is a great sales potential in the corresponding areas.

We have been talking about commodities policy for a long time and international agreements exist. The so-called totally free marketers - here too there are purists, as in other areas - the *Chicago boys*, are naturally opposed to all agreements and say they are nonsense. They say output, prices, production and quantities have to find their own levels by international price mechanisms. However, there are areas where in our opinion these international price mechanisms have to be embedded in certain overall conditions. In my view these include commodity agreements, about which we know a lot. After all, we do purchase 10 to 15% of the world's cocoa and coffee crop. We have always argued that international agreements that pay the commodity-producing developing countries a fairer price should be concluded. We are concerned here with long-term processes. A coffee plant takes five years to mature before it produces a return because it is difficult to cultivate. I do not think it is right that those countries should be beaten down to the last cent, only for billions to be sent back again in the form of development aid. We are therefore in favor of such commodity agreements, and we have said so publicly umpteen times. But there are still producers who are only cooperating hesitantly here in terms of their basic philosophy.

I am convinced we all have to learn more in this area and international cooperation has already improved in my view. Therefore I remain optimistic that people will gain a better understanding of these matters so as to make a decent contribution to these countries' development.

Perrin: It seems to me that there are a lot of ideas in a company that die or are killed off. I am responsible for creation in an advertising agency and my main job is to insure that ideas are actually put into practice once they have germinated. The real problem is not producing ideas but allowing them to survive. Is not the problem of idea survival one of listening? I have great difficulty insuring that people in a company listen to each other. Therefore it seems to me that creativity is a listening problem, listening has to be fostered. But I do not know how that can be done.

Maucher: I totally agree! An enormous number of people work in a large company and ideas are being conceived of or are present everywhere. I think it is very important to create a system or climate in which these ideas are adopted and put into practice without some corporal or anybody else shooting them down right away and saying "That's all garbage." Many of these things are blocked at the lowest level of management. This is one problem we face and it preoccupies me intensely.

We have a total of about 15,000 managerial staff and half of them belong to the lowest level of management. Yet these 7,000 or 8,000 people are the real *Mister Nestlés* for the 200,000 people whom we employ worldwide. But this lowest rung on the managerial ladder consists of people who, although they are closest to the employees, still have the least experience of management. On the one hand, this has the advantage that they understand their people's problems better; but on the other they have relatively little training in management. We often neglect these people because we concern ourselves with the higher responsibilities. It is a genuine problem because there is often a kind of - I do not want to offend anybody - corporal's or sergeant major's mentality. They make management easy for themselves. They give orders and instructions and have no time to express themselves in differentiated terms. They want things done their way and no other. Nevertheless I am convinced that our concept, *Employee Involvement*, will not work unless we get support from the 7,000 or 8,000 people in those positions. Doing more at this level will be an essential factor in insuring that ideas get a better reception and are pursued.

Of course, there has to be a *screening* process, for many of these ideas are not usable. But learning to appreciate that people do have ideas and taking up every idea that may possibly be worthwhile is an important objective for a company. The road to this goal is long. Many things are to be found on the road, in plants or in people's heads that are not put into practice. If all these ideas were implemented, a large proportion of the problems would already be solved; for there are not so many great, grandiose ideas in the world. It is often the little things that take humanity a step forward.

Guntern: I would like to support this view. The inventor Edison once said, "Genius is one percent inspiration and ninety-nine percent perspiration." It takes a lot of work to pursue an idea to its conclusion. And the road to the destination is littered with the relics of good intentions. Why do the good intentions often lead to nothing? As you said, people do not listen to each other and do not want to talk to each other because they think they know so much better.

A second reason why so many ideas fall by the wayside is that management frequently lacks the courage to fight vigorously for an idea as soon as major difficulties crop up.

A third reason for this problem is the "not-invented-here" syndrome that Mr. Maucher mentioned. In other words, people are envious of the person or group that has produced a good idea. Great ambition often leads - even in very clever people - to mutually competitive inhibition. And this, precisely, is what we are striving to curtail.

Works by Helmut Maucher
Leadership in Action, McGraw-Hill, Inc. New York, 1994.

KAZUHIKO NISHI
Japanese business executive

One of the few fervent advocates of integrating Eastern and Western ways of thinking and doing to meet together the challenges of our time, Kazuhiko Nishi has been lecturing Media System Engineering at Tokyo Institute of Technology since 1990.

Born in 1956 in Kobe City, Japan, he attended Tokyo's prestigious Waseda University. At the tender age of 21 he established ASCII Publishing Corporation, (the forerunner of the present ASCII Corp.), of which he was appointed Director and Chief of Planning. Two years later he was Vice-President of Microsoft in charge of the Far East, and soon afterwards held the same position at Microsoft in charge of new technologies and also became a board member. At 26 he could boast the creation of the world's first mass-produced portable computer, Radio Shack TRS 80/Model 100 and NEC 8201 A. His seven-year relationship with Bill Gates ended in a split which many analysts predicted ASCII would not survive. But survive it did, and beautifully. Nishi is currently President of the dynamic corporation and its subsidiaries, a half billion dollar group of companies that went public in 1989. He received the distinction of *Global Leader for the Future* in 1994.

Introduction by Gottlieb Guntern

The invention of the steam engine, the electrical light bulb and the automobile made energy the pace-maker of industrial development. Today information is increasingly taking its place on center stage. To generate information, to maintain, transform, distribute, and dissolve it again is becoming *the* core business of more and more industrial companies all over the globe. Within this business, Mr. Kazuhiko Nishi plans to play a major role, to win his company a leading edge, to widen up his strategic advantage. I venture to predict that we will be hearing a lot about him in the years to come.

Nowadays all kinds of information gadgets from video games to scanners, to computer screens, to the CD-ROM, to modems, to electronic mail and the like are becoming the preferred toys of children but also, increasingly, the preferred tools of adults. "Data highway" is the famous catch word that electrifies all those who are vaguely or intensely interested in computers and data processing. It seems that the same role that roads and highways once played for the transportation of matter-energy, data-highway will play for the transportation of information - and information, as you know, is the glue that holds together the fabric of a society.

Like Steve Jobs and Bill Gates, Mr. Kazuhiko Nishi belongs to those wonder kids who had highly innovative ideas very early, as well as the strategic power to put them into operation, at a time when other kids their age were completely absorbed by the traditional problems of puberty. He studied mechanical engineering at Waseda University, then started his own ASCII corporation at the age of 21. At 26 he created the world's first mass-produced portable computer. He then joined Bill Gates and became vice-president of Microsoft. He returned to Japan and now, at the age of 38, he is at the head of Japan's largest software firm, ASCII Corp. and its subsidiaries, a half billion dollar group of companies that went public about three years ago. There are four core businesses - but I shall leave that to Mr. Nishi.

I met Mr. Nishi last year at the World Economic Forum in Davos , where he was elected a "global leader for the future." Why? Because Mr. Nishi is very much appreciated by the Government of his country for being (a) a visionary and (b) a strategic thinker of very, very high caliber. He is now mainly interested in two things: digital compression of audio signals for the global transportation of this kind of information and digital compression of video signals for the same purpose.

My wife and I met Mr. Nishi, as I already mentioned, last year in Davos. He invited us for a helicopter ride and as we watched him observe the snow-capped peaks of the Swiss Alps, we could see that his mind is a high-speed multiprocessor unit. He seems to follow four kinds of thought very clearly and logically - as you will find out in the hours to come - each one independently, yet somewhere mysteriously connected all at once. So I am very pleased to welcome you, Mr. Nishi.

Kazuhiko Nishi

I would like to begin by saying that in Japan, journalists work long hours. When they retire, they start new businesses; and they all fail. It is a well-known fact that one should never let a journalist run a company. I do not know about Europe, but in Japan, journalists are regarded as typical non-businessmen. I wondered why they are so weak in business, and I have discovered this: the very basics of journalism is 5 W 1 H. This is the first lesson you are taught in the journalism class, whatever the college or whatever the university. 5 W means when? where? who? what? why? and 1H means how? But every time a journalist writes an article, there is a thing called a deadline. For instance somebody writes: "Yesterday a dog was run over by a vehicle in Zermatt and the dog is dead." The deadline is coming; the article has got to be sent in. So the journalists always forget to analyze "why." And this habit of just writing things as they are, repeatedly over 30 or 40 years, is going to result in a personality who never thinks about "why." This is the weakness of Japanese journalism.

When something goes wrong, many people just say: "Why did that happen? Why did you do it?" And sometimes I also say to myself, "If I had done this yesterday, or if we had made a more thorough inventory, we could have increased our sales." We use "if" for the future or for the past and "why" to grieve about and criticize the present. And we always think, "I don't know what is going to happen in the future." That is the typical attitude. But I think we need to change that attitude. We have to think about "why" for the past. Why this happened, why he did that and therefore why this is going to happen. Then we need to ask ourselves, "What if this happens? What if I do this?" If, if, if for the future. The transition lies in using "if" for the future rather than the past, and using "why" for the past rather than the present, trying to bridge "if" and "why" by "how." How can we cope with today? How much and how many? This is a very, very important viewpoint. And this is actually my daily

257

basic way of thinking. I love to read history, but I have a bad memory for remembering ages, dates, names. What I really enjoy when reading historical documents is wondering about why things happened. I also love to think about the future: **if** I do this, **if** this thing happens, **if** stocks crash again, and so on. This is the beginning. Now let me tell you a bit about my activities.

1995 marks my 20th anniversary of being in business, or I should say, of being independent. I left my family and became independent in 1975. I went to a college called Waseda, not because of the name, but because there was a very famous professor who was an expert in robotics. From the very beginning, I had very concrete ideas: I wanted to let robots play baseball, and let a robot make a home run. The reason is this: when you play baseball, the ball travels very fast from the pitcher's hand to the batter. And I was thinking about the speed of the ball and the speed of the nerve impulse. I had discovered in my high school years that the brain does not control the body. Of course, the brain triggers very important decisions and dictates your activities, but why are famous baseball players able to make home runs? If the baseball player's eyes recognize the ball coming and then the hands and body start moving, it is too late. The nerve impulse travels relatively slowly. I once read a book that some 65 million years ago, dinosaurs had multiple brains because they were so big; they had one brain here, one brain there. So I looked into the human body. As it appears, there is only one brain here, but I felt there may be something hidden in the nervous system. I felt we could make a robot that could cope with very high-speed action. So in the first year of college I proposed to my professor that we make an intelligent motor. Motors used to be very stupid; you would just connect them to a power source and they would rotate in certain directions. But if we add a computer to a motor, the motor suddenly becomes intelligent and we can train it. That was my concept of intelligent motors. My professor said, "Well, this is a good concept, but first of all you should make the computers. And I said, "Please, let me make robots." "No, you have to make computers for the Professor's project." So I had to help my professor first in order to be given my freedom, and I actually started my computer career in the Robotics Engineering Department.

In 1977 I started a publishing company to publish some articles I had written which were considered too "unique" at the time for publication. When I had about ten articles, I decided to start a magazine company. The first issue was easy and the second issue was pretty hard. I did not know about businesses at all, but I started to learn about them.

In 1978 I had the opportunity of designing a computer for a Japanese company. For that I needed to buy a software, and the only software company who had it was Microsoft. The company was headed by a gentleman called Bill Gates. He and I got along together very well. The first time I saw him, we sat down and talked for seven hours straight. We agreed to work together, and we put our agreement in writing in a one-page memo. This memo lasted almost ten years, but since it was so ambiguous, it caused us to separate.

In 1979 I designed the very first Japanese personal computer and launched the product for NEC and Oki Electric. Nobody in Japan knew how to use the computer, so I had to make a demonstration. On the first day a company came and asked to buy three sets of computers for the United States. The name of the company was IBM. Oki was counting on the fact that they could sell a lot of computers to IBM, whereas NEC asked Microsoft to design something similar for them. IBM was very productive, so they only asked to buy software from Microsoft, whereas Bill Gates and I proposed to IBM that they make a totally different kind of computer, using large micro-processors, large display, graphical interface, and joy-stick interfaces rather than small micro-processors. At that time IBM perceived computers as very high-level machines; for us, they were game machines. So we went to the radio shack on the corner of the street and bought a game joy-stick for a radio shack color computer and connected it to the IBM machine. That was all we had to do - there was no patent related to this. This really was the inception of the IBM personal computer in 1981. We also designed a software in the same year, although I was a member of the designing team for hardware. We went to IBM several times and talked a lot with them. We came up with the software called MS DOS and GW Basic. GW Basic stands for "Gee Whiz!" Basic, but everybody at Microsoft remembers it means Gates William, which is Bill Gates.

In 1982, after completing the project with IBM, I did a lot of traveling because many customers wanted to have a similar product. It was a nuisance to carry machines with me, so I gradually came to think that we had better make a portable one. A company called "Compac" made a so-called portable computer, but it was a very heavy machine. I insisted it was not portable, and the president of Compac would say, "Oh, it's portable within the office." So I said it was a **removable** computer. One evening a Compac machine was stolen from the office, and their comment was that it was indeed portable. After the computer was stolen, they decided to add a key locking system. In 1982 we designed a truly portable machine. That was the first time I flew to

Europe, to the Olivetti headquarters in Ivrea. I was very pleased with Olivetti, and the Olivetti people were very pleased with my machine, and they launched the portable computer as Olivetti's M 10 portable computer. In the United States it was sold as a handy portable computer; in Japan it was distributed by NEC.

After our success with portable computers, we started looking around for a new project. And we discovered that the big market was the home. So we began thinking about the requirements of a machine for the home. We considered VHS and many hardware companies - Sony, Matsushita, Toshiba - which manufacture different hardware but run the same software. Many different software companies create software which can run on different videos. At that point computer software could run only on some very specific machines. So, early in 1981/82 we introduced a new concept: a compatible machine with compatible software. This MSX-computer, which was the predecessor of 8 byte machines like Apple 2, made a successful entry into the entire computing in 1983. So you can see that during the first ten years of my computer experience, I was engaged in designing and engineering mostly software and some hardware.

In 1983 we faced the limitation of software, so the next step was to design semi-conductors. To do so, I wanted to have a customer and minimize risk. At that time semi-conductor designing was really in the hands of professional engineers and not in the hands of software people. But we designed the software, or chip, for AT&T. The first time I went to them, they saw me for only five minutes. They gave me several instructions and told me to come back in a week or so. The next time I went, they saw me two hours and said, "Please come back." The third time I went, they discovered I was flying in from Tokyo, Japan, so they gave me lunch. The next time, the vice-president came and we had a two-hour meeting in the afternoon. On the seventh visit they invited me to dinner and said they were happy to give me an order for quantity one. Here I was starting a very small business with AT&T which was to become very big.

At the same time there was a thing called a Microsoft mouse, which was my design, and the original patent was held by Stanford University and Xerox. We went to Xerox and we went to Stanford to get the license for the mouse. I asked how much the mouse cost, and Xerox estimated $ 5,000 a piece. Thank you very much. We bought only one. We took it apart and decided we could make it for $50. In the company everybody said, "Let K. Nishi take care of this." O.K. There were big debates: A Xerox mouse has three buttons. A Microsoft mouse has two buttons - you know, the famous PC mouse - and the Apple mouse has only one button. Let me disclose the story behind the number of buttons on the mouse. Originally Bill Gates said, "Let's have one button on the mouse." Somebody else said, "Well, Steve Jobs' mouse has one button. Then Bill Gates said, " Xerox has three buttons." I said, "Well, we probably should have two buttons." Everybody agreed. "By the way," somebody said, "a mouse has two eyes." Sold. That is the story of the decision of how many buttons to put on the mouse. Today our computer mouse has only one button. I am sorry for that.

We also started a project called "Windows" which has become very popular software, but I was beginning to be more and more inclined towards hardware. There was a big debate in the company over doing the hardware or sticking with the software. Microsoft decided it was a software company, and I wanted to sell hardware, so we said good-bye. I decided to return to Japan. That was in 1985 and marked the end of my first phase of experience.

I had been working part-time for ASCII in Japan and eventually became president. At the time ASCII was just a publishing company worth about 100 million dollars. We started a software business, semi-conductor businesses, communications businesses, and when we reached the size of about $150 million, we went public. At that point I felt I could not make every decision. The company was going in many directions, so in 1990 we adopted the division systems: a company within the company concept. I also felt that the ultimate future of software was movies. So I took the opportunity of editing the screenplay, directing the music and producing the movie called "Fried Green Tomatoes." Some of you might have seen it. It was a medium-sized movie, costing about $30 million and distributed world-wide. It made about $150 million in the US, so it was a relative success. Our company decided to get more involved in the movie business, which later turned out to be very tough. In 1992 we had to repay a compatible bond debt to our Swiss investors. In order to do so, I had to borrow from the bank. The bank demanded a profit ratio of five points more to repay the additional credit of about $150 million. So I had to restructure. This was a lot harder than in other Japanese companies. I started my restructuring not because of the bad economy, but to improve my profit ratio. Now ASCII is about $500 million in size and has approximately a ten percent operating profit. Unfortunately, I had to stop making movies, but I am thinking of coming back to that.

In 1994, after the computer wave, there was a big movement to connect communications to the computers, and American Vice-President Gore was supporting this concept of a National Information Infrastructure. Later he switched the slogan from National to Global, GII. I was fascinated by the concept, so our company made a special task force team to start analyzing what the intention of the Americans really was. We began thinking about information infrastructure and decided to get involved in the business. It was very interesting. Soon enough we discovered that communications is the key to putting a computer in every household, on every desk. Communications was our discovery. In 1995 this is our size and we are based in Japan and in the US. We want to start some operations in Europe pretty soon, perhaps. But let me briefly explain my view, my visions about computers and consumer products.

Computer history began in 1981 when IBM launched the personal computer. IBM believes that they invented the PC and that it sold because of their name. That is a mistake. The computer was bought because of the software called 1, 2, 3, Spread Sheet. This is a simple sort of calculator. And in 1985 a company called Sun Microsystems launched the product. Originally it was used as a scientific computer, but some people started to use these work-stations with the relational database software. The most popular software is from a company called Oracle.

Thanks to these work-stations, programming became very easy. We used to program computers in COBOL; we don't have to use COBOL anymore. By changing small portions of the text, the system can be very flexible, and this combination of relational database and work-station created the movement called down-sizing. This was the cause of IBM's downfall: it did not pay attention to this down-sizing until late 1992. In 1990 a company called Apple Computer announced a computer called Macintosh. A company called Adobe came up with Macintosh and launched a software called Desk Top Publishing. Many people bought Macintosh, and many people still buy Macintosh today because of Desk Top Publishing. Before Desk Top Publishing the thing was just a straight, very simple word processor using daisy oil printing or dotmaker printings or golf ball printings. The forms were fixed; size was fixed; there were no lay-outs. It was just a plain text. Today's computer is much more than that.

The years 1981, 1985 and 1990 are highlights in the computer industry, for they mark improvements in something old; somewhat like BASIC

Interpreter was improved to become Spread Sheet, computer processing improved to become Desk Top Publishing, and COBOL improved to become Relational Database. It is interesting to note that these three so-called inventions were big enough to create big companies. In the case of IBM, its personal computer business became very big. Some companies became very big thanks to a single product: Apple Macintosh made Apple Computer a large company. Lotus, Olaco and Adobe also became large companies.

If we think about the future, 1995 will be a milestone because these phenomena occur every five years. The next thing that is going to happen around 1995 will be in the category of work-stations. The key in predicting what is going to happen is to identify existing or hardly used applications. Today's application is electronic mail. If somebody comes and makes electronic mail as simple as opening ordinary mail, then that is going to be the big trend. I assess the future is going to be multimedia mail: not just sending a text, but sending a voice, a video and even software; anything. This is going to be important. The next invention will occur around the year 2,000, and the big thing is going to be PC. Many people expect PC will go into the home today. I say, no; it will be going into the home in the year 2,000; we have to wait another five years.

The next focus in computer industry is not the home, but the office and how to make the most of computers in office communication. This is my vision. Regarding consumer electronics, 1945, 55, 81 are Japanese dates, so it may be different in Europe. In 1945 and 1955 there were two big consumer products launched on the market: radio and television. In 1964 and 75 two interesting products were launched: Boss based on magnetic tape. One is called cassette, the other is called video-cassette or VCR. Radio and television were invented by many people: Marconi invented radio communication a long time ago, but it was RCA, the Radio Corporation of America, who really took the initiative of setting the standard in FM radio and television sets. For the cassette, Philips has been very active; for the video-cassette, Victor corporation of Japan; and Panasonic has been very supportive for the VHS, of course. In 1983 a thing called the compact-disc was launched by a Sony and Philips joint-venture. This revolutionized people's listening habits regarding music. I would expect that around 1995 or perhaps the following year , a digital video-disc will be appearing on the market, small, as good as the compact disc and carrying two-and-a-half hours or more of very high quality audio and video. That product is going to come, for sure, for the simple reason that 1995, 93, 83 were the years of wireless tape; the next step has got to be the disc. And audio, audio, audio, video, video, video: video-disc. A compact-disc is digital, so we'll have a digital compact video-disk. And by whom? There are lots of business opportunities, I think. In the year 2,000 I feel the price of this digital video-disc is going to be very low, more so after the device is popularized as a video disc player. It will be connected to the information network and thus, to the world. First the office will be connected and then the home.

Why is such great progress being made? Why do audio and video electronics become a cassette, and a cassette, a compact disc? Why does television encompass VCR and VCR become a distributor disc? When thinking about the future, thinking "why" is most important. And looking back over the history of consumer electronics, we can take the radio as an example. Radio was originally short wave and for listening to the news. Later it became FM and the major programs were musical. Then people wanted to tape the music. That was the introduction of the cassette tape. As the cassette tape became more popular, record software companies started to sell music recorded on tape. The transition was from radio to cassette. Then, as lots of people had lots of music tapes, Sony invented a thing called the "walkman" for people who want to listen to music with a small cassette tape recorder. But everybody complained that they wanted better quality, pure quality, so the compact disc was invented. The same story is repeating itself with video. Television used to be television just for news and sports, but when people started televising movies, everybody wanted to buy a video-cassette to tape the movie. As television VCR became popular, the chain of shops called video renter shops became very popular. The war between VHS and Better Brands was over. VHS won, not because of the quality of its hardware, but because of the variability of its movie coverage tape. So we are in constant transition. Yesterday Madam Ishioka demonstrated that the color quality in video movies is terrible but that it is good in slides. What if we had a video projection system with the quality of film? That is the product we are looking for, all right. But I was very happy I was not watching Dracula's last scene on a very vivid color projector. If so, my brain would have gone boom!

So, Ladies and Gentlemen, the next innovation is going to be the computer video-disc, which is going to be connected to networks in the 10 or 20 years to come. The next part of my speech is about businesses, because the second phase of my career concerns business. I would like to explain briefly how I have gone about developing my businesses by thinking. In around 1990 our company introduced the division system. The idea came from a very famous company called ABB. Last year I had the opportunity of seeing Percy Barnevik, the CEO of ABB, at the World Economic Forum and enjoyed his speech. ABB was the first company to go from a pyramidal to an orchestral organization, and I love that concept. Why do we need to switch to the orchestra? Why do we need to switch to the small company or company within the company? My reasoning is this: toward the year 2,000 or 2,005 there are going to be a lot of changes which I would call mega changes, in the economy, the weather, the exchange, all at the same time. We used to be able to predict what was going to happen, but when so many changes come at once, it is impossible to do so anymore. The only company who can survive such changes is the company that behaves small. It may be a large company, but it has to behave small, to move fast. That was the reasoning behind the division systems. I have been practicing division systems for over 5 - 6 years, and I would like to point out some of the problems.

Essentially a company within a company is a small group of 50 people where the general manager of the division is responsible for writing the business plan, for all the activities and for the independent balance sheet, profit-loss, and cash-flow. Every 6 months these managers show me the business plan. As I participate as executor of this system, I am aware of two things: first, everybody in the company focuses on the budget, the achievement levels, profits and sales. My scheme is to distribute copies of the business plan to everybody, including the receptionist. Some people felt that giving the business plan to the receptionist, who might leave the company tomorrow, was too dangerous. But I said: "Do it." My receptionist can easily remember that Company A, Company B, Company C are very important companies. So when people from these companies arrive, she is extremely nice to them. This is just one example of sharing the plans with everybody. I have discovered that working in relatively small groups of fifty is a very effective way of sharing objectives and creating a feeling of unity; the problem is creativity. Because people are always concerned about their achievement level of sales and profits, the more they think about that, the less they think about what is really new, really fun, what things we really have to do because our competitors are doing them. Many people think that as long as we get through the budget, we do not need to worry about our competitors. That is not so.

The second important thing is warmth as a company and the feeling of belonging. A group of fifty people is a small company within the company, and the feeling of belonging is belonging to that division but not to ASCII

265

Corporation. The company I run is relatively small, but if there is a company with some 200 divisions or 1,000 divisions, then I fear people will not feel any loyalty to the parent organization. I would be very interested in discussing this point with the ABB people. At any rate, my conclusion is that introducing the division scheme is going to activate people's creativity. I also personally go and talk to the employees and encourage them, so the personal touch in communications is the key for maintaining the warmth and a sense of belonging.

The International Zermatt Symposium on Creativity in Economics, Art and Science: just what is creativity in economics and business? A very straightforward answer is - profit! But is it really profit? I have seen many cases of profit-making companies, especially oil companies, where the people are very unhappy because the top-management will consider only stay-on profit-making projects. So let me switch from profit to prosperity. What does prosperity really mean? Does it mean tons of money? The answer is no. Prosperity is the drive toward happiness. In art, it is the search for beauty; in science, it is the search for the truth. I am not an artist, I am not a scientist; I am a businessman. So when I think about creativity in business or economics, I feel my target is this: creativity in business is the search for happiness. By the way, there is a company called IBM whose slogan is "Think." This company became very successful, very large and kept investing in large computers when many people were buying small ones. They felt that as they had been successful for the preceding forty years, they should go on in the same way. Suddenly there was a crash. Today IBM is under very, very severe restructuring. I am not the president of IBM, I have no relationship with IBM today, but if I were requested to give them a new slogan, I would add "Feel" to "Think." This would imply two changes. People may not be accustomed to doing so, but they have got to **feel** what is going on. Too much thinking is not good.

I would like to say here in this Symposium, that half of our time is spent in thinking, and half, in feeling. Please do not think when you are feeling; this is very important. I would like to propose the "3B's" that are very important in feeling, especially in generating inspiration. I speak from experience; let me explain: I asked my wife, "When do I really come up with good ideas? When I am very talkative, when I am really energetic?" She replied, "When you are in your bath, not moving. And also when you are in bed, you are very creative." These are relaxed situations. I also feel creative when I take off after work.

So I thought about it and came up with the "3B's": break, bath, bed. When you take a bath, you are so relaxed, you do not think about anything. You just relax. When I relax, sometimes I fall asleep, but sometimes I start thinking, "Wait a minute! This and this may be interesting." I have seen in the last twenty years that the secret for new ideas lies in the "3 B's." So much for my comments on creativity.

The next topic concerns global issues. My name is Nishi, and Nishi means "west" in Japanese. So from the very outset I am aware of what west is and what east is. Although Japan is in the Far East, my name is "west." I think the theme for the 21st century will be the amalgamation of East and West and North and South. This North-South-East-West issue is going to be the hottest topic of the new century. Why? Because thousands of years ago, man developed a Western style of culture and an Eastern style of culture. Take medicine: the Western approach to medication is to use drugs. If something is wrong with your organism, take the drug, fix it or cut it off. That is what the physicians prescribe, and the effect is felt within three hours. In China, which is almost the Mecca of Eastern medication, you change the organism, and you change the system. You eat some vegetables, you take some herbs, and gradually, slowly, your body changes. The effect takes three months. If you are seriously ill and cannot wait three months, you die. But then if you just take a very strong drug that kills part of your organism, that too, is bad. So in this case, a combination of Eastern and Western medication looks very interesting, and that is what many doctors are out to achieve.

Getting back to businesses, I was on the Board at Microsoft. I learned that if you do not speak up at the Board meetings for one year, it means that you have no opinion, and you are fired. Board meetings are almost a sort of fight. In Japan, typical Board members always listen to the President. If the President says "white," I am white, if the President says "black," I am black. Now that is a good Board member. Yet the Chairman is required to ask everybody's opinion before making a decision. This is a very interesting contrast: in the Western approach to management, individuals have to stand up and talk and insist; in the East, you do not really have to stand up and talk. You are respected, your opinions are listened to. That is a sort of totalitarian approach. I would say that ideally, we should combine both approaches. Thus everybody's opinion would be highly respected and everybody would be given the opportunity to speak out in a more non-competitive way. That is probably the future of management, and I feel it will really work well.

As regards feeling, there is a thing called "meditation" in Western culture. And there is an Eastern equivalent called "Zen." We have to take the good from the East and the good from the West and try to make them co-exist. That is probably the trend toward the 21st century.

Now let us talk about the contrast between North and South. Typically the North is rich and the South is poor. In the case of Italy, southern Italy does not have much industry, whereas northern Italy - Florence, Milano - is very rich. In Korea, South Korea is rich and North Korea is in trouble. Germany is not just North-South, but East-West; America's North and Asia's North, which is Japan, Korea, Taiwan, Hong Kong, are prosperous; the rest of Southeast Asia is relatively underdeveloped. Can we let North and South just drift apart? Of course not! Germany decided to re-unite. It is just a matter of time before Korea re-unites, and Italy has been united for a long time. My point is that even though we can expect a lot of trouble between North and South, people are going to come together despite that. We have to cope with the problem with a lot of wisdom, and this is another very important issue.

Let me point out briefly the great difference between China and India. I had a subsidiary in Beijing, China so I have had some experience there. The Chinese people are very sensitive to poverty and very sensitive to equality. If I pay a person some money for a job, and somebody else who is doing the same job is getting different pay, the people start to complain very strongly. There is a very great awareness of equality and of poverty, and that has been the headache of the company which operates in China.

Indian people are different. I take full responsibility for my statement when I say they don't really care about poverty. If they receive so much money and have to live on it for 2 weeks, fine. A rich person goes by; who cares? That is the general attitude of the people in India. This strong contrast in the perception of equality and money is probably going to be the most important success factor for the countries in the 21st and 22nd centuries. Many people feel that China is going to prosper most in the 21st century. I think that India is the country which is going to prosper, not because of its industrial power, but because of the mental power of the people plus their infrastructure which uses the English language.

The next point I would like to discuss is dreams. Today's topics are intuition and creativity, but the product of intuition and creativity is dreams. How can you have a dream through intuition and how can you make your dreams come true through creativity? When I look back on my almost twenty years of experience in business, they were dedicated to turning dreams into reality. I would like to disclose the know-how of making dreams come true. I have never done this before, and you may object, but please listen for a few minutes. You need a piece of paper for this, or a word processor. Now think about the greatest dream you ever had, the bigger, the better. Divide this big dream into small dream goals: in order to make it come true, I have to do this and this. In dividing dreams a word processor is quite useful, but you can do it on a piece of paper. It takes about two or three hours to write a list of 300 things to do. If you are really energetic, really creative, really enthusiastic, you can come up with 1,000. Include even the small things like saying "hello" to your boss or "thank you" to your customer. Then let them sit for a couple of days. The following weekend you spend another three or four hours subdividing these small acts to make a list of 10,000, maximum. And you start checking: this, I can do, this I have done, and there are several things which you do not know whether you can do or not. But you have got to make decisions: yes, I can do it or no, I can't do it, or I want to do it; make a strong positive imprint in your sub-conscience: I can do it. Then go to work. You forget everything, fine. You come back the following weekend and check again, and you discover at least five or ten things you have already done. You keep on in this way. (This is just some material stolen from a seminar on creativity.) The important thing is this: you will soon find that you are stuck, you cannot go any further. Before putting these documents into the shredder, wait a minute. Where you are lost, I recommend you start an inner conversation between your real self and your ideal or subconscious self. Try to activate your subconscious self and be the ideal person; and keep this conversation to yourself, or your family is going to think you are going insane and need a psychiatrist! My ideal self says, "You can do it, I know you can do it." My real self says, "No, I am tired, I am sick, I can't do it." The conversation can last twenty, thirty or even fifty or sixty minutes. But you will discover that your ideal self always wins. So you sleep it through and start making a new list, from the dream downwards. By repeating this and looking back on what you have already done, you will have continued energy. This process is very important in discarding the unnecessary objects listed. After careful examination, you find you do not really need to do 1,000 things. All you need to do are about 300. This process of forgetting is very important also. I would say a big dream is the sum of thousands of tiny dreams. The key is to have a big dream. You name the size of your dream. The company's limit is the limit of the president's dream. If the company is operated by a consensus of many people, the company's dream is the sum of all the employees' dreams. And believing "I can do it" is really most important.

Feeling is very important and so is moving. Impressions are very important and so is thinking. This is the approach I have discovered over the last 18 years. I recommend you try it, and I will probably come back next year. If something good happens, please let me know. If something bad happens, then give me a hard time.

The second key word I would like to mention after "dream" is "harmony." Harmony implies co-existence, acceptance. If there are left-wing people and right-wing people, a left-wing company will let the leftists dictate everything and rightists will not be allowed to exist. That is a problem. The basic theory of our society in future is to admit different kinds of people, different ways of thinking; the key is harmony. The basis of harmony is understanding, especially in North-South-East-West issues.

The last and most important key word is peace. We must understand our differences; we must allow others to exist. And after all, what are we striving for? Prosperity? Beauty? Truth? I would safely say everybody wants peace, in the true sense. The key to achieving peace is understanding and accepting our differences and building from there. If there is no communication, war will be inevitable. I respect this country, Switzerland, that declared permanent independence in the search for peace, and I would like to use this word peace to close my speech.

What about my expertise on computers and communications? We are geographically dispersed and we are different. We speak different languages. Some forty or fifty years ago, some people tried to make a universal language called "Esperanto," but in vain. English is getting to be a *de facto* Esperanto in parts of the Western world. Of course there is a whole sub-set of varieties in non-English speaking communities. I myself am making my speech in English which is not really English, but a sub-set of English. I would like to call "English 2,000" the Esperanto we may have been looking for for a long time.

By connecting computers and making sure that people can communicate, we are going toward better understanding our differences and coming up with a lot of new and rich ideas. That is probably the basis of building up good understanding toward peace. I would like to close my presentation with a network; not just a physical or electronic network, but a human network, in which people get together in a quiet place and talk, as we have done today. Thank you for inviting me and thank you for your attention.

Discussion

Guntern: When we began working here in Zermatt with these International Symposia, I was doing some thinking about vision. And I came up with the idea that to have vision is to look far into the future. Now you said something quite different today: vision is seeing the gaps in applications in the present. You have computers, you have software and you have to see what is lacking; this is your window to opportunity, and you go for it. What helps you to see these gaps? There are many people working in your business, looking at the same world, but they do not see them.

Nishi: I think the key is knowing the brighter side and the darker side of history. I have seen what has happened in the computer industry in the past 20 years. Many people write biographies or their autobiography. Ninety per cent of biographies are true, ten per cent are total lies, but they only look at the bright side of history. The only way to be able to identify the "why" of things that have happened, is to look at both sides. One of my hobbies is reading biographies and autobiographies. I have a huge collection.

Guntern: Napoleon, for instance?

Nishi: Some of them. But all of Napoleon's biographies are somewhat artificial, so they are not terribly interesting. The records kept by Napoleon's subordinates, however, are very interesting.

Guntern: What have you learned from those records?

Nishi: He was such a crazy man. He did too much. I like him very much, and what I have learned from his biographies is that you have to slow down. If you slow down, things are a lot better for you.

Guntern: Another strategic question: When people write something - books, novels, scientific papers, proposals, whatever - and they get a rejection slip once, they are disappointed. The second time, they are even more disappointed. The seventh time, many people just fall into resignation, bitterness, and stop there. Now you took this as a challenge to found a new business. What helps you to deal with rejection, frustration? What gives you the strength to go on?

Nishi: Let me explain this rejection episode: When I wrote the summary of my first paper, I went to the editor and he said, "Yes, go ahead." So I did. But when I brought in the finished paper, he said no, because the title was too journalistic and not academic. The paper was on a computer-graphic system and the title was *Making Video Games.* "The title is too childish," he said. So I said, "Well, what if I change it to *The Research on Interactive Computer Graphics and Animation?*" He said, "Accepted." So I said, "No thank you, I will do it by myself." My intention had been to explain to the public very simply, something which is complicated, hard to understand. That is my basic approach. I had no inferiority complex about my paper not being accepted. Many of you have noticed that my presentation uses no more than 2,000 words of English. Of course, I make mistakes. But I want to make things as simple as possible. That is my motto.

Guntern: And you fully succeed.

Nishi: Well, I am still making an effort.

Compernolle: I wonder if you should not add an "S" to your "3B's": break, bath and bed, but also stress. Sometimes you can be very creative when you are under stress, when you have to meet a deadline. This is what Gregory Batson called "creative frustration."

Nishi: You have just mentioned a very important point. The assumption behind the "3 B's" is that you have to go through prior very strong thinking. I am not saying you have to be under strong pressure, but that inspiration comes after intensive thinking, during the release from that intensive thinking, such as breaks, bath or bed. Then there is a hint, a light comes on. Without the stress or heavy thinking, if you just sleep, bathe, or spend all day at a break, nothing will come out of it.

I would like to make a point here. Once a year I go on a week's vacation with my family to a small island in the south of Japan. What happens is this: on the first day, you feel you want to call your company. On the second day, you don't want to call the company, but you still want to read the documents. On the third day, you want to send a memo, on the fourth day, you want to make phone calls, and on the fifth day, you are tired of making phone calls. On the sixth day, you are finally settled and have totally forgotten everything. You don't even know who you are. Then you have to go back to Tokyo and start re-habilitating your business skills. So when I go back home and go to work, I keep asking silly questions and people look at me like something's wrong; I am totally out of circuit. Going on vacation requires two weeks of re-habilitation back at the company. But changing one week's vacation into two weeks, gives you a totally different experience. That is, on the seventh day, when you are totally quiet, you are reset. On the eighth day, you feel you want to write something. On the ninth day, you start looking for a pen. On the tenth day, you start looking for a piece of paper - not just a small napkin, but a large piece of paper. On the eleventh day, you write a ten-page memo. On the twelfth day, you edit the memo. On the fourteenth day, you are fully charged and ready to go to work. So I strongly recommend you have two weeks of vacation and not one. That is called re-creation. And I think many of you already take two weeks. But here is this poor Japanese businessman who has never taken two weeks off for vacation. Now, finally, he has decided to do it.

Bellus: I am from Ciba-Geigy. Nishi-San, I would like to ask you something about the business part of your presentation concerning creativity. You pointed out that you have a company with small divisions and the managers have to think about budgets. They are under pressure regarding profitability, prosperity, so creativity is a problem. Certainly you have some vision or concept or perhaps some dream about how to overcome this difficulty. Let me ask perhaps just one question connected with this: of course, all your co-workers have their dreams. You said the limit of the company is the limit of the president's dream. These certainly conflict at times. How do you overcome this problem?

Nishi: Excellent question. That is a topic we actually discuss every day: to encourage the creativity of the general manager of the division who is responsible for running the division on the basis of the budget. One approach I have taken is this: If there is anything new, any new project which is not on the budget, they have to come to me and give me some small presentation, and we immediately agree on additional budgeting and fund the project. It is a small venture-funding kind of thing in the company. That is number one.

Number two is that nobody is born to be president. And nobody is born to be a successful general manager. You have to go through mistakes and you have to learn from them. What does success really mean? You have to have "hands on" experience. So, when I look at a general manager, I ask myself why he is so creative. These people have a track record of always achieving successful projects. So we intentionally put a potential general manager on a tough project, but one which we feel is going to be a success. We give him a special assignment to do with a limited budget. If there is an unlimited amount of money, then people do not think. So give them the experience of success. This is the answer. We create success artificially and imprint the experience onto general managers. The key is always to have room for some additional thinking. You know, if you just touch the trigger of a gun, it fires. This goes for very high-precision guns. But on low-precision small guns, there is a small thing called play, and you have to have play within the budget. About five percent. That is the point.

Q.: What if a co-worker, not only the head of the division, has a dream and you can't fulfill it, you can't allocate this 5 % to his dream? Usually that co-worker gets frustrated. And you cannot spend hours and days persuading him that your dream is better than his. How do you deal with this, how do you establish harmony here? In Japanese companies you probably have the same type of conflicts as we have in Western Europe. But somehow you seem to deal with them more successfully.

Nishi: Good question again. Well, the scheme I have adopted is that mainly the general manager is in charge of executing the budget. But we have another position called "coach," which is vice-president of a given sector. A coach is a person who just sits on the bench and watches how the players play. If something is wrong with the player, he says "time" and gives him a hard time and some instructions. The responsibility of distributing the "play" money is in the hands of the coach, on my behalf. I also said the limit of the company was the limit of the president's imagination; but I went on to say that the limit of the company was the sum of all the employees' imaginations. This is our philosophical approach. Western companies are owned by the shareholders; in Japan, the company is owned by the employees and some top-managers. The key is the close relationship between the company and the employees, who have mental ownership of it. Everybody feels like he is part of the company, and we can integrate the imaginations of all the people.

Guntern: Obviously the more you demand a higher rate and quality of innovation, the more you have to shift your order and control management to a management which is inspiring and motivating. Now, what we often see is that if something goes wrong, the CEO fires somebody.

Nishi: It is easy to fire people. But the mission of the CEO, staff president, and coach or sector vice-president if something goes wrong, is to observe the division and analyze what went wrong: what was expected from the budget, what happened, and try to fix it. If we see that the division is in a mess, then the general manager will still be called general manager but will have no responsibility. It is like an ambulance. When we set things straight again, the ambulance goes back in silence. That's our system. The issue is that there is nothing wrong with being sick, nothing wrong with making mistakes; it is how to recover from that state. Our approach is to send in a special mission to fix things.

Guntern: You also explained to me in Davos what you do with colleagues who are not very performant: you go and find out something that they do well. Could you explain that a little bit?

Nishi: Sometimes a general manager is performing below our expectations. We give him several chances, and if he is still underperforming, we ask him to step back from general manager to just manager. There he is going to do better than anybody else. Gradually, he regains his confidence. It may seem very tough demoting a general manager to manager, but as time goes on, after a month or two, he feels more energetic again. During the revitalizing period, we give him some training on how to be a general manager. Then he feels better and I guarantee him another chance with a new challenge. By accepting the new challenge and recovering from his mistakes, he regains confidence, and this is very important.

Q.: There is something I have often heard, and I would like to ask if you have experienced the same thing: the same amount of creativity is not needed in every phase of a project. I believe creativity is needed especially in the early phases. If you dream up something new, then creative people and input are required to get things moving. When things are structured, you need people to implement them; you need to get things done and respect dates and produce results. I don't think all people have the same talents. If you take successful implementers and put them on a new project because they were so successful earlier, you may be surprised that they fail in the new project because they are not the right person for that particular duty. So I think an important aspect is also to put the right people in the right phase of a project. Creativity might also be wrong in certain phases of a project or there may be too much of it. Do you agree or have you had similar experiences?

Nishi: I agree basically. There are two kinds of people: those who are leaders and those who are managers. Management-inclined people really do manage, and leadership-inclined people really agressively challenge things. In analyzing creativity, I believe there are two elements: one is creative, that is, if you think of something and you start moving, you feel you can do it. But another element in creativity which differs from the way of thinking is that there are certain skills you can learn. You can change your state of mind by learning. You can be very creative. Creativity is not an exclusive license for some highly talented people. A creative approach is something you can learn. My observation is you can have creative thinking, creative skills. I agree that the people who come up with the ideas and those who implement them have different skills. Some are more sensitive, some, more analytical. An architect is not always a good interior designer. An interior designer can be a terrible architect. There is a three-dimensional approach and a two-dimensional approach and these are complementary. Sometimes you find a good architect who is also a good interior designer, but that is something I still do not see a lot. I hope I have answered your question.

Q.: I have a somewhat complex question which I shall try to state clearly. It deals with the time factor you had, the issue of intuition and also experience. Let me start by explaining what I mean. I recently read an article about good tennis players. It said that the top ten tennis players have a reaction time which is about average. This reaction time is longer than the time from the service to hitting the ball back. So people were wondering why good tennis players are able to hit the ball back when it comes faster than their own reaction time. The answer was intuition. They have a certain intuition about how the ball is coming and therefore they can react in a shorter time phase. And then the question was, how do they acquire this intuition? The answer was that they have 100,000 templates of prior services in their mind with which they can immediately match the service coming in and hit the ball back. Now, if you put that on an industrial scale, some people have good intuition and this intuition is based, to some extent, on experience. Experience is probably having seen or done certain things a hundred times. If you relate this to our time of rapid social changes, such experience is basically diminishing because things are happening faster. With this in mind, my question is: do you think intuition is based on experience in terms of things that have gone wrong, or is it based rather on successes or is it a mixture of the two, or where does it come from? It has to come from somewhere, and to some extent experience must be related to intuition, because you cannot just be intuitively good. This good has to come from somewhere. Does it come from failures which you have gone through and analyzed or rather from successes?

Nishi: This is a very interesting question. You spoke about tennis players and their intuition based on experience. I do not do sports, but I watch them and have my observations. I think the key to sportsmanship lies in respecting the pre-determined formula and rules; but you have to be clever enough to identify the weakness of your opponent and shoot him within the rules. The definition of sportsmanship is searching for the opponent's weakness and aiming at that. That is one comment. It has nothing to do with creativity. I think the winning tennis player's intuition is not so much a physical skill, but rather being able to assess his opponent's weak point. Then there is the intuition about unexpectable things, things which are going to happen very fast or are changing very fast. I think people have different approaches to objectifying their experiences, extracting from them, defining the elements, storing them in their memory. Someone may store his experience simply as a series of actions; that is one approach. He may store his experience as a record of successes; that is another approach. Everybody must have a different approach in storing his or her past experiences as objects of memory. That is probably the key. So, there is an element which is independent of time. If you have enough time-independent elements as a basis for your intuition, your intuitive power will be independent of the changes in time. If your intuition comes from very time-dependent experiences, then it is not going to be effective for very long. That is my answer.

Guntern: Thank you, clear enough.

Lichtenberger: You said global networking was a good way of connecting creative people, but sometimes I think we are really running into an information overkill; there is too much information.

Nishi: No, no.

Lichtenberg: Let me give you an example: When I have a new idea, I want to find out if somebody has already had the same idea before me. I do not want to "invent" the same thing once again. So I do some text research, I go to this room where this guy is sitting and he tells me I have to be very, very subtle and write sixty lines of questions for this retrieval system. I think about it and I write sixty different topics or I try to find a very narrow one, and then he says it's great and he gives me ten tons of extracts from different journals. So I am sitting with 10,000 different people who thought about something somehow connected to my idea...

Nishi: Well, you are making a mistake in the way you search for information. The best way is to ask people who are experts in the area. That is one thing. Too much dependence on computer database is the big mistake. Ask people. First ask your professor, "Who knows about this and that?" Through the network, you contact the people and ask your question, and the answers start coming in. Well, this is merely technical advice, but I would not say that there is information overkilling. You go to a book shop; there is overkilling. You go to a record store; music is overkilling the music store, but somehow you identify the music you like, somehow you pick up the *Penthouse* you were looking for. So do not be afraid. Information never kills you. There is going to be a scheme which is going to make access to information very easy. It is just a matter of time. If you feel information is overkilling, yes, you are going to be killed. The way to bridge today and tomorrow, which is the time you really have to worry about, is finding the expertise in people.

Lichtenberg: The people who sit like synapses at the end of this network have this great tool for spreading information; but actually they are not spreading out information, they are just...

Nishi: That is correct.

Lichtenberg: If I publish, I exist. You ask a very little question and 10 million people scream different answers at you, all at the same time, and it takes so much time to find the jewels in this ocean of non-worthy information. I think as people we have to change also; we have to be capable of using this great instrument of global networking and sort out the information and just spread out what is really worth spreading out.

Nishi: Well, let me make three points. Number one is that Internet is incomplete and the French are making efforts to come up with an Internet called "hypernet." In American government policy bodies, they are not calling it Internet anymore, but "ODN" - open data network. So it is changing, and the French approach is more innovative. No doubt all the approaches will eventually be connected. I think it is going to be easier to use.

Point number two is: what will be the criterion of this network communication? Two things: one is network communication, not really people to databases, but people to people. I think you should really talk to people through the network, and not to databases. Just what is a database really? I would like to say it is an electronic book. You go to a bookstore and you buy a book; likewise, you go to the network and pick up a piece of information. It is a new type of book. If you think network is for meeting people and getting a new type of book, without complicated databases, then the world is going to be very simple. So I may be discouraging you, destroying your great ideas and dreams about network, but overexpecting is a bit dangerous. I would like to say that it is because of network that the computer is going to be everybody's device, like television and the telephone. My career over the past twenty years has been without networks. I have changed because I have seen the value of communications. If I make only computers, I am going to know only about computers, but because I am aware of communications, I am aware of people and I become aware of the differences between nations. That is really the beginning of thinking global.

Herzog: I should like to make a comment. I think the quality of communication is a very important issue. You apparently have the problem that when you open up a line, 500 people answer with a lot of junk just to show that they are there. There is a desperate need to be there and to show the world that you are there. Of course, the evolution of computer networks and information highways is evident for the next ten, fifteen or twenty years, and we will have an enormous flow of information through new channels, yet at the same time a strange thing is happening. Despite all the tools and instruments of communication - fax, telephone, handy, Internet and television sets - strangely enough people are lapsing into deeper and deeper solitude. At the same rate we are mastering new tools of communication, people are becoming more lonesome. So the 21st century will not only be the century of more communication, it will also create, paradoxically, more solitude. It is a question of the quality of information. Why, for example, do we become so lonesome and sad and unimaginative if we watch television for too long ? Children lose their fantasies because they are watching too much television. It's a very simple rule: those who watch television lose the world; those who read, gain the world. This is very obvious in the rich area of New York, Central Park West, at night. You can see the flats illuminated through the windows, and you barely see a TV flickering, but you see books from the floor to the ceiling. In every single apartment of the really wealthy people, they are reading. So when you talk about network, please use the information in the right way; use it as if it were a bookstore.

Nishi: Yes.

Herzog: We have not found the right attitude. Of course, many things that will occur to us will inevitably add to our solitude because we cannot introduce deep qualities and deep meanings to the kind of communication that we will master in the future. It struck me very strongly when I read recently the Chinese poetry from the Tang Dynasty of the 8th and 9th centuries. There is a poem by Tu Fu for example, where he describes how he takes leave of his friend. He takes a boat and departs on the Yellow River. He knows that he will not be seeing his friend for the next eight or ten years and there is no possibility of sending a letter or a messenger. Returning to your friend or your lover without having had any communication for so long had a very deep meaning at that time. For us, it is so different: when I return from Mexico, I pick up the telephone and tell my wife that I'm going to be back at 8.15 in the morning, and all of a sudden my return has no significance anymore. So because of the instruments of communication, we are losing depth and we are losing something very essential that makes us human beings. What you are proposing, your business approach and your vision, which is very deep and very clairvoyant, indicates the direction in which we are moving in computer technology, in the exchange of information. Yet nobody speaks about the quality of it, nobody speaks about solitude. Everybody thinks that communication is such a wonderful and great achievement. Of course it is, but we are not really mastering the tool. You have a clear idea how to do it and you suggest going to the bookstore rather than using the computer network. Yes, go to the bookstore and do not forget the importance of books. Those who read will gain the world. It is as simple as that. Tell that to your children. The same thing happens with television. Why is it that when I sit in a movie theater - well, my life does not change in a movie theater - but a movie all of a sudden becomes part of my existence, part of what illuminates me, part of what keeps me running? I see the same film a year later on television, and it just does not touch me anymore. It loses all its quality. How can we, for example, transpose the power of a movie into a different medium, into a different channel of information? How can we find a new quality to that? It is a question of quality and of overcoming solitude, and there are very few people who think about that. I believe we should start getting into that very intensively as well, at the same time. It is relatively easy to figure out what is going to happen in the next 5 or 10 years with information exchange and with laser discs and with certain networks and machinery and tools. This is not really a question; it is just a remark.

Nishi: About solitude. When you are wired on the network, you sometimes receive junk mail which is not addressed to you, but just randomly comes to your address. Something is happening in the ordinary postal system. So I may be a very superficial person and not really think about solitude or friendship over the network, but when I receive junk mail or nonsense mail, I do not respond. When I receive a deep message - even very short - which really touches my heart, I respond yes or no. Or sometimes I respond just with an exclamation mark: I once corresponded with a famous novelist; the electronic mail simply transmitted a question mark and my friend sent back an exclamation mark. So I responded with a second question mark. The answer came back in the form of five dollar signs, which is big news. I have discovered two things through this electronic interchange: if I do not start talking, nobody ever talks to me. So even when I am wired, I am alone. You have to start talking, you have to say hello to your people and of course there are all sorts of nonsense mail. A small "Hello, how are you?" is meaningless. But if you intentionally choose to respond to the mail which has a very deep significance for you, then your friend over the network is going to be your strong mental friend. If a departure in ancient China meant eight years of absence, eight years of loneliness, I prefer a thousand times, a million times over, to keep in touch with friends, with my family. I have had the experience of seeing friends again after twenty years, and this time lapse I can recover in five minutes or so. I have never really thought of solitude, but now that I think of it, I have such a feeling when I turn the switches off and everything is silent. By operating your network selectively, it is not a chaotic, but rather a very orderly and peaceful one, I would say.

One point I would like to mention is that I am thirty-eight and my children are ten and twelve, and I am seeing a totally different generation who has been living with computers and communication. My friend Nicholas Negroponte, the famous computer philosopher and a professor at Massachusetts Institute of Technology, recently wrote a book called *Being Digital*. It deals with many things, including this information networking society. In it there is a person who gets married over the network. A lady from Miami, Florida is in New York and meets a person who lives in Austin, Texas over the network, and they talk a lot. The lady feels this man is so nice, so understanding, and they would like to get together. So she jumps on the plane and flies to Austin without letting him know she is coming. Knock, knock. When he opens the door and she sees him, she discovers he is a bit different from what she was talking to. So she is disappointed, says good-bye, goes home and starts talking with another person in Frankfurt, Germany. She comes to like him and goes to Frankfurt. Knock, knock. She discovers a wonderful person, exactly the same as she was dreaming of, and they get together and talk a lot and decide to get married over the network. Many people join in on this network wedding. Some people say it is crazy, but things are changing like that. If there were no network, then it would be impossible to meet people like that. If there were no television, no movies, our life would not have evolved so much. But because we have invented these tools of culture, movies, television - the intensity, color and image in television - it's far different. Just compare Eiko Ishioka's presentation of the film versus the television projector. It is so different. Of course technology is not a perfect solution for everything, but my point is, there is a new age of people coming who understand the use of computers, and they lead pretty different lives and have pretty different styles. I am not in a position to criticize their approach, but we have to be very careful about the influence of these devices on society. I just want to say that our children are experiencing a totally new world with these digital devices, and I want to be open-minded about that.

Herzog: I am not against it, on the contrary. I am just trying to say we have to use it the right way. We have to find new ways of approaching it.

Nishi: Yes, I agree; thank you for your suggestions.

Guntern: O.K. I think we'll wrap it up here. Mr. Scholer, one last question.

Scholer: It is a very simple one, Nishi-San, I have a problem. You are a very busy company president, and you have time to read biographies. I am only a vice- president. I have virtually no time to read books and that is a pity; I do not watch much TV either. What am I doing wrong?

Nishi: Well, let me confess my style of life. I have very busy schedules, and my way of living may be a little extreme, but here goes: I have a library of about 50,000 books and a personal librarian. I have several thousand videos, a movie collection of some crazy movies, and 10,000 CD's. Do I read all my books? The answer is absolutely no. But I still go to the bookstore. There is a bookstore open at night, so on my way home from work, at around 11 o'clock or midnight, I stop over and buy three novels a week or every two weeks. Anything I am interested in, I buy. My wife always complains and kicks the book out of the bedroom, and it is automatically sent to the library to get classified. But I feel that some day I will have enough time to read them all, so I keep accumulating them; it is a crazy habit. From time to time, when I want to read about something, I go to my library and pick up about a hundred books on my topic and start reading. It does not take much time to read a hundred books. If you are really focusing on a specific subject like Greek architecture, reading very intensively does not take that long. If you want to watch a Disney movie, just grab the video and watch ten, fast forward. It may sound crazy, but it is really fun, like going to the buffet last night and picking out the food.

Until I got married, I was spending 99% of my life on business. I was counting how long it would take me to go from the company to my apartment, how much time I was spending on eating. Once I decided to eat breakfast in the car on the way to work, to maximize my working time, and that made for some really crazy years in my twenties. Then I met my wife and discovered I had different personalities. One is the businessman, nine to five; the other is K. Nishi, the person, the individual, without the title of president; just a simple individual; and the third is the husband of Midori Nishi and the father of her children. This change in my life from business to personal and family life, made it three times happier. The point is, I think you must have your personal life, you must have your family life, and I recommend that you do not read a business book on personal or family time. Please read whatever is of your personal interest on your personal time; that is my crazy advice.

Guntern: You have really illustrated, lived through, leadership today. A leader is a person who is able to inspire, to motivate other people - us, in this case - for outstanding performance. You can do that only because you have credibility; if not, we would not take up the signals you emit in the right way. Now you have got credibility because you have shown that you are a visionary, that you are a strategist and a patent-breaking Maverick, what you call a "crazy." I think the combination of all of these traits make up your personality and I would say that you belong to the category of real charismatic leadership. Now, "charismatic," like "creativity" and "intuition," is a very misused term, but it used to be an intelligent one with a very precise meaning. Charisma (*to Carisma)* in Greek means the irradiation of something you cannot capture in words, but which strongly touches you. And you have that.

Nishi: Thank you very much.

Guntern: You are a great leader. May I just say a few more words. Allow me to make two statements which may clear up a few things which have been said here. I do not believe that we live in an era of information overload. But we certainly live in an era of signal overload. And signal and information are two completely different things. If you take a president or CEO's desk, there are a lot of memos criss-crossing it. Many of them are quite insignificant. Why? Because some information is not true. Or maybe it is true, but it is ill-digested. So it is an art today to get to the core of what is relevant, to free oneself from the signal stream. But you never have enough information, and certainly never too much, as you never have enough creativity and of course you can never have too much of that either. You never have enough intuition, and you will never have too much of it. The second remark I would like to make is this: we have been speaking about intuition, and while you were talking, it was clear that your antenna kept scanning your inner horizon and your outer horizon - us, in this case. And you are really in touch with yourself; you are in touch with your instinct, your brain, your intuition, your emotions and you show it. Your rational thinking is very clear. Now, what is the difference between an intuitive person and a non-intuitive person, if both use words in their attempt to communicate? With an intuitive, authentic person like Mr. Nishi, you feel in touch and you feel that he is true. He compresses huge amounts of experience into very concise, well-formulated information that you can immediately understand. To play as simply as Bach, that is the greatest art, the greatest beauty: transparent simplicity, and Mr. Nishi has certainly shown that too. Now, beware of the other kind of talkers, the slick people who are very good with words, while their eyes keep flickering and avoiding your glance. A lot of cheating occurs in the industrial world, because slick talkers are making careers, and intuitive people are not always as good with words as Mr. Nishi. He belongs to another category. So intuitive people are often clumsy, circumstantial and somewhat vague. You should do everything to mobilize the resources of the intuitive people in your company and beware of the slick talkers. I have seen too many of these, and they are a pain in the neck in every company.

One last comment: experience. What is experience? Experience is not simply a memory of events. Experience is a memory of analyzed, organized, structured events. I will show you the interconnection between experience and intuition that you have alluded to in many different well-stamped formulations. Take a chessboard, and put twenty-five chessmen on it in specific, strategic positions. Now take two people, a grand chessmaster and a novice who does not know chess. Both are permitted to have a glance at the chessboard, then you block it and you throw the chessmen together. Ask your two people to reconstruct. The chessmaster will immediately place twenty-three to twenty-four chessmen in the right position; the novice will put about six in the right position. Now start a new game. Put the same number of chessmen on the board in a completely arbitrary way. Do you know what happens? The chessmaster will put six in the right place, and so will the novice. What is the difference? The difference is that paradoxically, you can have good intuition only if you have gone through a deep, repetitive analysis of facts and of inner and outer experiences. The chessmaster is a master, among other things, because he has done miles and miles of proper analysis. You can never be a person who operates well intuitively if you shun the hard work of deep analysis. Experience is something more. The deepest experience in life - we have all gone through this - is that you learn from your errors. One aspect of great leadership is allowing your colleagues to make errors. If you have decided on fixed or maximal precision instead of optimal precision, then you will kill your collaborators' imagination, intuition, and with it, their creativity, because they will be scared to death of making errors. So your open mind has opened ours a little bit, and this is vision: just one of the many qualities that gives you credibility as a great leader. Thank you.

EDNA O'BRIEN
Irish writer of fiction

Edna O'Brien is a daughter of County Clare in the west of Ireland - "a beautiful tragic country to be born into." To some she evokes James Joyce's Molly Bloom, for being Irish and lusty; for others, her literary genius recalls that of Colette. The author of five collections of short stories and thirteen novels, she has also been compared with Virginia Woolf, Yeats and Chekov. Her style, nevertheless, is hers alone: vivid, unique, one of words masterfully cascading through intricate plots. Enchanted, alarmed and deeply marked by the history and tradition of her beloved Erin, Edna O'Brien's first love affair was with her country. The mainstream of her novels and stories reflects domestic violence, the inner conflict in women, their complex, most often turbulent relations with men - set to the background of her heart-rending, war-ridden, passion-infested homeland. Her first novel, *The Country Girls*, was burned in the local parish courtyard. Edna O'Brien became notorious and went into self-exile in London, where she still lives and writes today.

Introduction by Gottlieb Guntern

For centuries Ireland has been a country welded together and at the same time torn apart by religious and patriotic fervor and antagonism. Now, to be torn apart seems to be a *conditio sine qua non* for becoming a good writer. Only a great writer is able to describe the lesion of identity, the torness and then to leap, with the help of ceaseless incantations, over the abyss of the ever- threatening self-destruction. Within the last hundred years Ireland, which has about half the population of Switzerland, has produced more outstanding writers than any other nation - or I would rather say culture - of this world: G.B. Shaw, Sean O'Casey, William Butler Yeats, James Joyce of course, Samuel Beckett, Brendan Behan and now, Edna O'Brien. During the last decade her reputation has been steadily growing to a point where the top press of the east coast in the United States has this to say, I quote: "Edna O'Brien ought to have her own stamp, her own flag. She is a country unto herself, a republic of letters." She has been compared to the French writer Colette, to Keats, to Yeats and to Chekhov. We heard yesterday from Wole Soyinka how difficult it is sometimes to face certain comparisons. But even if you are compared, you can still maintain your own identity, and if you read the work of Edna O'Brien, you are aware of the fact that she sings her own *canto hondo*, the song that comes from deep within. I have read a few of her eighteen books, and my general impression is this: Edna O'Brien is a painter who, like a Zen master, paints a whole landscape and the mood in that landscape with a few strokes of the brush. She is a musician with a very fine ear for the cadences of events; her language dances along with the rhythm of unfolding human encounters, fights and relationships. She follows a melody line that sometimes sinks down into the gall of bitterness only to climb up again, high into the sky of hilarity. She is a psychologist. With a few words she gives you the whole identity kit of a person or of an interpersonal relationship. She is a surgeon whose scalpel sometimes cuts quite deep below the skin into the flesh of hypocrisy and then she reveals the true face behind the mask of pretension, presumption and pomposity. She is last, but not least, a cultural anthropologist who has the honesty and the courage to call a spoon a spoon, a hammer a hammer, and a rat a rat. Her fertile imagination conjures up scene after scene. Her metaphors catch, with the same ease, the hues of a landscape, the mood of a soul and the texture of a human relationship.

Edna O'Brien

In the marriage feast of Cana, water was turned into wine, but in this century Soren Kierkegaard remarked that "Not only do we not make wine out of water, we make water out of wine."

Intuition: the power of the mind by which it immediately perceives the truth of things without reasoning or analysis.

This week we spoke of intuition versus rationality and more or less advocated its supremacy. But that is not the whole story, oh, no. It is too fallible, it is too circumscribed, it does not allow for the fact that we choose the definitions that suit us. Your intuition and mine are poles apart and what determines it is country, religion, ancestry and the sensibility which we cultivate in ourselves from the moment we are born. Is Saddam Hussein a man who works by intuition? Possibly he would think he is. Marat Sade believed that redemption was made possible by a complete debasement of the flesh. Fanatics who flagellated themselves believed the opposite. In both cases they must have responded to their intuition. Peter Abelard, when he submitted to being castrated to atone for his love of Heloise, was probably answering the voice of conscience, whereas she who waited for him all of her life was listening in vain to her own intuition.

Now my private history, like your private history, is a compound and a mishmash. It's the country we hail from, the locality, the known and unknown ancestors and the myriad impressions of childhood. Yet I have to tell you that my intuition and my mother's differed drastically and especially with regard to literature. I consider literature - and I always did - as an education, a salvation, a quickening of consciousness, and if one is very lucky, a transubstantiation. "Gaiety transfiguring all that dread," Yeats wrote in his irate older years. Literature is a magnification of life, that real life which all of us in our different ways are zealously fleeing from. "Mankind cannot bear too much reality," T. S. Eliot said. Literature, a deepening, a heightening, an ecstasizing, a peculiar magical leap by which an invented universe is made more intense; in Dante's

Inferno, more frightening; in Shakespeare's history plays, more bloody; in Emily Dickinson's poetry, more mystical. The entire spectrum of passion, of pain, of light, of feeling, of grace and of gross murder made more manifest, so that we as readers rise to it with the gusto that those great authors deserve.

"To read a book is to write it," Sartre said, and he was right. I did not grow up with books, in fact there were none in our village and in our house there were only prayer books and bloodstock manuals. There was a cookery book, of course. Yet I had an obsession with language, as if language was a Grail through which one would pass, a Holy Grail, leading to that frontier between sanity and insanity, between hope and darkness. Language was a key to discovery, the alchemy.

Now my mother saw literature as sin, naked unredeemable sin. It was as if in a previous incarnation she had read James Joyce's *Molly Bloom*, or had been Molly Bloom and privy to the prodigal lust which Molly permitted herself. Yet I shared my mother's and my community's feelings about other things, about God, Him of whom Samuel Beckett has said, "The bastard, he doesn't exist," therefore conferring on him existence. I believed God watched every moment of our lives because He was both omniscient and omnipresent. I was once told by a doctor that all Irish Catholics who were venturesome enough to take LSD underwent a crucifixion experience. I can vouch for it. Blood, Christ's blood and the mother's blood, along with the flames of hell were what engulfed me, complete with a plethora of language that married litany and obscenity, that believed the tabernacle housed holy and unholy things. It is interesting that some countries are mothers and some are fathers. We say Mother Russia, we do not say Mother Germany. Likewise I think that there is male and female intuition and that they strike differently. It is not a fixed thing, it is changing just as the atoms and cells in our bodies are altering as we sit here. What we feel about something today, we may not feel so insistently tomorrow, or am I wrong?

I want for a moment to refer to something that Mr. Brodsky said the other day. It was an example of his intuition which is also an extension of his hopes and could ultimately be called a wish. He said that in Czechoslovakia, if all the newspapers, instead of printing their political tosh, had decided to serialize *A Man Without Qualities* or *Remembrances of Things Past,* society there would have been changed. I don't believe it. I would like to believe it but I don't believe it. People, all of us, are changed only when we are willing to be changed. The unwilling are not. Roman Roland said that "Art is a great consolation to the individual but that it is useless against history." W. H. Auden put it differently: "For poetry makes nothing happen." It does and it doesn't. It survives history, it challenges it, but it could not or has not prevented wars, the holocaust and the ongoing catalogue of butchery. The most that one could hope for is that through suffering we learn and produce greater poets, and more devoted readers, people who will want not just to read but to re-read, not out of duty, not out of fashion, but by coming to realize that the secular world for all its pleasures and all its flatteries, is just not enough. We have a spiritual entity and in times of crisis we meet it. "Go seek a draught to slake thy thirst, go seek it in thy soul," Matthew Arnold said. It's good advice.

There is something that often irks me and it is this condescending distinction between prose and poetry. There isn't any difference. Prose if it is any good, has the rhythm and cadence of poetry and a great poem induces in the reader the sudden complex escalation of feelings as say *War and Peace* or a three act play. They filter in and serve the unvoiced necessities within us, they speak directly to the imagination and lift us to another region of consciousness.

"A sweetheart from another life floats there
As though she had been forced to linger
From vague distress or arrogant loveliness
Merely to loosen out a tress
Among the starry eddies of her hair."
W.B. Yeats

Five lines so dexterously wrought and with such rich imagery that we too shudder over this absent creature. Language alone does not constitute the miracle. There must be the unleashing of emotion, "the shiver in the spine," as Kafka termed it. Literature is a strong brew and teaches us things we would rather not know. "For the last time, I learn what I already know," Camus said and when I re-read a great work that also seems to happen to me.

So what have I learnt from my masters, Joyce and Chekhov? From Chekhov I learnt to try and not be afraid, to penetrate the deepest recesses of soul and psyche, to borrow. Everyone goes there, writer, non-writer, painter, cook, thief, lunatic - everyone goes there and many live there. It is there where deep work or deep despair is met. If one is lucky, something extraordinary evolves. A poem or a piece of prose or a thought. It is man's small stab at being God. It should not have vanity in it, but neither should it have humility, it is a moment of absolute power.

And from Joyce I learnt not to be afraid to reap from my own experience, but also to be audacious, to play with language, to recognize its potential, simply by not using it in the old and tired way, but in a new dynamic way. "Darkness is in our souls, do you not think? Our souls shame-wounded by our sins, cling to us yet more, a woman to her lover clinging, the more the more. She trusts me, her hand gentle, the long-lashed eyes." There's a sentence.

I worked in a pharmacy in Dublin because my family wanted me to have a practical career. One day, for four pence, I bought a second hand book called *Introducing James Joyce* by T. S. Eliot, and in between serving customers and making pills, I read a few pages of *Portrait of the Artist as a Young Man*. It was for me (I hope this does not sound grandiloquent) a revelation which in my giddy innocence I likened to that of Saul of Tarsus on his horse, seeing the light. It was the account of a Christmas dinner, the fire banked high and red, the ivy-twined branches of the chandeliers, a Christmas table with big dishes, a plum pudding studded with almonds, a bluish flame on top, and then an eruption, the eruption that shatters the Irish hearthstone, the old wrangles, sex and politics; the raising of the ghost of Parnell who was both hero and adulterer. And I thought this is our life, this is my experience, this is home and I don't any more have to write about things I do not know. Joyce gave me the key, or should I say a glimpse of the key. He was a genius, but he also considered himself a slave. Every day he went, as he said, to the far Azores and in the evening he came back. The loneliness that he must have felt is incalculable. He was a man almost penniless doing something radical with language, dissembling it, assembling it and daring to write a work such as *Finnegan's Wake*, which would put him beyond the boundaries of literature as it was known, or maybe ever will be known. Dublin, the Roman Catholic God and the body of a woman are his obsessive themes, at least when he started out. He described her as the sow who eats her farrow. He left Ireland, but she did not leave him. The streets, the ash pans, the snotgreen sea, the snorting of the horses on the Guinness drays, these and every feature of Dublin filled his mind. If he could not remember something, he had his poor brother or his poor sisters or a relative go down a street to check the awning over such and such a shop or the declivity of a bit of pavement in Bachelor's Walk. He scrutinized every feature of Dublin and then he remade it, gave it a mythic permanence. For me that city is as much Joyce as it is the actual city. He stalks it, he haunts it. To compound matters, there are little snatches of Leopold Bloom's cogitations engraved in bronze in the pavements but not very well cemented, so that one is likely to fall over them. He would like that. "First we feel and then we fall," he once said. It would seem as if he knew everything and the phenomenon is how. The other day I was delighted when Professor Kadanoff, speaking of physics, told us "...that the particles are always there, they do not go away." For me, that represented in the human psyche the lodestar of memory. The memory is always with us even if we lose touch with it. It does not go away. This is where a writer gropes in search of the half-remembered things, early sounds, non-sounds, figures glimpsed, emotions so deep that we have buried them. I am thinking in particular of Samuel Beckett and his play, *Footfalls*. A woman is pacing the floors in order to reach something vital, some clue to the pathology of her life. She thinks that by walking, she will walk her way back to it, but of course she can't. The writing journey is always about that. Freud wrote a long and engrossing essay about a bird, the web, the breath, the feathers and the flesh of a bird that skimmed the face of Leonardo da Vinci when he was in his cradle. Freud saw in it some illusive connection between the moment of trauma and the great works. Memory, for all the sorrows it brings, is our deepest muse and is as well the mother of intuition. It is what gives any work its impetus, its potency and of course the underlying sense of tragedy that constitutes human life.

Creation is not a happy thing, and writers are not happy beings. Having to do it again and again and again is the nightmare; having to make the journey to the unknown regions and come out with maybe a mere fragment. If we knew what we were doing, we would not need to do it. It is a search through the unconscious for what is only dimly apprehended. It is also an excitement. It is a discovery. You climb mountains not because you know what you are going to find, but because you do not know. So what makes one write, what makes one persist with this unhappy occupation? Who is it for? The self, the gods, the big world? I do not think one knows, no more than any of us know what it is we will dream tonight. Talking of dreams, I would like to tell you a tiny joke. My dreams are rarely comic; in fact were they to be painted, I am afraid that Hieronymus Bosch would be the appropriate person. Most nights in dream I am making a journey to an unknown destination. It might be an asylum, it might be a hotel, it might be a theater or a church. I dread going, but I have to go. Often I don't arrive, but one night lately I did arrive and was given my key and I wakened up shouting out the room number - it was 2684. And I thought "Ha ha ha, two sick parents ate four children." I mention it not to castigate my dead parents, but to remind myself that they too play a strong part in causing one to be a writer. My father told stories, he reveled in telling stories and my mother wrote me shoals of letters - in fact one every day - that had in them an empathy with nature alongside a morbid dread of offending God. I, too, am afraid of God even if I am not sure He is there. I write to keep myself this side of dread. At first, I believed I was writing to escape them and indeed rebellion towards them and towards country was a whetstone, but not the whole story. Anger is one ingredient of writing, so is frankness, but it is only part of the story. Mystery is the most important thing, mystery at life itself, the source of it, the termination of it, mystery at the complexity of human beings and the way fate catches up with us all. All children are artists by nature because they have this wonder about life and then, sadly, it fades. To remain an artist one has to remain a child and this is a perilous state, especially in a world where feelings are so readily and barbarously mocked; but keep them we must, they are our life spring.

I don't have a beautiful film or ravishing slides to show you or Wole Soyinka's skill with drawing, so therefore I just have to read you a story. First I will tell you how I think it came about. Every year when I went home, my sister met me at the railway station, and driving out the road we would pass a particular field where there was a woman going up a hill or down a hill with buckets. She was always carrying these two buckets and she wore a torn raincoat. One day I said to my sister, "Who is that woman?" "I don't know, she never goes to Mass," my sister said and then added: "She lives with her brother." An imaginary life for her came to me then. Not a wholesome life, not her as a paragon of the community but someone whose secret was such that she had to shun society. Yes, writers do make assumptions and work does have an element of criminality, but these are essential if we are to look into the pith of any human being. The story is called "Brother."

Brother

"Bad cess to him. Thinks I don't know, that I didn't smell a rat. All them bachelors swaggering in here, calling him out to the haggart in case I twigged. 'Tutsy this and Tutsy that'. A few readies in it for them, along with drives and big feeds. They went the first Sunday to reconnoitre, walk the land and so forth. The second Sunday they went in for refreshments. Three unmarried sisters, all gawks. If they're not hitched up by now there must be something wrong; hare lip or fits or something. He's no oil painting, of course, my brother. Me doing everything for him; making his porridge and emptying his worshipful paw, for God knows how many years. Not to mention his lumbago, and the liniment I rub in.

'I'll be good to you, Maisie', he says. Good! Good! A bag of toffees on a holy day. Takes me for granted. All them flyboys at threshing time trying to oggle me up into the loft for a fumble. Puckons. I'd take a pitchfork to any one of them; so would he if he knew. I scratched his back many's the night and rubbed the liniment in. Terrible old smell, eucalyptus.

'Lower... lower. Down there. Down to the puddiny bits, the lupines. All to get to my Mary. He had a Mass said in the house after. He said he saw his mother, our mother; our dead mother, something on her mind. I had to have grapefruit for the priest's breakfast, and I had to de-pip it. These priests are real gluttons. He ate in the breakfast room and kept admiring things in the cabinet, the china bell and the bogoak cabin, and so on. He thought I'd part with them. I was running in and running out with hot tea, hot water, hot scones; he ate enough for three men. Then the big handshake. My brother Matt giving him a tenner. I never had that amount of money in my whole life. Ten bob on Fridays to get provisions, including sausages for his breakfast. Woeful the way he never consulted me. He began to get hoity-toity, took off that awful trousers with the greasy backside from the sweating and lathering on horseback, tractor and pushbike; threw it in the fire, cavalier-like. Had me airing a new suit for three days. I had it on a clothes-horse, turning it round and round every quarter of an hour, for fear of it scorching.

Then the three bachelors come into the yard again, blabbing about buying silage off him. They had silage to burn. It stinks the countryside. He put on his cap and went out to talk to them. They all leant on a gate, cogitating. I knew 'twas fishy, but it never dawned on me that it could be a wife. A wife? I'd have gone out and sent them packing. Talking low they were, and at the end they all shook hands. At the supper he said he was going to Galway Sunday.

'What's in Galway?' I said.

'A greyhound', he said.

First mention of a greyhound since our little Deirdre died. The pride and the joy of the parish was she. Some scoundrels poisoned her. I found her in a fit outside in the shed, yelps coming out of her, and foam. It nearly killed him. He had a rope that he was ruminating with, for months. Now this bombshell: Galway.

'I'll come with you, I need the sea breeze', I said.

'It's all male, it's stag', he said and grinned.

I might have guessed. But why they were egging him on I'll never know, except 'twas to spite me. Some of them bachelors have it in for me; I drove bullocks of theirs off our land, and I don't give them any haults on bonfire night. He went up to the room then and he wouldn't budge. I left a slice of griddle bread with golden syrup on it outside the door. He didn't touch it. At dawn I was raking the ashes and he called me, real soft-soapy, 'Is that you Maisie, is that you?' Who in blazes' name did he think it was - Bridget or Mary of the gods! 'Come up for a minute', he said, 'there's a flea or some goddamn thing itching me, maybe it's a tick, maybe they've nested'. I strip the covers back and in the candlelight he's like one of those saints that they boil, he's thin and raky. Up to then I only ventured to him in the dark, on windy nights when he'd say he heard a ghost and I had to go to comfort him. So I reconnoitre his white body while he's muttering on about the itch, he says, 'Soldiers in the tropics minded itch more than combat'. He read that in an almanac.

'Maisie', he says in a watery voice, and puts his hand on mine and steers me to his shorthorn. Pull the stays off me. Thinking I didn't know what he was after. All pie. Raving about me being the best sister in the wide world and I'd give my last shilling and so forth. Talked about his young days when he hunted with a ferret. Babble, babble. His limbs going into jelly, and then the grunts and him burying himself under the red flannel eiderdown, saying God would strike us both. Us both?

Next Sunday he was off again. Not a word to me since the tick mutiny, except to order me to drive cattle or harness a horse. Got a new pullover, a most unfortunate colour, like piccalilli. He didn't get home that Sunday until all hours. I heard the car door banging. He boiled himself milk, because the saucepan was on the range with the skin of cold milk on it. I went up to the village to get meal for the hens and everyone was gassing about it. My brother had got engaged for the second time in two weeks. First it was a Dymphna and now it was a Tilly. It seemed he was in their parlour - pictures of cows and millstreams on the wall - sitting next to his intended, eating cold ox-tongue and beetroot, when he leans across the table, points to Tilly and says, 'I think I'd sooner her'.

Uproar. They all dropped utensils and gaped at him, thought it was a joke. He sticks to his guns, so much so that her father and the bachelors drag him out into the garden for a heart-to-heart. Garden. It seems it's only high grass and an obelisk that wobbles. They said, 'What the Christ, Matt?' He said, 'I prefer Tilly, she's plumper'. Tilly was called out and the two of them were told to walk down to the gate and back, to see what they had in common.

In a short time they return and announce that they understand one another and wish to become engaged to be married. Gink. She doesn't know, she doesn't know the catastrophe she's in for. She doesn't know about me and my status here. The Dymphna one had a fit, shouted and threw bits of beetroot and chicken gizzard all about and said, 'My sister is a witch'. Had to be carried and put in a boxroom, where she shrieked and banged with a set of fire-irons that were in there. Parents didn't care; at least they were getting one gawk off their hands. Father breeds herds, French herds, useless at it. A name like Charlemagne. The bachelors said that Matt was a brave man, and drink was mooted. So all the arrangements that had been settled on a Dymphna were now transferred to a Tilly. My brother drank port wine and got maudlin. Hence the staggers in the yard when he got home and loud octavias. Never said a word at the breakfast. I had to hear it up in the village. She has mousey hair and one of her eyes squints, but instead of calling it a squint the family call it a 'lazy eye'. It is to be a quiet wedding. He hasn't asked me, he won't. He thinks I'm too much of a gawk with my gap teeth, and I'd pass remarks and make a disgrace of him, remarks that he'd like to give him a rise and a cheer on wet evenings. All he says is, 'There'll be changes, Maisie, and it's for the best'. Had the cheek to ask me to make an eiderdown for the marriage bed, rose-coloured satin. I'll probably do it, but it will only be a blind. He thinks I'm a softie. I'll be all pie to her at first, bringing her the tea in bed and asking her if she'd like her hair done with the curling tongs. We'll pick elderflowers to make jelly. She'll be in a shroud before the year is out. To think that she's all pretty now, like a little bower bird, preening herself. She won't even have the last rites. I've seen a photo of her. She sent it to him for under his pillow. I'll take a knife to her, or a hatchet. I've been in Our Lady's once before, it isn't that bad. Big teas on a Sunday and fags. I'll be out in a couple of years. And he'll be so morose from being all alone, he'll welcome me back with open arms. It's human nature. It stands to reason. The things I did for him, going to him in the dark, rubbing in that oil liniment, washing out at the rain barrel together, mother-naked, my bosoms slapping against him, the stars fading and me bursting my sides with the things he'd say. Dotey no less. I might do for her out of doors. Lure her to the waterfall to look for eggs. There're swans up there and geese. He loves the big geese eggs. I'll get behind her when we're on that promontory and give her a shove. It's very slippery from the moss. I can just picture her going down, yelling, yelling, then not yelling, being swept away like a newspaper or an empty canister. I'll call the alarm. I'll shout for him. If they do smell a rat and tackle me, I'll tell them, I'll tell them that I could feel the beads of moisture on my brother's pole without even touching it. I was that close to him. There's no other woman could say that, not her, not any woman. I'm all he has, I'm all he'll ever have. Roll on, nuptials, for daughter of death is she."

I mentioned the word criminality. Many people in my home town and in the environs felt that I had betrayed them. I had revealed their secrets. My first book, *The Country Girls* scandalized them and there was even a humble little burning in the chapel grounds of two or three copies. My mother told me that women fainted during this ritual. I was too frightened to say that perhaps they fainted because of turf smoke. She also told me that the post mistress who happened to be a Protestant - very relevant - told my father that I should be kicked naked through the town. The naked was also very relevant. I could not defend what I did to my mother, but neither could I apologize for it. I went on to write another book, and the opinion was that by comparison, the first book was a prayer book. Nor could I explain - I still can't - that to me writing was as important as existence. I did not write to disgrace them, but they thought I did. At least I was not silenced, only rebuked and as time went on, a little change came about, and it was all to do with celebrity or semi-celebrity. The moment one went on television, the subversive nature of the books was quite forgotten. I found that as disquieting as I had found the insults a few years earlier. Andy Warhol, I fear, was clairvoyant when he suggested that everyone wanted to be famous for fifteen minutes. Fame or the hunger for it often supersedes the truth of the work. But I have not come here to preach.

I was interested when Wole drew three circles to define the ancestors, the living and the unborn. When we are born and while we are still young, the hunger and thirst for life is very raw in us. It's everything. We leave home, we take examinations, we are desperate to succeed either at work or at play. Very often we also want to escape the world we grew up in, to wipe it out. I wanted cities, glitter, nightclubs, illusion, I wanted everything removed from fields and cattle and fodder and homemade bread. I think I believed that I could remake myself and make myself, if you like, more presentable in the big world, but of course I was mistaken. I ignored the ancestors and I ignored the unborn. These are stronger in me now and become stronger with each passing day and were in fact the hidden impetus for my last novel, *House of Splendid Isolation*. I made a journey back to my father's family house. It was not there. There was nothing there, there wasn't even a pillar or a mound of stones - only nature, the crows and the old trees and the lake, a mad moiling lake at that. For some reason the total absence of a house induced in me a kind of shock, a shock that I could not quite explain. It was about family and it was about history and the writer's compulsion to compensate for loss through words. I knew that I must write about it, but only had half of my story. The same day in my sister's house there was much talk of post office raids, of hold-ups, with everyone insisting that this was the work of the IRA. Then I heard a story of a particular raid, a hooded young man, armed knocking at a post office door and a woman through sheer exclamation giving him such a fright that he dropped his gun and ran for it. The woman, by the way, has since been called Annie Oakley. She telephoned the police, a car chase ensued and the young man was shot dead at the corner of a country road, which up to then had seen only a few cars or tractors or a school bus. I decided to pay a call on the policeman who did the shooting. I was curious to know about it and above all to know what he felt. He brought me to the spot where it happened and the scene was just the same - mist, the odd deer, quietness and a world that looked as untouched as the beginning of time. He described it in considerable detail, the speed he drove at, coming on the enemy car around a corner, getting out, the first shots, the "fella" falling over the bonnet of the car and his balaclava flying off into a ditch. I asked him what he felt and he thought about it. "When you're shootin', it's fifty-fifty, but when you've shot him, half of you hopes you got him and the other half hopes you didn't, because we are all Irish under the skin." It was a very profound thing to say, it was also very honest and it gave me the thrust for my story. It was as if history and politics were made human for me instead of being distant and theoretic. I wanted to tell the story of Ireland today through two voices, the voice of a woman in the big empty house and the voice of the terrorist who invades it. But that would only consist of the present. I also wanted to convey the past and it seemed to me that the voice of an unborn child would be the way to do that since it could touch on things beyond time. This is how it began:

"History is everywhere, in rain, or hail, or snow, or blood. A house remembers, an outhouse remembers, a people ruminate. The tale differs with the teller.

It's like no place else in the world. Wild. Wildness. Things find me. I study them. Chards caked with clay. Dark things. Bright things. Stones. Stones with a density and with a transparency. I hear messages. In the wind and in the passing of the wind. Music, not always rousing, not always sad, sonorous at times. Then it dies down. A silence. I say to it, have you gone, have you gone. I hear stories. It could be myself telling them to myself. Or it could be these murmurs that come up out of the earth. The earth so old and haunted, so hungry and replete. It talks. Things past and things yet to be. Battles, more battles, bloodshed, soft mornings, the saunter of beasts and their young. What I want is for all the battles to have been fought and done with. That's what I pray for when I pray. At times the grass is like a person breathing, it hushes things. In the evening the light is a blue black, a holy light, like a mantle over the fields. Blue would seem to be the nature of the place though the grass is green, different greens, wet green, satin green, yellowish green, and so forth. There was a witch in these parts that had a dark-blue bottle which she kept cures in. She was up early, the way I am up. She gathered dew. Those that were against her had accidents or sudden deaths. Their horses slipped or their ponies shied on a hill that ran down from her house. She had five husbands. Outlived them all. I feel her around. Maybe it is that the dead do not die but rather inhabit the place. Young men who gave their lives, waiting to rise up again. A girl loves a sweetheart and a sweetheart loves her back, but he loves the land more; he is hostage to it...

> *Gurtaderra is the Valley of the Black Pig and the last battle will be fought there and the Orangemen will meet the Irish Army at Cloonusker and Sruthaundalunach and the rivers will run blood. The Irish will be driven back through Gurtaderra and Guravrulla, but the tide will turn at Aughaderreen and the Orangemen will be driven back and defeated. In the morning it would be as easy to pull an oak tree out of the ground as to knock an Orangeman off his horse, but in the evening a woman in labour could knock him dead with a tassel of her shawl.*

It says that in the books.

"Bastards, Bastards ..." he says it again and again in each end every information available to him, says it without moving a muscle or uttering a syllable - "English bastards, Free State bastards, all the same."

My mother is listening and she is objecting.

Discussion

Guntern: Edna O'Brien built up a lot of music, a lot of tension, and there were some abysses in it, that made you feel a little bit uneasy, so that below the laughter, there was also some fear. She will now take your questions, your comments, whatever you have to offer in your dialogue with her.

Compernolle: You said you didn't bring a movie, but you have created a movie. This is the first time somebody reads some poetry to me and I could see it happen before me, so although you did not bring a movie, you have projected a movie in my mind. Thank you.

O'Brien: Thank you.

Q.: I'd like to say that you really brought this atmosphere of mystery that Ireland has. I remember when I was a child, I was probably seventeen, and lived in a town in Ventura, Brazil, and I was exposed to that mystery river when I read the *Portrait of a Young Artist* - an artist by the name of James Joyce. And then all of this stayed in my mind. But I was in your country after being exposed to *Finnigan's Wake* and to our James Joyce. It was the definition of the word that he gave, that magic word, what is pornography, what is not, what is the word by its own meaning? But when I was in your country and when you sent that fellow today, the bastard, under the bastard of not being born there... Thank you very much.

O'Brien: Thank you. I think the question is, aren't we all bastards? Probably, yes. But there are degrees of bastardom and also a distinction between thought and deed. The person I wrote about, who was to some extent based on an actual person, a terrorist, was a bastard to some and a hero to others. Now you may ask why I chose to write about him. Two reasons. I wanted to amplify the fate and the history of my country insofar as I could, to write of a situation imposed on Ireland against the will of her people. By that I mean the dividing of the country in 1922, a division which has resulted in twenty-five years of war, and also to learn as much as I could about a man who was killed for his cause and how it might have damaged him. It was not an easy subject. However, I would say that one of the privileges along with one of the duties of a fiction writer is to explore those very dangerous territories. Newspapers report things, but the writer needs to examine the human toll. This man told me a lot about his life, his decision to join the IRA, having been interned at the age of fifteen, his commitment to his own community and the recognition that by killing he would one day himself be killed. He told me one story that I will never forget. His wife was shot while he was in gaol. On the evening she was shot he had gone to bed early and went to sleep. The warders knocked on his door. He didn't hear. He slept until seven the next morning when the news was about to be broadcast, and his door was broken in. They said to him, "Your wife was shot," and for a minute he did not believe them, because as he said, they were always trying to break you. Then they turned on the radio and he heard it. He believed it then. His grief was enormous, even though he did nothing to emphasize it and I remembered something I had read by a young American soldier in Somalia who, writing to his parents, said, "War is a terrible thing and kills everyone in some way." It does.

And now I will tell you another story from that blighted province, and it is about a Protestant Paramilitary who let me be privy to some of his history and his doings. He was 14 years of age and still at school when he joined a Paramilitary organization. One evening their leader said, "We have a job - hands up, who'll drive the van?" A hand went up. His hand went up. He told me that as his hand went up, he felt such a hero. He felt proud and he felt afraid. So now four or five days pass, he goes to school, he goes home in the evenings, and it is Saturday evening, the evening on which the job is to be done. And he looks at television, a program called "Top of the Pops" so somebody is singing "Youpidoupidou," or whatever they sing, and it's time to go. And he meets his man, that he was arranged to meet. It's all done very harmlessly, he walks down a street, they wait for a car, it's a stolen car. He gets into the stolen car and he described it with such exquisite precision. The cylinder is in the car, the man has already come in the stolen car who has the cylinder with the explosive in it. There is a shawl in the stolen car, rather beautiful. Detail is always fascinating. There is a shawl, he spreads the shawl over the cylinder the way you might, in a sitting room, put it over a lamp shade. They drive to the pub, a Catholic pub, Ormeau Avenue, he gets out, places the cylinder and puts a match to the fuse, hurries down the steps, drives off, one street away he hears the explosion. And he thinks, "I'm a hero, I've killed Catholics." It could be the other way around, so I'm not taking sides, I'm just telling the story. They drive off, he's okay, goes back to school on Monday. Nothing happens for two to three years. He's betrayed. Betrayal usually comes from within. He is in his own house, mother and father, it's three o'clock in the morning. The policemen, Royal Ulster constabulary, RUC break the door down, that's how they come in. No need to knock. He's brought to the police station, he's interrogated, he says: "No, no, no it was not me, it was not me." Again another detail, the guard who is interrogating him, he's a bit rough with him, takes out - the guard does, the policeman - takes out a photograph of his own children, babies and children. The Irish are big families, usually the Catholics are bigger ones. Anyhow, he shows Ronnie this photograph and he says: "Will you swear on the lives of my children, that you did not do it?" And he broke. He couldn't swear, so he admits it. And the next day, he described again, a boiling summer's day and he's in a van, a black Maria with about ten or fifteen, a hulk of other men, all going to this prison, called "Long Kesh," and they're all heaped in over each other, like sacks of potatoes or meal or anything, cursing and blinding, different offenses, not all terrorists, some, and it's a summer's day and he knows, daylight, sunlight is gone for a long time. He's in for ten or eleven years. Now this young and very sensitive man said to me: "A couple of wonderful things happened to me while I was in there." And I said: "What was that?" "Well, " he said, "I studied, I learnt to read, I took a University course." Open University, which quite a lot of them do, some paint, some draw and some, like Wole was describing yesterday, realize that the mind is the last saving post. And he said: "Another wonderful thing happened to me. I was sick and I went to the infirmary, and I met a tyge," (A "tyge" is a Protestant word for Catholic, a kind of derogatory word, it's like when people say a "paddy" or a "mick.") "I met a tyge in the infirmary," - because they are in separate parts of the prison, for fear of riots. And he said: "You know, the guy didn't have two horns," meaning he wasn't the devil. He said: "I found out I could talk to him." And I said: "Ronnie, this is a wonderful thing." And then he said: "I would not want a Protestant government in the North again. Because our Protestant leaders are the most obstinate and bigoted men." I said: "In that case then, you, as a Protestant former paramilitary say, that you are, you would support a United Ireland." "Oh no," he said, "Oh no, no, no. I couldn't imagine being in a country where the currency was different. I want the Queen on the English pound note." Now this, to me, spoke more than multitudes of political dogma. He wanted the talismanic, ritualistic, mythic symbol. I said: "But Ronnie, we are all supposed to be joining the European Common Market. There are a lot of problems about it. It seems as if there's going to be a single currency." He didn't want to know that. He wasn't ready for it.

So what am I trying to say? Prejudices, wherever they flourish, lead to hate and hate leads to war and the only single chance we have of countering this is through openness, through enlightenment, through compassion and through fiction. Towards the end of *House of Splendid Isolation* the unborn child says, "To go in, within, is the bloodiest journey of all. Inside you get to know that the same blood and the same tears drop from the enemy as from the self, though not always in the same proportion. To go right into the heart of the hate and to sup from it and to be supped. It does not say that in the books. That's the future knowledge."

Q.: You said before that for you, memory is the mother of intuition. For me, memory is the father of intuition and the deep feelings and the deep pictures of the soul are the mother. And my question to you is, if you write a book, do you make a plan with your brain, or do you just begin to write with your intuition? **O'Brien:** Do I make a plan? No. My mind is too askew. A plan would not work for me. Writing is a bit like water divining or sleepwalking. You venture into it. You have maybe a first line or the germ of an idea, but that is all. Some books are planned. Thrillers, I expect, are planned, but the sudden moment of radiance through language is a visit from the gods. One day lately I was asked if I were reincarnated again would I be Irish and I said, "Three quarters... I would like to be a quarter French for the logic!" but I was not serious.

As a writer, one is always waiting for the hidden impulse. You cannot order it and you cannot say when it will come. One lives with the fear that one has gone dry, that one has lost the sap. It's like listening for a footfall or waiting for daylight or maybe even waiting for dark. You can't plan it. Sometimes a crisis or some kind of separation brings it on. When I left Ireland and came to England I only knew then how much my country and my actual family mattered to me. I was given the huge sum of £50 and I spent it on very practical things because I was very much under the tutelage of my husband. I bought curtain material and a sewing machine, but of course I had to write the book. I wrote it each day after my children went to school, it wrote itself in a matter of weeks and it seems to me that I was crying most of the time. It begins with, "I wakened quickly and sat up in bed abruptly, it is only when I am anxious that I waken easily and for a minute I could not remember what it was that worried me, then I remembered, the old reason, he had not come home. My father. My cold, mad, feary father I go back to you," Anna Livia says. I was attempting the same thing, going back to look for the father who could not be. Writing is a kind of retrospect. Yesterday I took a small walk here and I could not stop thinking of one of the great retrospects in literature, *A Farewell to Arms*. It reminded itself to me because it is set in a landscape such as this, high snowy mountains, the pine trees, frost in the pitchers of water, the stones and boulders washed and whished by the streams. It was as if I was living the book yet again. That is what writing does. It enables us to see how others feel and think, it is the last banquet between minds and it is as essential to us as any religion might be.

Guntern: At the end of these beautiful incantations going from life to death and back again, touching us deeply, making us laugh, and exhausting your energy and ours too, let us come to an end of this meeting. For when Kiros, the fleeting fellow, the god of the right moment is gone, you cannot catch him any longer. So whatever I could add, I would take away from you. Thank you very much for your participation.

Works by Edna O'Brien

August is a Wicked Month, Penguin Books, London 1967
The Love Object, Penguin Books, London 1970
A Pagan Place, Penguin Books, London 1971
A Fanatic Heart, Farrar Straus Giroux, New York 1985
The Country Girls Trilogy and Epilogue, Farrar Straus Giroux, 1986
The High Road, Farrar, Straus, Giroux, New York 1988
Lantern Slides. Short Stories, Penguin Books, London 1991
Time and Tide, Farrar Straus Giroux, New York 1992
House of Splendid Isolation, Farrar Straus Giroux, New York 1994

WOLE SOYINKA
Nigerian poet, writer and playwright
Nobel Prize laureate

Wole Soyinka was born in Abeokuta, Nigeria on July 13, 1934, into a family with a staunch sense of tradition and engagement. He studied literature and theater in Leeds, England and founded a theater group in his country in 1960. Five years later he dared openly to protest against the sham government elections and was promptly arrested. During the civil war in Biafra he stood up for the union of the rival parties - and was compensated with 28 months in solitary confinement. He taught literature at the University of Ibadan for a short period before being forced into exile from 1971 to 1988 in England, Ghana and Paris. Known to many as the "Shakespeare of Africa," Wole Soyinka was awarded the Nobel Prize in literature in 1986. But he is also a man of many talents, a socially and politically outspoken poet, writer, director and playwright, who has the courage to speak out against the totalitarian regimes and corruption which plague his country.

Introduction by Gottlieb Guntern

Wole Soyinka was born the son of a headmaster and of a very intelligent and caring mother, whom he calls "the wild Christian" in a memoir about his childhood in Aké, Western Nigeria. From the very beginning he was faced with two kinds of cultures: the Black man's Yoruba culture and the White man's culture of British colonialism. He must have heard more than once, I suppose, Rudyard Kipling's arrogant phrase of "the White man's burden," while sighing under the Black man's burden. Soyinka insists that before having been an author he was already a human being; but he is a very specific human being. He is also a political animal, but not somebody greedy for power. He is a real leader in his own right. He tried to prevent the war of secession in Biafra because he understood that if he did not fight tribal chauvinism, the ensuing genocide organized by a Mafia of power gamblers and economic parasites would destroy the country and its people. He paid for that with twenty-eight months of solitary confinement in a four-by-eight-foot cell. For the time being Wole Soyinka has left his country - or to put it more succinctly, he was forced to emigrate illegally. That is the official version. He knows that if a passport is withheld in his country, it may be a prelude for things worse to come. He is now traveling with a passport issued by the United Nations.

In 1986 Wole Soyinka won a Nobel Prize for his unique and complex work. What is a complex work, what is a complex personality? Yet another term often used and very often ill-defined. A work is complex not because there are many books or other entities produced per unit of time. Complexity is defined by the amount of information it takes to describe approximately and explain a work. Wole Soyinka is also a complex, multi-dimensional personality. He is a poet, a playwright, a dramatist. He was dramatic advisor at the London Royal Court Theatre, he is a short story writer, he is a novelist. He has been or is a professor of literature at the Universities of Cambridge,

Sheffield, Yale, Ife and Ibadan. His book *Art, Dialogue and Outrage,* is the best book on art criticism and social criticism I have read in the last twelve or fifteen years. He is a philosopher and a social critic. He is a very astute mind, and his mind can operate like a razor blade, sharp, sometimes full of irony because he hates pomposity, phony behavior and pretension. Although he is firmly rooted in his native Yoruba culture, he has been a transcultural nomad for many years now, at home everywhere that he chooses to be.

He dedicated his Nobel Prize acceptance speech to the Leader Nelson Mandela with whom he has many things - including solitary confinement - in common. Many of those present in Stockholm must have been shamefully aware of the fact that the leading men of European philosophy - like Hume, Locke, Montesquieu, Hegel and Voltaire - preached across the centuries the gospel of the White man's supremacy, which is one of alienation. In the name of White man's supremacy, some stupid and narrow-minded military and ecclesiastic missionaries have invaded the Black continent, destroying the "lesser gods" and replacing them by a better God, the Lord of Jewish-Christian tradition - in whose name, in turn, a lot of atrocities have been committed.

Wole Soyinka once wrote: "A tiger doesn't walk around in the forest proclaiming his tigritude. He jumps and catches his prey."

Wole Soyinka has taken many a leap and has caught many a prey. He will go on taking one leap after the other, for his work is still very much in progress and in process.

Wole Soyinka

Creativity is a subject which has always intrigued me. I think, in addition to being creative persons, most people at a certain stage also become critics. Now to be creative, you have to be critical from the very beginning. There is a kind of systemic criticism in which one looks over the process by which one produces and by which one's colleagues, friends and even ancestors did produce. It becomes a fascinating subject in itself. Fortunately, there are writers who are also critics and artists who are also critics. I think, in the story of creativity and intuition, they are a bit better than the millipede which one day stopped to count its feet and after that just never walked again.

I think we, as human beings and as creative people, can indulge ourselves from time to time in pausing and trying to understand the process by which we operate, even if we are not asked to do so. We must just try to understand the process by which we prepare to function or, at least, the foundations from which we draw the resources which we then try to present to the world as a kind of discovery, some kind of vision. Unfortunately, due to some unpleasant political uncertainties, I have not been creative lately. I do not even feel cultured, simply because of the very sinister directions in which my mind constantly appears to be moving. Not just over the past few months, but in fact close to about three years now, since we began to see the tenacity of an unproductive, very vicious, repressive dictatorship, which was not only negative in itself, not only static in its thinking, but the ramifications of whose existence have gone to deflect minds away from what should be their major concerns. By minds, I am not speaking merely about critics of government, I am talking about productive people: professionals, technocrats, businessmen, many of them even apolitical, but who have come to realize that the extension of this situation is inimical even to their own survival as businessmen, their continued productivity as lecturers, technocrats, even as students, market-women, or factory workers. So increasingly, the tempo of opposition has come

311

about, and as always, one gets drawn into this, to a point where very truthfully, I am not even feeling cultured, let alone artistic.

Creativity, whether we like it or not, is a very subjective process. It takes place from within an objective reality and a very multiple one, but the elements of choice, priorities, imaging and so on, is a highly subjective one. Let me say a few words about a certain leader who thought he was creative. When he came to power, he seemed a generally creative leader. There were certain moves he made, certain original paths he seemed determined to tread that, dictator as he was, the majority of Nigerians, including intellectuals, business people, students and workers, were prepared to give him a chance. Even I said: "Watch this being. He seems determined to make history." So he started off marvelously.

Of course at the same time, given our objection to dictators in general, we were watching every single step that he took. But there was optimism, especially as he came after a singularly vicious dictatorship, one of the most fascistic ever known, at least in uniform. So he arrived, knocked off this brutal military regime, and made a number of quite intelligent moves, both in the economic field and also in what seemed to be a very conscious attraction to himself, more capable and finer minds. In other words, he seemed absolutely determined to cut a different swathe from his predecessors, both civilian and military. For a long time it was a bit of a mystery. Its collapse reminded me - again I may go into the artistic world - of an experience that I once had. At this point everything began to fall apart, and we wondered how on earth he had made it during the first two, even three years.

I recollected my experience when I was directing a play, *The Road*, in the Goodman Theater in Chicago. There was an actor who was playing the lead role. I was very suspicious of him, but as those of you from the United States know, when you have an artistic director in charge of a theater, and you come in as a guest director, absolute autonomy is virtually non-existent. I thought that I could live with this actor, but within the first few days of rehearsal I became conscious of the fact that I had made one of the most terrible mistakes of my life. I described him as a "black hole," like the ones in our galaxy. He absorbed light, but never gave off energy or anything that even came close to it. It was a desperate experience. We shared the same hotel, and I said to him: "You can call me at anytime at all of the day or night and I will go over this interpretation of this particular line, of this particular move, this gesture." I devoted hours and hours to this actor. Finally I got my assistant to keep working on him. Two weeks into rehearsal I called the management of the theater and said: "We've hit a dud. Let us cut our losses very quickly and get another actor." They were not convinced, so they set up a small rehearsal. The actor must have somehow known what was to happen. The first act of the play was a kind of run through, and he gave a performance which made me look like a fool. Both my assistant director, the stage manager, the other actors looked at this man and said: "Where on earth has this been all the time?" But I knew something was wrong. I could not really place it, but nobody could find fault with the performance of the actor. So the artistic director and the management looked at me and said: "Well, you are a slave-driver. How could you have got such a performance out of this man in two weeks? God what do you do? The Union will be after you. We don't believe this." So I had no choice; I had to go back to rehearsals, and of course the moment we resumed, the moment the pressure was off, everything fell to pieces once again. Again the agony of individual rehearsals, of explanations over and over again. I did a lot more demonstrations. I think anybody who is a director here knows that most directors hate to demonstrate a gesture. They prefer to interpret, to explain and then allow the actor to find his own way of physically interpreting what they said. Well, I was actually compelled to demonstrate, to walk from here to there, to pick up a glass from the table, to take up a walking stick … and this went on and on and on. Of course by opening night, I knew we were in big trouble. There was one thing, though, which kept nagging at me. How had he achieved that one performance, that act? And as I watched another disastrous performance on stage, I suddenly knew what he had done. He had memorized, he had made a selection of the various gestures and demonstrations. I felt there was something familiar in what he was doing, but without sequence, without meaning, without relationship: I said, "This is familiar." Then I realized I was looking in a mirror. I had made that gesture, but it was not necessarily in that context. I had walked like that, but not necessarily in that context. What he had done on that trial day was simply to sit down, watch me very closely and memorize the demonstrations I had given him. He had learned by rote - like some people learn certain scriptures. He had actually mimicked me, and with some element of cohesion for that portion of the play.

Now the dictator reminded me very much of that character, but only after we began to look into his background, to what he had done before coming into power . I realized that his was a long-standing ambition. He had been involved in a number of military coups before, as manager, facilitator, conspirator, signals man. He was a very charming dictator, very generous, with my money and yours, Nigeria's money. So he had built up a large followership over there, and he had converted what was supposed to be a leadership institute which we had worked on with an earlier regime; a kind of think-tank place where technocrats, artists, writers, intellectuals, economists and so on could come together, into a strictly military one: the Institute of Strategic Studies. It was for the military, but which civilians were periodically invited. He had cultivated some of the civilian scholars there and given them assignments, working papers. "Prepare me an economic blueprint. What would you do if you were president of this country? What would you do with the private sector? What are your views on fiscal policies? You criticize the military for not doing this, if you were in the position of the head of state, what would be your foreign policy towards remote areas, in which we have no interest, like Alaska?" Then he would say: "By the way, on the way from Alaska why don't you pass by the Latin American congress and see how they take care of this?" He built up a very efficient, competent dossier on many aspects of national life, using the human material which was invited to this caucus, and which was a monopoly of the military. So when he was ready to come into power on his own, he was armed with a number of answers to lots of national questions. I thought this was a very intelligent proceeding. But of course he was not creative. He lacked the capacity to link these various disparate elements of what constitutes nation building. He lacked the aptitude, the knowledge, the intelligence to piece it all together, at least for any appreciable length of time. He had the ability to divert himself in view of the unexpected, within the country, outside the country. So he continued following these ill-digested scenarios and manifestos which had been placed before him. At the beginning he was like that actor of mine, who was able to present a similarly intelligent facade.

He was cunning, not stupid, do not misunderstand me. He was very cunning and quite intelligent, but there was something missing, and that is what I tend to describe as the creative element. He lacked that element of creative leadership, creative control assessment, the ability to take a different route, something which had not been prepared ahead of time. Not just prepared, but *pre*-prepared. So when he was faced with unexpected economic problems, he stubbornly held on to the principle that this must be right. This has been prepared by some of the finest minds of the country. This has been prepared by an economic adviser, who works for the World Bank. This has been prepared by somebody who is acknowledged as a cultural mind, and who attends lots of festivals and so on. This has been prepared by a student of

314

comparative religions as an answer to the various religious polarizations, and the other has been prepared by a social anthropologist. For any issue of ethnic conflict or ethnic uncertainties, he could only operate by a blueprint. Eventually he fell, and his fall was quite spectacular, quite disgraceful. So with this anecdote I hope you have at least a little insight into my thinking about what actually constitutes - let us not call it the divine spark - let us just call it the creative spark which sets the meticulous planner apart. Meticulous planners are capable of amassing to themselves some of the finest minds, but they just lack the ability to infuse into that creative element that resolves any crisis at any time; indeed that does not need to wait for any crisis, but just moves an organism, a very complex organism like a society, along in recreative directions.

We ask, where does creativity come from? What world view is its world view? Where does it take its inspiration? How does it confront the various bombardments of experience, of knowledge that an individual is bound to encounter in all his wanderings in libraries or physically across the globe? I am a Yoruba and I shall give you a little insight into the Yoruba world view.

The Yoruba world view is not absolutely unique, but there are certain elements that are worth noting. Especially in view of the fact that unlike many religions, which were taken by the slaves across to the Americas, the Yoruba has the distinction of being the most resilient, one that has certainly survived albeit, in some cases in syncretic form, with Christianity, especially Roman Catholicism. In Brazil, in Haiti, in Cuba, in Colombia and in certain parts of America, you will find that the Yoruba religion, and elements of its world view have actually survived and were active - in one form or another - long before the American Blacks themselves began to rediscover Africa and to be proud of the African continent. It did not astonish me at all the last time I was in Cuba to hear Fidel Castro very proudly pronouncing himself an African and saying that he believes he is a Yoruba. It has to do with the acceptance of a reality which in some cases strenuous efforts have been made to crush, but which has somehow survived. Now, to present the Yoruba world view in images, I want you to imagine three amorphous spheres floating in a much larger sphere floating in infinity. I have to draw lines, but I want you not to mind for a moment that these are rigid lines. Imagine one, two, three not hermetic, yet at the same time self-sufficient, unique in themselves. This, let us say, represents the world of the ancestor; this represents the world of the living, the present; and this, the world of the unborn. Now, the Yoruba believe that these three worlds are interconnected, they move into one another

315

continually. In other words there is no rigid separation in the world of the ancestor, the world of the living, the world of the unborn. This is not just a theoretical approach to existence. Some of you may be aware, for instance, if a child is born with certain remarkable characteristics to a departed person - and you know you do have strange children like that, who are wise from the moment of their birth - that child is often treated like an ancestor, like a baba. He is called baba, and he can get away with murder, like many American children do, but in a different sense. He is indulged because there is a feeling that something is hidden here, which came from the ancestor world and which should not be disturbed. There is a kind of autonomy accorded to that child, which is not tolerated in other children.

We have, within the unborn, a syndrome related again to this notion of the mutual transmission of the world of the ancestor and the world of the unborn. We have a syndrome, which you might decide to call infant mortality, but which we call "Abiku." This is a syndrome of the child of *obanje,* a child who is born, dies, is born again and is considered to be the same ancestor trying to come back to the world of the living. However, it resides in the world of the unborn, whose inhabitants are constantly calling the child back. So when that child is born and is recognized as an "Abiku," certain things are done - some of them quite nasty, I am afraid, depending on which particular society - to try to keep the child within the world of the living. Scarification is one of them. Sometimes a child is compelled to lead out the parents, the entire family and the neighbors and indicate where the original placenta has been buried. They feel that there is a mystery placenta buried somewhere and until it is discovered and destroyed, this child will continue to go into the world of the unborn. Ben Okri in his novel, *The Famished Road*, uses this as a kind of structure for his entire novel, the repetitive cycle which is at once both tragic but at the same time quite optimistic because it promises a kind of continuity between the world of the living and the ancestor world.

In addition there is the masquerade Egungun, another device for keeping, for at least simulating contact, with the world of the ancestor. At certain seasons there is a whole parade of masked people who speak in guttural voices, emerging from groves all over the town or the village or wherever. Each family, for instance, can actually have its own Egungun mask which is representative of an ancestor. That Egungun comes out and arbitrates all the various quarrels which have been going on in the past year, advises about planting, names children and afterwards disappears into the world of the ancestor. This way the rites of death, of separation and absence, become a kind of collective therapy for the anguish which is normally experienced by the living when they lose somebody who is dear. Now these are the three main provinces which exist in a very concretely manifested way in the world of the Yoruba.

One of the questions which I asked myself trying to penetrate the philosophy of the Yoruba world view and the world of creativity is what happens around these worlds. The passage from one to the other - what does it entail? What forces, what inimical forces exist that are so powerful that there have to be ritual enactments to ease the passage from one world to the other? Either from the world of the living to the world of the ancestor or from the world of the unborn to the world of the living. There are so many very complex, very poetic rituals, which actually exalt in accompanying the living into the world of the ancestor. These can be some of the most elaborate ceremonies and rituals, with sacrifices. What in the collective unconscious of the Yoruba is it that is so strong as to warrant these community rituals which can last days and in fact are repeated almost annually? How does one articulate the space, this realm? For me it seemed that it could only be a correlation to a space occupied by the creative elements, the creative forces, the creative genius. Because it is an act of creation, an act of creativity to pass from the unformed world of the unborn to the world of the living. And equally so must it be actually to transcend the mortal constraints and pass into the world of the ancestor. So I named this "the equivalent of chthonicrealm," where the energies of creativity are lodged and the process of creativity requires an imaginative leap through this area of transition, because I think most people will admit that there is an element of the psychological or at least psychic transformation during the process of intense creativity. Some people even lose their minds and have to be institutionalized. But there is a kind of correlation at least between the sense or the hidden instinct of coming into being which is allied to the process of creativity in one form or the other, and this area of transition where the forces of creativity are lodged.

This is not as original as it sounds. I shall explain in a moment, when I come to the details of a specific deity, why I named it the realm of transition. While we are on the subject of creativity, I felt that one could correlate this ancestral area with the territory of memory: here, actuality and here, vision. Now that can be interpreted sociologically, but in fact the act of creativity is, of course, a way of engendering a new species. I leave that to you. But these seemed to be a natural way of looking at existence and creativity. I shall explain why they are not original in a moment. I must talk about our gods a little bit to amplify this and then come to a particular god, who for me gives us the clue to this creative zone, this dark and dangerous realm of transition which has to be appeased before its hoards, its very mystic hoards can actually be rifled by the creative mind. Of course the process of rifling can be methodical, systematic or intuitive. This is acknowledged by all creative people.

Now with the deities - I cannot go through all of them, for we are as prodigal in our deities as the Greeks were - we come to another most interesting aspect of Yoruba world view. Myth has it that life, being, the essence of being, was once one. However - and this also the Yoruba consider a creative process because it led to a multi-dimensional perception of reality - there came what you might call an internal revolution within the original being, which led to the creation of gods, demi-gods, demiurges and the mortals. There are parallels everywhere; in the Judaic tradition, it is the apple that was eaten. Knowledge came and the gap between the angels and the gods on the one hand and humanity on the other became wider and wider until you had to die to go and meet the people on the other side. However, among the gods there was one who recognized the persistence of an anguish, a sense of incompletion among the deities. This god was Ogun, the god of lyric, of metallurgy, the god of war and creative agent. All the other gods, Oshuni, Edumar, Oya, Shango had sensed for a very long time a missing element in their being. Finally they wondered if this was not an element essential to their own sense of completion. The suspicion was in this missing element and not in fact the part that went with the human beings, the mortals who became totally separated from them. So the gods, who of course occupy both spheres - because we have the anthropomorphic deities, who occupy both the ancestral area and at the same time they are essences of some of the most creative energies within the realm of transition - looked for a way of reuniting with the mortals.

Everything was tried: sacrifices, incantation; the whole lot. It was impossible because in the meantime the primordial jungle had become totally impenetrable. Only one deity had the knowledge, the perception to forge what was indeed a technological tool - a machete, but of course a mystic machete which hacked through this primordial jungle and penetrated the realm of transitional chaos to the living, where for the first time in eons, the gods were able to reclaim an element of themselves, which had been lost since the separation of the divine being from its mortal elements. This deity was Ogun, the god of metals, of metallurgy in general. Ogun is the deity of the blacksmith,

318

the warrior, etc. (I shall fill in the etc. in a moment in describing another aspect, a very crucial aspect, of the Yoruba world view.)

I once used an expression which stated in effect that the Yoruba world view does not really admit any impurities in its digestive system. What this means is that it does not reject any experience. It is very selective, but it accepts, it admits that phenomena exist outside its knowledge at any given time. In that sense - and I believe that this is one of the reasons why this religion survived in the Americas - it is able to confront any new experience and absorb it into its own existence and constantly expanding systemic understanding of phenomena in general. I call it a cultural rootedness or cultural security. Now, the result of this is that when I am confronted by people who over-emphasize the differences between the technological world - what I call the CP Snow syndrome - and the humanistic world; when I encounter those who tend to exaggerate this in a kind of intellectualized way, I am often just baffled because this is not my experience. My experience, our experience, which is that all of those deities, is that when the Yoruba encounter a new phenomenon, something totally unrelated to their existence, what they do is look inwards to find some kind of correlation. Usually this co-option takes the form of enhancing the existing area, the territory of one of the deities, using the fundamentals and simply absorbing the news as part and parcel of an aspect of something that has always been and that can actually belong, and not what others would describe as coming from a totally alien region. Thus Sango, who is the god of lightning, the equivalent of your Thor or Jove, for instance, becomes the god of electricity. The moment the Yoruba encountered electricity for the first time, they simply attributed it to Sango. So you find many electrical workers in urban areas that are followers of Sango. The same is true for Ogun. The railway worker today is a follower of Ogun. As for the astronauts, I have no doubt at all they have to divide themselves between Sango and Ogun. Certainly the rocket engineer will be a follower of Ogun, and this way the Yoruba have absolutely no problem in accommodating even what seems to be the most disparate elements in alien experience. It is rare, I believe, to find the Yoruba feeling alienated by any new encounter. All the religions - that I call the comparatively closed religions: Islam, Christian, Roman Catholic, Baptist and so on - which have come into Africa, find out that sooner or later they absorb elements of the Yoruba world view. Either in ceremonies or in festivals, in religious images, in anything at all. Of course this is not beloved by the religious purists. Especially the more fundamentalist kind, and they go to all sorts of lengths to extirpate from their own religion these elements that have crept in from the Yoruba culture.

To get back to Ogun, he had to prepare himself. If this experience of Ogun had taken place in modern times, within contemporary conscious time and not the timeless time we are talking about, I believe that he would have invented the laser beam and blasted the ethonic realm to get the gods reunited to the other world. This is very typical of the approach of the Yoruba to technological experience. Within that reality, however, Ogun experienced what I consider the essence of tragedy. When I was studying the dramatic medium, tragedy in Leeds, I always found it very strange to read categorical statements about the origination of tragedy in Greece. I do love their myths and find correlations in them with the Yoruba culture. Their gods are just as reprobate, just as mortal, as the Yoruba deities, and of course the Athenian culture was a source of endless fascination. The works of Aeschylus, Sophocles, etc. are all beautiful interpretations of human intuition. But how could any society, how could anybody claim that the tragic experience began at any one spot of the globe? I found it very strange, and particularly strange because I could understand tragedy through the experience of Ogun. To pass through this malstrom of psychic energies, Ogun had to be destroyed, and this is reflected in the rituals that celebrate his passage. He had to be destroyed. And he could transcend this void and arrive at a landing point only by reassembling his scattered pieces through an exercise of willpower. Now, you recognize echoes of nature's eternal tragedy in this. But I understood, on reading that really astonishing piece of poetic insight into the origins of tragedy by Nietzsche, I could understand perfectly through the experience of Ogun in this world, the ripping apart of the protagonist. The protagonist as actor and the reassemblage of that actor through an exercise of the will. The experience of catharsis and the accumulation of wisdom as a result of this process of submission to the most inimical forces that exist in the universe. Of course the resolution of Ogun's tragedy is very different from the resolution in European classical tragedy. But the process is exactly the same, and certainly the accumulated wisdom, the very special knowledge that is acquired in the process.

So in a nutshell, this is the Yoruba world view and this is how the Yoruba world actually encounters the outside world. Of course the Yoruba world also has known how to defend itself against those who insist that its own world is inimical to theirs and should be destroyed. But again, as I have always emphasized, the Yoruba have a certain unique aspect to their history. The Yoruba religion has never waged a jihad or a crusade. It is one of these nonproselytizing religions. It is there and it explains much of human phenomena. There is a whole corpus of Ifa. Ifa, if you are looking for parallels, is the equivalent of the Delphic Oracle, except that Ifa has a tradition of a corpus, of verses which provide the answers to the seeker in whatever form, whatever the problem may be. Ifa actually contains verses which deal with Christianity, with Islam, with technological discovery. I am sure today if I go back to the odu of Ifa, I shall find that space conquest is part of it. This is done without any kind of overt mystification of the Nostradamus kind. It does not operate in that way. It just synthesizes, distills human experience enabling it to accommodate whatever is new.

Among the other significant deities is Esu, the element of chaos. Even in the tidiest of scientific or technological programs, and certainly most primarily in any kind of human engineering that attracts - or at least attributes - to itself any kind of absolute, Esu is the deity who reminds one that there is no absolute at all where the organism called humanity or human society or human community is involved. It inserts constantly the kind of caution which Ifa the corpus of knowledge might be tempted to ignore, the kind of certitude Ifa may attempt to apply to its operations with human beings who seek guidance from it. Esu is that element at the cross-roads where the wrong road may be taken in spite of the most efficient map.

Other deities have to do with rivers. Osanying, another interesting one, is the medical one, the local Aesculapius if you like. Osanying is the god of the herbs, of medication in general, of ecology, whose pharmacopeia exists in Ifa's verses which deal with the most efficacious sometimes forgotten herbal treatments to which I believe Europe is now beginning to turn. They are calling it natural medicine or something like that. Well, it is all in Ifa, if you ever come across it or care to investigate what it has to offer.

So where does a writer or an artist get his images from? Where do the images of the traditional sculptors and the modern sculptors, the modern painters, the craftsmen and women, the clothmakers, come from? They come, of course, from an acknowledgement of the viability of experience, as long as it can be made organic and integral to the overall work; the viability of any kind of image which has contributed to the formulation of the human community. Even if it is merely in retrospect. It may be in a traditional theatrical enactment. Similarly in some of the carvings, there is the image of a European with a helmet on horseback and the purists will say: "What is that doing here? Surely that's not a traditional carving." Of course it is a traditional carving. It is very much a traditional carving. It is history. History that goes back to the very first encounter of the Yoruba with White men in the fifteenth, possibly the fourteenth century. It is not an impurity at all - depending, of course, upon how the artist uses it. The same thing goes for music. Sometimes, in my view, it goes a little bit too far. Maybe this is one of the areas in which I am a purist, and who can fail to be purist when one listens to the noises that pass for music in the commercial world these days? But those are exceptions. The important thing is the world view, from which we all operate in the creative world in that part of a country. That world view is one which ingests, selects and adapts new experiences. That is why if you go to the headquarters of the Nigerian Electric Power Authority, NEPA, you will see the figure of Sango, who presides over electricity. Actually I think this is a blasphemy against Sango, because I think Sango is far more efficient than our electrical system has proved to be in the past few years.

Guntern: We are now in a state the French call "dépaysé." For somebody who has lost his country and said that he isn't even cultured anymore, we have just witnessed a process of self-induced "enculturation." You went back to the mythological roots of your existence, of your identity as an artist. I would like to connect a few of the issues which have been discussed during these days with what I know from your work.

You have often emphasized that European expressionism and other art forms - for instance, cubism - and others - have stolen from your continent without ever acknowledging where they took what from. You called a certain Mr. Frobenius a famous vulture in the long chain of archaeological robbery. He was able to admire the Yoruba sculptures as being extraordinary, beautiful, creative accomplishments, and at the same time he described the people who had done them as stupid plebeians. A first question: what blocks the intuition of such people? Obviously they are not able to analyze facts, but at least they could have an intuitive judgment that would not permit such statements.

Soyinka: Well, it is a point which I have always found quite remarkable. Some of the artists, the expressionists for instance, just to be fair to them, did not fail to acknowledge *within their own circle* the source of influence in some of their paintings and sculptures. There is no other way to describe Frobenius, than that he suffered from the virus of racism. There he was, defying even the most common denominative level of the practice of acquisition. If you want to acquire something, you at least have to approach and negotiate. You are told you can take this, but you cannot have that. He was a robber. He would go back, bribe his way among the courtiers, the guardians, and excavate even on prohibited sites and carry away these bronze, clay, terracotta figures.

He would take quite an army with him, including a bronze caster. In some cases he was so desperate, he would have his bronze caster make replicas of these busts and bury those there instead, with the connivance of the usual corrupt elements which I think all societies can boast of. But you quite rightly put your finger on what I consider his greatest crime. When he found the origin of the actual producers of these works of art, he refused to give them credit. He insisted that they were some degenerate people who must have wandered on to the sites and established themselves there. Even though the evidence was before him. Now the art of bronze-casting still existed in Ife and Benin while he was in Nigeria. He wrote in a way to insure that no one coming after him would even attempt to accord to the autochthons of this area that very specialized skill and knowledge and beauty which they produced. This is why I singled him out for castigation in particular. Not only did he physically rob, he did a disservice to the cause of scholarship. First of all by substituting his own contemporary and absolutely inferior works cast by his assistant, then by trying to destroy what should be called the scholastic continuum of knowledge by fantasizing about the possible origins of this world. Without any proof, he stated his fantasies categorically.

Guntern: Art critics and journalists, some at least, are able to do the same thing. What blocks their intuition? There are a number of journalists here, and I must say in general we and what we do here are treated in a generous way by them. But every now and then somebody shows up with a mask of hostility. A person who has never been here, does not know what we do, but somehow knows that it is very stupid, not done with competence. I often wonder how can they possibly ignore what they translate in their facial expression. Why does their intuition not tell them something, where obviously their analytical power leaves them outside in the field? What happens there?

Soyinka: I have a feeling that you are going to have to get those journalists up on this platform so we can ask them that question. But I would like to see them actually, because I know the kind of journalists you are talking about. Unfortunately it does not happen just with journalists. I had this experience as a student when I began to attempt to write. I remember one of my very early plays which I showed to one of my lecturers. He said: "To read this is interesting, but surely natives do not talk like that. This is too sophisticated for natives." And I said: "Oh yes, but they would not be using the English language." But you see, I had to listen to them. In the play, they were speaking the English language. If I were to translate Shakespeare into Yoruba, I assure you they would understand that language, and the thoughts of that language.

A similar kind of attitude exists in the world of theater directors and even publishers. Some - especially paperbacks - feel that a work by an African can only be introduced to the world if there are grass skirts on the front cover and a bone through the nose even if what is inside bears absolutely no relation. There is another example farther up the scale of those from whom one expected better. I was inducted into an Academy of Arts and Sciences, of a country which shall remain nameless, and my citation is something which should be framed: " Soyinka writes about the folklore of his society in native English language" - or something like that. I wondered if whoever wrote that had ever read anything I had ever written. It was obvious in his imagination, if somebody came from that society and deserved to be inducted into that academy, it could only be because he was translating his folk tales into some kind of crude English language. That was the citation which was sent to me. So it is a common phenomenon and of course it is an attitude of rejection. You just cannot come to terms with the fact that people you encounter actually come from a very old and self-sufficient civilization. It is just the question of what language, what medium of translation has been used. That is all.

Guntern: A third instance where obviously analytical power is not big enough and even intuition fails normally intelligent people: in *The Man Died* you wrote a footnote to the Red Cross. Could you please comment your experience there and the footnote as well?

Soyinka: I was in prison in Lagos before I was taken to Kaduna. It was during the civil war and the Red Cross - who did a lot of wonderful work - had succeeded in persuading the Nigerian Government to allow them to visit the prison and the prisoners of war. That morning we were all woken up very early. I was in my own cell upstairs, looking at the proceedings, and everybody was given soap that morning and a new uniform. I know that probably an effort had been made to remove all the weevils from the beans which were served that morning. Then they were let out. These were prisoners who had been locked up in over-crowded, filthy conditions. The reek of their bodies used to ascend to my cell upstairs. They were out in the sun. They were given game cards, checkerboards and so on. We knew something was happening. Eventually a group of people from the Red Cross arrived and they had a look, smiled, talked to these prisoners. I was expecting that they would know, if not from experience at least intuitively, that this was an unnatural scene. It was not real, it was a faked scene. Anybody could see that. But they came, they nodded, smiled, shook hands and went away. I could not believe that they did not ask to see inside the cells or how many of those people could be accommodated in that building with any kind of comfort. That was the footnote to the Red Cross. Next time, please do not even go near places like that if you are not prepared to ask for all doors to be opened and to have unrestricted interviews with the prisoners. Go into a corner and talk to them and learn the real truth.

Guntern: To take up your word "weevil," the extreme stress, strong emotions, above average expectations, burden and pain do to intuition what the weevil does to a granary. This is a general experience about intuition. We have to come to grips with the terms we have used during this congress. Now let us go to something where intuition was right. I was very struck by many scenes in your book, *The Man Died*. One was very strong. You were told that by Christmas you would be out. They offered a barber to come visit you and shave you. You had not seen yourself in a mirror for more than a year. You were once again uncultured, out-cultured, outrageously alienated from what is dear to your heart. Then all of a sudden, while everything was being prepared to cut your hair, you knew you would not be out by Christmas. Have you had often had such intuitive experiences?

Soyinka: Yes, this was one remarkable instance of intuition. I had been in there about a year. It was around Christmas and the entire atmosphere, the director of the prison was only too happy, and it was impossible not to be infected by everybody's happiness. Somehow they had taken to the way I was conducting myself there. So they sent for new clothes and for a barber, because for a long time I had refused to touch my beard or my hair. I was seeing my face in a mirror for the first time in over a year, and suddenly, I do not know what happened. Up to that point I had accepted the information. The evidence was there on their faces; it was no trick. I had accepted the fact that I was leaving and I was quite glad, and then I looked in the mirror and saw my face. I looked into my eyes and that instant, I just knew that I was not going to be released. Not that year, not for another year at least. So I told the warder to send the barber away and take all the clothes away and to leave me alone. I knew I was not going to be released. Moments like that are very common in my existence. I describe one such instance in my new book *Ibadan*, a continuation of *Aké*. It takes my life up to the early sixties, just before the civil war began. I was taking one of the respites I used to give myself in the midst of all the problems in Nigeria at that time. We had so many political crises in that country that it is no good my trying to tell you which particular one it was. At any rate, it was one before the civil war. One of the respites I used to enjoy was to get in my Land Rover and drive to Oshogbo, which is a

325

small town, inhabited by a very strange and unusual Austrian painter and sculptor, Susan Wenger, a very spiritual person. She took to this Yoruba religion as if she had been born into it. In fact, she became a priestess of Oshun and used to spend a lot of time creating new sculptures for the Oshun grove, which had a very peaceful atmosphere. I used to enjoy just escaping to Oshun grove within Nature itself. I found also that Susan Wenger had become a part of that place. The way she worked, she exuded a kind of serenity in her studio, and one of my treats was to go to Oshogbo and just sit in her studio and watch her at work, drinking palm-wine and not saying anything, or maybe saying something. I would just sit there and then, when she finished work in the evening, we would all go to this local night club, listen to juju music, drink more palm-wine, eat some venison and so on. On this occasion, I had made sure I had no engagement for the week-end, so I was completely at ease. I was driving along, looking forward to my periodic treat, when suddenly I found I did not want to go. I could not explain it. I tried to fight it for a couple of miles, and finally I just turned around and went home. I had a sense of something not being quite right. When I got back by evening, I checked all the doors, I checked all the windows, made sure my family was safe and went to bed. That night the house was attacked by the thugs, an illegal police sent by one of the government party men to which we were in opposition and who objected to some things I was writing and doing. I was attacked by a bunch of twenty to twenty-five people in the middle of the night. We managed to frighten them off. They believed I was better equipped than I actually was in the house, and they all scattered.

This is another example, which is when my mother died. I was going to Ghana. I was teaching in the university of Ife at the time. I slept in Ibadan, because I had a very early flight from Lagos in the morning. I got to the airport in Lagos, and queued, accompanied by a driver. Soon the people in the queue were getting very angry because the plane was to leave at eight thirty, and by eight o'clock, there was still nobody at the check-in counter. Finally the man came, and we all abused him roundly and started moving. I was just about the third person to the desk and suddenly I said: "No, I'm not traveling. I can't travel." I turned round, and my astonished driver asked, "Why not?" I said: "Let's just go back." We drove straight to Ife, got to my house and I sent him for my mail. "Don't tell anybody I'm back. Go and bring all the mail in my office." He brought the mail, and I was going through the mail, wondering where "it" was. You have not defined anything, but it is that question! Where is it, what is it? So my colleague in the office saw the driver when he came for the mail and managed to get out of him the fact that I was back. I went through all the mail and nothing was there. So I decided, "Well, I'll just wait in the house." Afterwards my colleague came and broke the news to me gently, that my mother was dead. I knew that was it.

Now what is even more interesting was the fact that, as I told you, I had stopped in Ibadan, at the home of some friends, the Aboyade family. When the news chased me to Ife that morning and I could not be found, the messenger went to that house in Ibadan. Professor Aboyade told the man that I had traveled and the messenger told them what the matter was. His wife, who incidentally is a very sensitive person said: "No. Wole has not traveled." Her husband said: "What are you talking about? He left this morning. You saw him, he left very early in the morning before dawn, so as to catch his flight." She said: "No, because his mother is dead. Wole has not traveled, I'm telling you, Wole has not traveled. That's all." And she was absolutely certain that I had not traveled. A case of double intuition, from two different directions.

Guntern: Let me just make a remark or two on that. General experience shows that your intuition works very well when you are relaxed, when you are not highly goal-oriented, but rather in a situation of non-attachment, when you have feelings of serenity, no very strong burden or pain or anger, or anything of the kind. So knowing this, you can train your intuition to work better. Second, if you are capable of empathic identification with another human being or situation, then your intuition will work better. If you alienate yourself from the world and look up on it, as though it were an insect and you had a microscope, you will not be capable of intuition. Third, for some reason that nobody knows, good intuition is most often linked to a very strong feeling of absolute certainty. It seems that the right hemisphere of most people is more linked to the emotion brain than the left one. No one has the slightest hint of understanding why, but the fact does exist. So away from this, just as a side remark, in prison, under very, very extreme existential situations you became very, very creative in a very specific way. You wrote things, you made sculptures, you baptized the four walls "Wall of Flagellation," "Amber Wall," "Wailing Wall" and the fourth I have never found out. There must have been four walls, you wrote about three only. You did many more things to keep you from going crazy, even re-invented the whole of algebra. Could you say a little bit more about the creative process in extreme conditions?

Soyinka: Well, the first thing in a situation like that is that one is determined to survive intact. By survive, I do not mean stay alive, I mean survive mentally. That is the first thing that occurs to one in that kind of situation. Before I was thrown into solitary confinement, I had gone through a very harrowing internal turmoil which was related to a story which had been made up, that I had attempted to escape from prison. That, of course, was related to another lie - which was that I had made a confessional statement. A so-called confessional statement from me was released to the press. I think this was one of the most agonizing moments of my stay in prison. When a government goes to that extent of lying against an imprisoned individual and that individual has a very strong imagination, he does not stop at the lie alone. He thinks, what is linked with it? What is the next step, what are they about to do? What other lies are they about to tell? And against who? If a confessional statement was attributed to me, it is possible that it is going to be used to implicate others, as if it were I who was implicating them. I think it is one of the times when I became really mortally afraid of being killed. All I could think was, if these people can go this far, they plan to kill me, and kill me before I can expose this fabrication. Now I think it is probably the only time in my life I was really terrified of dying at a particular time. I just wanted to make sure I did not die until I exposed that lie. After that I did not mind. So I had been through this and I knew that, and I felt the impact because of that helplessness, that sense of impotence and my fear about what was about to be done in my name. I already knew what - how -the imagination can actually act to destroy an individual, especially if it is a negative one, one that is very much afraid of certain courses of action. And of course the story about my trying to escape was linked to that, because they did attempt to eliminate me, while I was there. I got wind of it and was able to take some kind of preventive actions and send a message outside.

After that I was at peace with myself, but being thrown into solitary confinement was their response to that event. I knew that they would attempt to take vengeance on me, and the only cause of action left for them, the only reason they would put me in solitary confinement, was to make sure that my mind was destroyed before they released me. It was as simple as that. I had to make sure I survived with my mind intact. It meant setting myself a task and dividing up the time. Looking at my barren environment, the first thing that occurred to me was that there was one thing I could do to save my mind, and that was to keep that mind occupied in as rational a way as possible. Since I was a writer, the first thing to do was to look for means of writing. That is how I came to save some bones from the food which came and start making nibs, which I attached to sticks, and then I discovered some properties of coffee which could be concentrated in some way, and actually it is very good

328

ink. I still have examples of what I wrote. The early, early versions were sticky, so some pages were disfigured. But as I improved, it was a really marvelous thing.

Guntern: In your technology.

Soyinka: A marvelous thing in my new technology. Then, strange things happened. I described in one of the poems when a crow flew over the yard and dropped a quill. There were lots of crows and vultures and egrets, and I sometimes watched them flying past at sunset through the bars. On this occasion this group of birds flew past and I saw this quill spiraling down, so as soon as I was released to go and take my bath in the morning, I grabbed it and fashioned a very old-fashioned quill out of it. That is the story behind the poem *Crow - Quill.* But the most interesting activity for me was mathematics. Because in school I had loathed mathematics, I decided that that very discipline would be the one which would challenge my mind. So I began to rediscover all the simple laws of equation, geometry, the Pythagoras theorem, square roots, all those things which I had refused and just hated to do in school. I would do some of them, just enough to pass exams, and after that I dropped mathematics just like that. Here I began to put myself through a kind of school. I still hate mathematics. The moment I left prison I did not want to see mathematics again.

Sometimes I would watch ants. I could have written a treatise on the activities of ants: soldier ants, small ants, sugar ants, oh yes, I used to detail them and I even thought I could recognize some of them individually. But the dangerous part was when my mathematical experiments took me into very strange territories. I began to think that there was an equation which solved the relationship between time and space, and that was very dangerous ground. I remember days when I would work frantically, not eating. I was convinced I was on the verge of discovering a formula which finally tied up the quantities of time and space. Then one day I snapped out of it and looked at all the sheets of toilet paper I had covered with these things. I was frightened, so I tore them up and never went in that direction again.

Guntern: Could you quote a stanza from *Crow and Quill?*

Soyinka: No I cannot. I am different from Brodsky in that aspect. I cannot remember my own poems.

Guntern: You once wrote that literary style is like a fingerprint, like a burglar's method, that you can identify the person behind it. Now, when I read your plays, there is the same ancient noble power, the same song it seems to me, I found when I was a young student reading Euripedes, Aeschylus,

Sophocles in Greek. It reminds me of that. You have been compared to them. You have been compared many times to William Shakespeare. Now, after all this supercilious ignorance with respect to your rich culture, to the culture of your continent, how do you deal with such a mixed blessing as being compared to William Shakespeare?

Soyinka: Yes, I do not even call it a mixed blessing at all. For me it is highly inconvenient. I suppose if I were not a teacher, it would not matter. But being a teacher, I am always struck by such thinking that is diverging from the obvious task of accompanying a work of art to its sources. I always find it strange, because when I read the literature of other cultures, just as when I discovered for the first time Japanese Nō-theater - that was a comic episode in itself. When I discovered it, I was immediately curious about Japanese culture in general and then went into Japanese history and so on. The colonial education was such that it tried to direct your mind only in one direction towards the colonial culture. Like the French, you know how Francophone Africans are taught to say, "our ancestors the Gauls." That is one of the first things that the Africans learn in the French colonies. Anyway, the same goes for English literature.

Where I cannot, for want of time or means, pursue the background of a new work from a culture which I am encountering for the first time, my tendency, which I consider the natural thing to do, is to project rightly or wrongly into that culture through the literary evidence which is before me. Naturally it must have echoes here and there, but I believe that it is something which has come organically from a certain culture of which I am ignorant. So when I encounter this sort of "African Shakespeare," the African Euripedes, and so on, I say, "Why can't these people behave like my students? Why is it that they choose the easy way out and refuse to understand that they've encountered something which exists in its own right?"

I was not going to talk about this, just the humorous episode of my discovery of the Japanese Nō-theater which is when I was in Leeds. All I knew about the Japanese was that they were the kamikaze war pilots who wanted to bomb the American warships out of existence and join the Nazis. They fought on the wrong side during the war and so on. The existence of a culture, called Japanese culture, was something which I did not know of, ironically, until I escaped from the confines of Nigeria into England. I went to the Brotherton library just to read outside the curriculum. There was no such thing as Japanese theater in that curriculum. I got to the Japanese section and saw a book on Japanese Nō-theater. If there is no theater in Japan, why write about it? So I took it down. It was pleasant, rich in dramas and remarkable theatrical idiom which has a number of affinities with my own traditional theater. I think I read everything there was in that Japanese section that day before going home. After that, of course, I became far more curious about Japanese culture, even acquiring a Samurai sword on my first visit to Japan.

Guntern: Taking your expression as a writer in my own right, it seems that your autonomy began very early and also your courage to fight for it and to defend the boundaries of your identity. It seems that mother, the wild Christian, often wondered about your brooding, your being lost; she thought that you were reading and doing things because maybe for other things you were not worth very much. I remember one scene made me laugh aloud when I read it; you were chattering as a little boy in church in the afternoon service and then the sexton came to rebuke you and you took a firm stand - oh, you tell the story.

Soyinka: This is one of those episodes that made everybody say I was going to be a lawyer because I was so argumentative. I really must have been a pest. I confess it. What they took from me I cannot take from my children. I would have beaten them up years ago if they behaved like I behaved as a child. But apparently I just would not accept, I would not let go, I challenged any kind of proposition which I felt had a chance to be challenged. On that occasion I was making noise in church. As usual, I got carried away in my conversation with my friend sitting next to me. I had actually forgotten my environment, which I used to do quite a bit. So I was caught, pants down, there was no question about it. But when the sexton then challenged me, I felt he should have done better. He did not prove my guilt to me. So I said: "Look at the church filled with all these people. And you were seated over there, right next to the pastor. How could you have identified my voice in all that crowd?" I mean, how could he prove that it was I who was chatting among all the children who were there? Of course all it did was earn me a whipping because he was never going to tolerate that kind of argument. But of course he also found it very charming and so on and so forth. For him it meant in essence that I was destined to be a very truculent lawyer. I had many other instances like that. I never like to use the word *rebel*, but I think I probably was a bit rebellious as a child.

Guntern: It would seem so, yes. We had an obnoxious kid and now we have a little pest.

Concerning your rebellious fighting spirit, you wrote that once somebody does not accept the political power any more, each family unit should, in place of or after its Regulation every morning, quote, "... make a ritual of throwing their breakfast slop at the pinned-up photograph of the symbol of power before going out to earn a living under an insupportable system." I find that very strong and to the point.

Soyinka: When a political situation is unacceptable and even when people believe that at the moment there is nothing they can do to break that pattern, to force that impostor, that predator out of power, I think that an immediate process of preparation should be commenced by all those who do not accept that imposition, whatever form it may take. That was the immediate action that sprang to my mind: that the family should pin up a picture of the tyrant and ritualistically fling the slop at it and then go out to earn their living every day. It is the opposite of what happens to our friends the journalists these days when everybody is talking about democracy. I am always shocked at their attitude when some uniformed thug takes over power in an African country and then goes to an assembly, the Commonwealth assembly or the United Nations assembly, or whatever. He is accorded the same kind of respectful attention by the press corps and becomes a glamor boy. I remember the last Commonwealth Conference when Strasser of Sierra Leone had just taken over and all the journalists were swarming around and he became *the* star of the occasion. This nothing but a miserable, third-rate mutineer who acceded to the seat of power simply because the former person lost his nerve. They were just mutineers, it was not even a planned coup, nothing. They were striking for more pay and got angry. The pay had not arrived in time, so they marched to the presidential palace and the president, who had no spunk, fled, because he felt a coup was in the making. So this fellow, purely by accident, found himself in the seat of power. There he was at the Commonwealth Conference, being treated as a head of state in his own right. The press adopted this sycophantic approach. I know that journalists have to do their work. He was a story, but then he should have been treated just as a story. The cause of democracy and the cause of the struggle against oppressive, arbitrary, mindless forces is simply not assisted by non-selective and unreflective kind of adulation - and I use the word deliberately - which is paid by voluntary courtiers to somebody who is probably a cretin anyway. I find that very strange. So to counter that kind of tendency, the least those who know, who are most directly involved, can do is draw their blinds and throw their breakfast slop at the picture. I believe that dictators should be stripped of all dignity. Certainly it is one of my weapons, it is what I do all the time. When I speak publicly about them, I refer to them in the most unflattering terms deliberately because I want to counter the aura of dignity in which they are cloaked by other people. It is necessary to cut it down and to reduce them to what they really are: just mindless adventurists.

Discussion

Vontobel: What is the most important thing in life for you?

Soyinka: Oh, dear.

Guntern: That is an important and good question.

Soyinka: Can I think about it? If you are kind enough to ask later on, maybe I shall have an answer.

Q: Could it be that something deep inside your being is the, in quotation marks, "only creator" of all your realities? And if so, what consequences would you draw from that?

Soyinka: One special issue of the journal *Liberation* sent a questionnaire to several writers. The question was, "Why do you write?" The answers were published, some long, some short, some cryptic, some witty. I wanted to answer that question as honestly as I could, but found it very difficult to do so. As the deadline approached, suddenly I thought - and genuinely felt it at the time - "The masochist in me, I suppose." Now that was a truthful answer and at the same time not quite accurate. There are times when it is definitely accurate. When you ask yourself: "What is this compulsion? Why do I write? Why must I write? Why don't I do something else?" it is very different from: "Why do I write this particular thing or this particular way?" That only makes life a bit more complicated for me. So in trying to answer your question, I experience the same difficulty. Is it something deep in me which makes me want to create reality? I can only speak in general terms when I say that I think the creative person is someone who is not satisfied with appearances; who believes that there is something beyond what is materially visible around him. I think in a way the creative person is an explorer. I was giving an interview in my room this morning. My window directly overlooks the mountain ranges, the hills. Because of the closeness of the buildings, which is just as if they were in ranges like little hills themselves set against the huge mountain, one sensation you could have, I was thinking objectively, was: "Oh, this is a claustrophobic atmosphere. I feel suffocated." On the other hand you could say: "Oh, this limitation to my immediately visible world is exactly what I need; just the solitude, the sublimeness, especially when the light plays on it in a particular way." The very existence of the range contains the seeds of its own destruction, in the sense that you feel there must be something beyond that range, something which might hold the risk of reducing this magnificent range in size, both qualitatively and quantitatively; of even diminishing its grandeur. If you do not want to diminish its grandeur, it is quite possible you will be content to stay there. But if you are not, if you feel that despite this grandeur you are experiencing and enjoying for the moment, you must tunnel underneath it to see what is on the other side, or climb over it to peek beyond, then you could take this as an act of restlessness, masochism. It is very comfortable just to stay there and not attempt to pierce beyond this material repletion - because it is replete in its own self. On the other hand you know you cannot rest until you explore, physically, if you are an engineer or a mountain climber or a speleologist. In the end you might discover other realities which you never suspected existed, but which somehow, intuitively, you know must lie there beyond. No matter how satisfying this is, no matter how sufficient or efficient it is, there must be something beyond. I want to take the risk of exploring that other reality. Of course as a writer you transmute that into words. As a painter you transmute it into images, physical images. That is the answer I can give you. I hope it is satisfactory.

Kadanoff: I wondered whether you were hopeful that Africa could put together its traditions with democracy to make something good for itself.

Soyinka: That is a useful question because the truth is that even within certain monarchical structures on the African continent, we have had institutions which can be considered democratic. What is democracy? Democracy is accountability, a possibility of change. A change of personnel, a change of direction. It is a plurality of options, whether in the field of economics or culture. It is choice, it is a certain leveling of power and hierarchies in order to respect the dignity of the human being, the equality, the egalitarian principle of human association. So within traditional society, we do have those examples. In fact some tyrants, whether civilian or military, on that continent have even tried to use tradition, because you can always select from tradition. They use tradition to suggest that Africans do not have any such thing as democracy, but of course they have been conveniently selective. Africa suffers exploitation and still has some very repressive feudal structures even today. At the same time it has some democratic structures. The essence is there. You can modernize it any way you want, cope with global intercourse to make it tidier, more scientific or whatever. The democratic instinct is not at all strange to traditional African society. And African leadership and African policy makers, sociologists, political scientists and power contenders can actually create any society based on these principles.

Sykorskaia: What do you think is the difference between intuition and instinct?

Soyinka: That is a very, very gray area there. I would say that every human being does have the faculty of instinct. Instinct can apply, for instance, to human gravitational pull. Instinctively I am mad at this man, I don't know why. I call this the gravitational force of attraction or repulsion on one level or the other. Choices, I think, sometimes have to do with instinct. Intuition, I suggest, is a far more mystical quality. Mystical is a word I use as sparingly as possible. But I suggest that one can find certain mystical imput into what intuition is. It is certainly a more complex conclusion to many, many processes of which sometimes we are not even aware. But instinct, I believe, is more an activity of choice as I said, of gravitational pull in one direction rather than another. Whereas intuition is a process of both mind and body which can be set into almost any parameter of human experience. Instinct is, I think, far more specific. And very often it has to do more with choice, instinctively I went this way rather than that.

Guntern: In scientific language we define instinct as a genetically heart-programmed behavior, entailing perception, elaboration of information, decision-making and reaction. For instance when one talks about movement in football, it has to do with space perception and therefore one immediately thinks of intuition. But it is probably more proper to say that this was an instinctive reaction. That is one thing. Second, the instinct brain is about 285 million years old, philogenetically, a very old, primitive brain. Intuition is a neo-cortical thing. I am speaking as an anatomist, physiologist. It appears that it is quite strongly linked to the so-called non-dominant brain hemisphere, which is only about five million years old. Nobody really knows how intuition functions, but we do know a few things: it takes a lot of analyses, carefully works them out, and after a while it crosses the corpus callosum, which is an atomic structure between the two halves of the reasoning brain. Information travels there and the picture is formed; when the holistic, monistic thing is done, you know with a sudden flash: I shall not be released by Christmas. Now this is the viewpoint of the scientist.

Soyinka: I would not use the description *instinct* for the experience I had when my mother died, anymore than I would for my trip towards Oshogbo, when for no physical, tangible reason, no signs on the road, no omens, no dark bird or black cat that ran across the road, I turned back. There was no explanation at all. I was inside my own mind, looking forward to something and suddenly... Now, for that I would use intuition, definitely not instinct. Instinct has nothing to do with it.

Guntern: But telepathic communication.

Soyinka: That could probably be in the same area.

Steinmeyer: I would like to take up on Leo Kadanoff's question once more and come back to your circle in terms of past, present and future. I think the unborn part is vision, you said, and future. Could you tell us a little bit more about the desired future for Africa, the mission you have?

Soyinka: This mission which I believe I have, this territory of the unborn, is getting very, very stale and very wearisome for me in the sense that it is almost like a receding oasis. I have said in a different context that during the colonial struggle, when we left and went to study abroad to acquire different skills - the engineers, doctors, surveyors, bankers and so on - we felt that we were the renaissance people. We had only one concrete problem and that was the liberation of Southern Africa. We saw ourselves as a part of an international brigade, European style, who would march down, liberate Southern Africa and put into effect all the various dreams we had: construct a Black paradise on Earth, outpace, outstrip the development of Europe. Nothing was beyond us, we were giant in our minds. We could not wait to get back home, we were impatient with our studies, aiming to finish quickly and get back to building that society. Nothing, nothing was beyond us. Well that vision has become somewhat muted right now in Nigeria. I think I would be satisfied if there were running water for everybody, if we had a shelter for everybody, if we could clear all the beggars off the streets, meaningfully, not through class-sanitation, please understand. If we could get rid permanently of these rapacious dictators, if we could move from one part of the African continent to the other and find that the standard of living is not beneath what is acceptable as appertaining to human dignity, I would feel that we were not doing so badly. I think I would leave the next generation to complete that vision of paradise which we had when we were students, but certainly not to accept and not to act in any way which suggests that we accept what exists at this moment. That, for me, is the ultimate surrender.

Guntern: What could be done not to stop fundamentalism in its tracks, because obviously that cannot be done, but to counterbalance this terrible influence?

336

Soyinka: The fundamentalist question we have just mentioned is one which I think the entire world community had better address in very stark terms. I am not talking about Islamic fundamentalism alone; the massacres which take place, not all of which are reported, regularly between the Sikhs and the Hindus in India for instance; the kind of extremism that leads to the massacre of Moslems in the mosque in Israel; the arbitrary, mindless killings of journalists and writers in Algeria; the complete oppression, suppression of women in many societies. This is half the world's productive population and I do not mean in the sense of child-bearing at all. For any kind of religious mentality to insist upon this kind of exclusiveness and mete very severe, even capital punishment on members of the other sex simply because they insist on being human beings and taking their place in the world is unthinkable. And it is spreading. It is in Nigeria. I received a report when I came through London and I phoned to pick up the latest news at home, that some fundamentalist had cut off the head of somebody in the North simply because he was accused of using pages of the Koran in a disrespectful way - something like that. This man was put in prison for his own safety. They went in, broke down the walls, cut off his head, impaled it, danced around the streets and went to the mosque, where the mullah preached for about two and a half hours. It really is a menace and some people do not want to give it its proper name because of this other disease called *political correctness*.

Guntern: It is another form of fascism.

Soyinka: You know we are dealing with real enemies of humanity. The sooner we come to terms with that and with all strategies to deal with it in the most drastic manner, I think the better for us because it is something which is spreading all the time. It is human regression in any religion. One thing which has cheered me, however, in the case of the Islamic fundamentalists, is that the orthodox world of Islam itself is finally recognizing that they in fact are in the front line of the menaced people and they are now beginning to hold conferences and take action. This is one encouragement.

Guntern: This is another form of totalitarianism and psychological atrocities. You begin with language, you call somebody a sub-human being, for instance, and all of a sudden you are told you are the fourth Black person to be here on the podium in five Symposia. It used to be correct to say a *Black* person. All of a sudden we were told that with respect to the United States, you can only speak of an Afro-American person. I find it awful because it is a kind of control that kills individuality, kills dignity and then in a second step will permit all kinds of inhuman atrocities. With respect to this political correctness, you also used a term, the *emasculation of language* and then you added a hyphen *pun-intended*. Could you say some more about the chain, the causal chain and the chain of rational implications, leading from language to concepts, to operational bases for certain strategies and actions that ultimately destroy human beings psychologically, physically or in whatever form?

Soyinka: The word is fascism and again I have recalled what I call a cultural rootedness which makes it impossible for me ever to submit to any totalitarian trend in any form from other cultures. I repudiate it in totality. For instance this Afro-American and Black thing you mentioned. Where was the decision taken? Under what democratic means was a conclusion arrived at that Black people were no longer black, but Afro-American? Look at the progression of this particular form of linguistic progression or retrogression. There is nothing wrong with it; in fact I believe in plurality. If one writer feels comfortable, for the purposes of poetic scansion with colored rather than Afro-American, then for heaven's sake, as long as that writer enhances language and whatever he is writing by this particular selection and it jells, then I do not see that individual has committed any crime or that it is a cause for me to set up a linguistic Nuremberg to try such a writer for crimes against Black humanity. Once it was colored, then it was Negro. Then Negro was passé, it became Afro-American. From Afro-American it became Black and then in recent times from nowhere you suddenly hear that it is politically incorrect for me to describe myself as Black, and I say that the world must be going mad. What bothers me is the atmosphere of terror and self subjugation you encounter among your colleagues who last year were very comfortable with this word and suddenly, "Oh, no, no you mustn't say that here anymore." It is like the liberal culture in certain societies which is very dangerous, pernicious and self-diminishing. When I talk about cultural rootedness and politically correct, I sent in an article once and the editor actually edited out, politically quote - unquote, "incorrect expressions" in there and I warned: "If you publish that article with your editing, I will sue you in the international court of human rights. So you better put back my politically incorrect expressions, right there. That's my stamp, that's my style and everybody knows it. I sign it, it's me, and anybody who wants to pick a quarrel, fine, but please do not insert, quote-unquote, 'politically correct' things."

In Yoruba we have an annual New Year's greeting, "Odún á y'abo," which means, "May the New Year be female." In the American and European world of political correctness, this would be totally objectionable. Now am I supposed to go and change that New Year's greeting because you are uncomfortable, you feel I am discriminating against women? I say I want the New Year - as does my society - to be female. We want it to be procreative, productive, gentle. Now, if the women in other parts of the world want to deny themselves this aspiration of gentility and share it with a man, fine, that is good for their societies. Let them not make it a universal principle. This is what I object to with political correctness. It is a peculiarity which can be explained in psychological terms, in terms of cultural insecurity, in the historic guilt of misogynist societies, in oppression, racism, etc. but not as universal ideas. It cannot be universally defended, and is not necessarily correct, and by correct I mean correct, viable strategies for correcting certain sociological ills. Very often it becomes an end in itself, distracting from the really serious social iniquities which are plaguing those societies. People now occupy their minds with expunging the dots, the commas, the "isms," the "esses" of language, and as a result, nobody pays attention anymore to the proliferation of beggars, indigent people, the homeless, and so on. All the intellectuals and politicians are now worried, everything is subsumed, you cannot explain. You do not have to think any more, all you have to say is: "Oh, I don't want to do this. It's politically incorrect." You do not have to justify it. You do not have to relate it to the context in which that particular activity is suggested. It is totally pernicious, and I find it completely unacceptable. Of course, to end where we began, it also prevents the real crimes against humanity from being addressed. Take the knifing of people like the elderly writer Mafouz. In my culture, we do not worship elders, but we highly respect them. We believe they have a certain treasury of experience from which we can draw. When I use the word *subhuman,* I use it very deliberately. Anyone who is so contemptuous of the act of creativity or the creative potential of another human being is subhuman. That is the only language I can use to describe those who carry out the act and those who sit in the comfort of their homes, the authority, the majesty of their minuscule selves and send out individuals to commit such acts. They are an enemy of humanity. I do not care for what religion they are operating, be it Judaic, Sikh, Hindu, Islam, Christianity, or even Yoruba Orisha, which suddenly grows a kind of aberrational aspect and indulges in this kind of thing. Those of us who believe in the authentic Yoruba religion must fight and call things by their proper names, not by any quote-unquote "politically correct" expression. Evil is evil.

Bollo: I want to ask you if in your country or culture there is the practice of sexual excision of little girls and women.

Soyinka: Yes, in a very tiny part of Nigeria; it does not exist in my part of Nigeria at all. Perhaps you were thinking about the Yoruba woman who asked for political asylum on the grounds that if she returned with her daughters to Nigeria, they would be excised. There again we had a "politically correct" judgment whereby the judge did not even inquire. He did not request evidence to see if a whole people were being slandered by this woman who just wanted a U.S. green card. But she knew what sort of society she was dealing with. She had had a quarrel with her husband and had divorced or something like that, and wanted to remain in the States, (just like many Nigerians who are fleeing from Nigeria for economic reasons and going to places where they can be on welfare or get a job). So having studied this gullible society, she cooked up this story which was a lie. I was interviewed by a *Time Magazine* reporter who has been in Nigeria for a long time, and he called me all the way from the States. He has had quite a few Nigerian girlfriends and he said he had not encountered any sign of excision in all their relationships. He wanted to do a story on that and I spoke to him and interestingly enough, his story was not published because it would have been politically incorrect. So I agree there are certain pockets where this practice of excision takes place, but it is such a lie to suggest that it is the tradition in all Nigeria.

Q.: Until now we have heard only about positive experiences of intuition. Are there any experiences of intuition which have put you on the wrong track?

Soyinka: I have to think very hard about that. My suspicion is when the result of an experience, a moment of decision proves wrong, one tends not to call it intuition, but I cannot think of any example offhand.

Guntern: Yes, intuition can lead you to negative, wrong decisions, especially if you are under stress, if you have tremendous expectations which are not justified by any factors in your environment or within yourself. If you are very highly emotional for whatever reason, then it just does not function. There are many examples of bad intuition. Another particular aspect was pointed out by Socrates. Since his childhood he had had on and off a voice that told him, "Don't do that." And then he remarked that the voice never told him what to do. He states the case of a certain Carmides who intended to go to the Nimean games. His voice told Socrates: "Don't go there, Carmides." He told Carmides, who went anyway and he was killed. Another example is Churchill. He was in London when it was being bombed in 1941. His driver opened the car door for him as usual, but all of a sudden a voice told Churchill, "Don't get in here." So, to the utter amazement of his driver, he went around to the other door and got in. They drove away and a few meters farther on a bomb hit the car exactly on that side.

Intuition can also make you do stupid things, but not if you are relaxed, serene. Now, we live in a society where many people are very much lost about values. For example, on television you have a highly dramatic story where a mother of seven children is about to die; all of a sudden, cut, and Mickey Mouse comes on in an ad, and then all of a sudden the dramatic story takes off again. Now people do all kind of things because they are disoriented with respect to values. Some use a hysterical language of extremes. Other people just resign themselves, enter slight depression, helplessness even hopelessness, despair. Some people enter religious fundamentalism to seek their salvation, or in our parts of the world, even intelligent people may fall prey to sects like Scientology . So it is an important issue. Where do we find our proper scale of values? What do we put high up, and this was the gentleman's question, unless I am mistaken. What is medium and what is negligible?

Soyinka: I believe that there has to be a set of acceptable human values. We can begin from the most obvious. I think that all of us here and in most parts of the world would believe that it is wrong, unacceptable to curtail arbitrarily the existence of another human being. Therefore if there is any system of belief that says this is permissible, then we have a responsibility to challenge and contest it. We can move on from there and say that on this basis, society has an obligation to structure itself in such a way that the day-to-day existence of children, of the needy, is not curtailed for lack of resources. Any society which operates any system of social organization - be it capitalism, socialism, "welfarism" or whatever - and in the process of attempting this acceptable level of existence arrogates to itself the right to say that it is perfectly all right to indulge in ethnic cleansing or - to use my favorite expression, *class-sanitation* - which is what happens in the barrios of Brazil where the faceless police go and round up and kill children for being beggars and potential social menaces - such a society is criminal. That society does not take the option of structuring itself, its economy, in such a way as to guarantee the existence of those children. So it believes that, in the higher cause of insuring a superficial, deodorized, acceptable level of human existence, it must conduct class sanitation. But if we respect the fundamental basis that no system of government, no system of social organization has the right to cut off the existence of individuals or collective groups in that manner, then we have a responsibility to voice our opposition and to take action on one level or other

341

against that system of government. From there we can move on to different levels, we can talk about the activities of religion within society. Anybody can worship anything. If a group of people decide that this piece of carpet is imbued with divine powers and they want to prostrate themselves on it and to lick it and roll themselves in it, it is not my business. But when it gets to the point where we cannot walk on the carpet, which we all collectively own, where you say you must cut my throat because you believe that carpet is divine and therefore anybody who so much as walks on it or paints an imitation of it is desecrating the divine spirit and that therefore you must curtail my existence on that account, then obviously we are compelled, in defense of our own existence of an accepted lowest common denominator of respect for human lives, to take collective action against it. We can go on and on in all different levels like that.

Guntern: By some strange coincidence which was unintentional on our part and which makes sense within the framework of our topic of intuition, we have two speakers this year who have had personal experience in prison and both for the same reason: because they took an autonomous stand. They did not accept being in the fangs of what I call "mediocracy," over-adapting to whatever a majority of people apparently or *de facto* want or say or do. They go their own way and they have paid dearly for it. All of a sudden it strikes me that within the topic of intuition it makes strange sense that the two of them have come together. Although they have missed each other in time and space, in our minds they have come together: Joseph Brodsky and Wole Soyinka. I was deeply moved when I read Brodsky's work. I was deeply moved when I met him in Rotterdam where he read poetry together with a Dutch, a British and two Russian poets. Then there was such a difference when Wole Soyinka began to talk; it was just another world. (To Soyinka) While I was watching you talk, going back to your cultural, spiritual, mythological roots, the Yoruba culture, I thought, he looks like a tree. I tried to think what kind of tree, but couldn't find one. Of course, I don't know very many African trees. And then I thought, "He's a whole forest." Intuitively I felt this picture that fits you perfectly. You are a great forest. In spite of your precarious living conditions, you have accepted to come to Zermatt and share a few hours with us. Thank you very much.

Soyinka: As usual I have succeeded in leaving half of myself behind. I was going to read some passages today and narrate experiences in relation to those passages. It suddenly occurred to me that among the people who brought books for an autograph, somebody somewhere might have a book of poems.

342

And - here is another piece of intuition - the moment I voiced my request, a young lady over there said: "Yes, somebody there has." So I happen to have *Idanre* in my hand, which is a remarkable work for me. I shall only read the last section and tie it up with yet another instance of some similar experience. Even as a creative person, I have always been fascinated by the way the mind operates, the way the spirit responds to particular moments, to flashes or intuition or whatever you want. When I was a student in England, I was in bed with my girlfriend and in the morning she said to me: "What was that cry? What was the shout? What was it about? What were you dreaming last night?" I said, "What did I shout?" And she said I shouted: "Throw meat to the Valkyrie." I said: "Throw meat to the Valkyrie?" I couldn't understand it. So for days I walked around, trying to recover what strange dream it was that had led me to shout, "Throw meat to the Valkyrie." I never recovered the dream, but a few days later I just got up and wrote a long poem which was based on that. I remember it was in rhyming couplets and was published in one of the college journals. I have lost it since. I wish I could find it, but at any rate, it was a Gothic poem, a horror poem. I remember two lines from that poem which went:

> And there within the belfry, her visage calm and mild,
> They stood anon across the nave, eating up the child.

I can't explain it, but I can't find the poem. This other experience was slightly similar yet dissimilar. I was working in Ibadan in my study one night. (I live very much at night.) I got up, could not explain why, became very, very restless. I lived near the bush, as usual. I found my feet directed into the very thick bush around there. I walked and walked and came out in another part of the town I had not traversed, near a palm-wine shack , which was just opening up in the early hours of the morning, at dawn. It was an experience I could not explain, but I got home and wrote the long poem "Idanre," finished it virtually without tampering with a word, without serious corrections, without locking it somewhere and going back to it later on. I felt that night I had walked in the presence of my favorite demiurge, Ogun, whom I spoke about earlier. That was the main physical thing I could sense about that walk that night. I got home and I started writing this poem. It is a very long one, so I shall just read you the last section.

Night sets me free; I suffer skies to sprout
Ebb to full navel in progressive arcs, ocean
Of a million roe, highway of eyes and moth-wings.
Night sets me free, I ride on ovary silences
In the wake of ghosts

Ogun's mantle brushed the leaves, the phase of night
Was mellow wine joined to a dirge
Of shadows, the air withdrew to scything motions
Of his dark-shod feet, seven-ply cross-roads
Hands of camwood, breath of indigo

Night sets me free, soft sediments on skin
And sub-soil mind. . . Dawn came gradual, mists
Fell away from rock and honeycomb, Idanre woke
To braided vapours, a dance of seven veils
The septuple god was groom and king.

Mists fell to mote infinities from mountain face
Retrieved, were finely gathered to a sponge
Of froth murmurs in palm veins, he rinsed
The sunrise of his throat in agile wine; I took the sun
In his copper calabash

Dawn, He who had dire reaped
And in wrong season, bade the forest swallow him
And left mankind to harvest. At pilgrim lodge
The wine-girl kept lone vigil, fused still
In her hour of charity

A dawn of bright processions, the sun peacocked
Loud, a new mint of coins. And those were all
The night hours, only dissipated gourds,
Rain serried floor, fibre walls in parcimonious
Sifting of the sun, and she . . .

Light burnished to a copper earth, cornucopia
Fell in light cascades round her feet. Our paths
Grew solemn as her indrawn eye, bright of Night
Hoard of virgin dawns, expectant grew her distant gaze
And Harvest came, responsive

The first fruits rose from subterranean hoards
First in our vision, corn sheaves rose over hill
Long before the bearers, domes of eggs and flesh
Of palm fruit, red, oil black, froth flew in sun bubbles
Burst over throngs of golden gourds
And they moved towards resorption in His alloy essence
Primed to a fusion, primed to the sun's dispersion
Containment and communion, seed-time and harvest, palm
And pylon, Ogun's road a "Mobious" orbit, kernel
And electrons, wine to alchemy.

Thank you.

Works by Wole Soyinka

Collected Plays 1, Oxford University Press, New York 1973
Idanre and Other Poems, Hill and Wang, New York 1987
The Man Died, The Noonday Press, London 1988
Aké: the Years of Childhood, **Vintage International Edition,** New York 1989
Ìsarà: A Voyage around "Essay," Vintage International, New York 1991
Art, Dialogue, and Outrage, Pantheon Books, New York 1994

Below is a list of the Symposia and their dates.

Maya Angelou	The Creative Process	13.06.1990
Joseph Brodsky	Intuition and Creativity	12.01.1995
Gerald M. Edelman	Playful Immagination in the Creative Process	16.01.1994
Gabriel García Márquez	The Factors which Favour or Inhibit Creativity	18.12.1991
Jane Goodall	Playful Immagination in the Creative Process	13.01.1994
Helmut Maucher	The Factors which Favour or Inhibit Creativity	17.12.1991
Kazuhiko Nishi	Intuition and Creativity	14.01.1995
Edna O'Brien	Intuition and Creativity	15.01.1995
Wole Soyinka	Intuition and Creativity	14.01.1995

DATE DUE

346